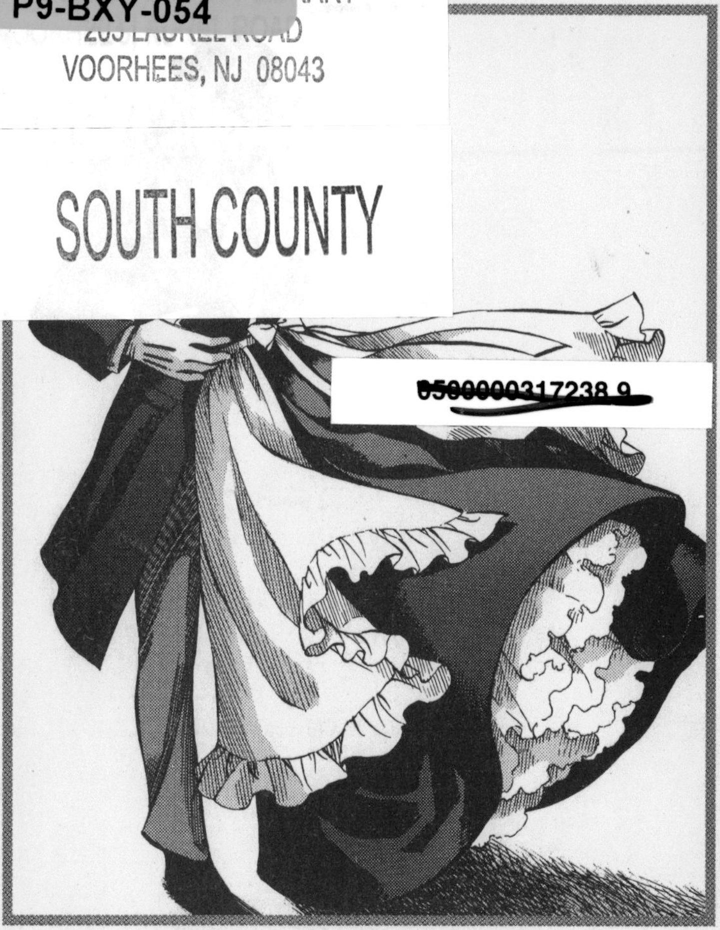

EMMA

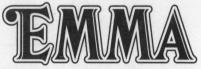

Volume 5

By Kaoru Mori

-Contents-

GRAPHIC
NOVEL
F
vol. 5

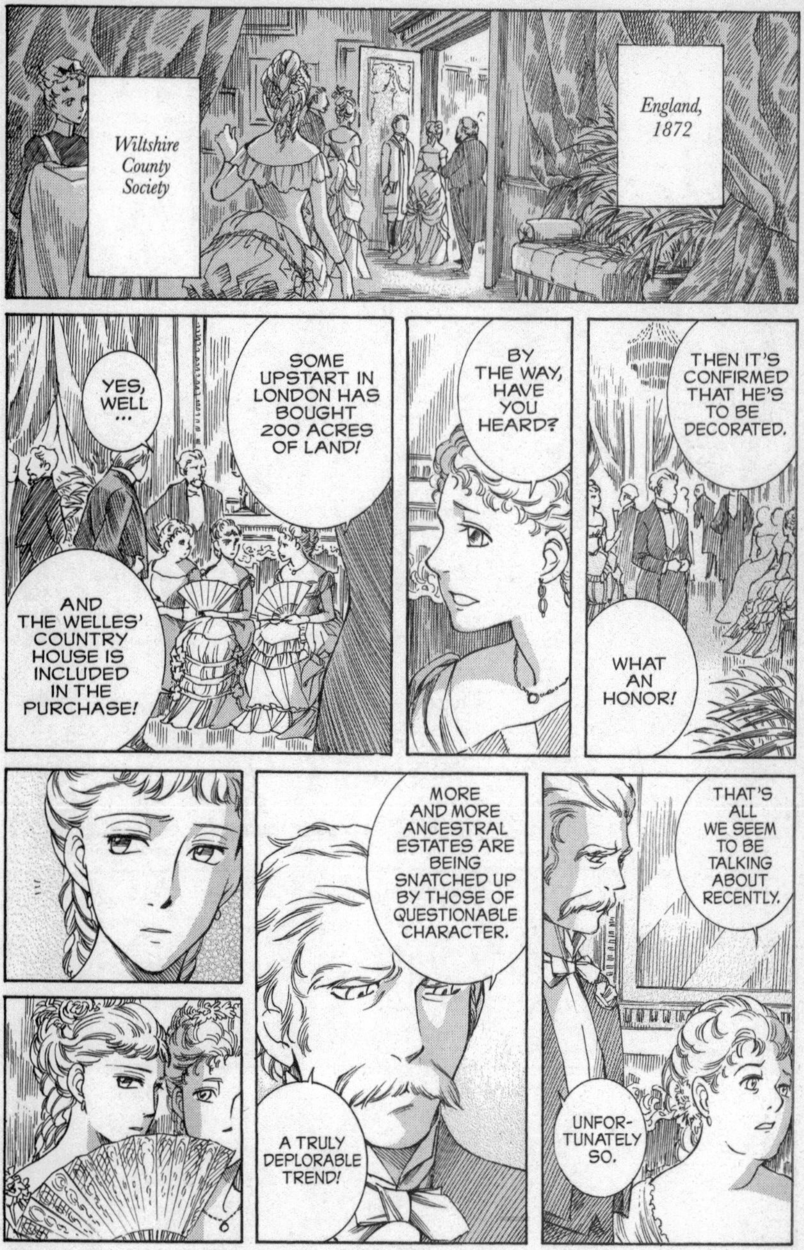
England, 1872
Wiltshire County Society
THEN IT'S CONFIRMED THAT HE'S TO BE DECORATED.
WHAT AN HONOR!
BY THE WAY, HAVE YOU HEARD?
SOME UPSTART IN LONDON HAS BOUGHT 200 ACRES OF LAND!
YES, WELL ...
AND THE WELLES' COUNTRY HOUSE IS INCLUDED IN THE PURCHASE!
THAT'S ALL WE SEEM TO BE TALKING ABOUT RECENTLY.
UNFOR-TUNATELY SO.
MORE AND MORE ANCESTRAL ESTATES ARE BEING SNATCHED UP BY THOSE OF QUESTIONABLE CHARACTER.
A TRULY DEPLORABLE TREND!

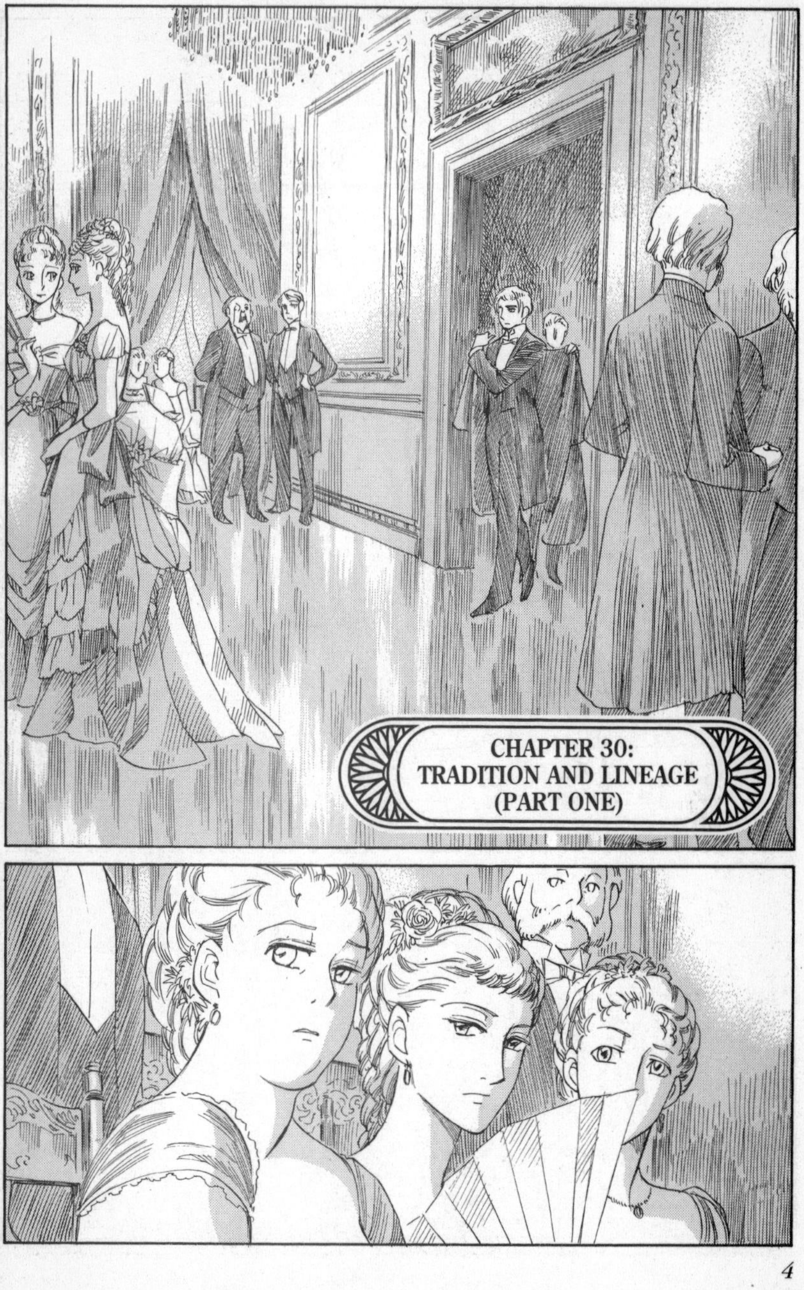
CHAPTER 30:
TRADITION AND LINEAGE
(PART ONE)

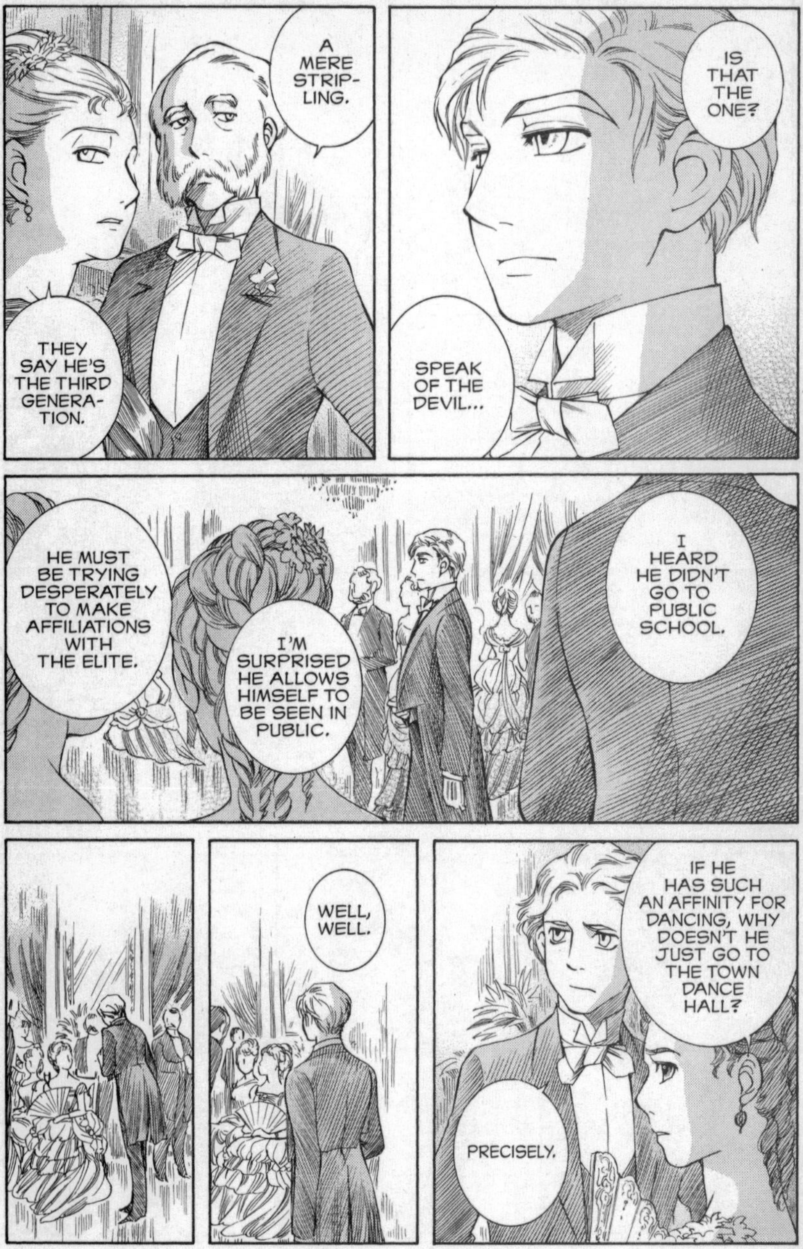
IS THAT THE ONE?
SPEAK OF THE DEVIL...
A MERE STRIP-LING.
THEY SAY HE'S THE THIRD GENERA-TION.
I HEARD HE DIDN'T GO TO PUBLIC SCHOOL.
I'M SURPRISED HE ALLOWS HIMSELF TO BE SEEN IN PUBLIC.
HE MUST BE TRYING DESPERATELY TO MAKE AFFILIATIONS WITH THE ELITE.
IF HE HAS SUCH AN AFFINITY FOR DANCING, WHY DOESN'T HE JUST GO TO THE TOWN DANCE HALL?
PRECISELY.
WELL, WELL.

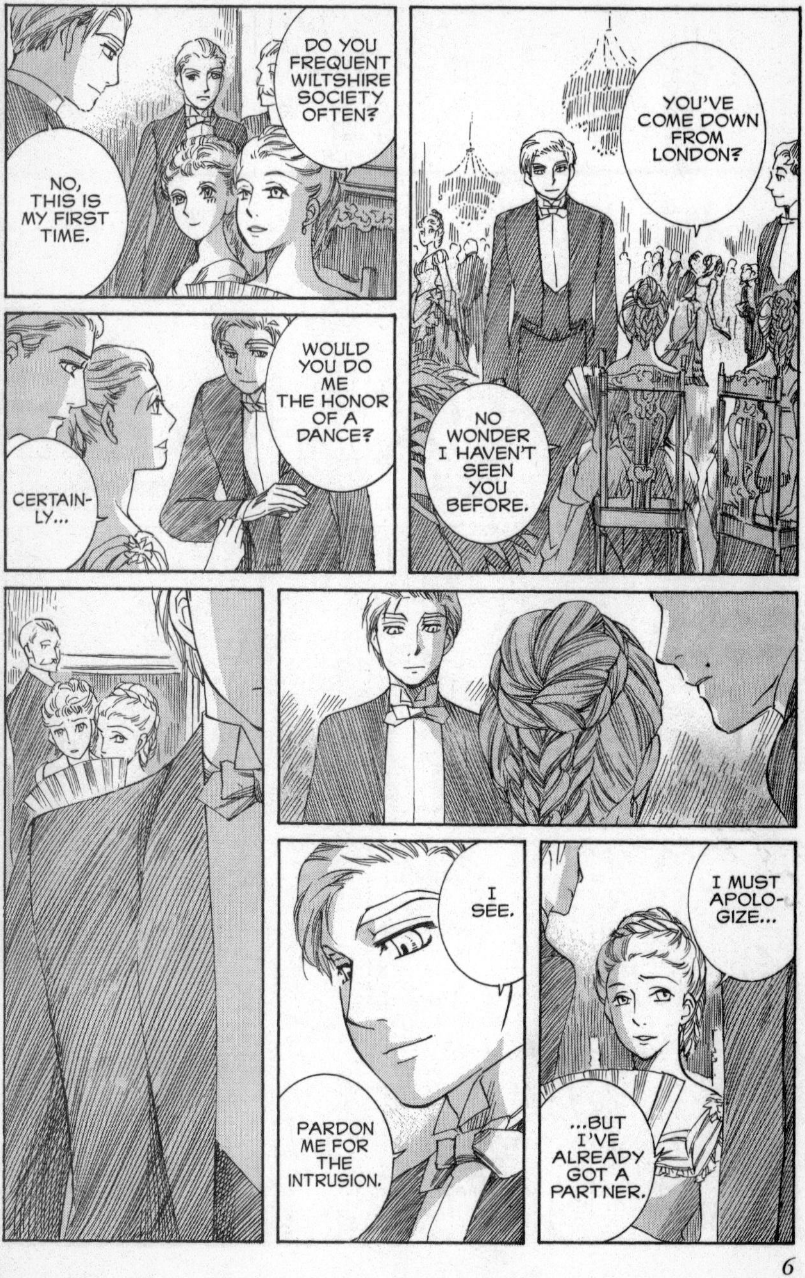
YOU'VE COME DOWN FROM LONDON?
NO WONDER I HAVEN'T SEEN YOU BEFORE.
DO YOU FREQUENT WILTSHIRE SOCIETY OFTEN?
NO, THIS IS MY FIRST TIME.
WOULD YOU DO ME THE HONOR OF A DANCE?
CERTAIN-LY...
I MUST APOLO-GIZE...
...BUT I'VE ALREADY GOT A PARTNER.
I SEE.
PARDON ME FOR THE INTRUSION.

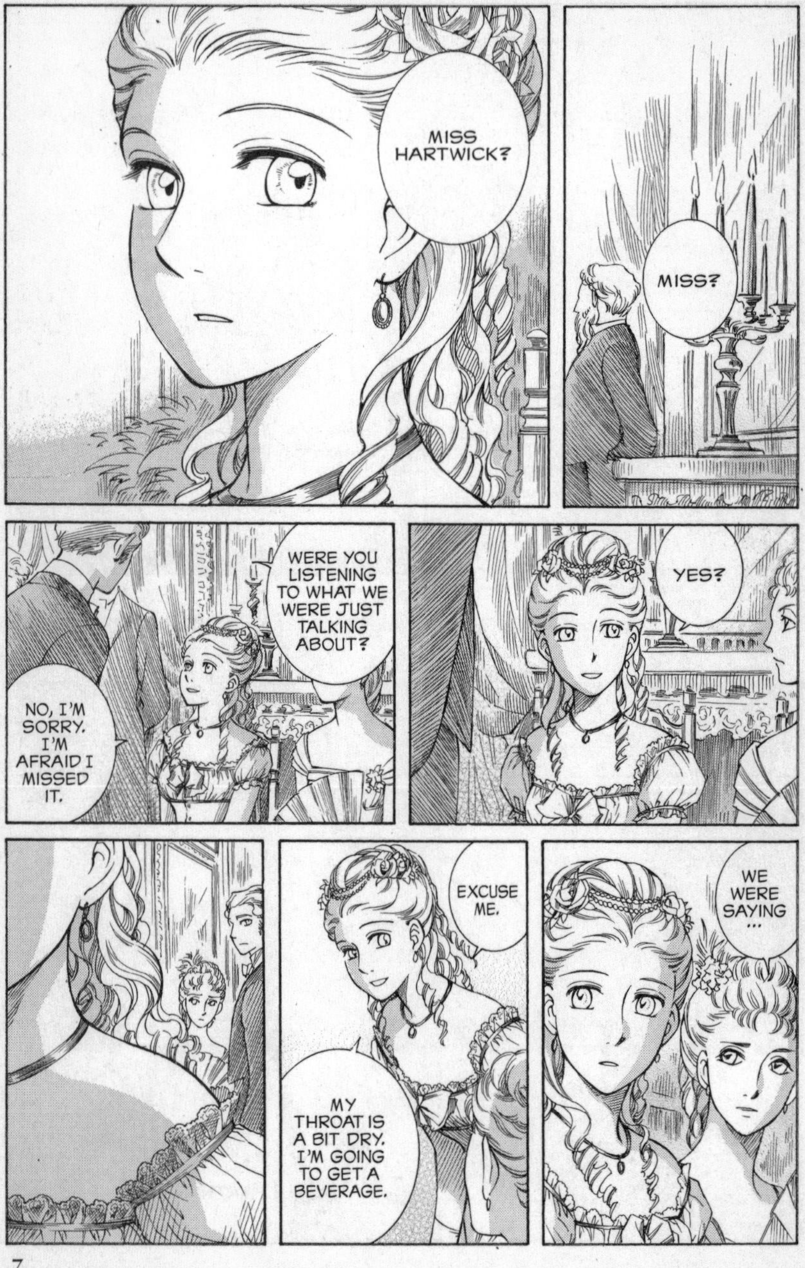
MISS?
MISS HARTWICK?
YES?
WERE YOU LISTENING TO WHAT WE WERE JUST TALKING ABOUT?
NO, I'M SORRY. I'M AFRAID I MISSED IT.
WE WERE SAYING ...
EXCUSE ME.
MY THROAT IS A BIT DRY. I'M GOING TO GET A BEVERAGE.

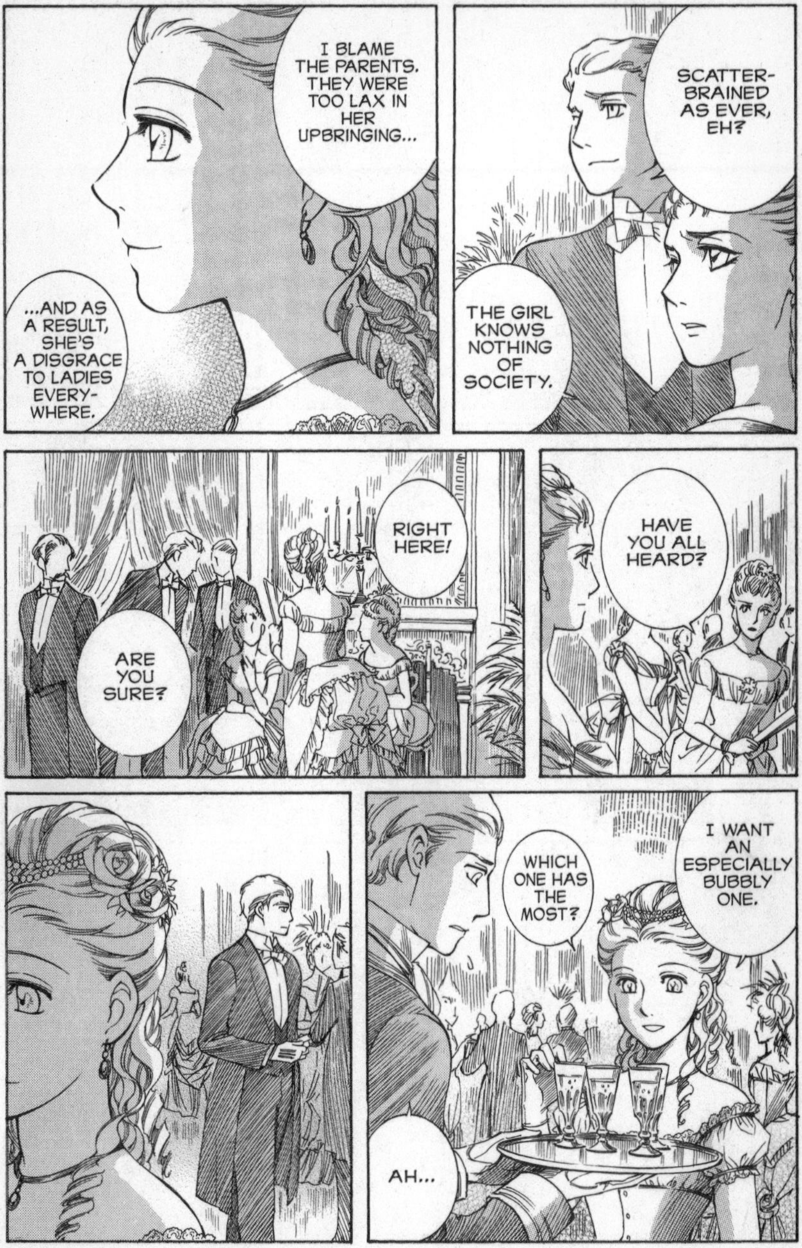
SCATTER-BRAINED AS EVER, EH?
THE GIRL KNOWS NOTHING OF SOCIETY.
I BLAME THE PARENTS. THEY WERE TOO LAX IN HER UPBRINGING...
...AND AS A RESULT, SHE'S A DISGRACE TO LADIES EVERY-WHERE.
HAVE YOU ALL HEARD?
RIGHT HERE!
ARE YOU SURE?
I WANT AN ESPECIALLY BUBBLY ONE.
WHICH ONE HAS THE MOST?
AH...

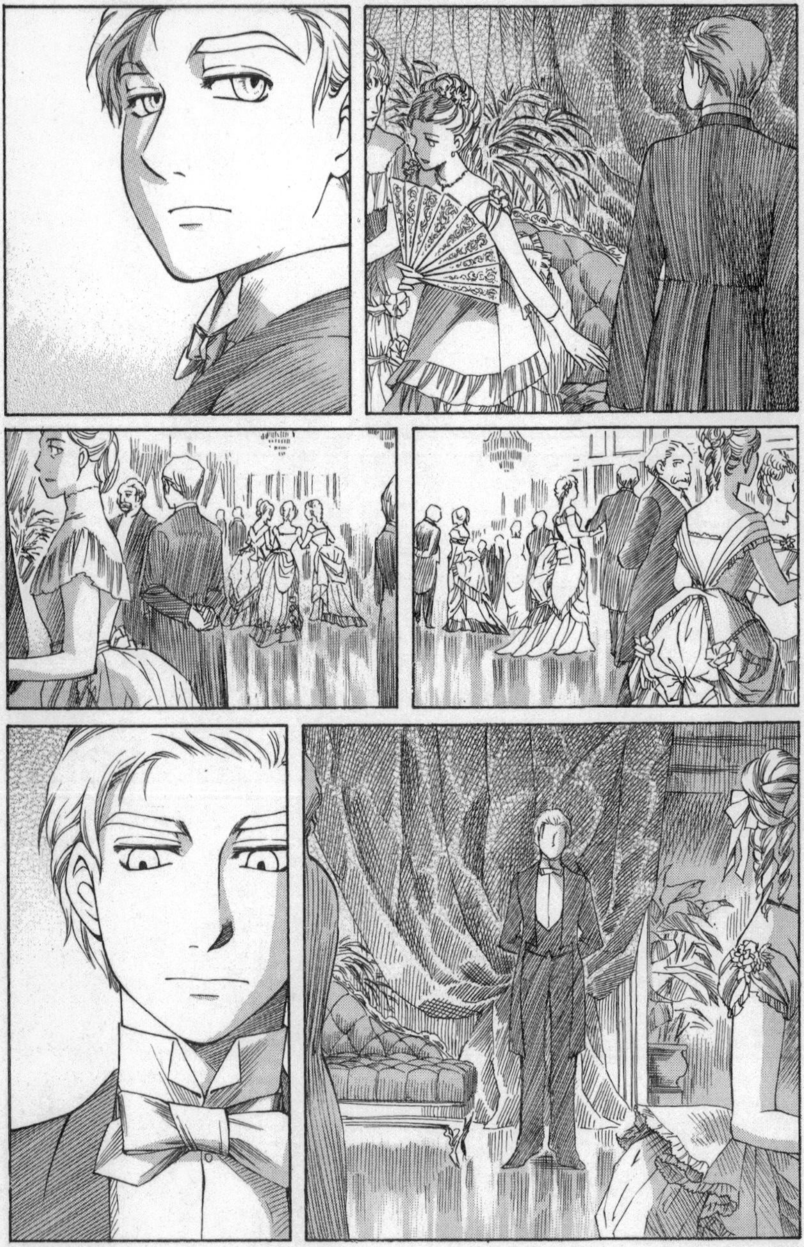

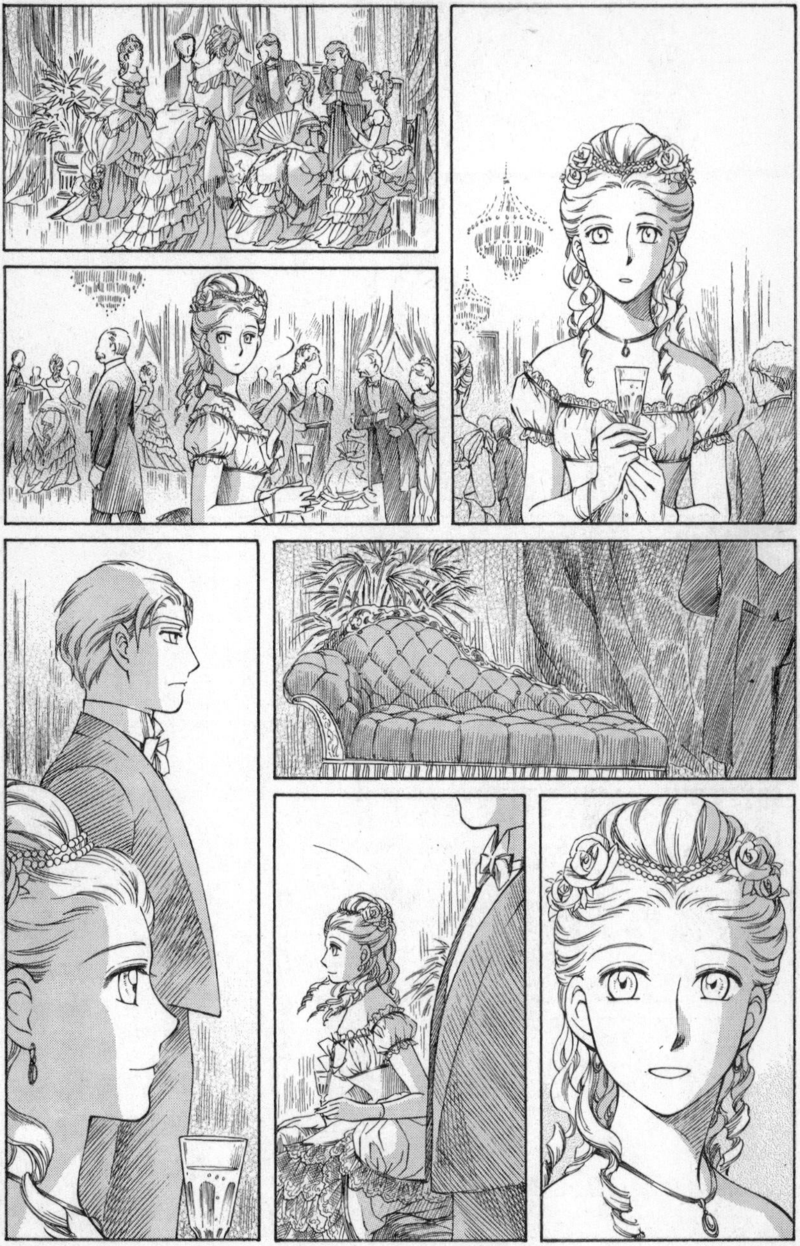

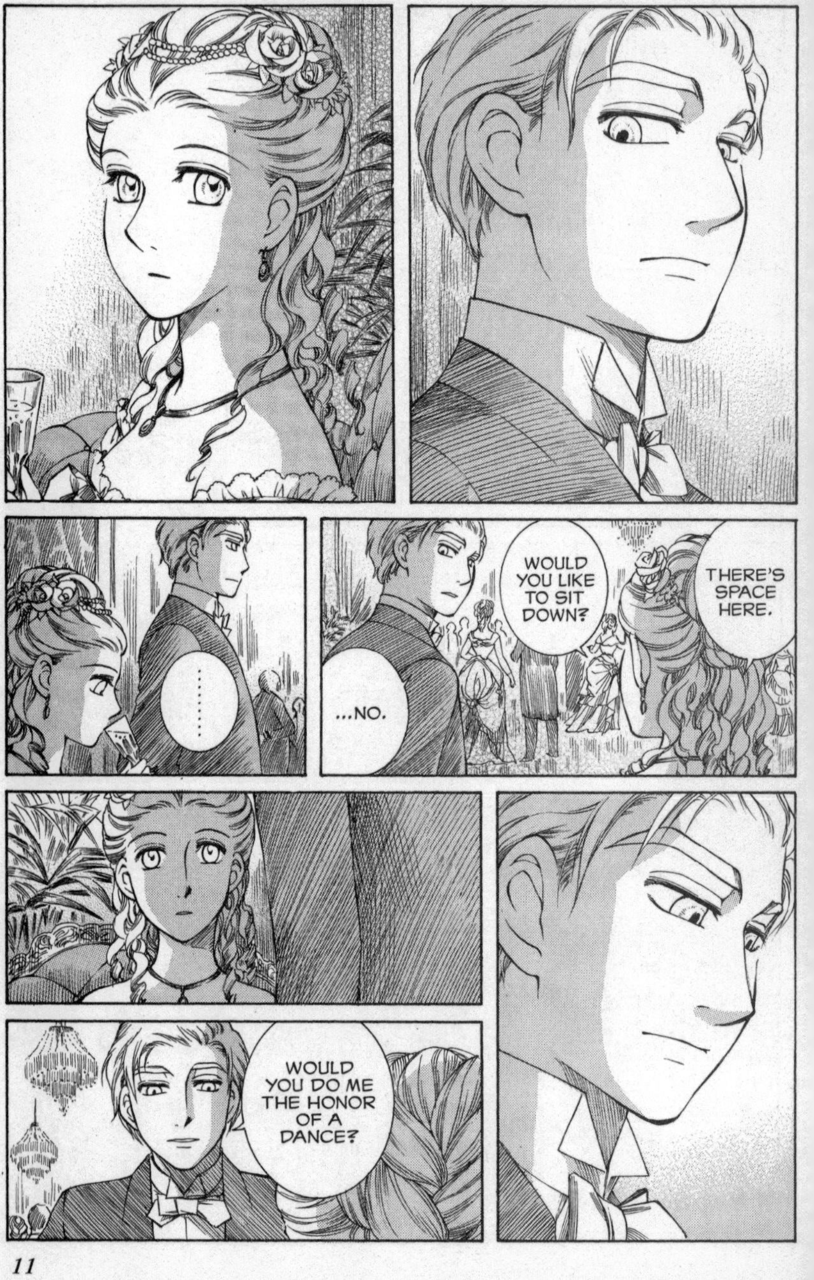
THERE'S SPACE HERE.
WOULD YOU LIKE TO SIT DOWN?
...NO.
......
WOULD YOU DO ME THE HONOR OF A DANCE?

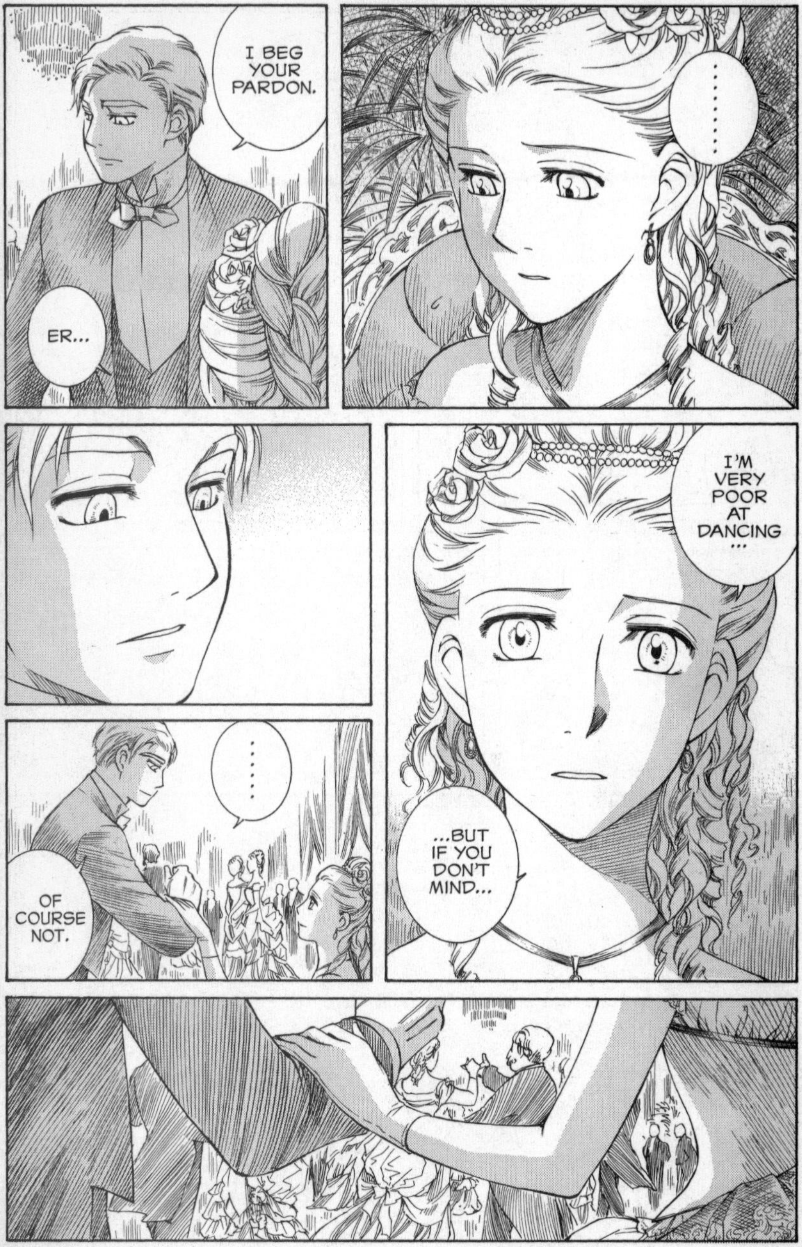
......
I BEG YOUR PARDON.
ER...
I'M VERY POOR AT DANCING...
...BUT IF YOU DON'T MIND...
......
OF COURSE NOT.

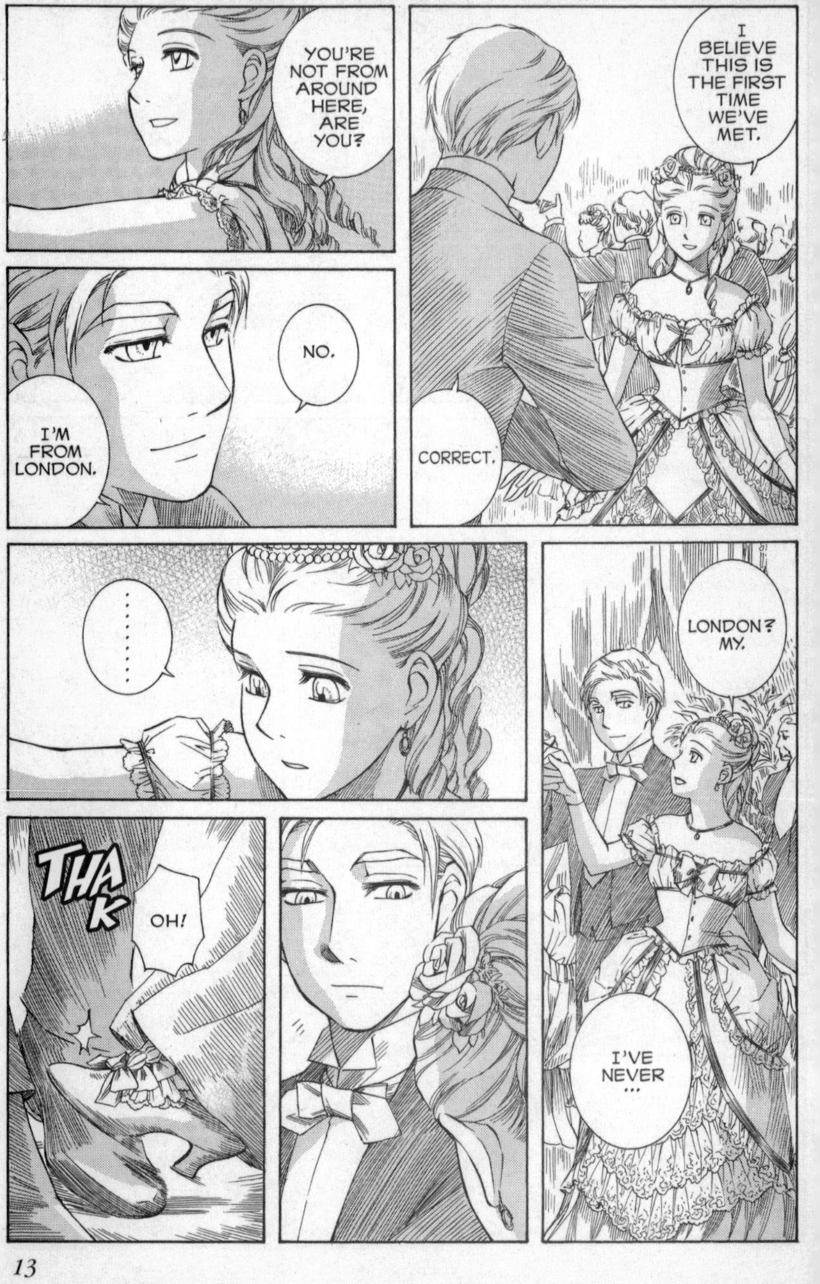
I BELIEVE THIS IS THE FIRST TIME WE'VE MET.
CORRECT.
YOU'RE NOT FROM AROUND HERE, ARE YOU?
NO.
I'M FROM LONDON.
LONDON? MY.
I'VE NEVER ...
......
THAK
OH!

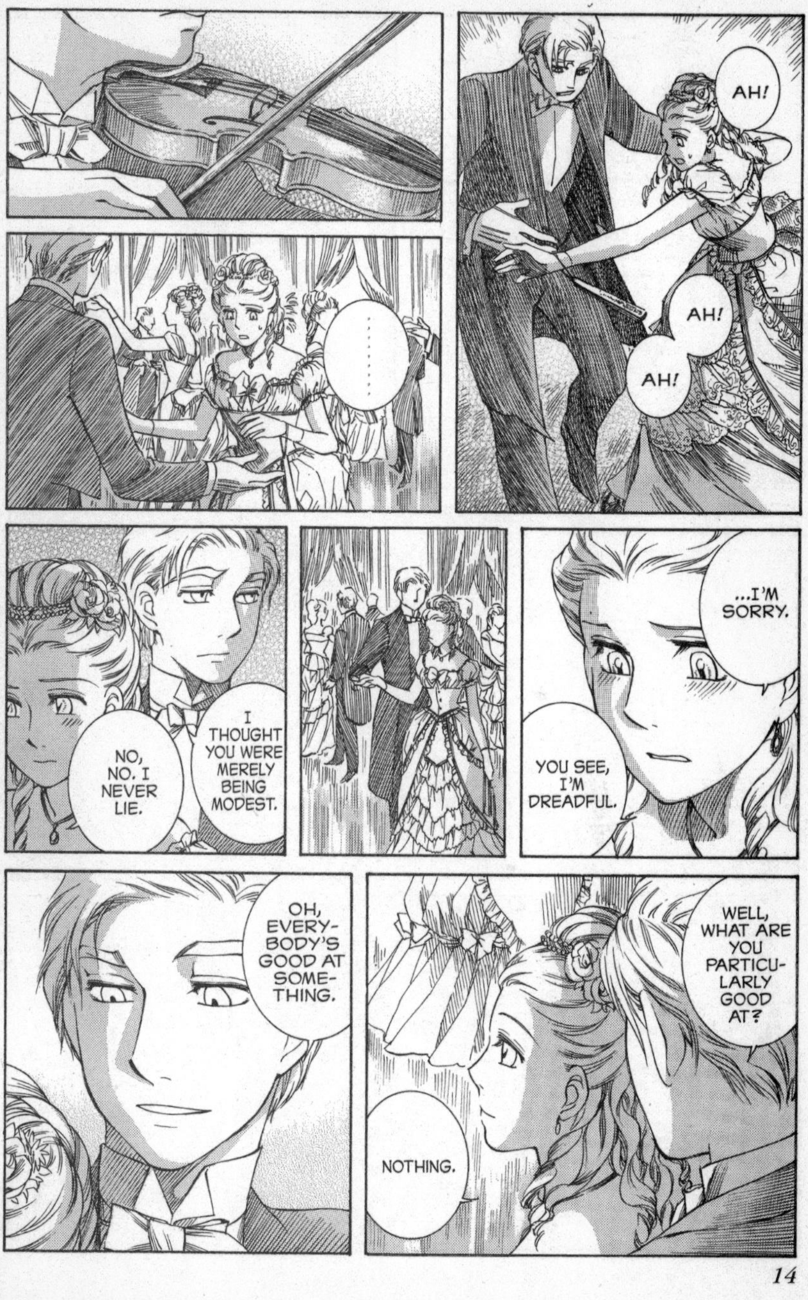
AH!
AH!
AH!
......
...I'M SORRY.
YOU SEE, I'M DREADFUL.
I THOUGHT YOU WERE MERELY BEING MODEST.
NO, NO. I NEVER LIE.
WELL, WHAT ARE YOU PARTICU-LARLY GOOD AT?
NOTHING.
OH, EVERY-BODY'S GOOD AT SOME-THING.

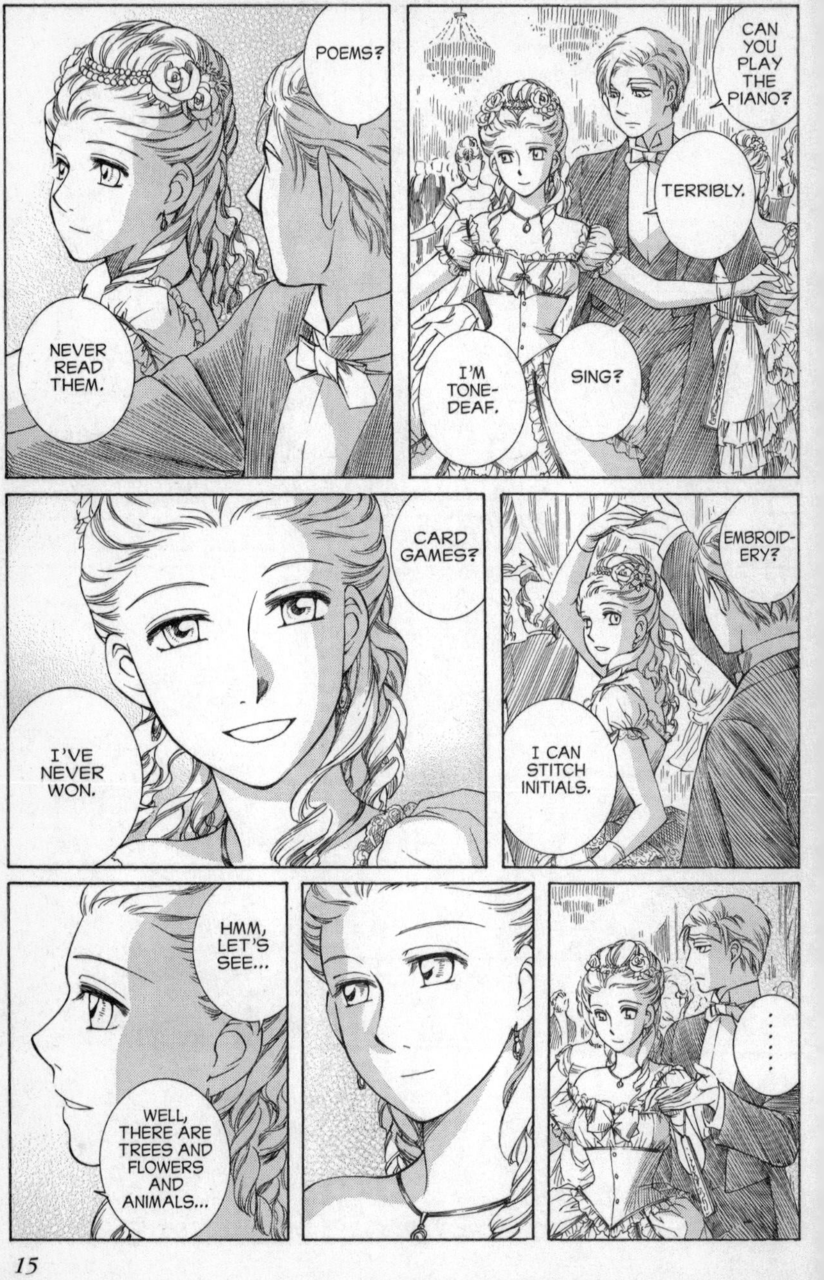
CAN YOU PLAY THE PIANO?
TERRIBLY.
SING?
I'M TONE-DEAF.
POEMS?
NEVER READ THEM.
EMBROIDERY?
I CAN STITCH INITIALS.
CARD GAMES?
I'VE NEVER WON.
......
HMM, LET'S SEE...
WELL, THERE ARE TREES AND FLOWERS AND ANIMALS...

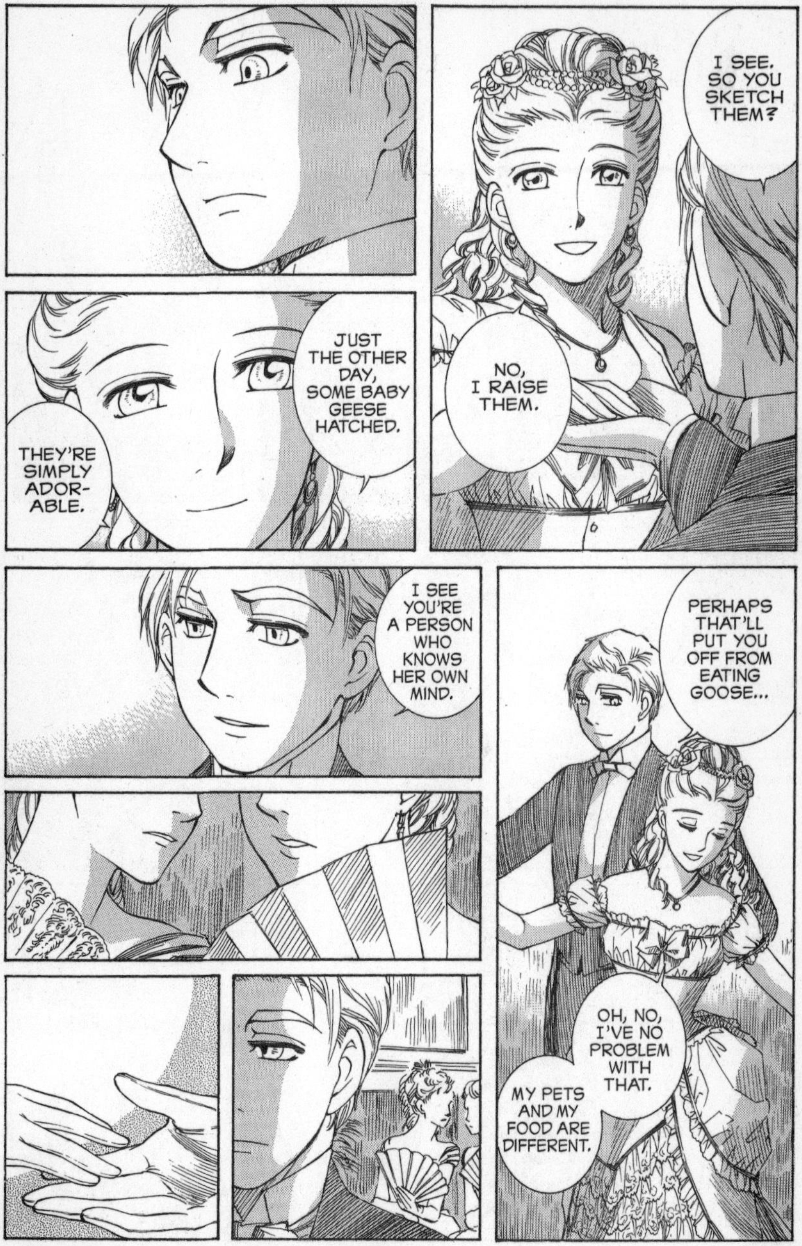
I SEE. SO YOU SKETCH THEM?
NO, I RAISE THEM.
JUST THE OTHER DAY, SOME BABY GEESE HATCHED.
THEY'RE SIMPLY ADOR-ABLE.
PERHAPS THAT'LL PUT YOU OFF FROM EATING GOOSE...
OH, NO, I'VE NO PROBLEM WITH THAT.
MY PETS AND MY FOOD ARE DIFFERENT.
I SEE YOU'RE A PERSON WHO KNOWS HER OWN MIND.

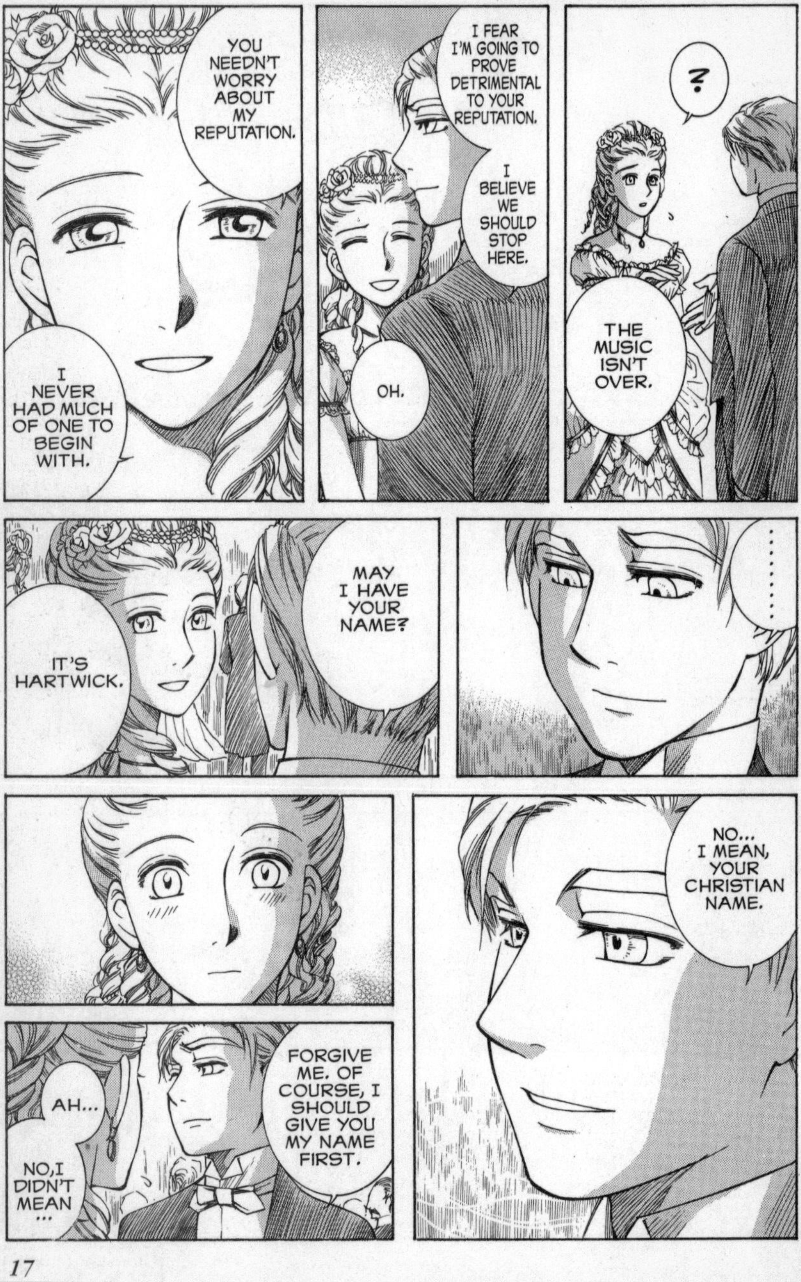
?
THE MUSIC ISN'T OVER.
I FEAR I'M GOING TO PROVE DETRIMENTAL TO YOUR REPUTATION.
I BELIEVE WE SHOULD STOP HERE.
OH.
YOU NEEDN'T WORRY ABOUT MY REPUTATION.
I NEVER HAD MUCH OF ONE TO BEGIN WITH.
......
MAY I HAVE YOUR NAME?
IT'S HARTWICK.
NO... I MEAN, YOUR CHRISTIAN NAME.
FORGIVE ME. OF COURSE, I SHOULD GIVE YOU MY NAME FIRST.
AH...
NO,I DIDN'T MEAN ...

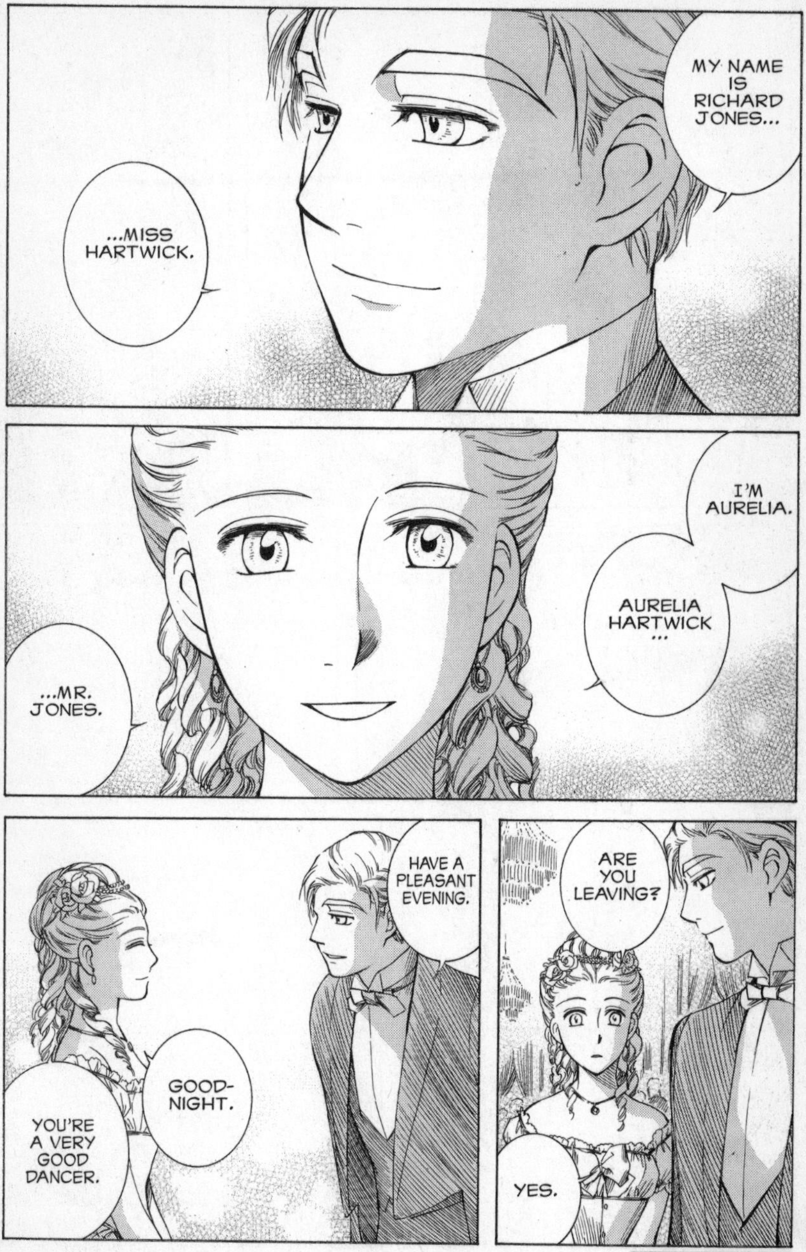
MY NAME IS RICHARD JONES...
...MISS HARTWICK.
I'M AURELIA.
AURELIA HARTWICK ...
...MR. JONES.
ARE YOU LEAVING?
YES.
HAVE A PLEASANT EVENING.
GOOD-NIGHT.
YOU'RE A VERY GOOD DANCER.

Chapter Thirty: The End

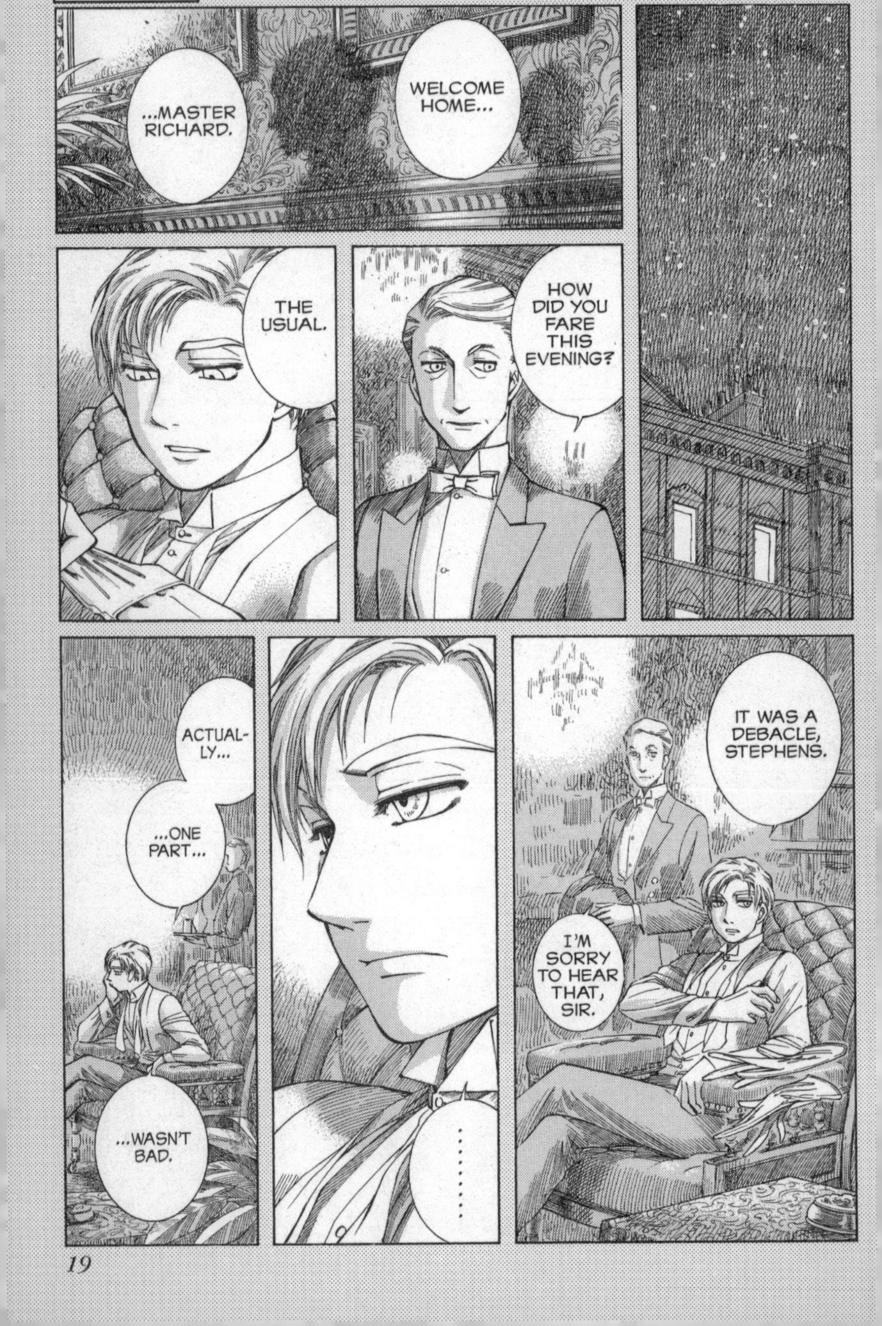
WELCOME HOME...
...MASTER RICHARD.
HOW DID YOU FARE THIS EVENING?
THE USUAL.
IT WAS A DEBACLE, STEPHENS.
I'M SORRY TO HEAR THAT, SIR.
....
ACTUAL-LY...
...ONE PART...
...WASN'T BAD.

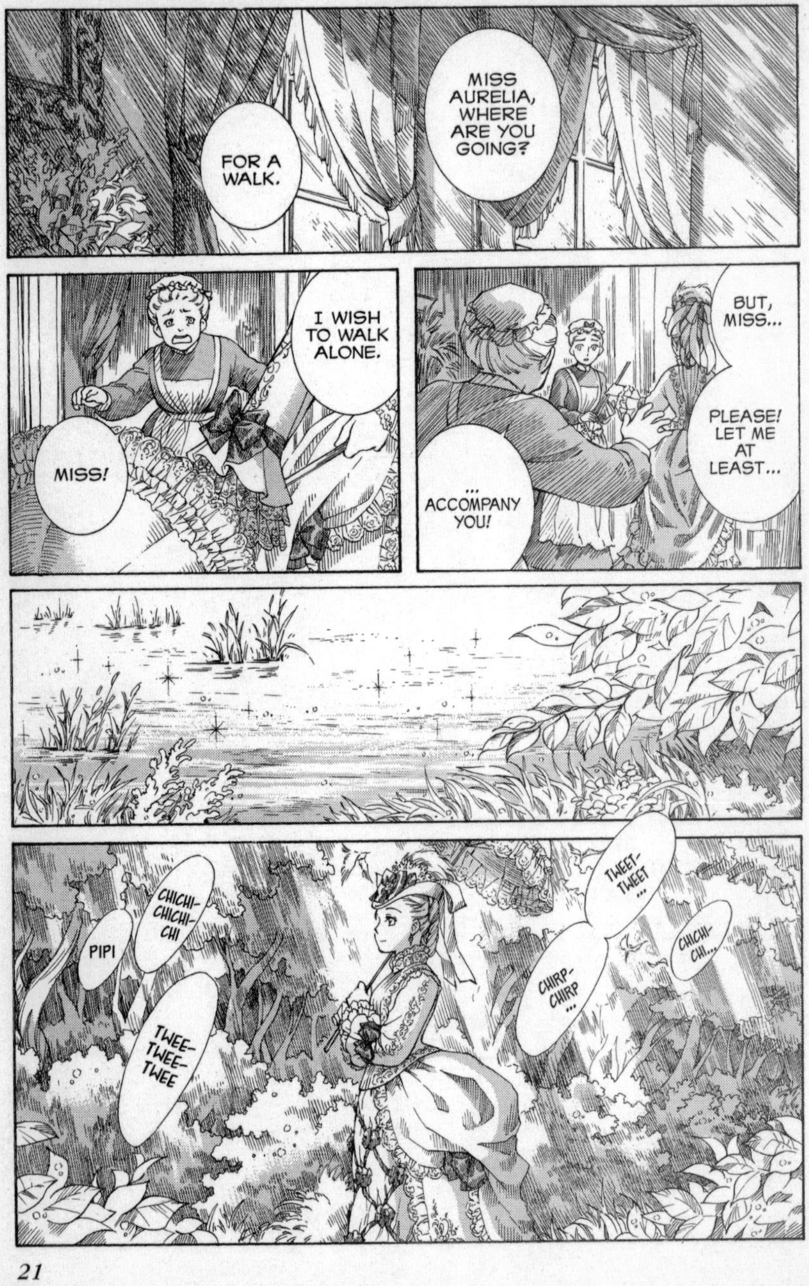
MISS AURELIA, WHERE ARE YOU GOING?
FOR A WALK.
BUT, MISS...
PLEASE! LET ME AT LEAST...
... ACCOMPANY YOU!
I WISH TO WALK ALONE.
MISS!
TWEET-TWEET...
CHICHI-CHI...
CHIRP-CHIRP...
CHICHI-CHICHI-CHI
PIPI
TWEE-TWEE-TWEE

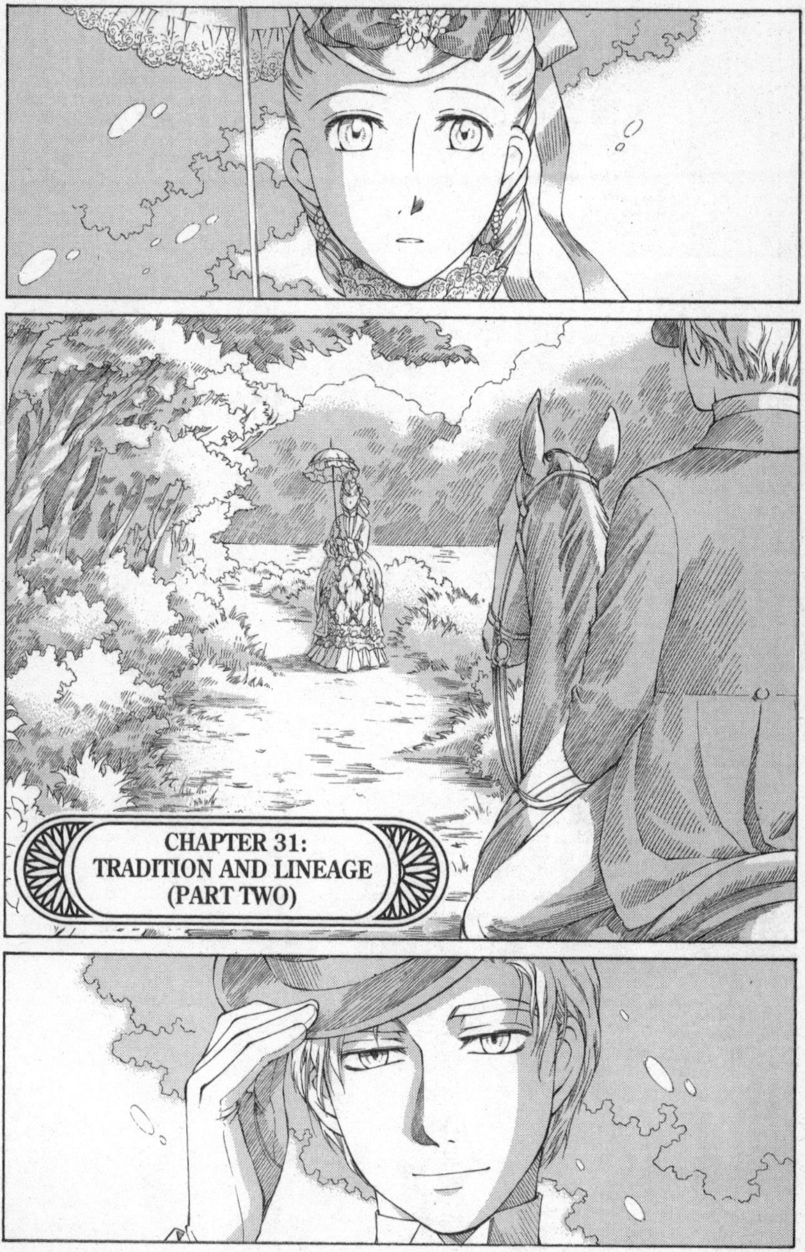
CHAPTER 31:
TRADITION AND LINEAGE
(PART TWO)

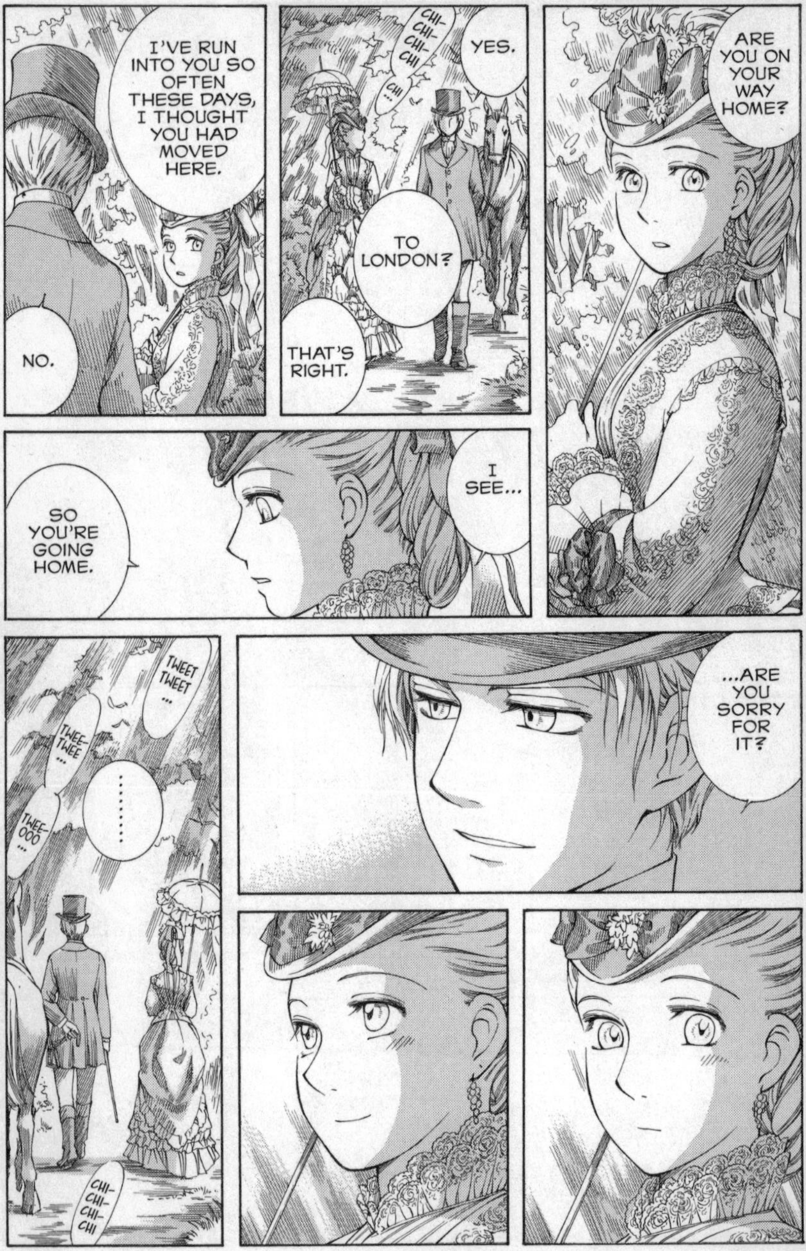
ARE YOU ON YOUR WAY HOME?
YES.
CHI-CHI-CHI-CHI
CHI...
TO LONDON?
THAT'S RIGHT.
I'VE RUN INTO YOU SO OFTEN THESE DAYS, I THOUGHT YOU HAD MOVED HERE.
NO.
I SEE...
SO YOU'RE GOING HOME.
...ARE YOU SORRY FOR IT?
TWEET TWEET ...
TWEE-TWEE ...
......
TWEE-OOO ...
CHI-CHI-CHI-CHI

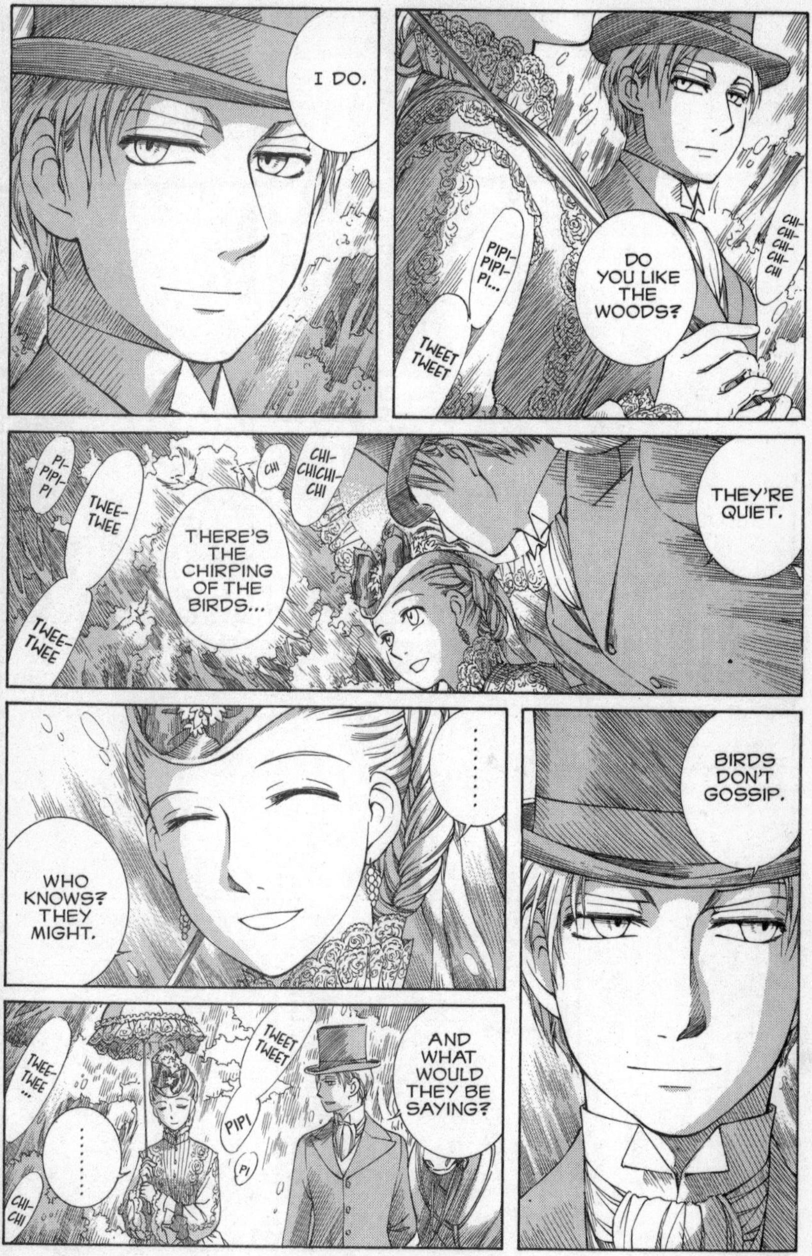
CHI-CHI-CHI-CHI-CHI
DO YOU LIKE THE WOODS?
PIPI-PIPI-PI...
TWEET TWEET
I DO.
THEY'RE QUIET.
CHI-CHICHI-CHI
CHI
THERE'S THE CHIRPING OF THE BIRDS...
PI-PIPIPI-PI
TWEE-TWEE
TWEE-TWEE
BIRDS DON'T GOSSIP.
......
WHO KNOWS? THEY MIGHT.
AND WHAT WOULD THEY BE SAYING?
TWEET TWEET
PIPI
PI
......
TWEE-TWEE...
CHI-CHI

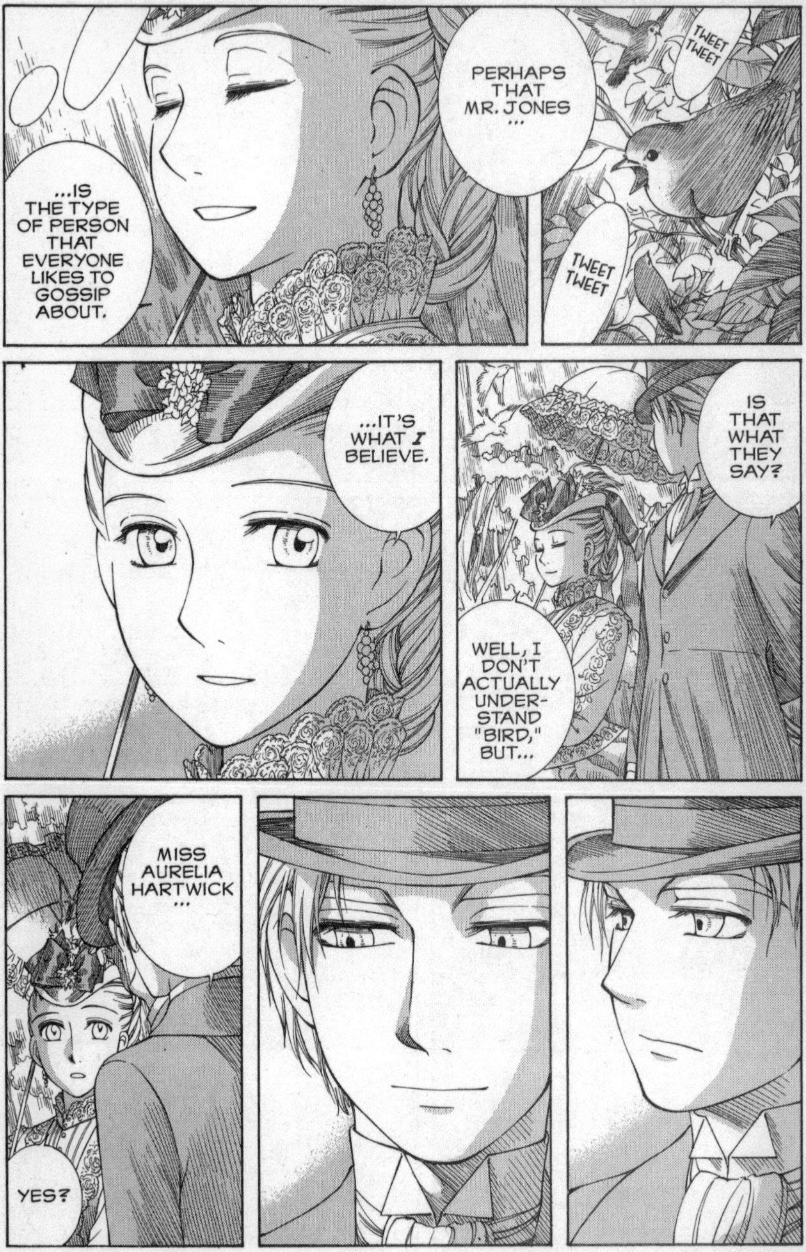
TWEET TWEET
TWEET TWEET
PERHAPS THAT MR. JONES ...
...IS THE TYPE OF PERSON THAT EVERYONE LIKES TO GOSSIP ABOUT.
IS THAT WHAT THEY SAY?
WELL, I DON'T ACTUALLY UNDER-STAND "BIRD," BUT...
...IT'S WHAT *I* BELIEVE.
MISS AURELIA HARTWICK ...
YES?

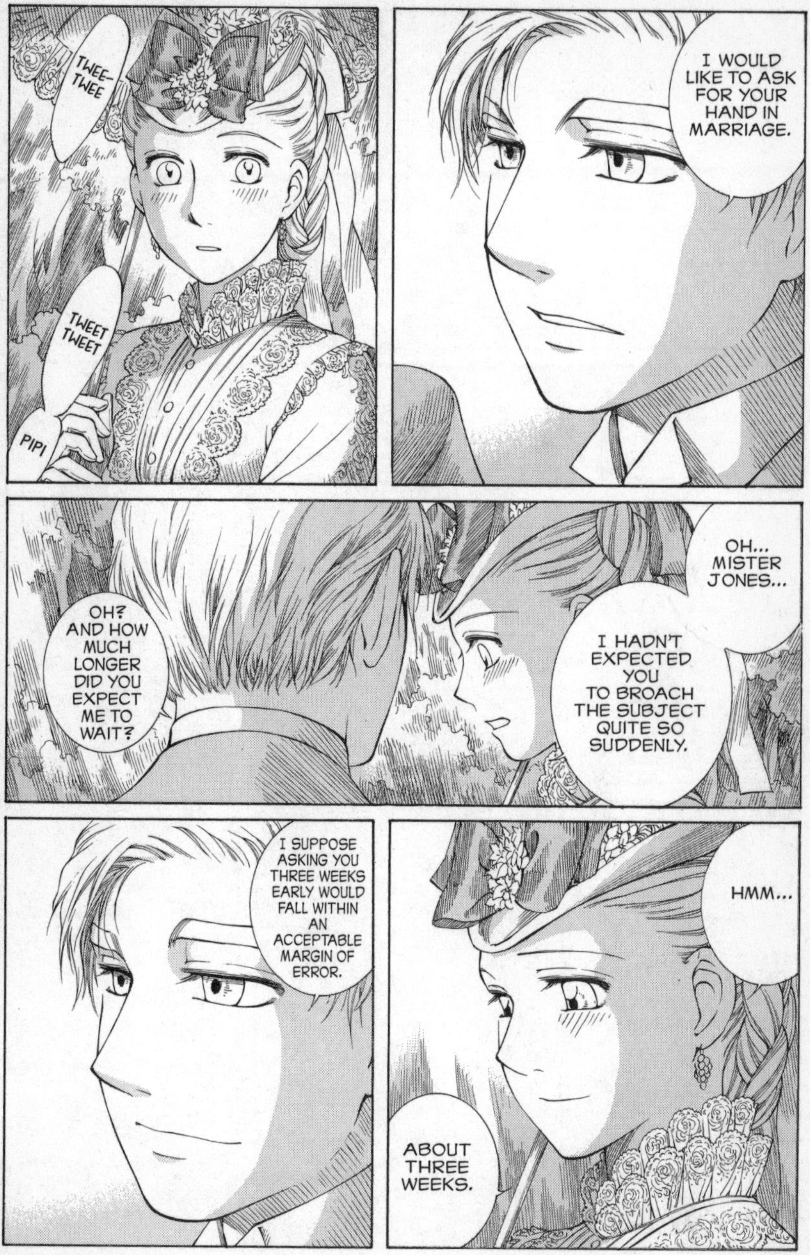
I WOULD LIKE TO ASK FOR YOUR HAND IN MARRIAGE.
TWEE-TWEE
TWEET TWEET
PIPI
OH... MISTER JONES...
I HADN'T EXPECTED YOU TO BROACH THE SUBJECT QUITE SO SUDDENLY.
OH? AND HOW MUCH LONGER DID YOU EXPECT ME TO WAIT?
HMM...
ABOUT THREE WEEKS.
I SUPPOSE ASKING YOU THREE WEEKS EARLY WOULD FALL WITHIN AN ACCEPTABLE MARGIN OF ERROR.

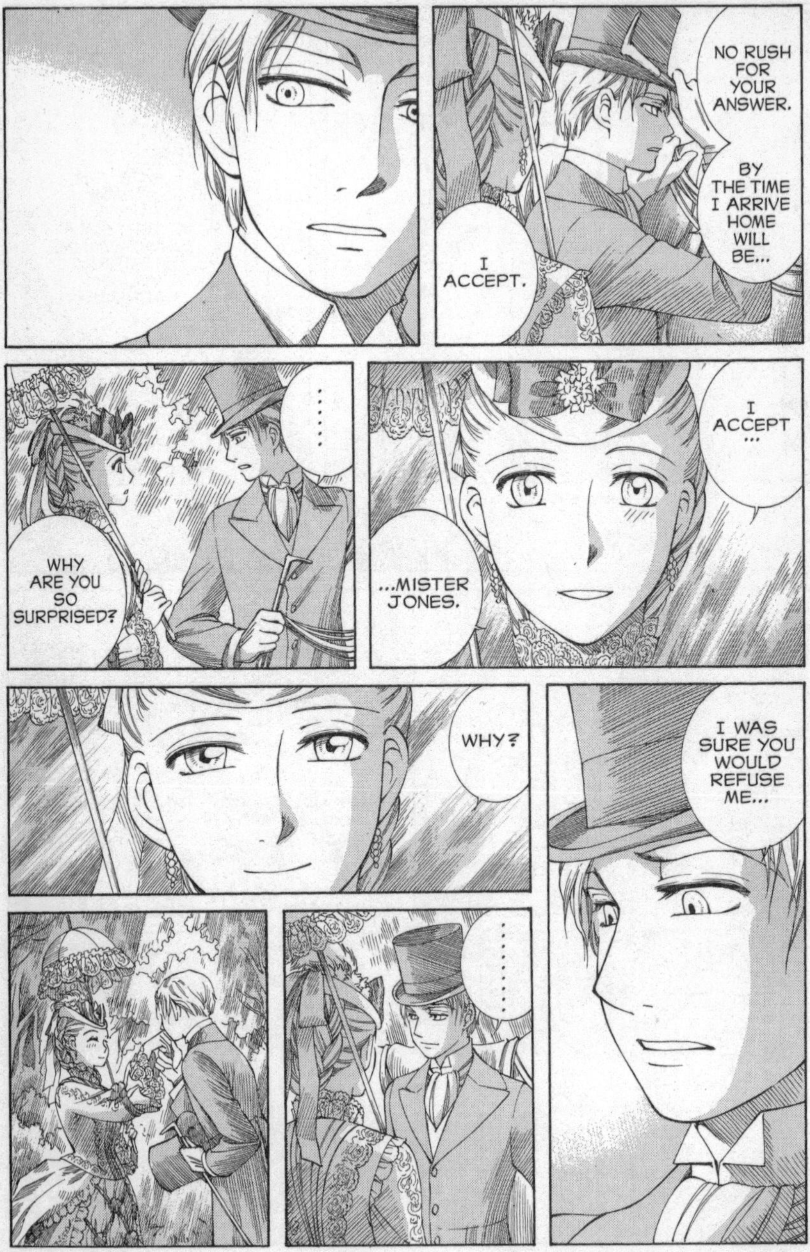
NO RUSH FOR YOUR ANSWER.
BY THE TIME I ARRIVE HOME WILL BE...
I ACCEPT.
I ACCEPT ...
...MISTER JONES.
......
WHY ARE YOU SO SURPRISED?
I WAS SURE YOU WOULD REFUSE ME...
WHY?
....

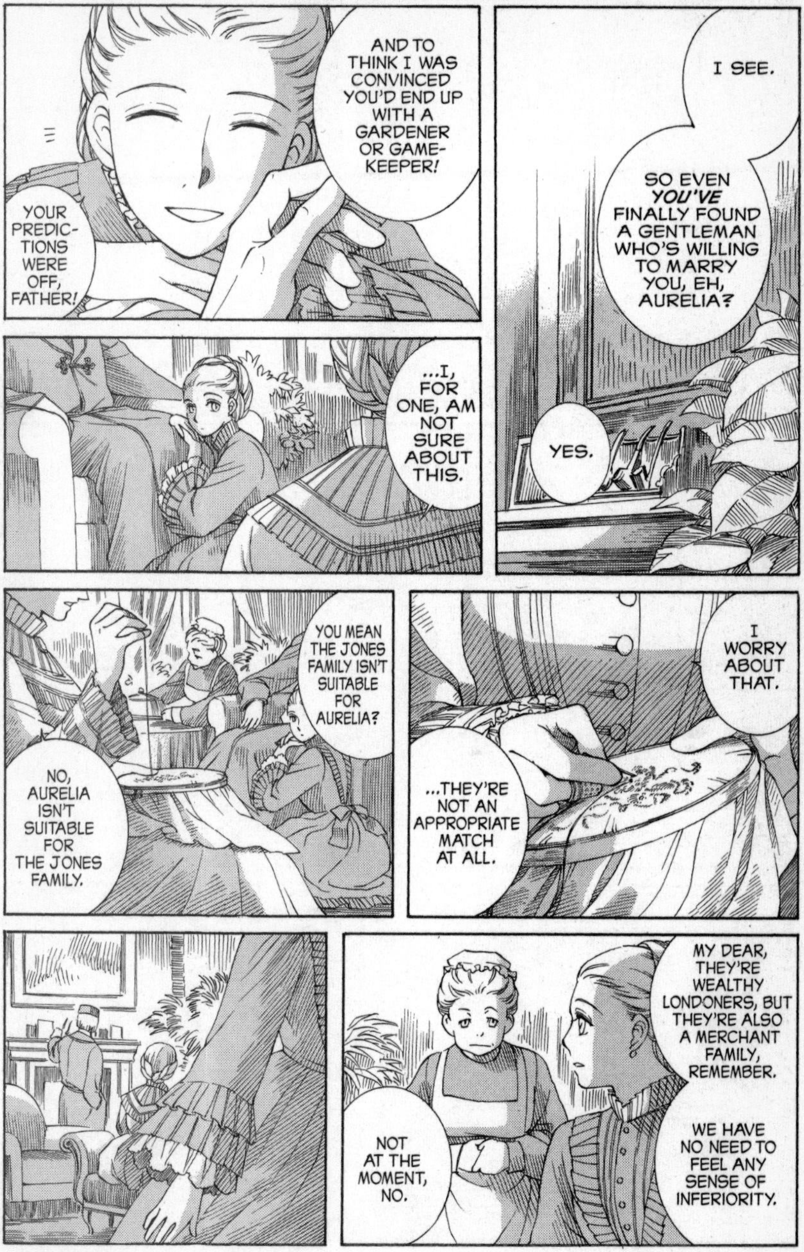

I SEE.
SO EVEN *YOU'VE* FINALLY FOUND A GENTLEMAN WHO'S WILLING TO MARRY YOU, EH, AURELIA?
YES.
AND TO THINK I WAS CONVINCED YOU'D END UP WITH A GARDENER OR GAME-KEEPER!
YOUR PREDIC-TIONS WERE OFF, FATHER!
...I, FOR ONE, AM NOT SURE ABOUT THIS.
I WORRY ABOUT THAT.
...THEY'RE NOT AN APPROPRIATE MATCH AT ALL.
YOU MEAN THE JONES FAMILY ISN'T SUITABLE FOR AURELIA?
NO, AURELIA ISN'T SUITABLE FOR THE JONES FAMILY.
MY DEAR, THEY'RE WEALTHY LONDONERS, BUT THEY'RE ALSO A MERCHANT FAMILY, REMEMBER.
WE HAVE NO NEED TO FEEL ANY SENSE OF INFERIORITY.
NOT AT THE MOMENT, NO.

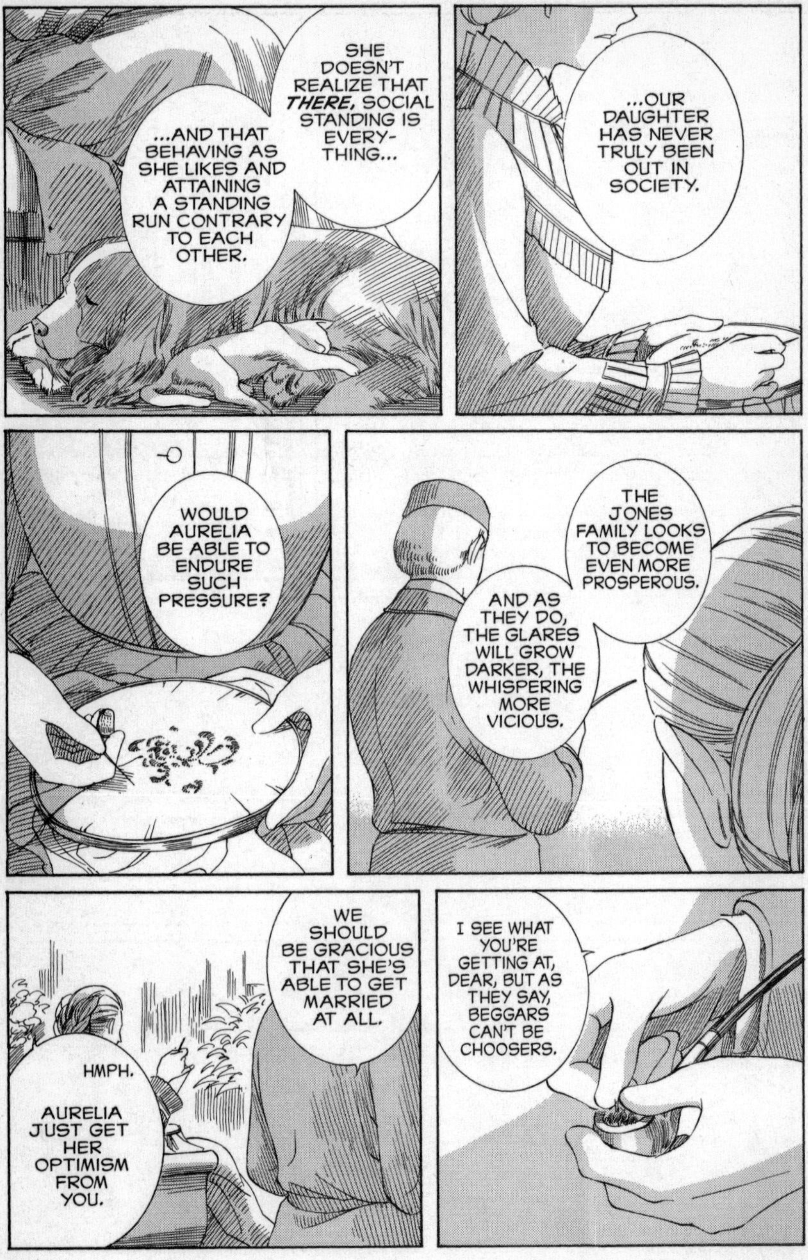
...OUR DAUGHTER HAS NEVER TRULY BEEN OUT IN SOCIETY.
SHE DOESN'T REALIZE THAT *THERE,* SOCIAL STANDING IS EVERY-THING...
...AND THAT BEHAVING AS SHE LIKES AND ATTAINING A STANDING RUN CONTRARY TO EACH OTHER.
THE JONES FAMILY LOOKS TO BECOME EVEN MORE PROSPEROUS.
AND AS THEY DO, THE GLARES WILL GROW DARKER, THE WHISPERING MORE VICIOUS.
WOULD AURELIA BE ABLE TO ENDURE SUCH PRESSURE?
I SEE WHAT YOU'RE GETTING AT, DEAR, BUT AS THEY SAY, BEGGARS CAN'T BE CHOOSERS.
WE SHOULD BE GRACIOUS THAT SHE'S ABLE TO GET MARRIED AT ALL.
HMPH.
AURELIA JUST GET HER OPTIMISM FROM YOU.

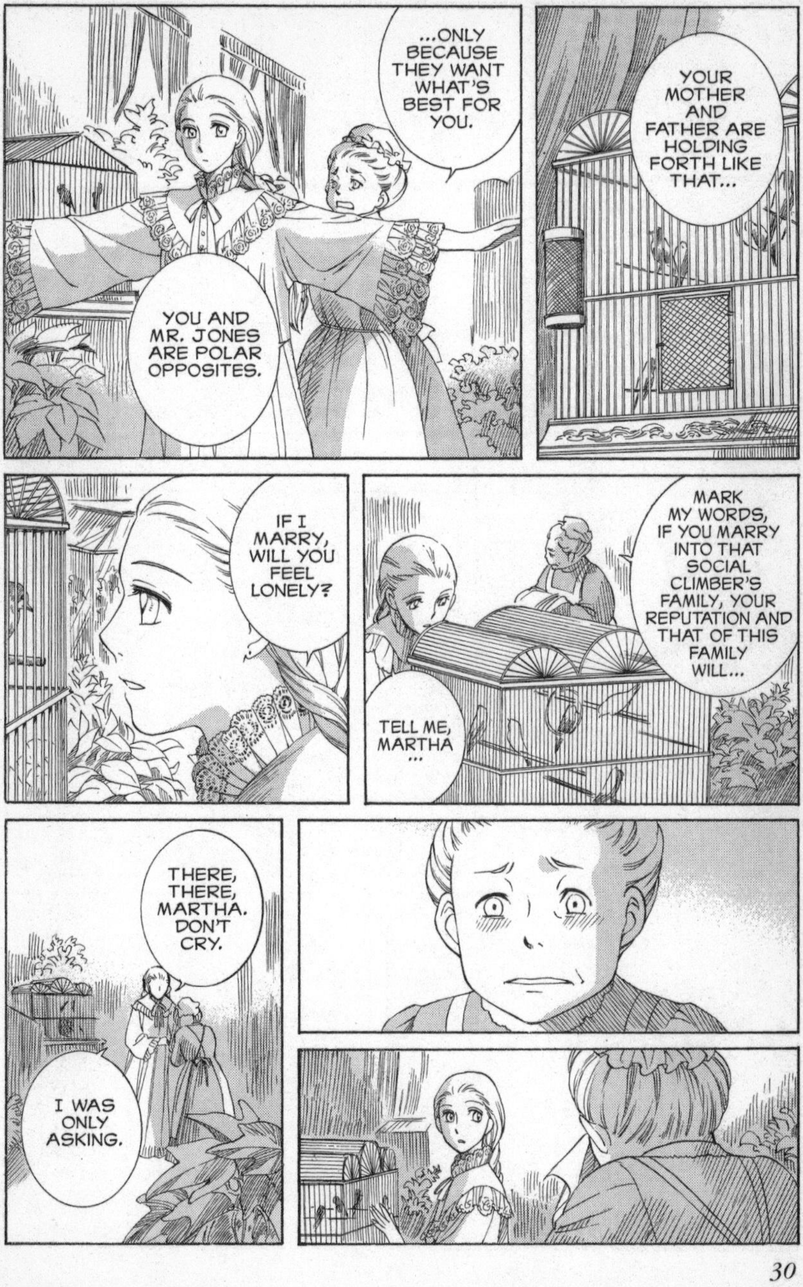
YOUR MOTHER AND FATHER ARE HOLDING FORTH LIKE THAT...
...ONLY BECAUSE THEY WANT WHAT'S BEST FOR YOU.
YOU AND MR. JONES ARE POLAR OPPOSITES.
MARK MY WORDS, IF YOU MARRY INTO THAT SOCIAL CLIMBER'S FAMILY, YOUR REPUTATION AND THAT OF THIS FAMILY WILL...
TELL ME, MARTHA ...
IF I MARRY, WILL YOU FEEL LONELY?
THERE, THERE, MARTHA. DON'T CRY.
I WAS ONLY ASKING.

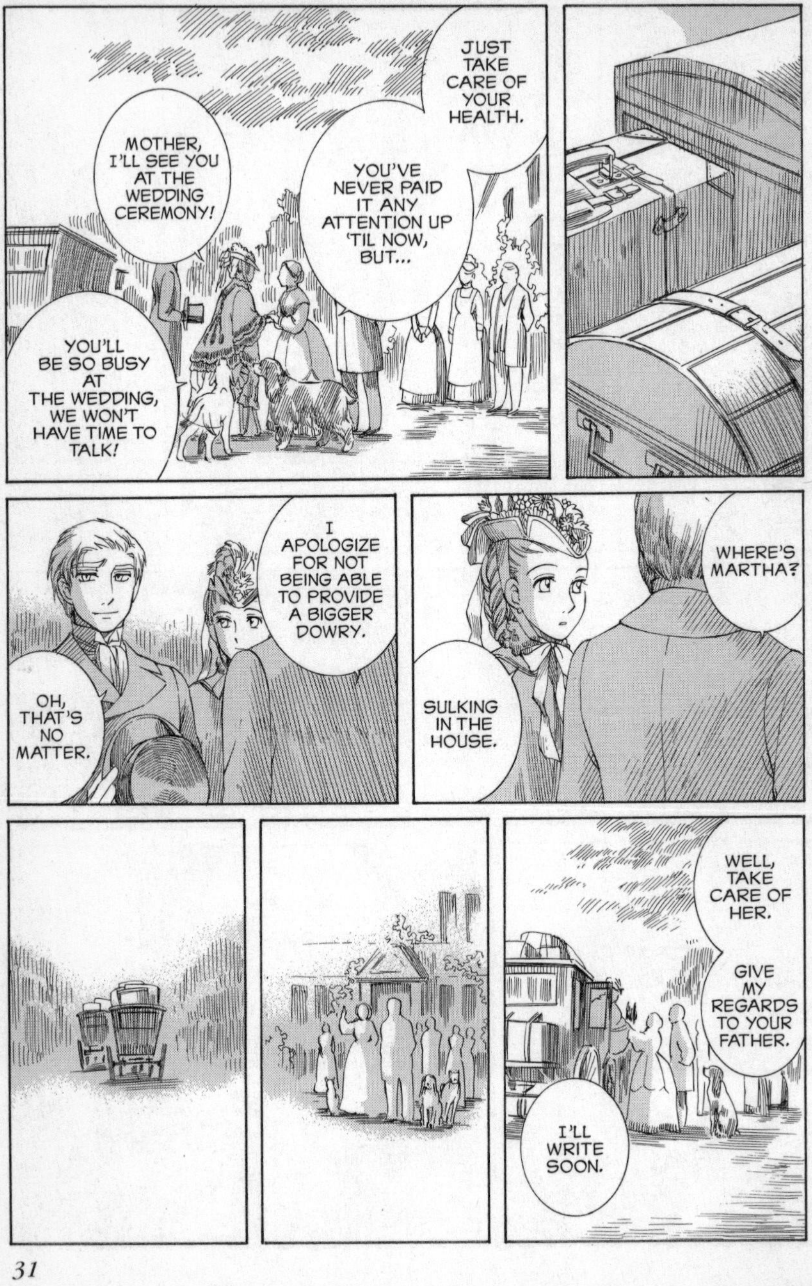
JUST TAKE CARE OF YOUR HEALTH.
YOU'VE NEVER PAID IT ANY ATTENTION UP 'TIL NOW, BUT...
MOTHER, I'LL SEE YOU AT THE WEDDING CEREMONY!
YOU'LL BE SO BUSY AT THE WEDDING, WE WON'T HAVE TIME TO TALK!
WHERE'S MARTHA?
SULKING IN THE HOUSE.
I APOLOGIZE FOR NOT BEING ABLE TO PROVIDE A BIGGER DOWRY.
OH, THAT'S NO MATTER.
WELL, TAKE CARE OF HER.
GIVE MY REGARDS TO YOUR FATHER.
I'LL WRITE SOON.

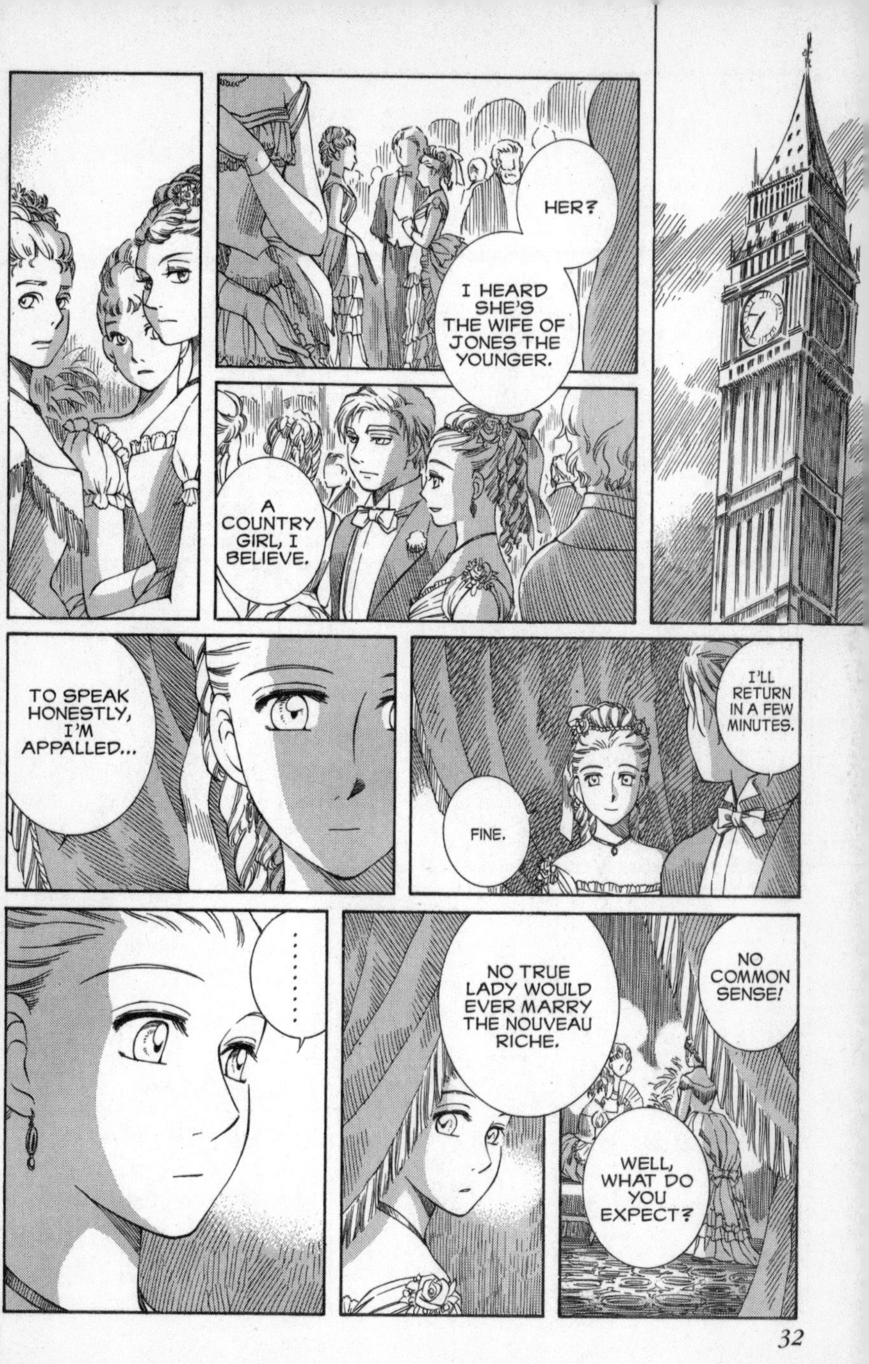
HER?
I HEARD SHE'S THE WIFE OF JONES THE YOUNGER.
A COUNTRY GIRL, I BELIEVE.
I'LL RETURN IN A FEW MINUTES.
FINE.
TO SPEAK HONESTLY, I'M APPALLED...
NO COMMON SENSE!
NO TRUE LADY WOULD EVER MARRY THE NOUVEAU RICHE.
WELL, WHAT DO YOU EXPECT?
......

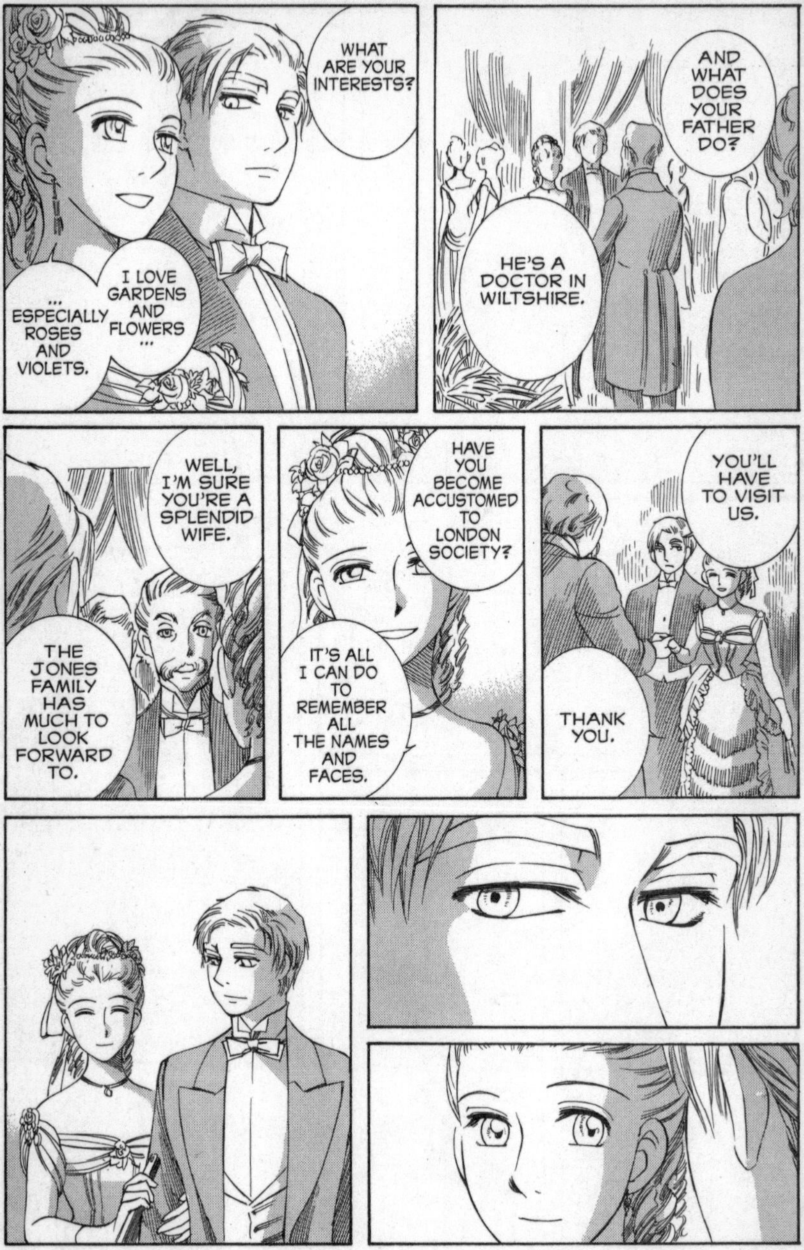
AND WHAT DOES YOUR FATHER DO?
HE'S A DOCTOR IN WILTSHIRE.
WHAT ARE YOUR INTERESTS?
I LOVE GARDENS AND FLOWERS ...
... ESPECIALLY ROSES AND VIOLETS.
YOU'LL HAVE TO VISIT US.
THANK YOU.
HAVE YOU BECOME ACCUSTOMED TO LONDON SOCIETY?
IT'S ALL I CAN DO TO REMEMBER ALL THE NAMES AND FACES.
WELL, I'M SURE YOU'RE A SPLENDID WIFE.
THE JONES FAMILY HAS MUCH TO LOOK FORWARD TO.

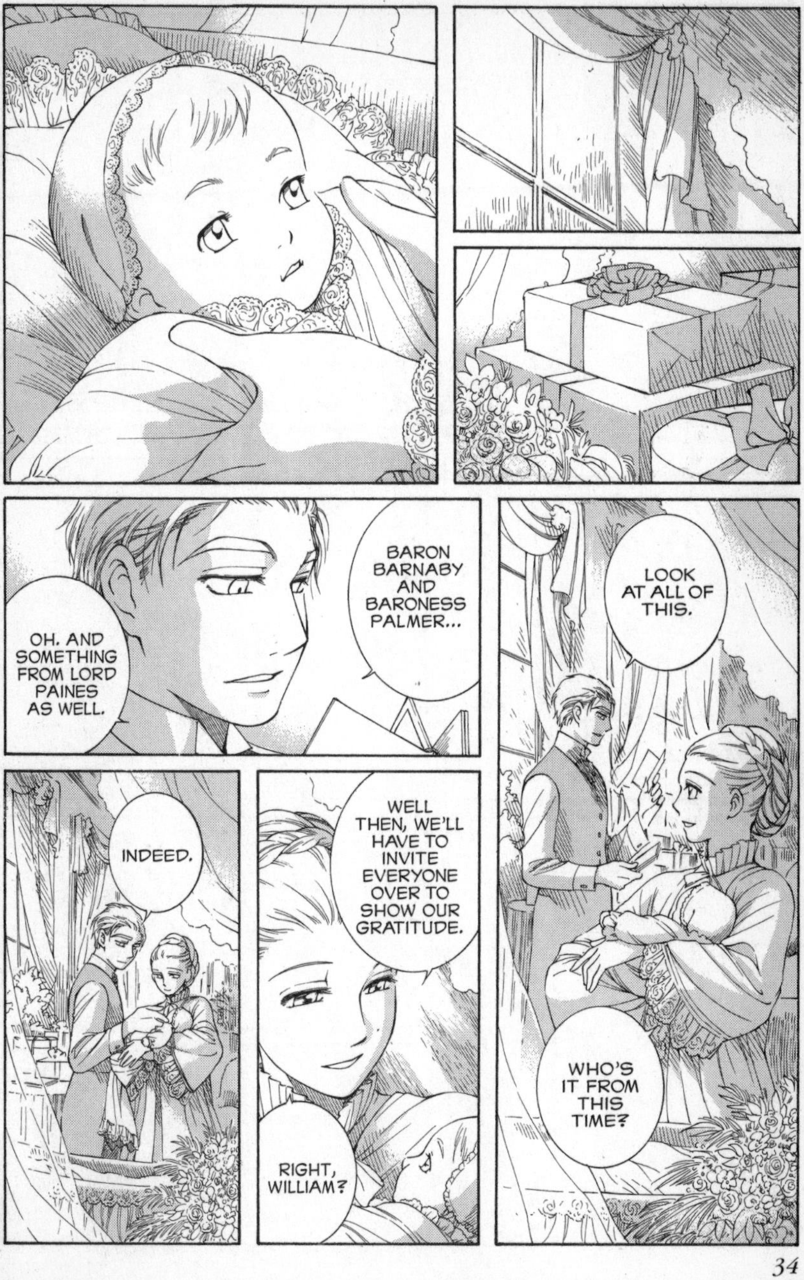
LOOK AT ALL OF THIS.
WHO'S IT FROM THIS TIME?
BARON BARNABY AND BARONESS PALMER...
OH. AND SOMETHING FROM LORD PAINES AS WELL.
WELL THEN, WE'LL HAVE TO INVITE EVERYONE OVER TO SHOW OUR GRATITUDE.
RIGHT, WILLIAM?
INDEED.

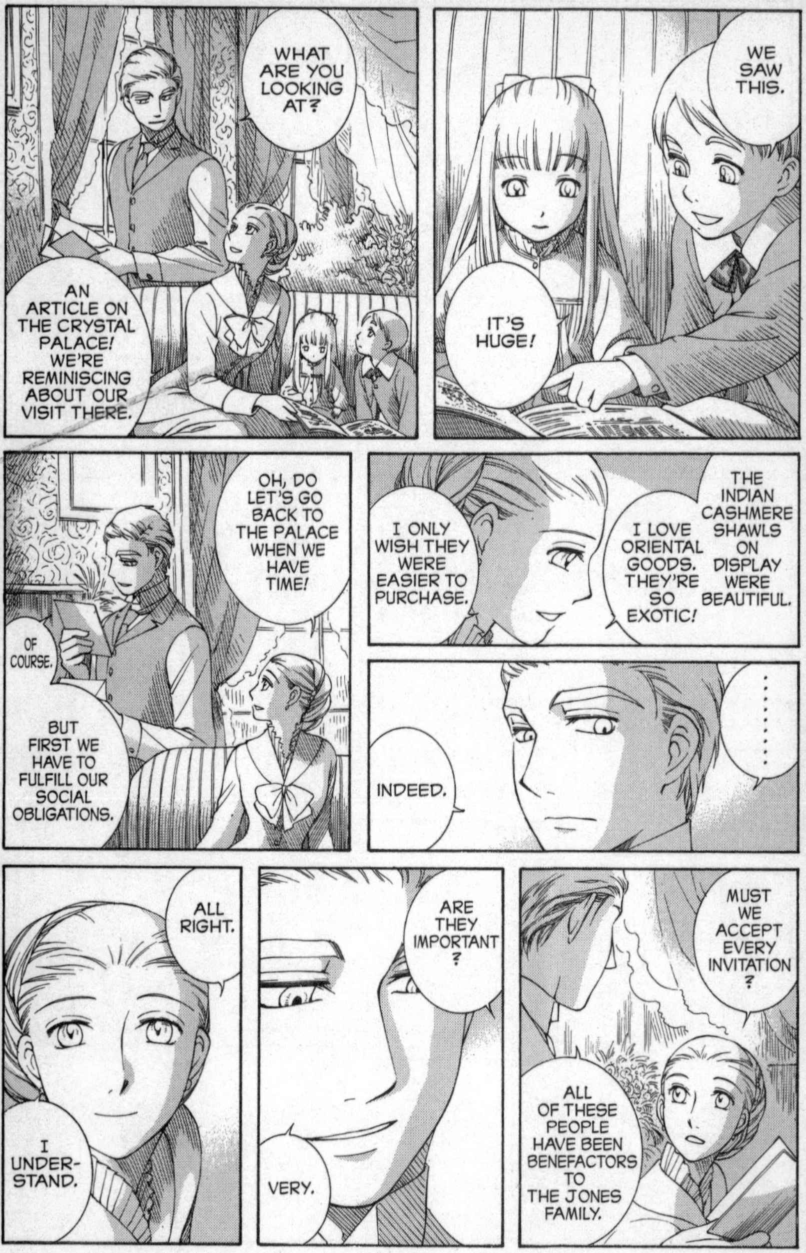
WE SAW THIS.
IT'S HUGE!
WHAT ARE YOU LOOKING AT?
AN ARTICLE ON THE CRYSTAL PALACE! WE'RE REMINISCING ABOUT OUR VISIT THERE.
THE INDIAN CASHMERE SHAWLS ON DISPLAY WERE BEAUTIFUL.
I LOVE ORIENTAL GOODS. THEY'RE SO EXOTIC!
I ONLY WISH THEY WERE EASIER TO PURCHASE.
....
INDEED.
OH, DO LET'S GO BACK TO THE PALACE WHEN WE HAVE TIME!
OF COURSE.
BUT FIRST WE HAVE TO FULFILL OUR SOCIAL OBLIGATIONS.
MUST WE ACCEPT EVERY INVITATION?
ALL OF THESE PEOPLE HAVE BEEN BENEFACTORS TO THE JONES FAMILY.
ARE THEY IMPORTANT?
VERY.
ALL RIGHT.
I UNDERSTAND.

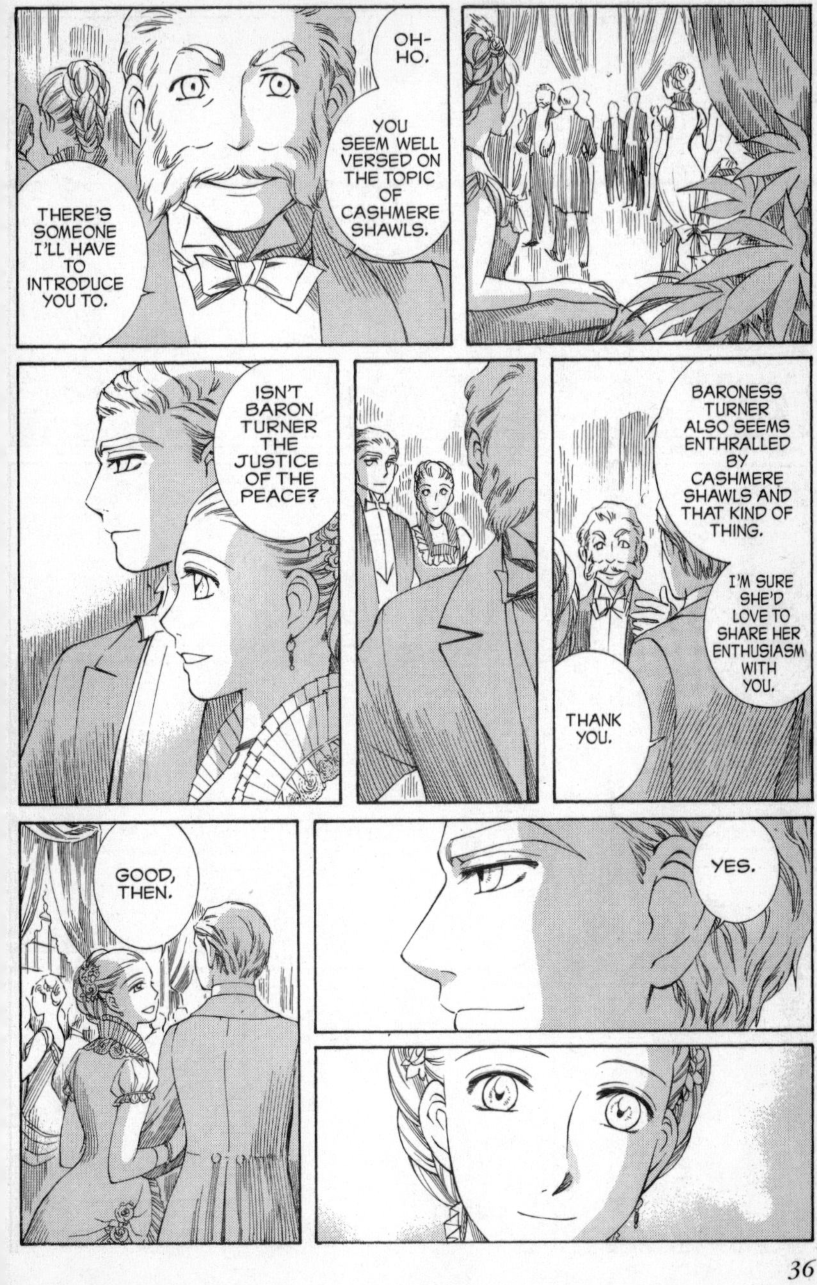
OH-HO.
YOU SEEM WELL VERSED ON THE TOPIC OF CASHMERE SHAWLS.
THERE'S SOMEONE I'LL HAVE TO INTRODUCE YOU TO.
BARONESS TURNER ALSO SEEMS ENTHRALLED BY CASHMERE SHAWLS AND THAT KIND OF THING.
I'M SURE SHE'D LOVE TO SHARE HER ENTHUSIASM WITH YOU.
THANK YOU.
ISN'T BARON TURNER THE JUSTICE OF THE PEACE?
YES.
GOOD, THEN.

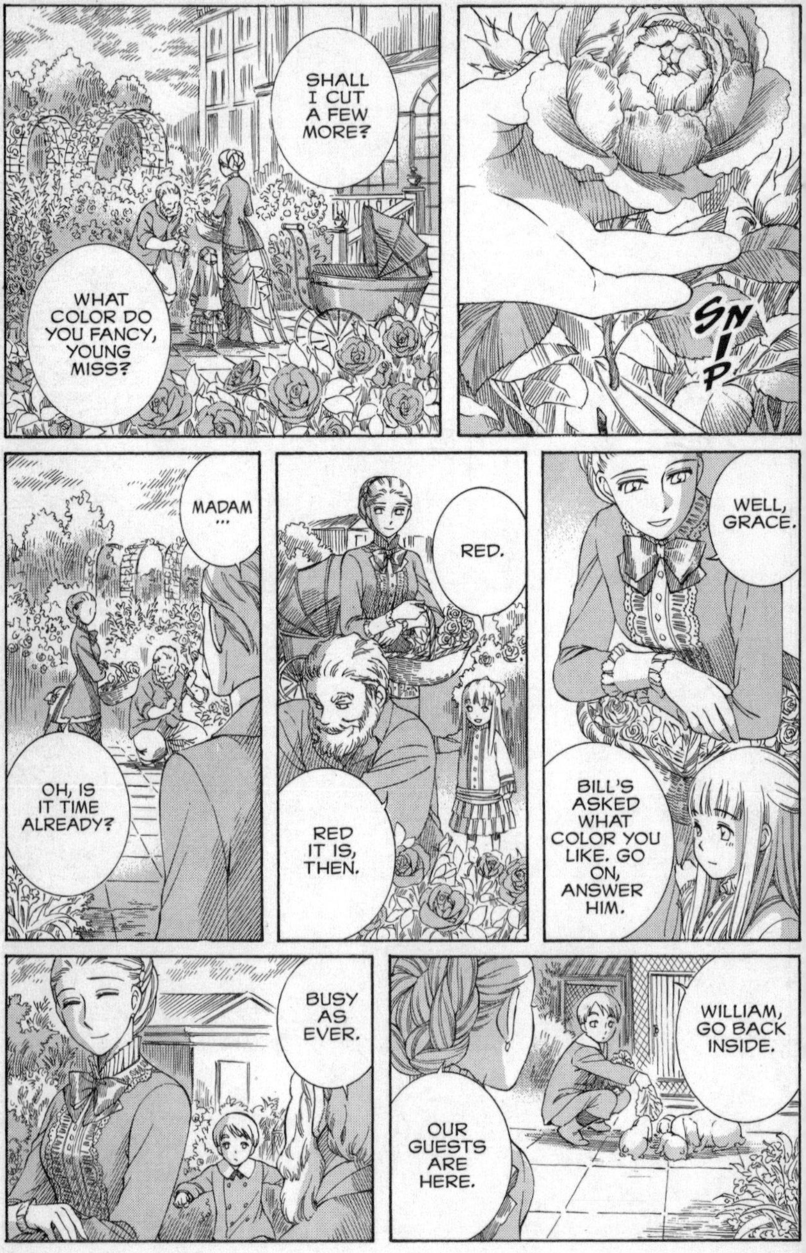
SNIP
SHALL I CUT A FEW MORE?
WHAT COLOR DO YOU FANCY, YOUNG MISS?
WELL, GRACE.
BILL'S ASKED WHAT COLOR YOU LIKE. GO ON, ANSWER HIM.
RED.
RED IT IS, THEN.
MADAM...
OH, IS IT TIME ALREADY?
WILLIAM, GO BACK INSIDE.
OUR GUESTS ARE HERE.
BUSY AS EVER.

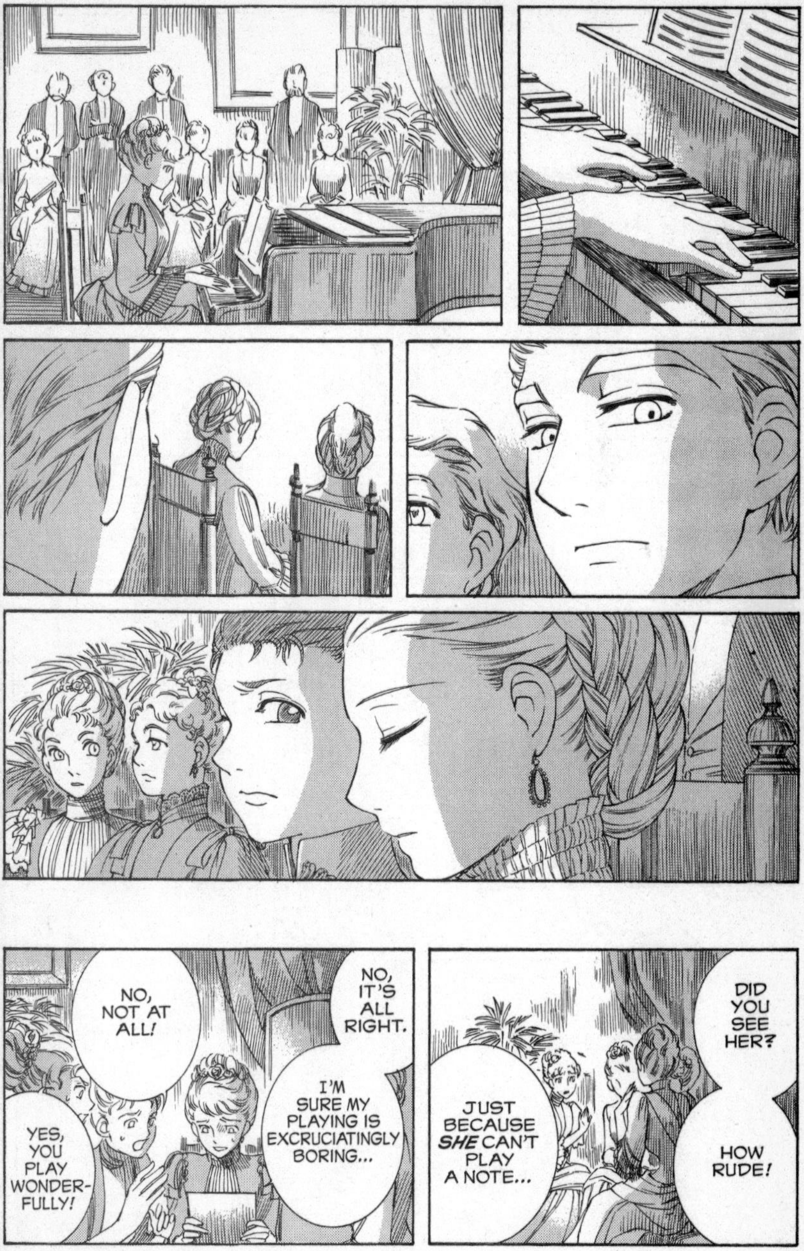
DID YOU SEE HER?
HOW RUDE!
JUST BECAUSE *SHE* CAN'T PLAY A NOTE...
NO, IT'S ALL RIGHT.
I'M SURE MY PLAYING IS EXCRUCIATINGLY BORING...
NO, NOT AT ALL!
YES, YOU PLAY WONDER-FULLY!

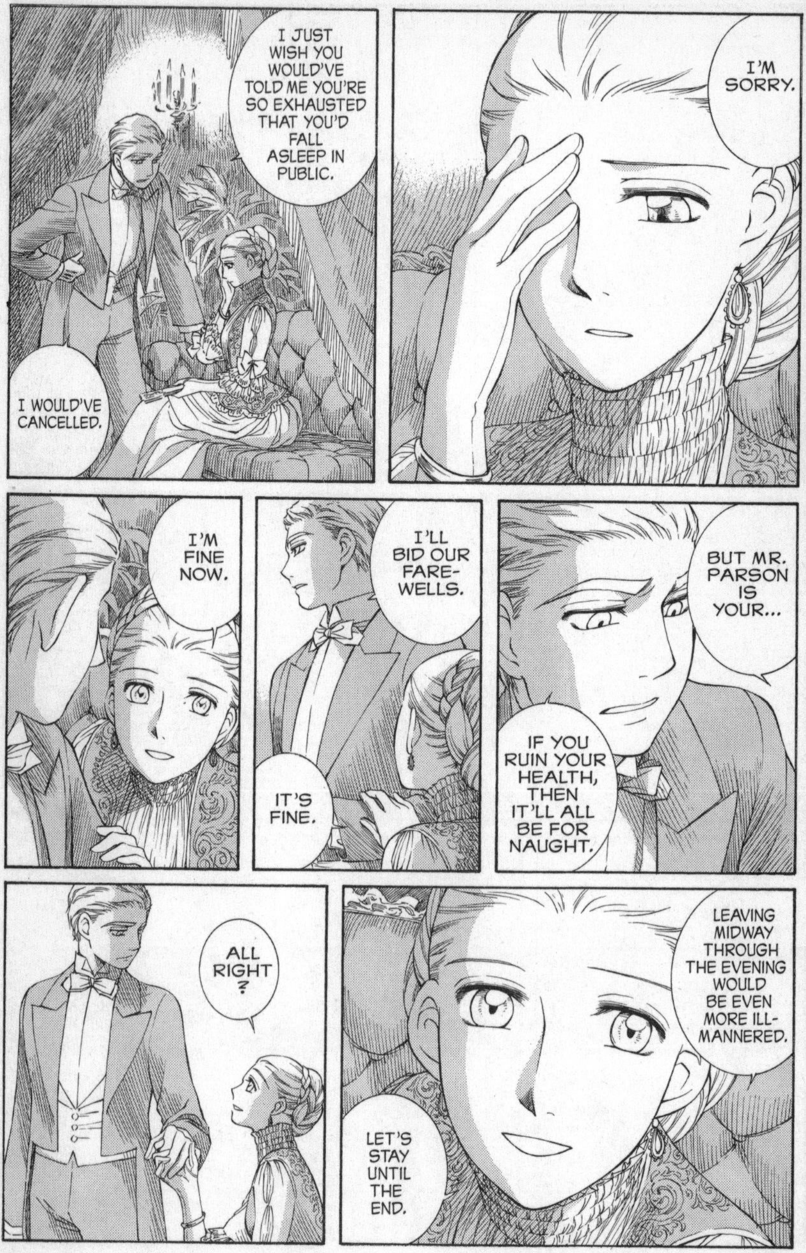
I'M SORRY.
I JUST WISH YOU WOULD'VE TOLD ME YOU'RE SO EXHAUSTED THAT YOU'D FALL ASLEEP IN PUBLIC.
I WOULD'VE CANCELLED.
BUT MR. PARSON IS YOUR...
IF YOU RUIN YOUR HEALTH, THEN IT'LL ALL BE FOR NAUGHT.
I'LL BID OUR FAREWELLS.
IT'S FINE.
I'M FINE NOW.
LEAVING MIDWAY THROUGH THE EVENING WOULD BE EVEN MORE ILL-MANNERED.
LET'S STAY UNTIL THE END.
ALL RIGHT?

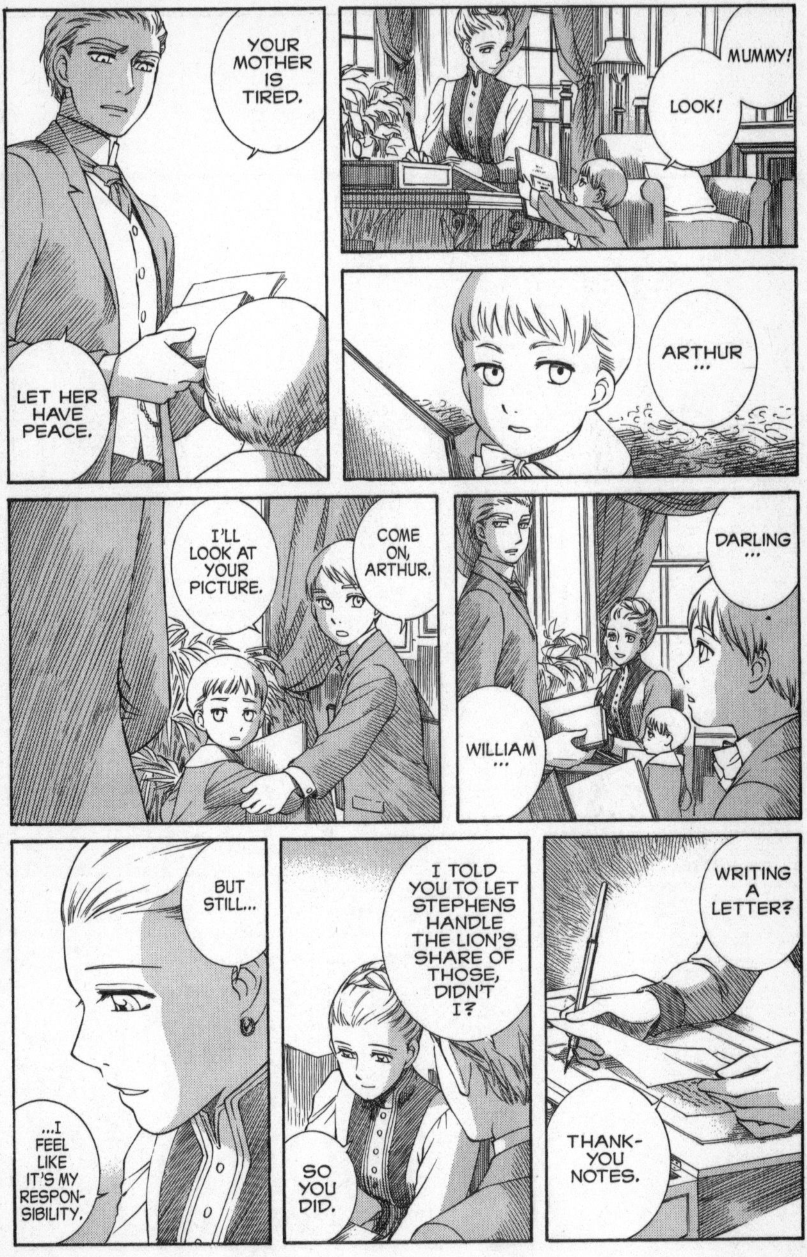
MUMMY!
LOOK!
ARTHUR ...
YOUR MOTHER IS TIRED.
LET HER HAVE PEACE.
DARLING ...
WILLIAM ...
COME ON, ARTHUR.
I'LL LOOK AT YOUR PICTURE.
WRITING A LETTER?
THANK-YOU NOTES.
I TOLD YOU TO LET STEPHENS HANDLE THE LION'S SHARE OF THOSE, DIDN'T I?
SO YOU DID.
BUT STILL...
...I FEEL LIKE IT'S MY RESPONSIBILITY.

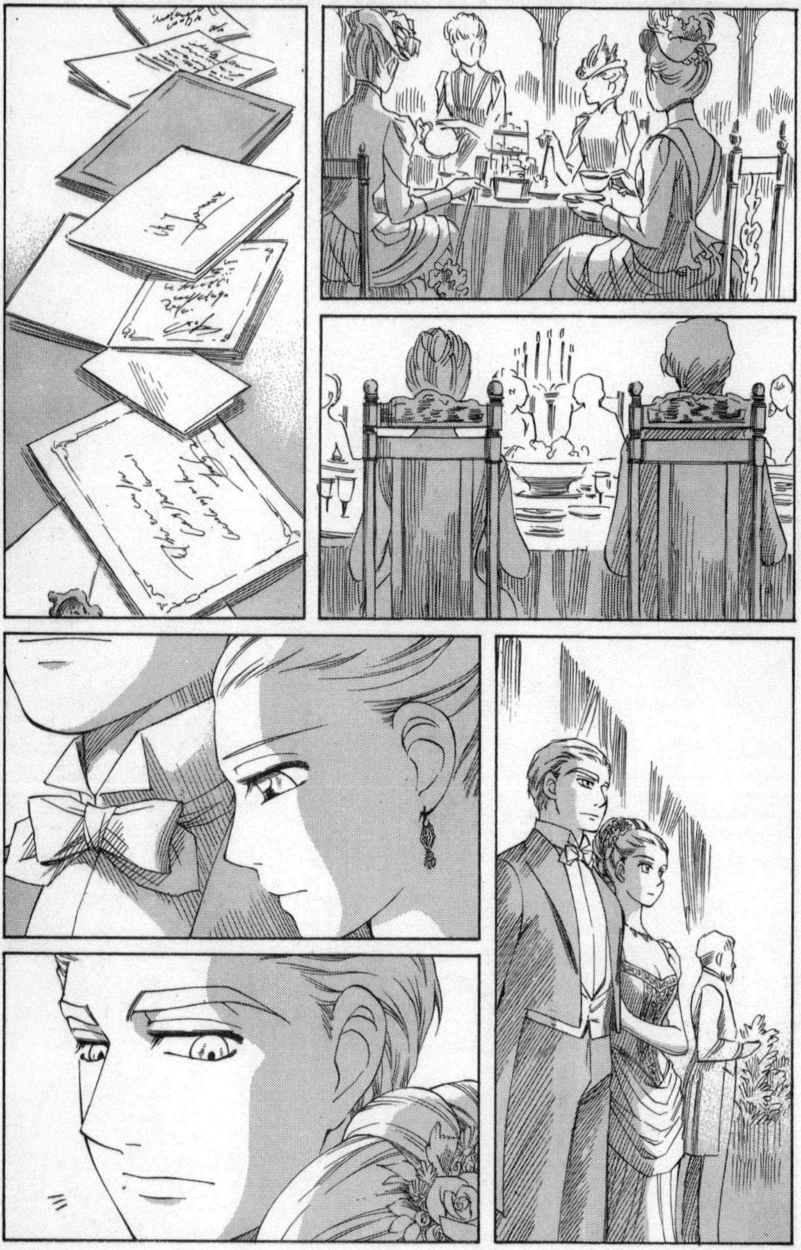

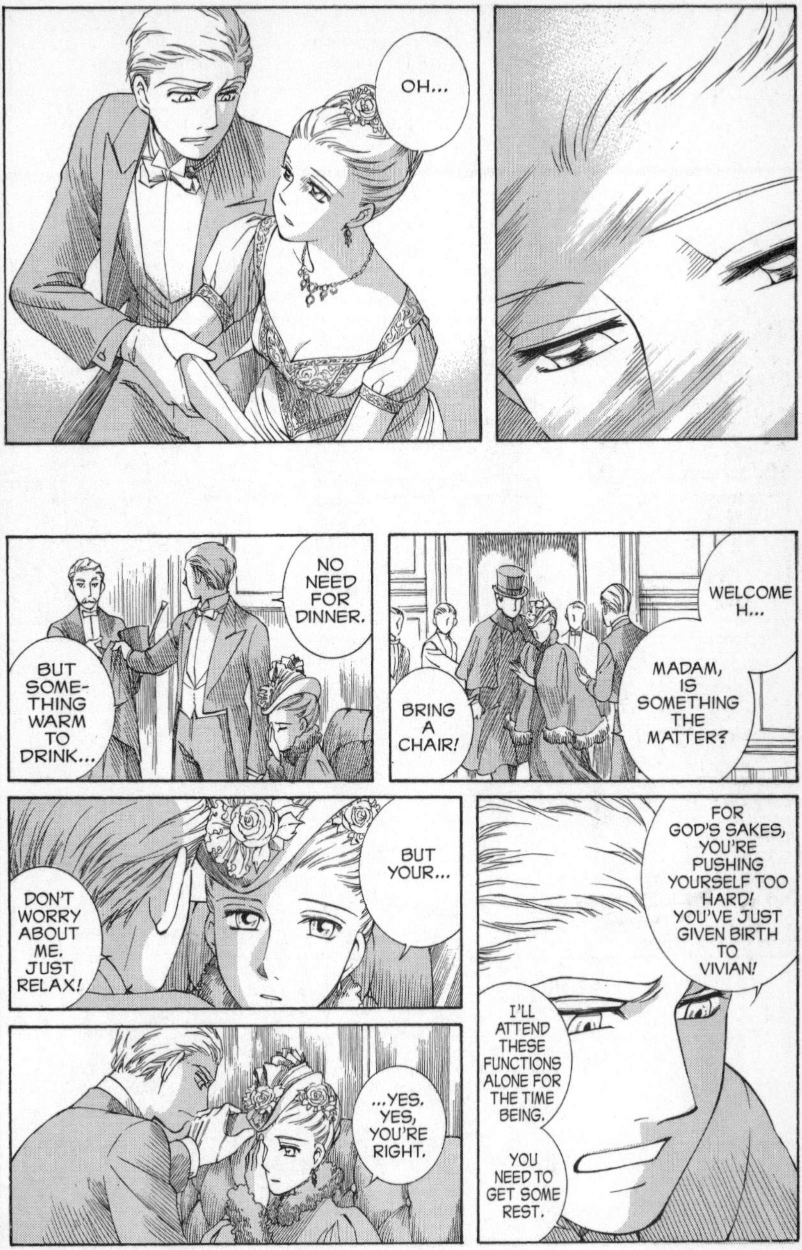
OH...
WELCOME H...
MADAM, IS SOMETHING THE MATTER?
BRING A CHAIR!
NO NEED FOR DINNER.
BUT SOME-THING WARM TO DRINK...
FOR GOD'S SAKES, YOU'RE PUSHING YOURSELF TOO HARD! YOU'VE JUST GIVEN BIRTH TO VIVIAN!
I'LL ATTEND THESE FUNCTIONS ALONE FOR THE TIME BEING.
YOU NEED TO GET SOME REST.
BUT YOUR...
DON'T WORRY ABOUT ME. JUST RELAX!
...YES. YES, YOU'RE RIGHT.

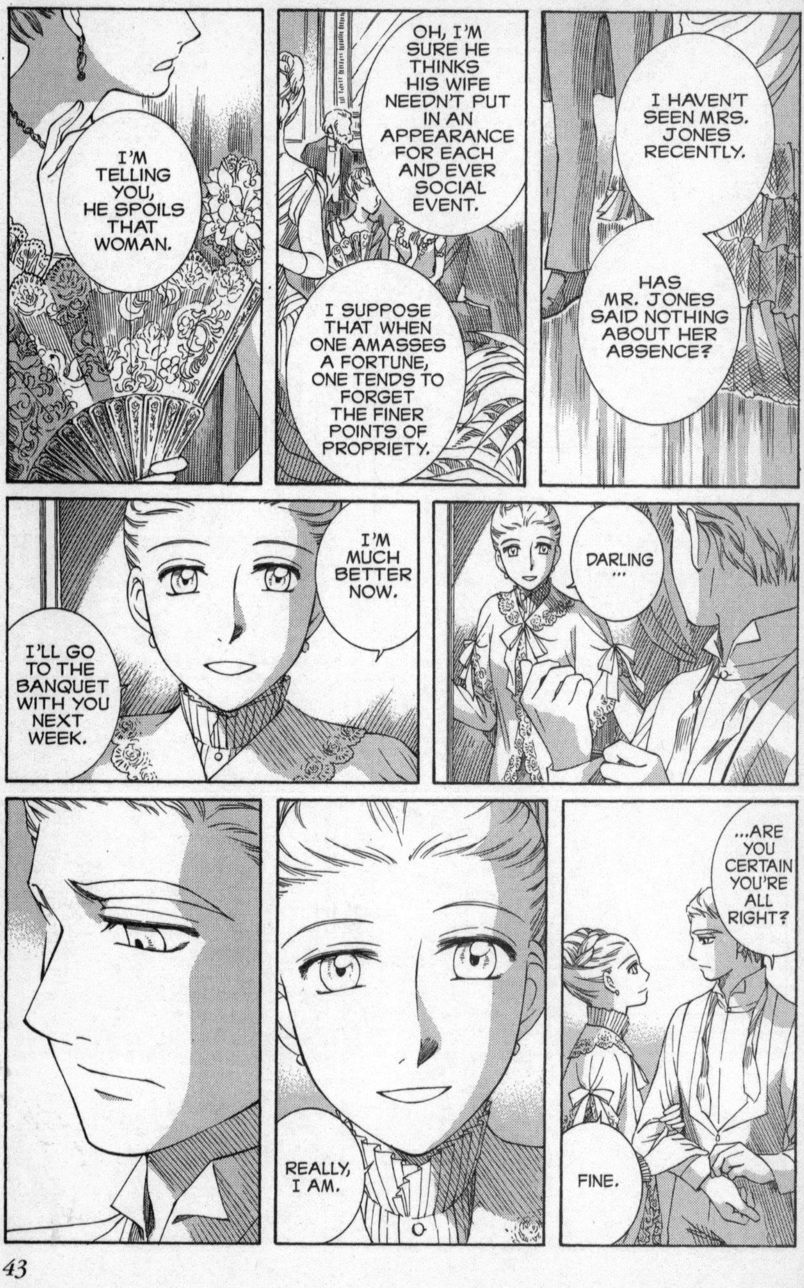
I HAVEN'T SEEN MRS. JONES RECENTLY.
HAS MR. JONES SAID NOTHING ABOUT HER ABSENCE?
OH, I'M SURE HE THINKS HIS WIFE NEEDN'T PUT IN AN APPEARANCE FOR EACH AND EVER SOCIAL EVENT.
I SUPPOSE THAT WHEN ONE AMASSES A FORTUNE, ONE TENDS TO FORGET THE FINER POINTS OF PROPRIETY.
I'M TELLING YOU, HE SPOILS THAT WOMAN.
DARLING ...
I'M MUCH BETTER NOW.
I'LL GO TO THE BANQUET WITH YOU NEXT WEEK.
...ARE YOU CERTAIN YOU'RE ALL RIGHT?
FINE.
REALLY, I AM.

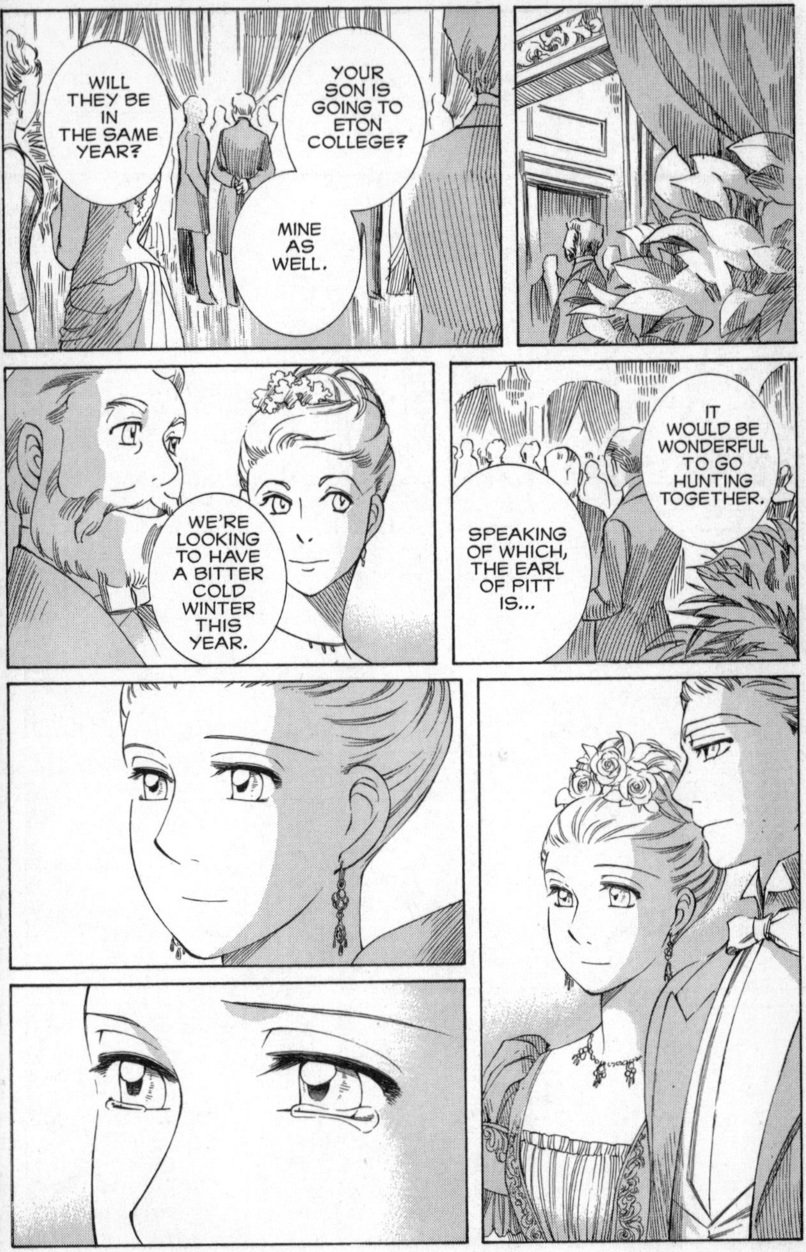
YOUR SON IS GOING TO ETON COLLEGE?
WILL THEY BE IN THE SAME YEAR?
MINE AS WELL.
IT WOULD BE WONDERFUL TO GO HUNTING TOGETHER.
SPEAKING OF WHICH, THE EARL OF PITT IS...
WE'RE LOOKING TO HAVE A BITTER COLD WINTER THIS YEAR.

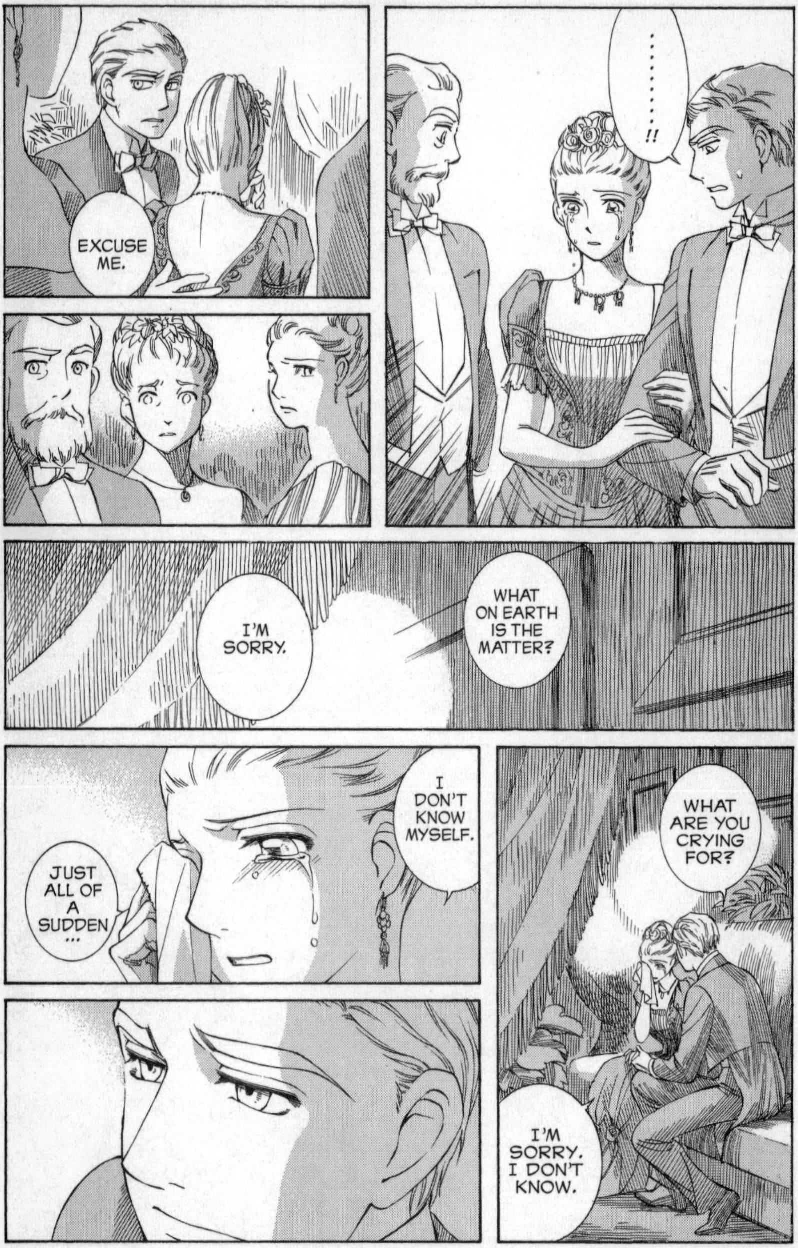
......!!
EXCUSE ME.
WHAT ON EARTH IS THE MATTER?
I'M SORRY.
WHAT ARE YOU CRYING FOR?
I'M SORRY. I DON'T KNOW.
I DON'T KNOW MYSELF.
JUST ALL OF A SUDDEN...

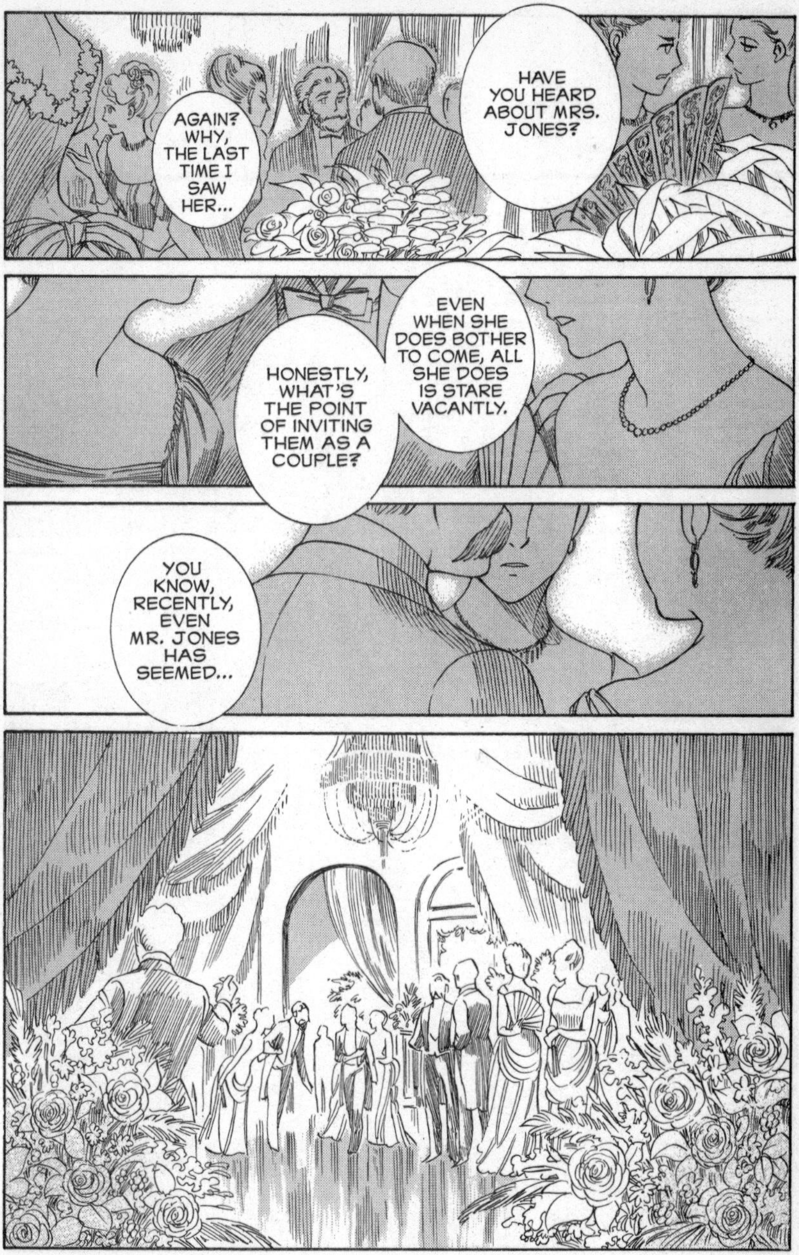
HAVE YOU HEARD ABOUT MRS. JONES?
AGAIN? WHY, THE LAST TIME I SAW HER...
EVEN WHEN SHE DOES BOTHER TO COME, ALL SHE DOES IS STARE VACANTLY.
HONESTLY, WHAT'S THE POINT OF INVITING THEM AS A COUPLE?
YOU KNOW, RECENTLY, EVEN MR. JONES HAS SEEMED...

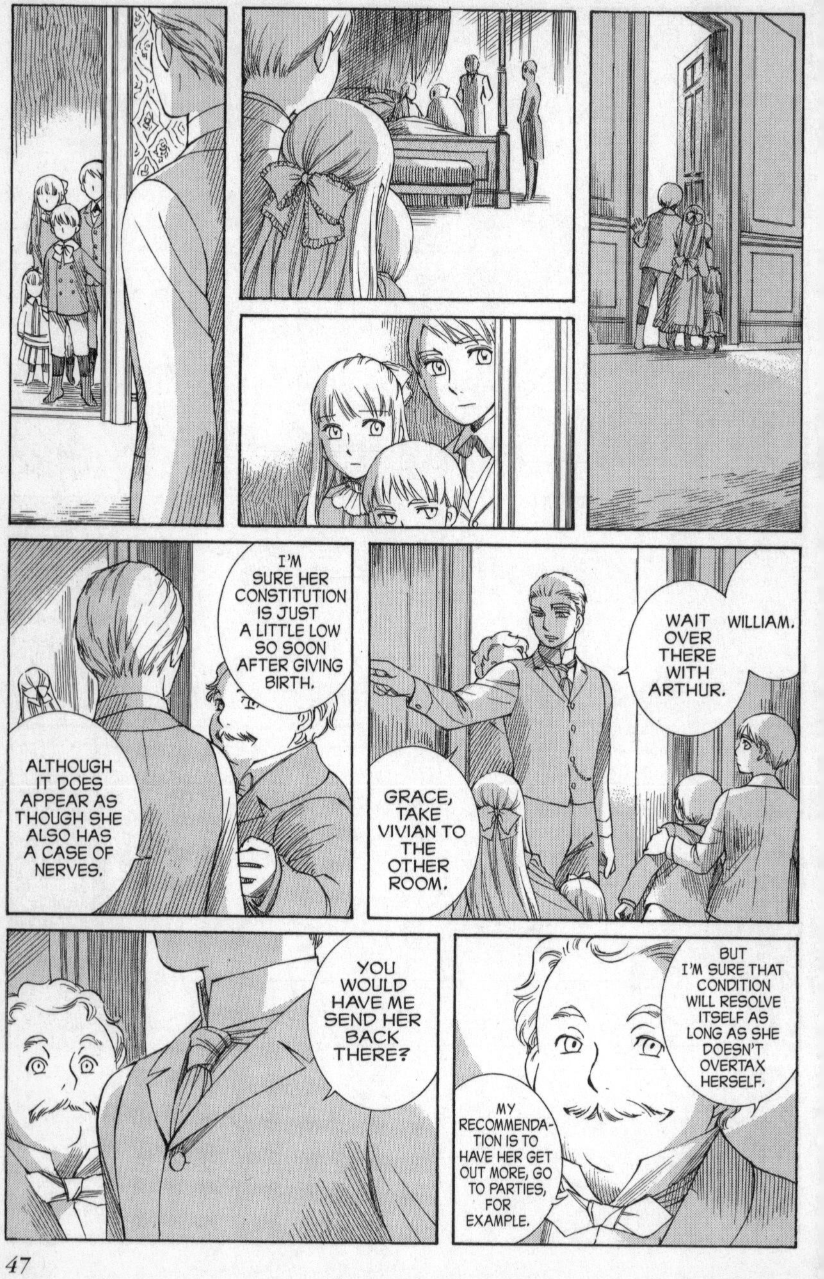
WILLIAM. WAIT OVER THERE WITH ARTHUR.
GRACE, TAKE VIVIAN TO THE OTHER ROOM.
I'M SURE HER CONSTITUTION IS JUST A LITTLE LOW SO SOON AFTER GIVING BIRTH.
ALTHOUGH IT DOES APPEAR AS THOUGH SHE ALSO HAS A CASE OF NERVES.
BUT I'M SURE THAT CONDITION WILL RESOLVE ITSELF AS LONG AS SHE DOESN'T OVERTAX HERSELF.
MY RECOMMENDATION IS TO HAVE HER GET OUT MORE, GO TO PARTIES, FOR EXAMPLE.
YOU WOULD HAVE ME SEND HER BACK THERE?

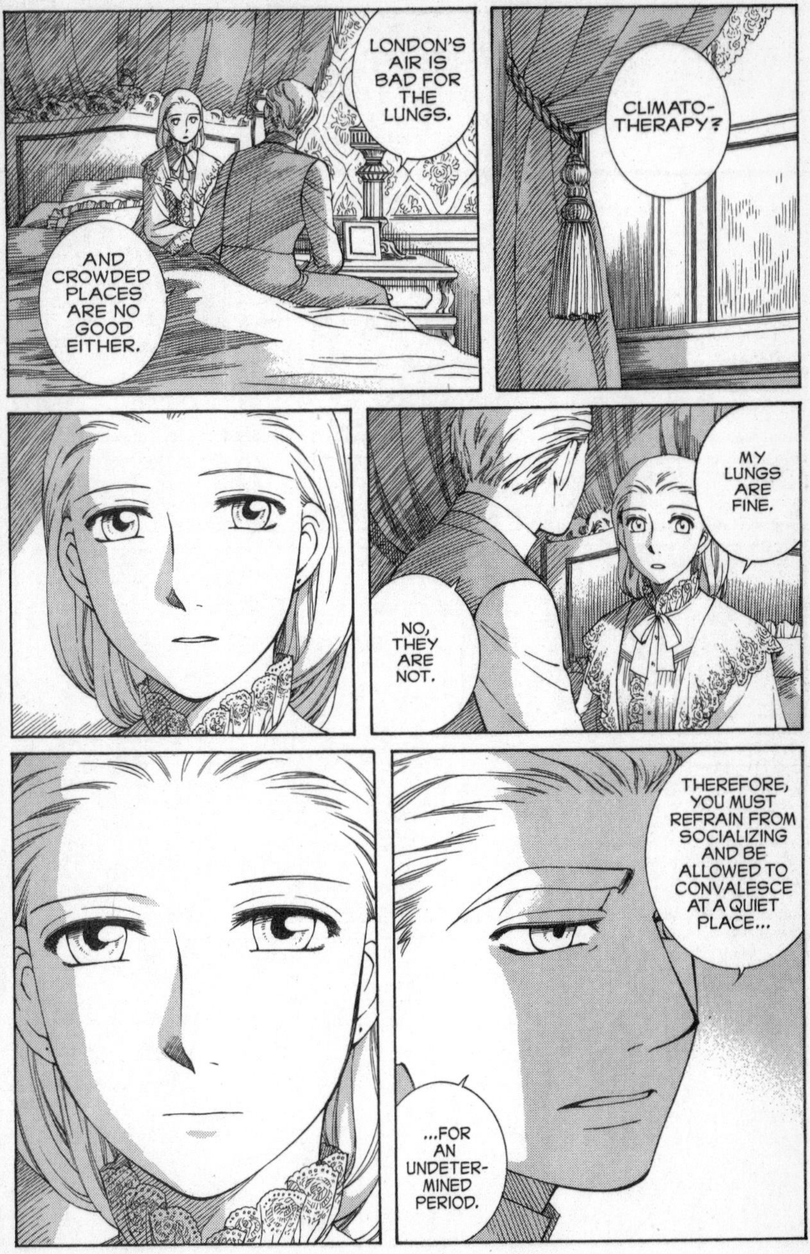
CLIMATO-THERAPY?
LONDON'S AIR IS BAD FOR THE LUNGS.
AND CROWDED PLACES ARE NO GOOD EITHER.
MY LUNGS ARE FINE.
NO, THEY ARE NOT.
THEREFORE, YOU MUST REFRAIN FROM SOCIALIZING AND BE ALLOWED TO CONVALESCE AT A QUIET PLACE...
...FOR AN UNDETER-MINED PERIOD.

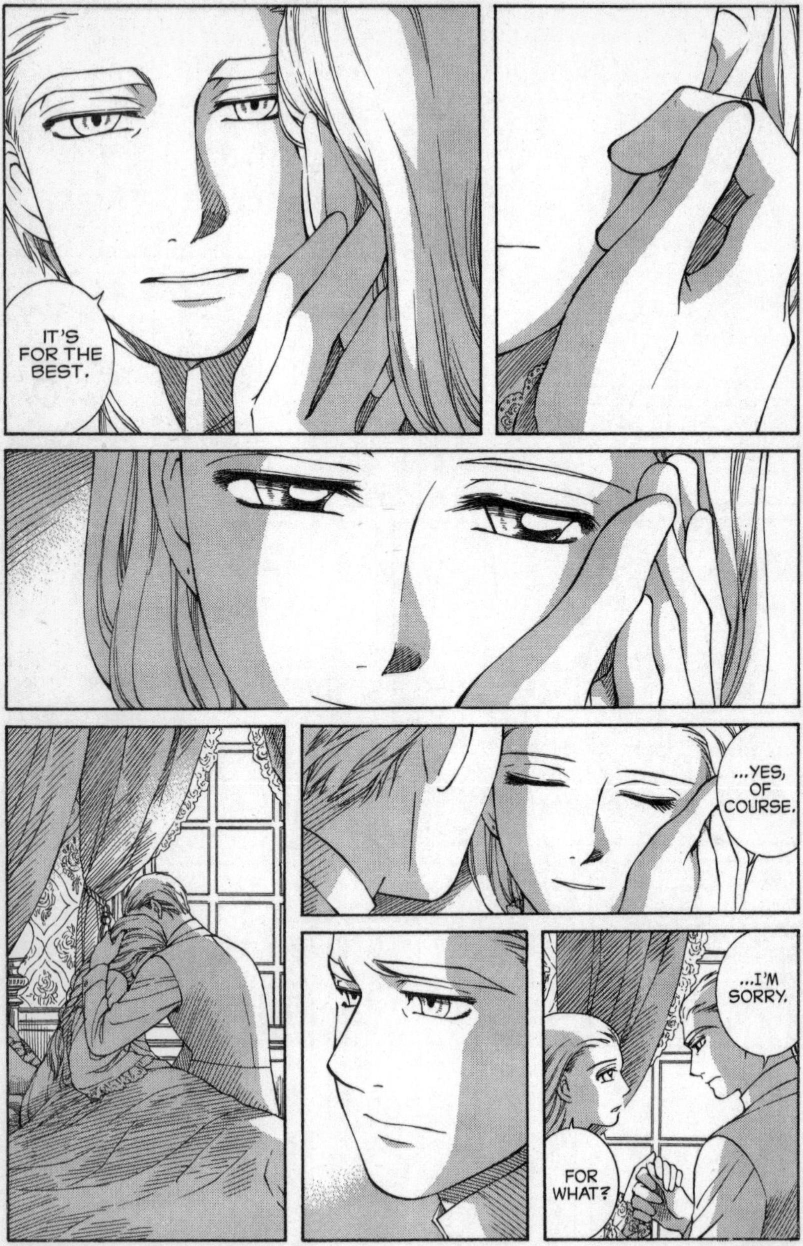
IT'S FOR THE BEST.
...YES, OF COURSE.
...I'M SORRY.
FOR WHAT?

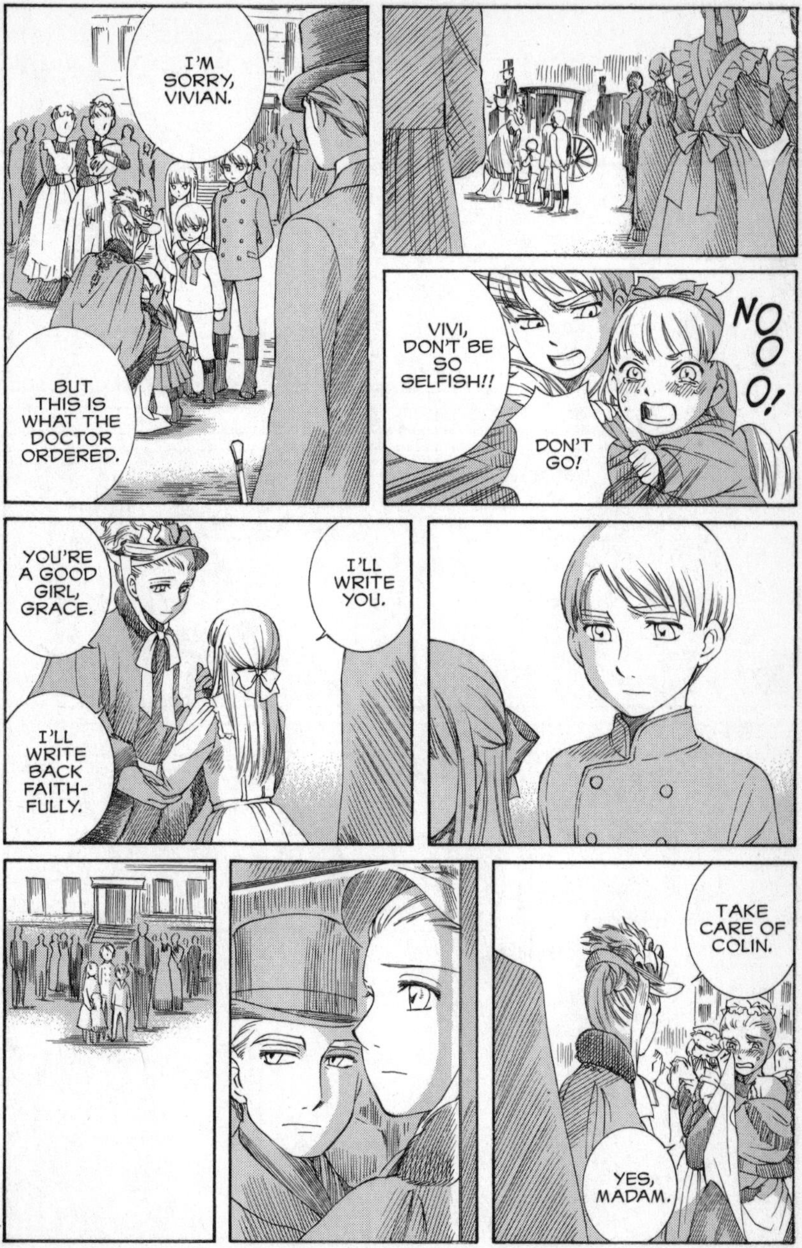
NOOO!
VIVI, DON'T BE SO SELFISH!!
DON'T GO!
I'M SORRY, VIVIAN.
BUT THIS IS WHAT THE DOCTOR ORDERED.
I'LL WRITE YOU.
YOU'RE A GOOD GIRL, GRACE.
I'LL WRITE BACK FAITH-FULLY.
TAKE CARE OF COLIN.
YES, MADAM.

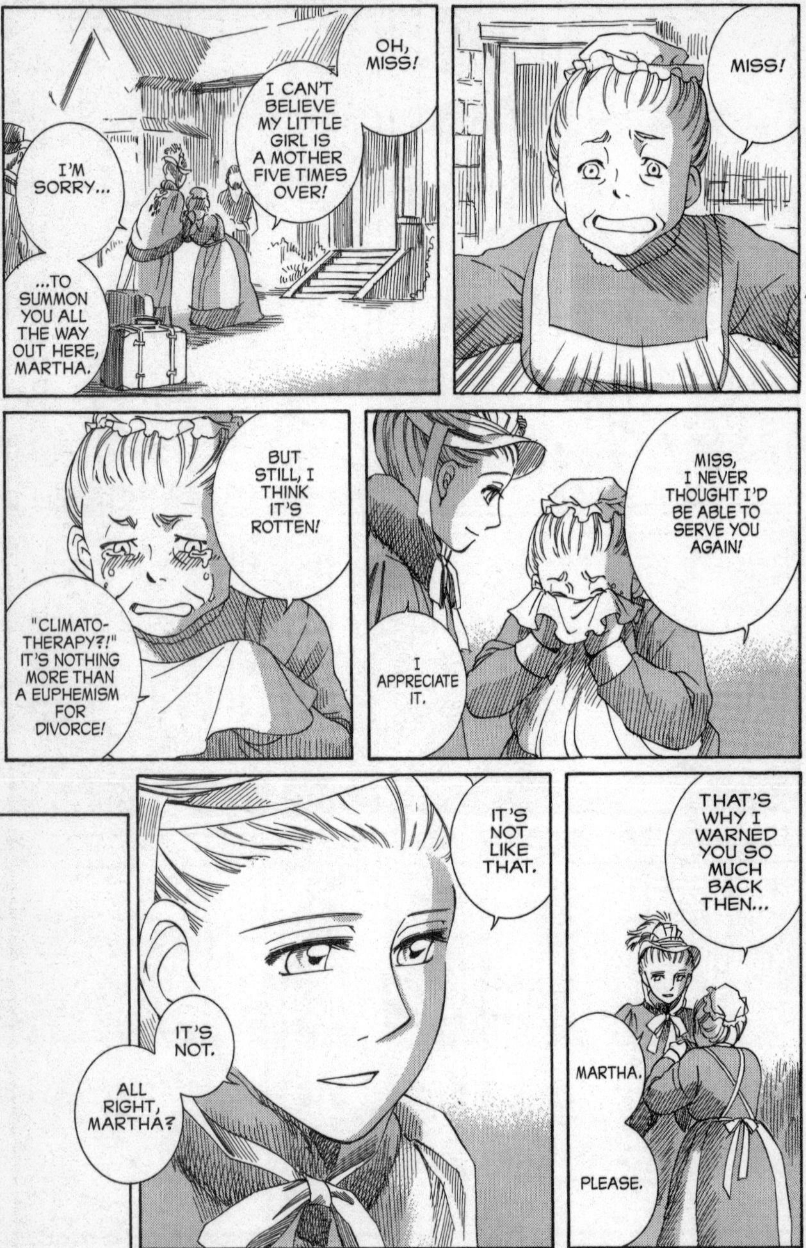
MISS!
OH, MISS!
I CAN'T BELIEVE MY LITTLE GIRL IS A MOTHER FIVE TIMES OVER!
I'M SORRY...
...TO SUMMON YOU ALL THE WAY OUT HERE, MARTHA.
MISS, I NEVER THOUGHT I'D BE ABLE TO SERVE YOU AGAIN!
I APPRECIATE IT.
BUT STILL, I THINK IT'S ROTTEN!
"CLIMATO-THERAPY?!" IT'S NOTHING MORE THAN A EUPHEMISM FOR DIVORCE!
THAT'S WHY I WARNED YOU SO MUCH BACK THEN...
MARTHA.
PLEASE.
IT'S NOT LIKE THAT.
IT'S NOT.
ALL RIGHT, MARTHA?

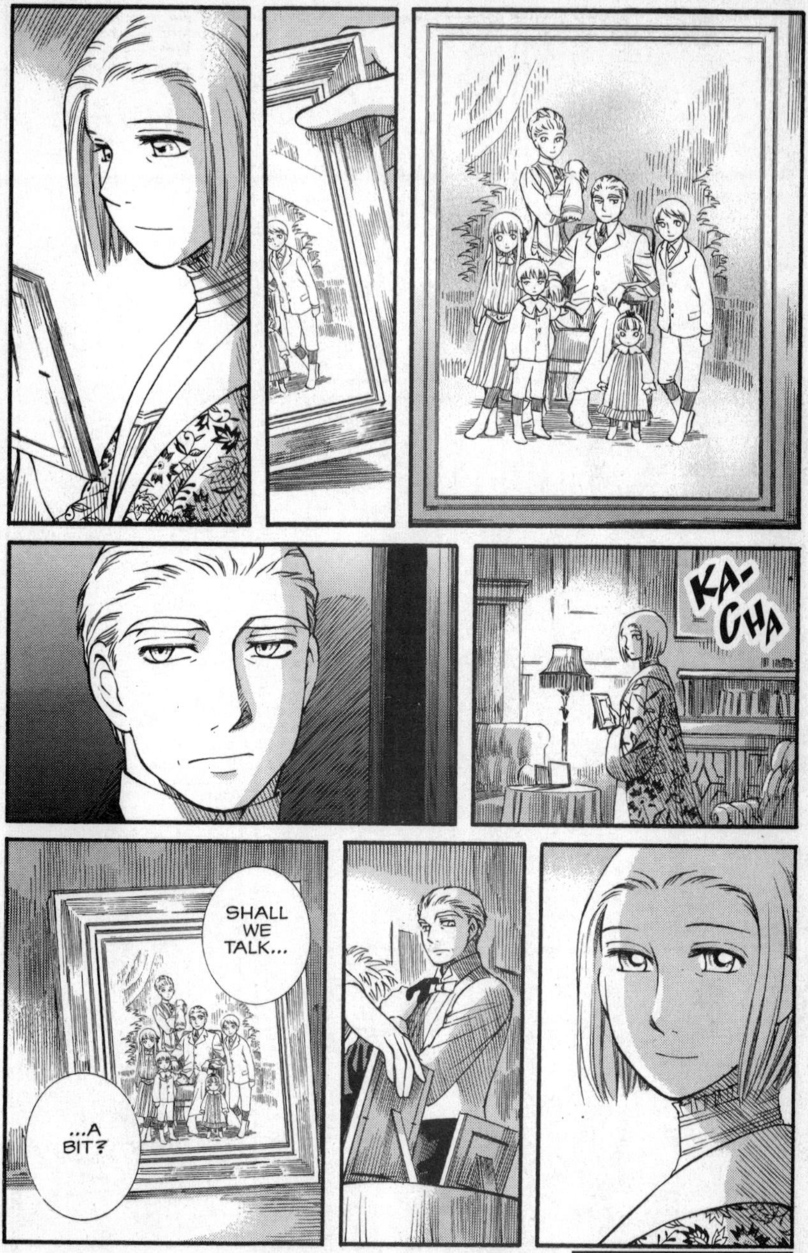
KA-CHA
SHALL WE TALK...
...A BIT?

Chapter Thirty One:
The End

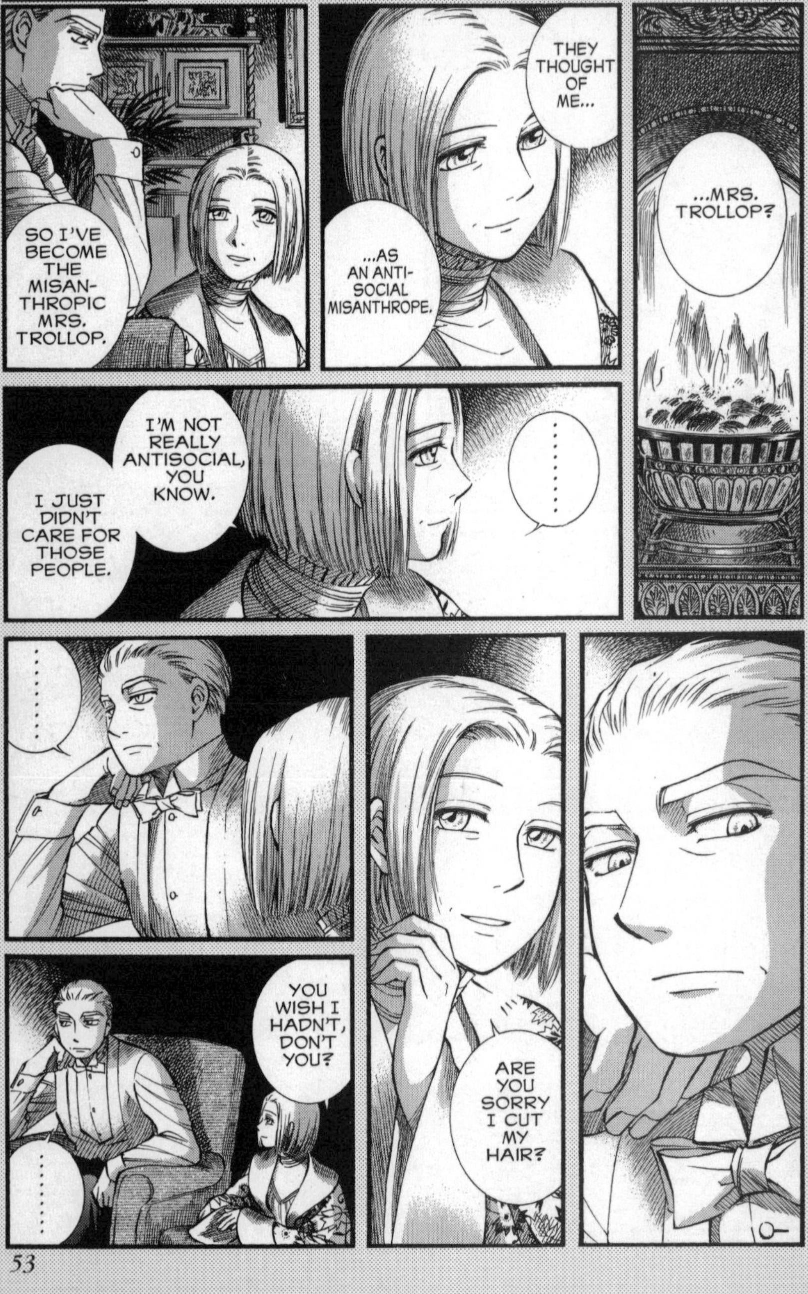
...MRS. TROLLOP?
THEY THOUGHT OF ME...
...AS AN ANTI-SOCIAL MISANTHROPE.
SO I'VE BECOME THE MISANTHROPIC MRS. TROLLOP.
......
I'M NOT REALLY ANTISOCIAL, YOU KNOW.
I JUST DIDN'T CARE FOR THOSE PEOPLE.
ARE YOU SORRY I CUT MY HAIR?
......
YOU WISH I HADN'T, DON'T YOU?
......

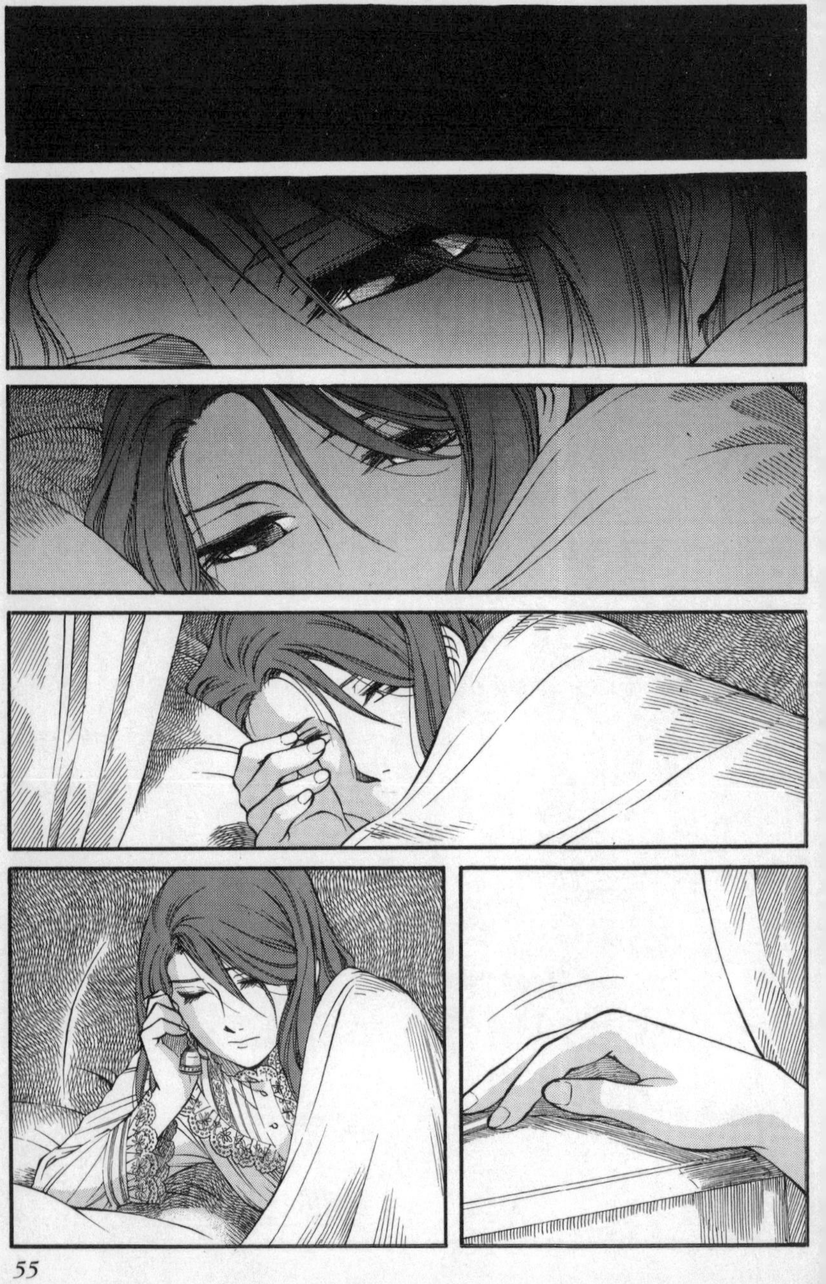

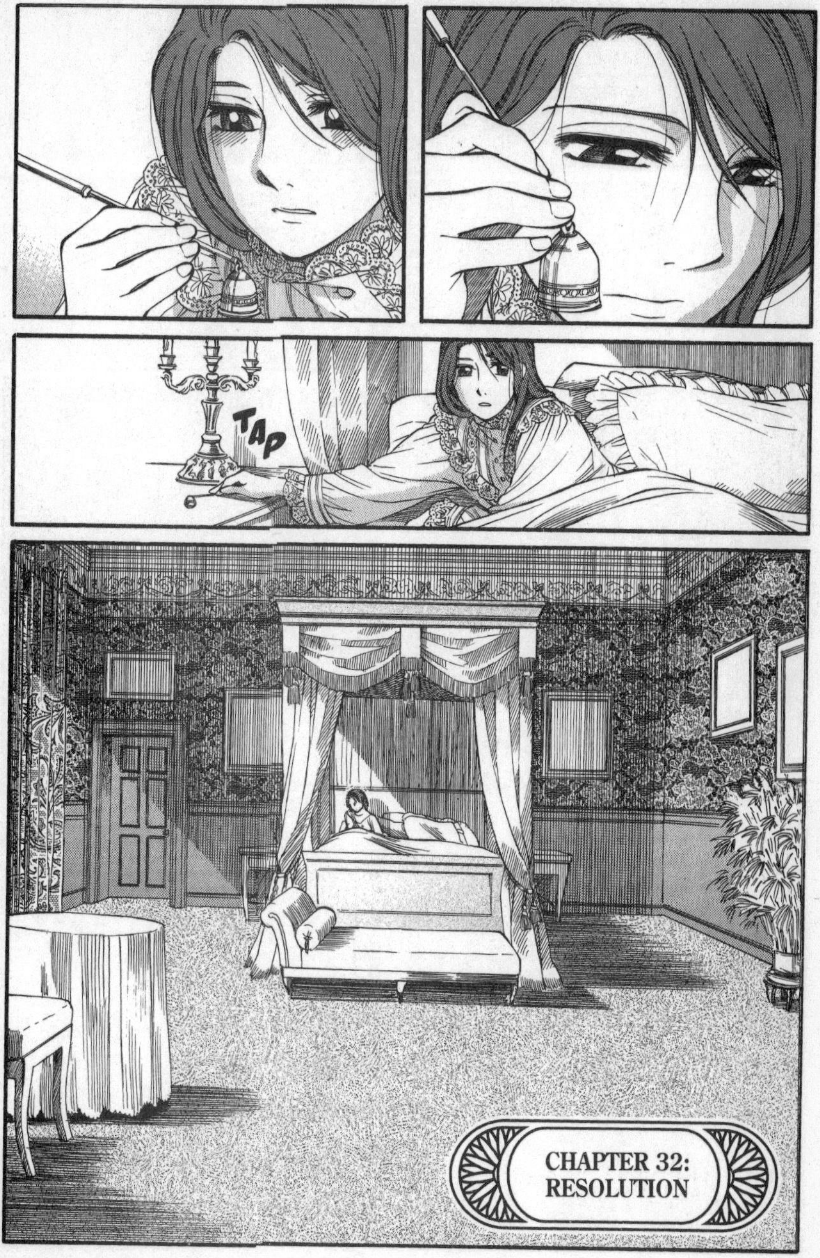
TAP
CHAPTER 32:
RESOLUTION

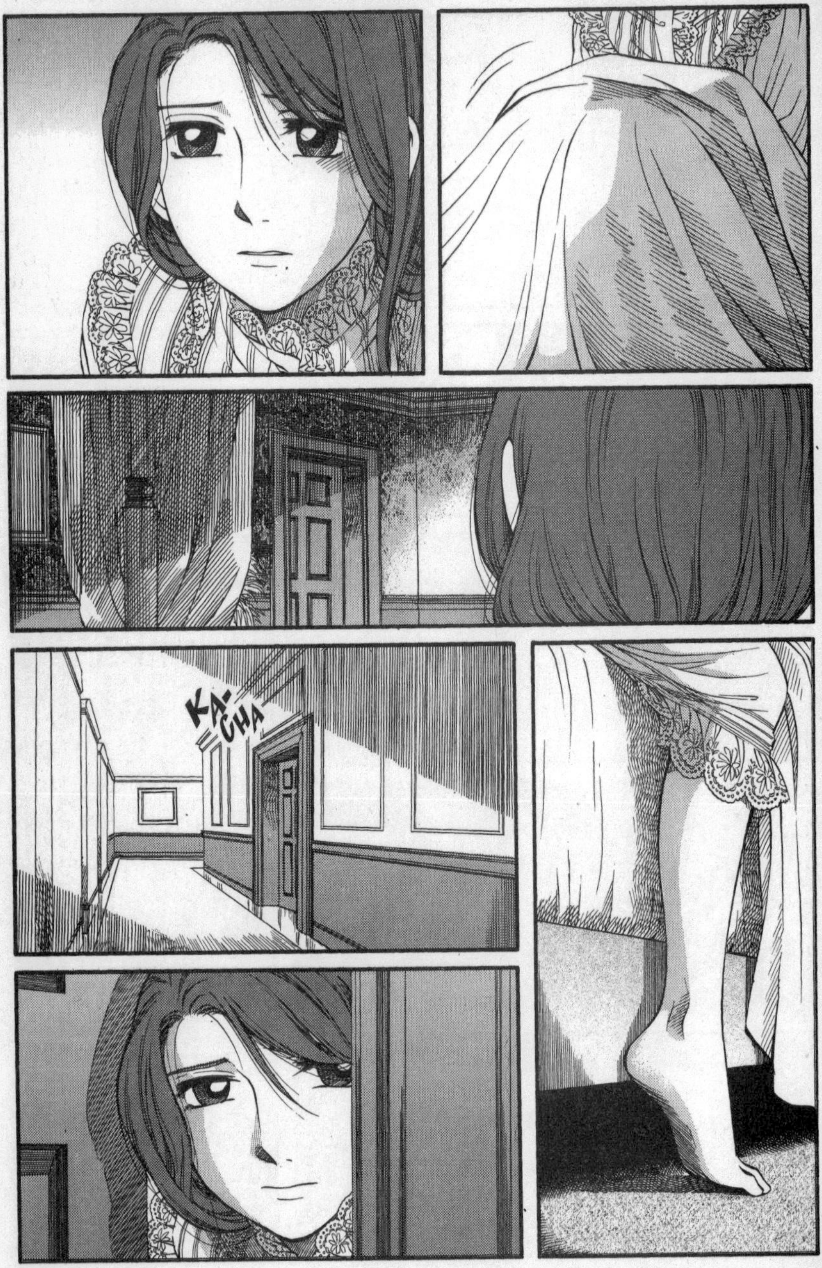
KA-CHA

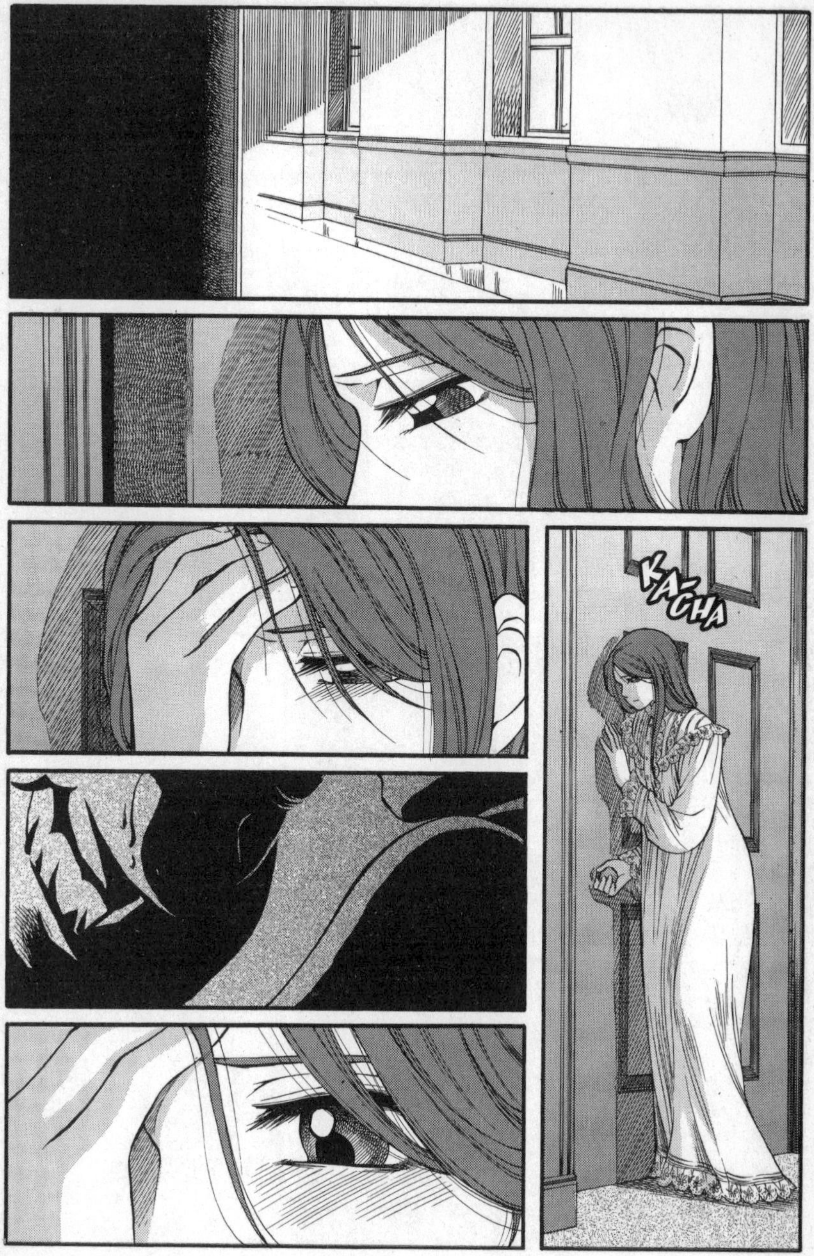
KA-CHA

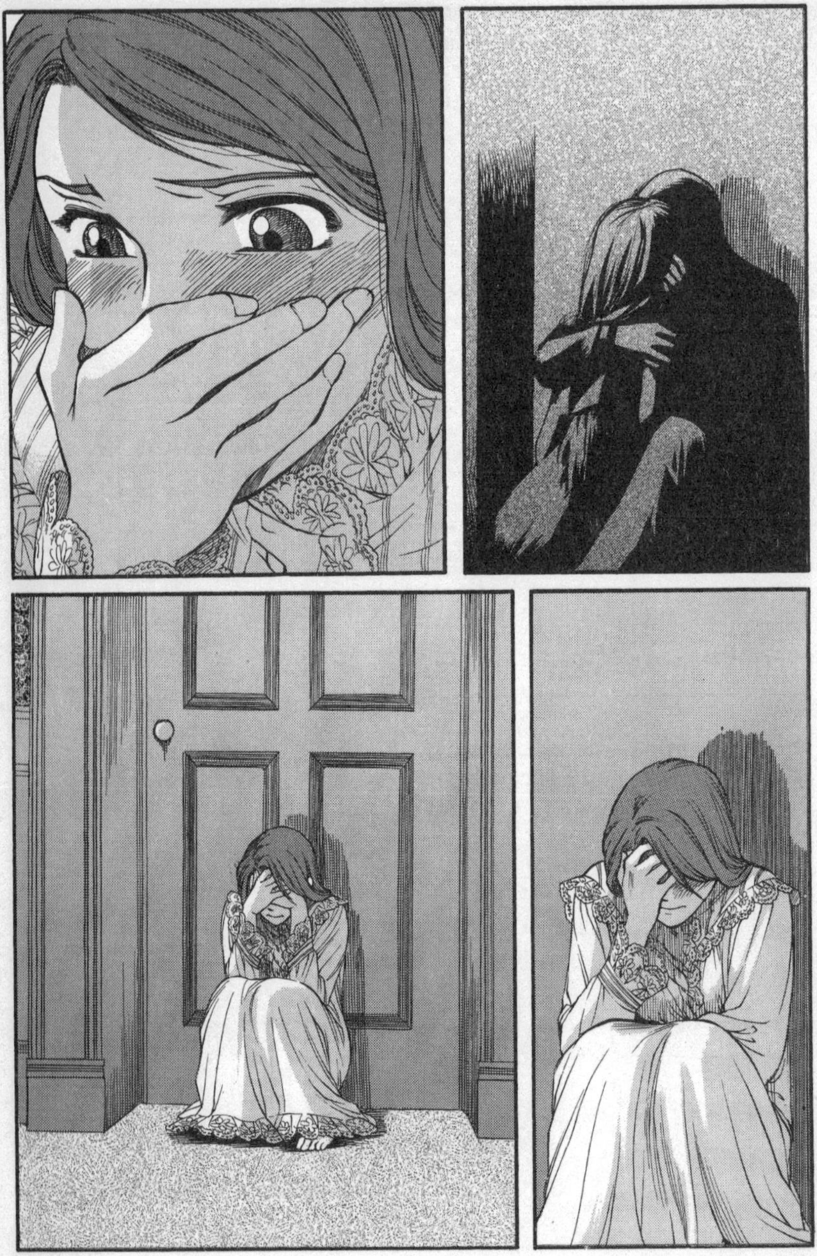

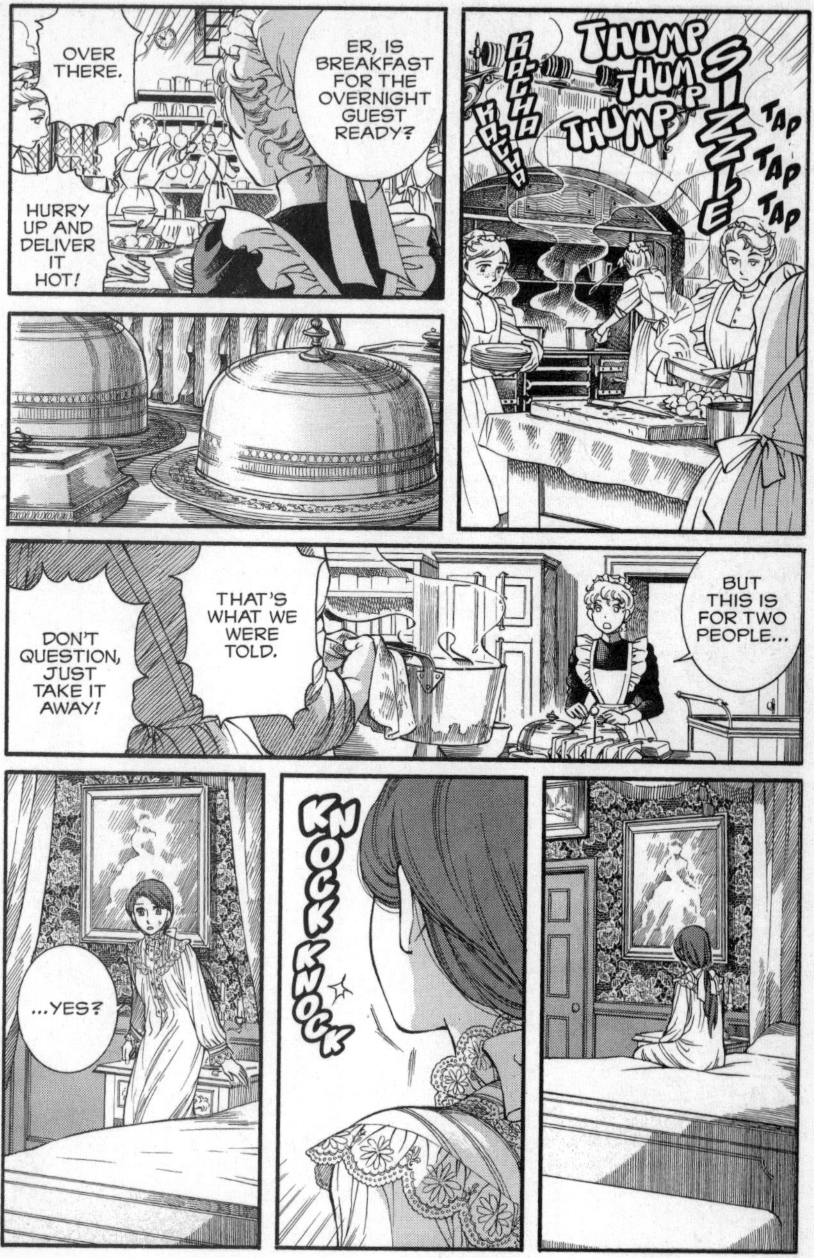
KACHA KACHA
THUMP THUMP THUMP
SIZZLE
TAP TAP TAP
ER, IS BREAKFAST FOR THE OVERNIGHT GUEST READY?
OVER THERE.
HURRY UP AND DELIVER IT HOT!
BUT THIS IS FOR TWO PEOPLE...
THAT'S WHAT WE WERE TOLD.
DON'T QUESTION, JUST TAKE IT AWAY!
KNOCK KNOCK
...YES?

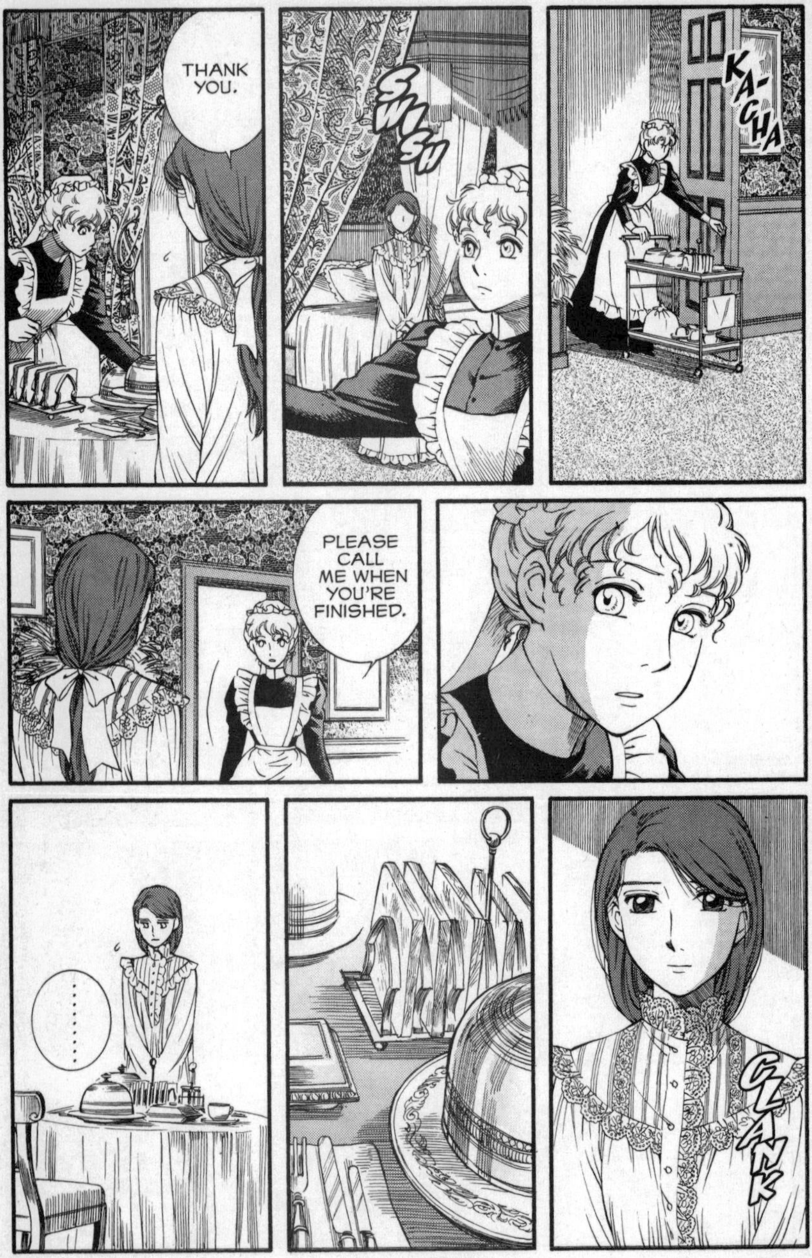
KA-CHA
SWISH
THANK YOU.
PLEASE CALL ME WHEN YOU'RE FINISHED.
CLANK
......

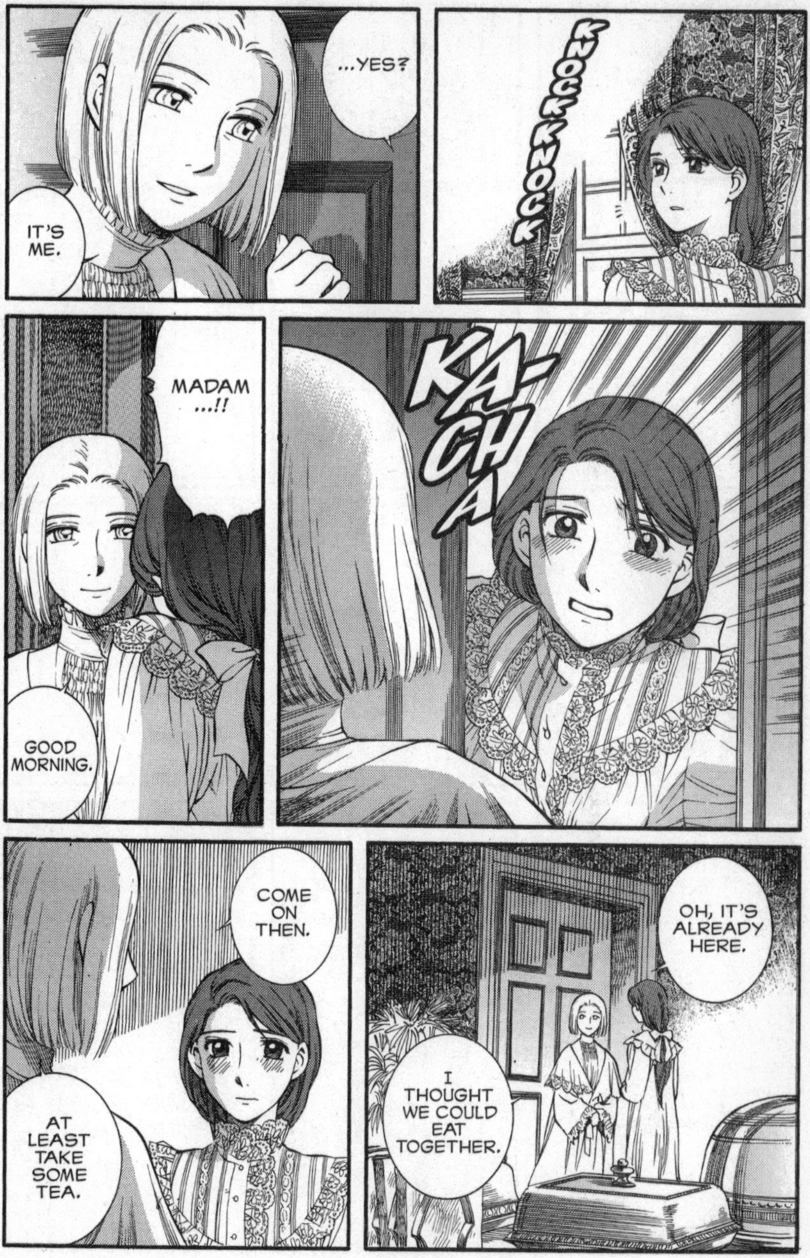
KNOCK KNOCK
...YES?
IT'S ME.
KA-CHA
MADAM ...!!
GOOD MORNING.
OH, IT'S ALREADY HERE.
I THOUGHT WE COULD EAT TOGETHER.
COME ON THEN.
AT LEAST TAKE SOME TEA.

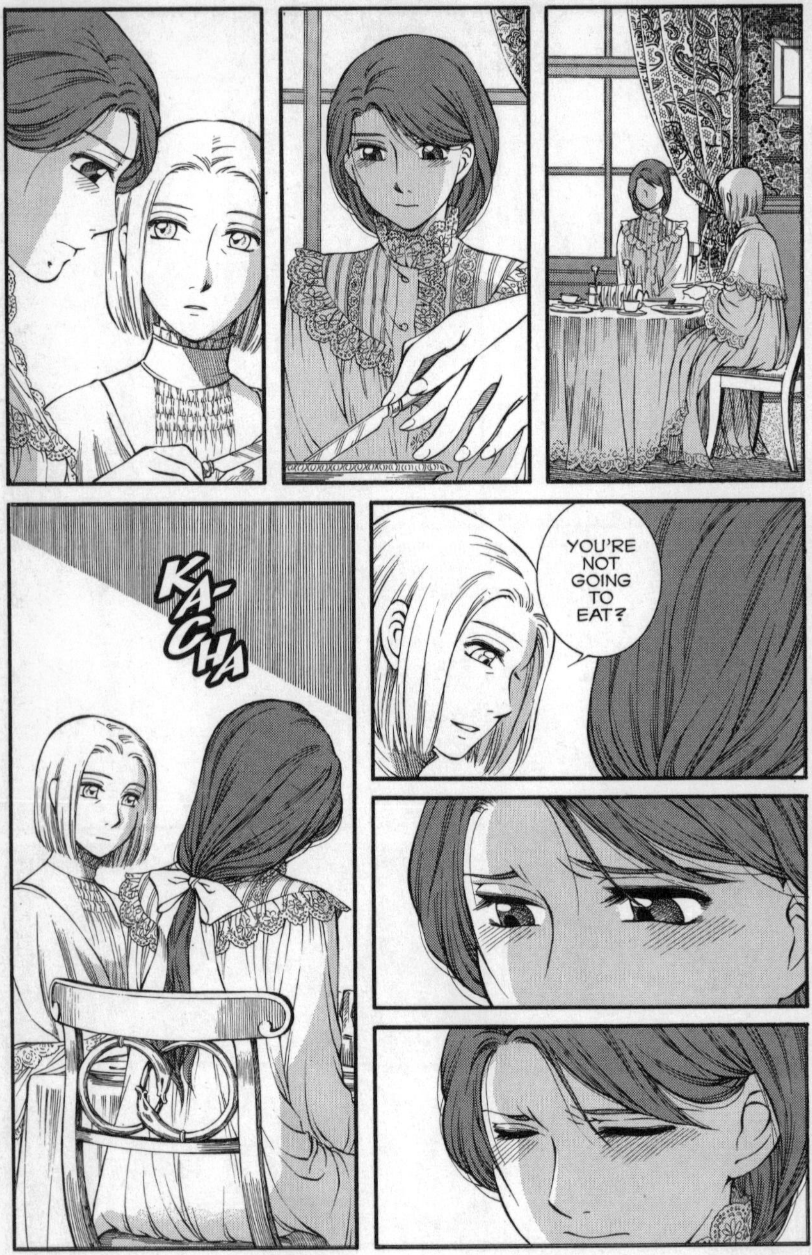
KA-CHA
YOU'RE NOT GOING TO EAT?

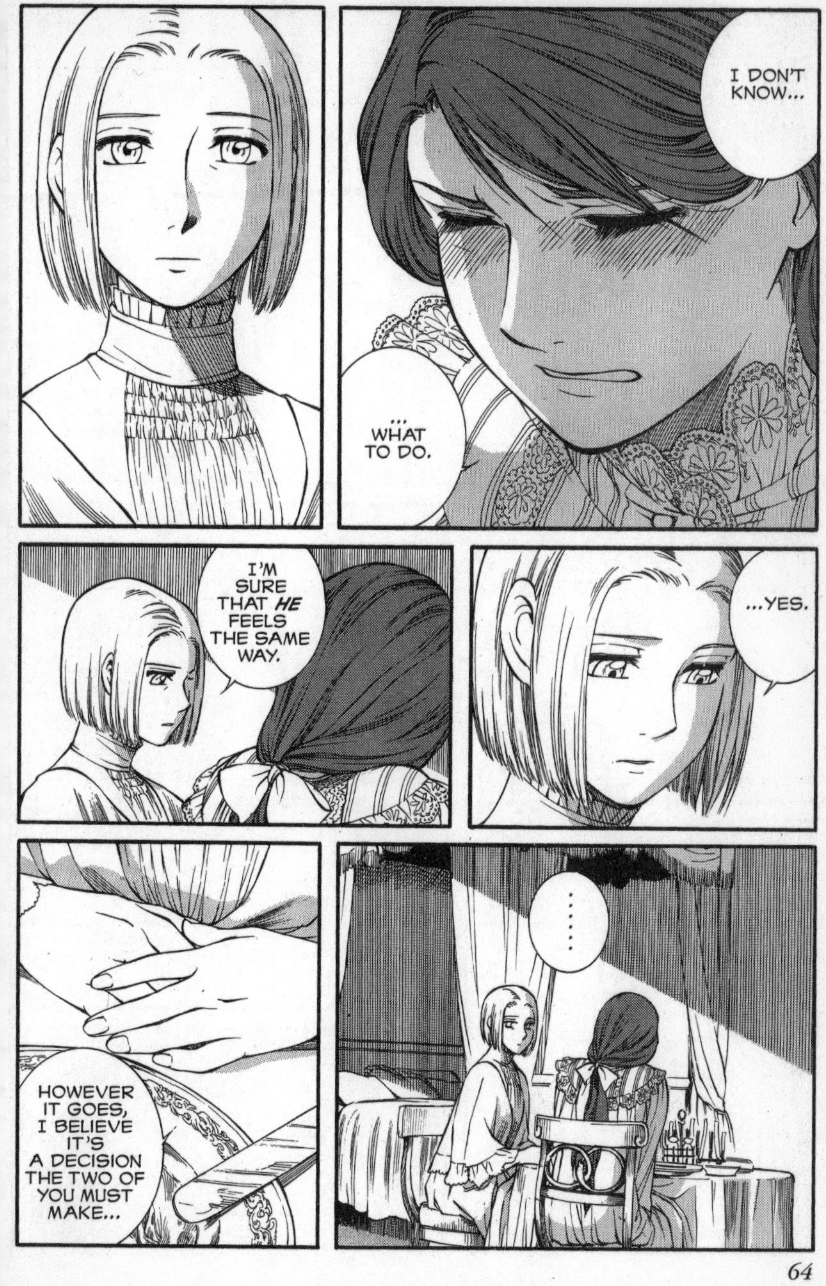
I DON'T KNOW...
... WHAT TO DO.
...YES.
I'M SURE THAT *HE* FEELS THE SAME WAY.
......
HOWEVER IT GOES, I BELIEVE IT'S A DECISION THE TWO OF YOU MUST MAKE...

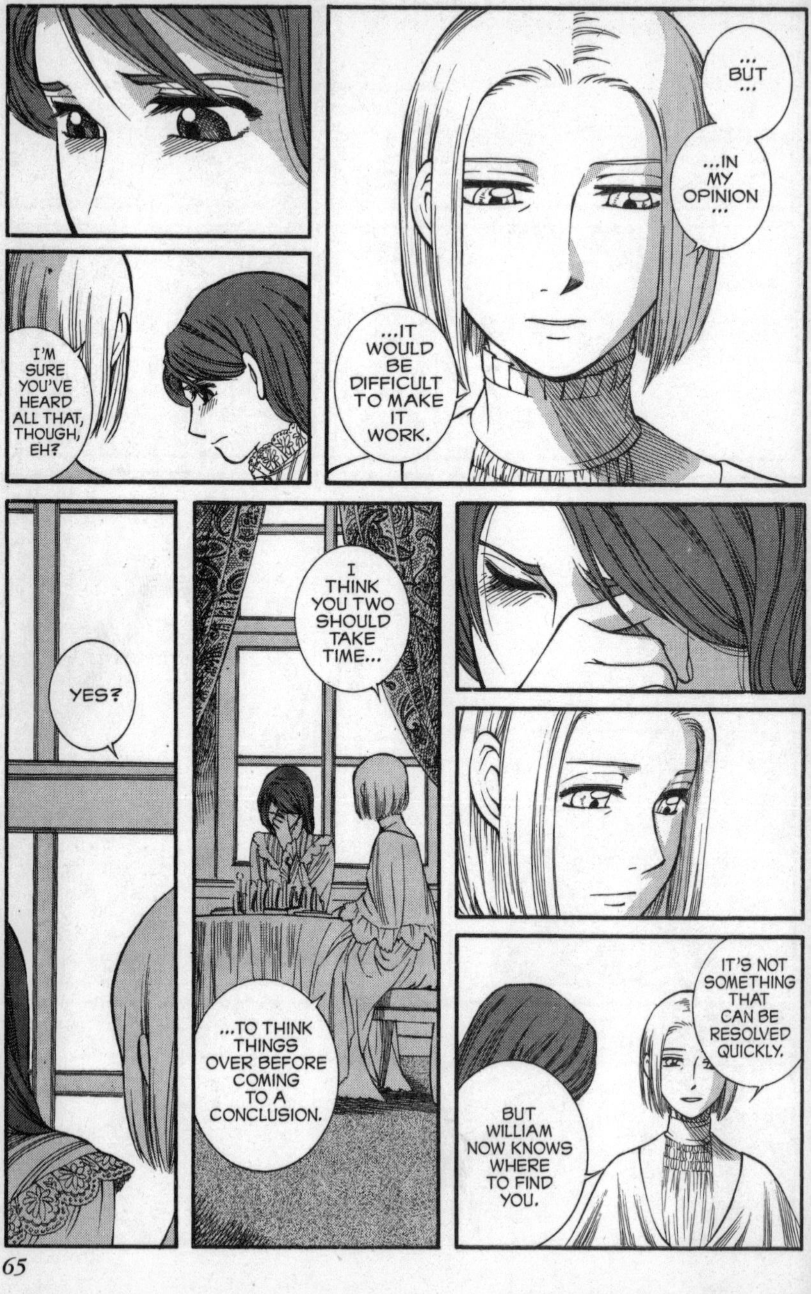
...BUT...
...IN MY OPINION...
...IT WOULD BE DIFFICULT TO MAKE IT WORK.
I'M SURE YOU'VE HEARD ALL THAT, THOUGH, EH?
IT'S NOT SOMETHING THAT CAN BE RESOLVED QUICKLY.
BUT WILLIAM NOW KNOWS WHERE TO FIND YOU.
I THINK YOU TWO SHOULD TAKE TIME...
...TO THINK THINGS OVER BEFORE COMING TO A CONCLUSION.
YES?

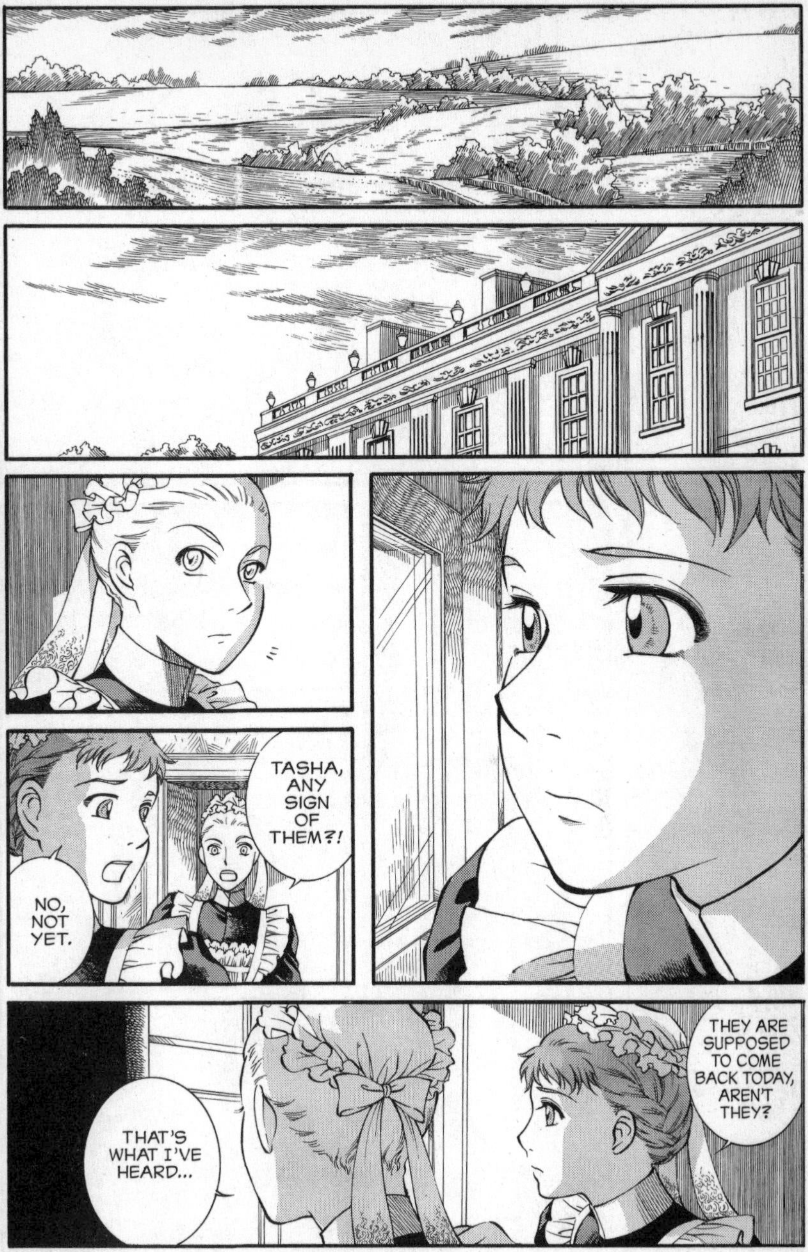
TASHA, ANY SIGN OF THEM?!
NO, NOT YET.
THEY ARE SUPPOSED TO COME BACK TODAY, AREN'T THEY?
THAT'S WHAT I'VE HEARD...

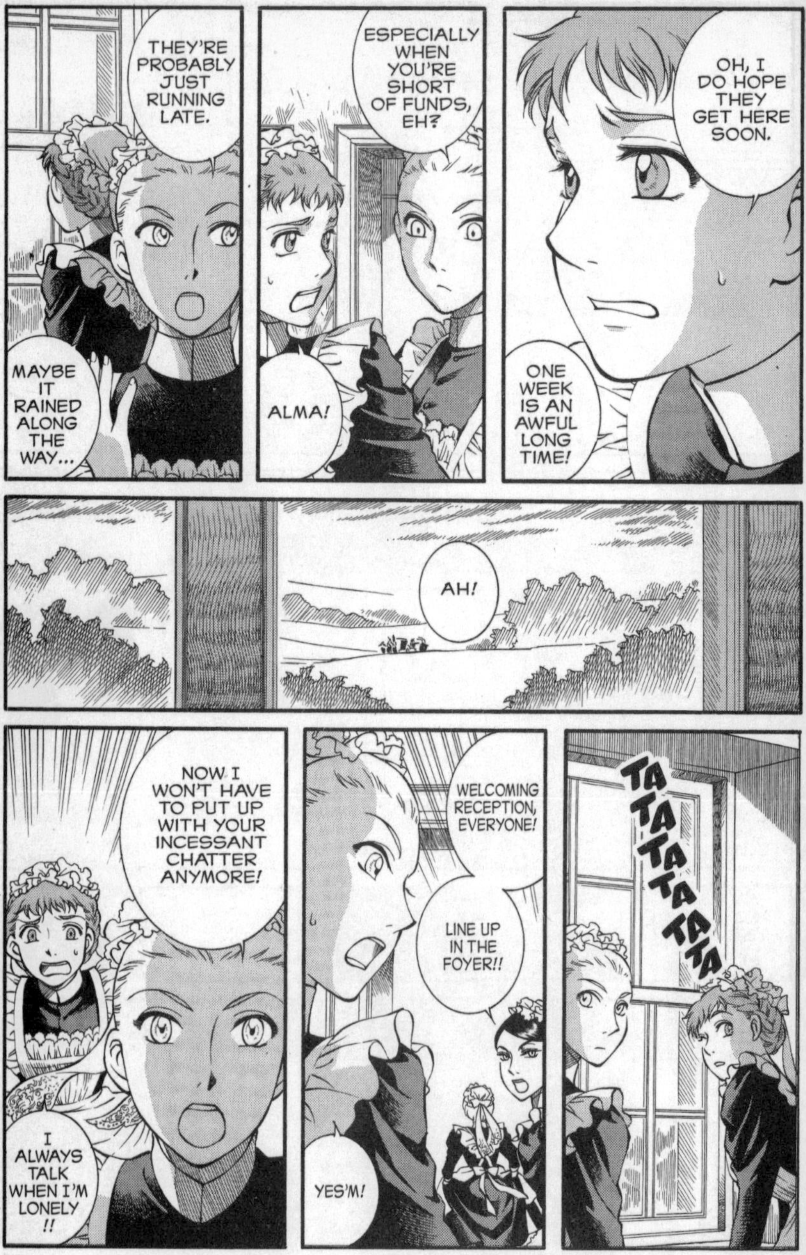
OH, I DO HOPE THEY GET HERE SOON.
ONE WEEK IS AN AWFUL LONG TIME!
ESPECIALLY WHEN YOU'RE SHORT OF FUNDS, EH?
ALMA!
THEY'RE PROBABLY JUST RUNNING LATE.
MAYBE IT RAINED ALONG THE WAY...
AH!
TA TA TA TA TA TA
WELCOMING RECEPTION, EVERYONE!
LINE UP IN THE FOYER!!
YES'M!
NOW I WON'T HAVE TO PUT UP WITH YOUR INCESSANT CHATTER ANYMORE!
I ALWAYS TALK WHEN I'M LONELY!!

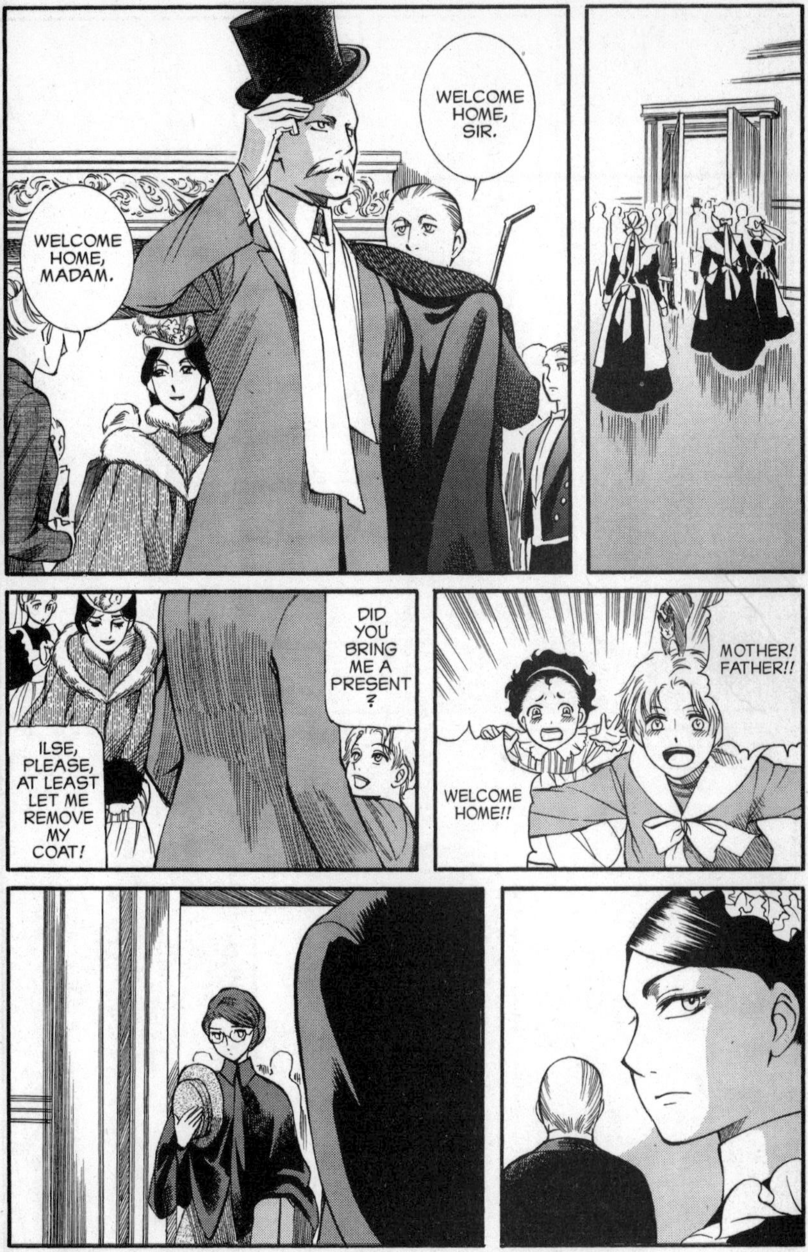
WELCOME HOME, SIR.
WELCOME HOME, MADAM.
MOTHER! FATHER!!
WELCOME HOME!!
DID YOU BRING ME A PRESENT?
ILSE, PLEASE, AT LEAST LET ME REMOVE MY COAT!

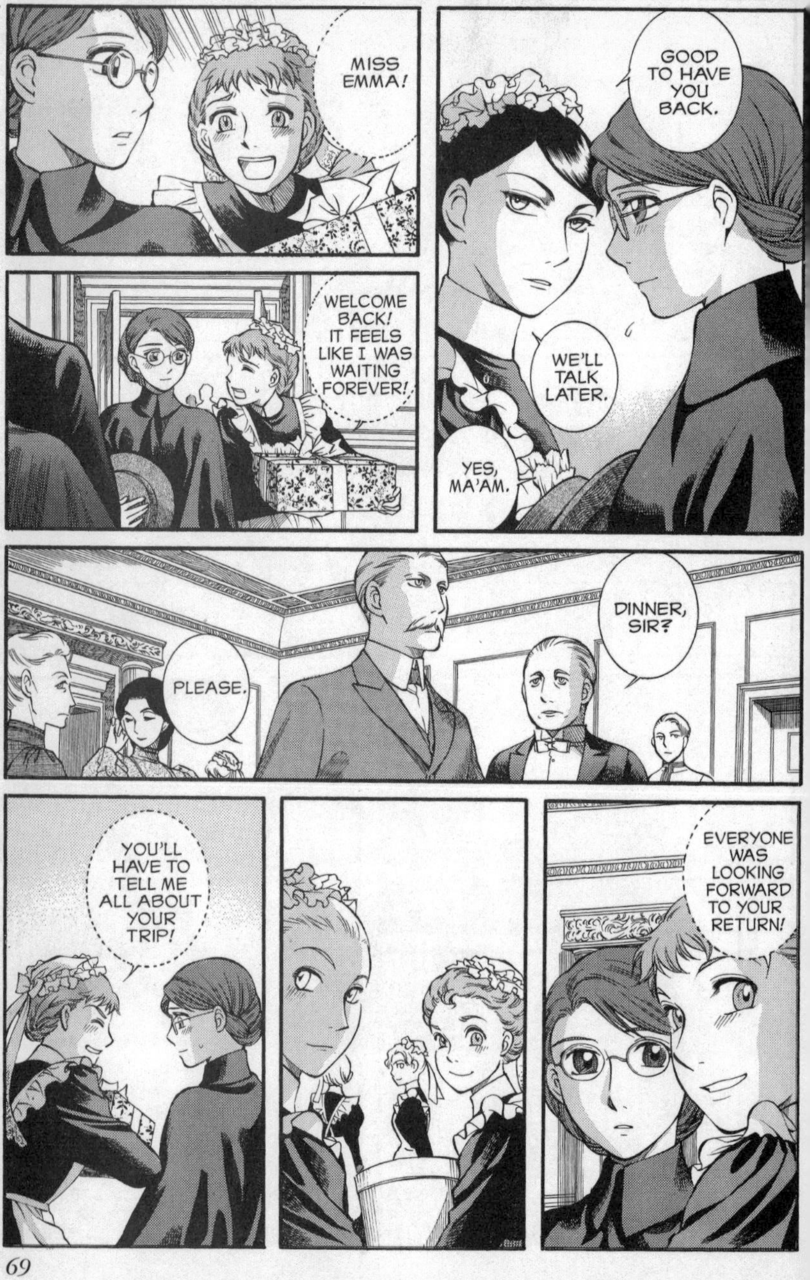
GOOD TO HAVE YOU BACK.
WE'LL TALK LATER.
YES, MA'AM.
MISS EMMA!
WELCOME BACK! IT FEELS LIKE I WAS WAITING FOREVER!
DINNER, SIR?
PLEASE.
EVERYONE WAS LOOKING FORWARD TO YOUR RETURN!
YOU'LL HAVE TO TELL ME ALL ABOUT YOUR TRIP!

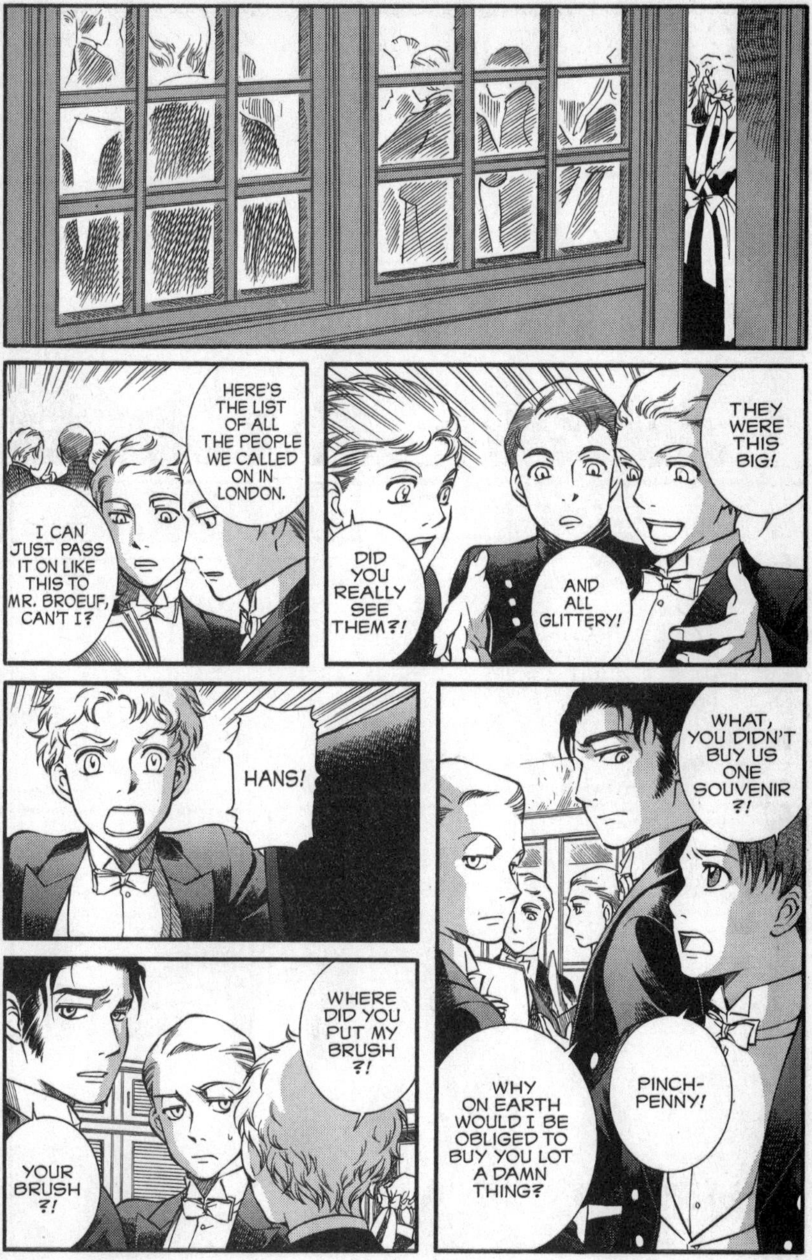
THEY WERE THIS BIG!
AND ALL GLITTERY!
DID YOU REALLY SEE THEM?!
HERE'S THE LIST OF ALL THE PEOPLE WE CALLED ON IN LONDON.
I CAN JUST PASS IT ON LIKE THIS TO MR. BROEUF, CAN'T I?
WHAT, YOU DIDN'T BUY US ONE SOUVENIR?!
PINCH-PENNY!
WHY ON EARTH WOULD I BE OBLIGED TO BUY YOU LOT A DAMN THING?
HANS!
WHERE DID YOU PUT MY BRUSH?!
YOUR BRUSH?!

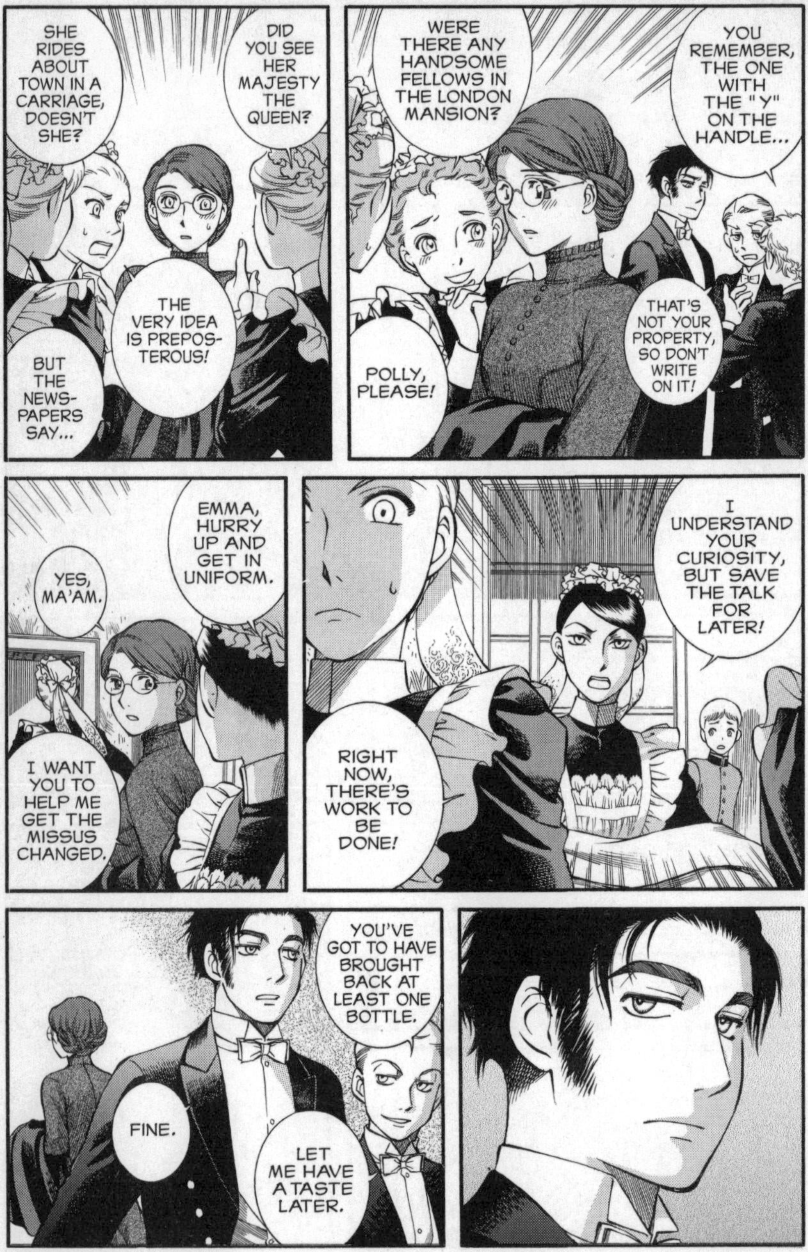
YOU REMEMBER, THE ONE WITH THE "Y" ON THE HANDLE...
WERE THERE ANY HANDSOME FELLOWS IN THE LONDON MANSION?
THAT'S NOT YOUR PROPERTY, SO DON'T WRITE ON IT!
POLLY, PLEASE!
DID YOU SEE HER MAJESTY THE QUEEN?
SHE RIDES ABOUT TOWN IN A CARRIAGE, DOESN'T SHE?
THE VERY IDEA IS PREPOSTEROUS!
BUT THE NEWSPAPERS SAY...
I UNDERSTAND YOUR CURIOSITY, BUT SAVE THE TALK FOR LATER!
RIGHT NOW, THERE'S WORK TO BE DONE!
EMMA, HURRY UP AND GET IN UNIFORM.
YES, MA'AM.
I WANT YOU TO HELP ME GET THE MISSUS CHANGED.
YOU'VE GOT TO HAVE BROUGHT BACK AT LEAST ONE BOTTLE.
FINE.
LET ME HAVE A TASTE LATER.

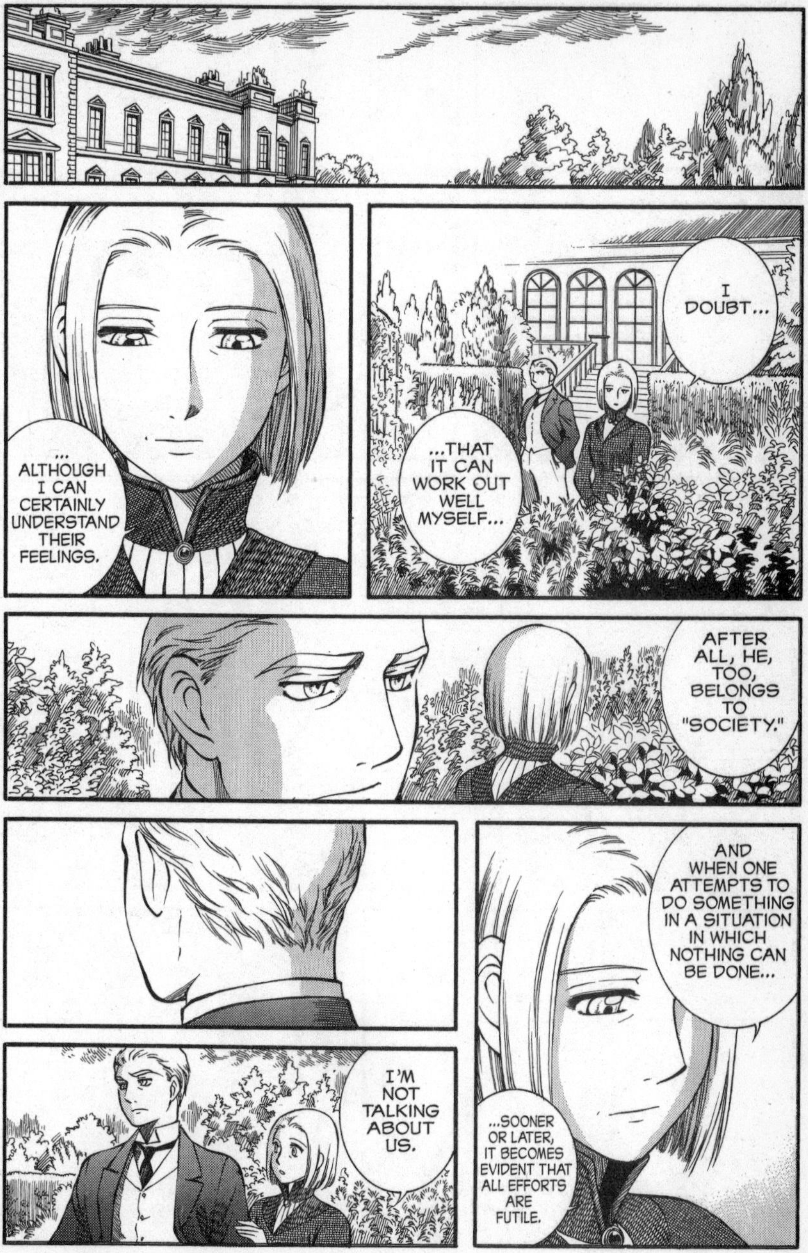

I DOUBT...
...THAT IT CAN WORK OUT WELL MYSELF...
...ALTHOUGH I CAN CERTAINLY UNDERSTAND THEIR FEELINGS.
AFTER ALL, HE, TOO, BELONGS TO "SOCIETY."
AND WHEN ONE ATTEMPTS TO DO SOMETHING IN A SITUATION IN WHICH NOTHING CAN BE DONE...
...SOONER OR LATER, IT BECOMES EVIDENT THAT ALL EFFORTS ARE FUTILE.
I'M NOT TALKING ABOUT US.

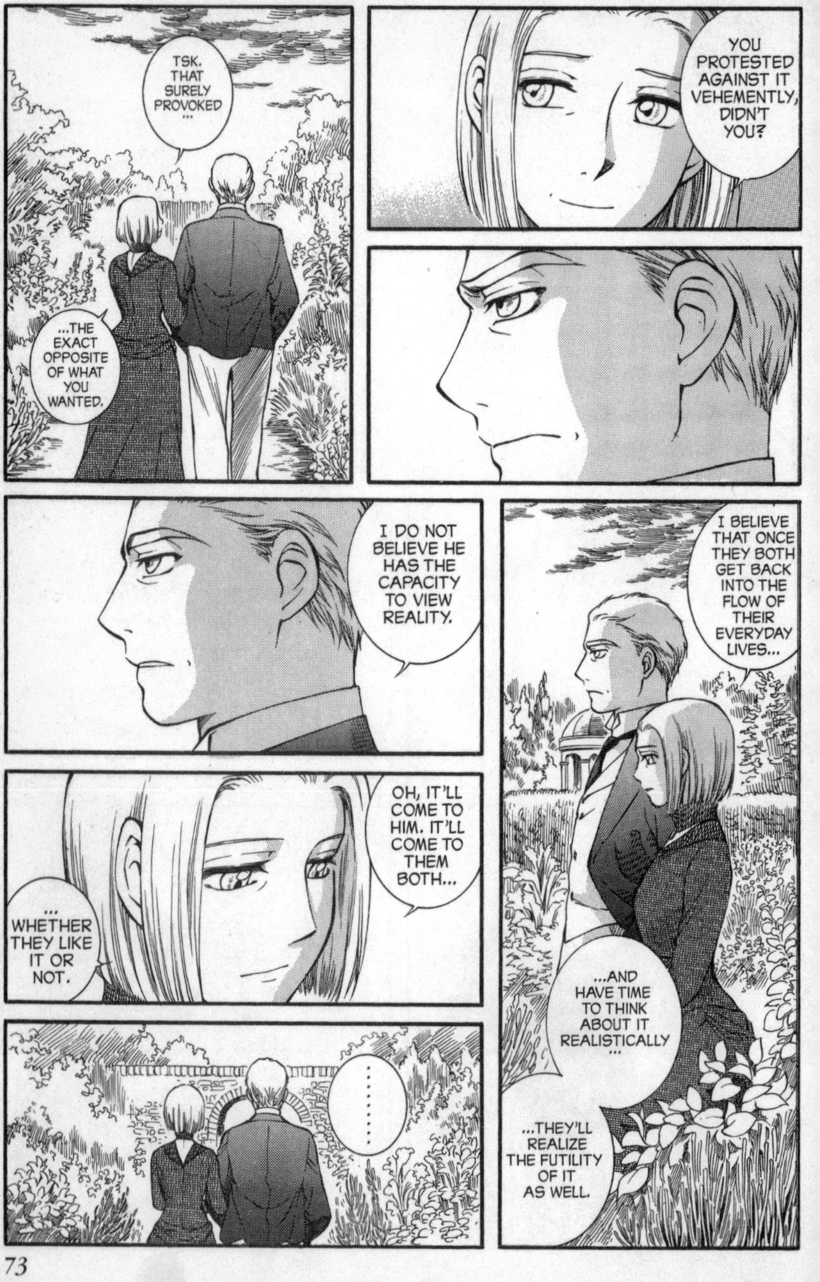
YOU PROTESTED AGAINST IT VEHEMENTLY, DIDN'T YOU?
TSK. THAT SURELY PROVOKED ...
...THE EXACT OPPOSITE OF WHAT YOU WANTED.
I BELIEVE THAT ONCE THEY BOTH GET BACK INTO THE FLOW OF THEIR EVERYDAY LIVES...
...AND HAVE TIME TO THINK ABOUT IT REALISTICALLY ...
...THEY'LL REALIZE THE FUTILITY OF IT AS WELL.
I DO NOT BELIEVE HE HAS THE CAPACITY TO VIEW REALITY.
OH, IT'LL COME TO HIM. IT'LL COME TO THEM BOTH...
... WHETHER THEY LIKE IT OR NOT.
....

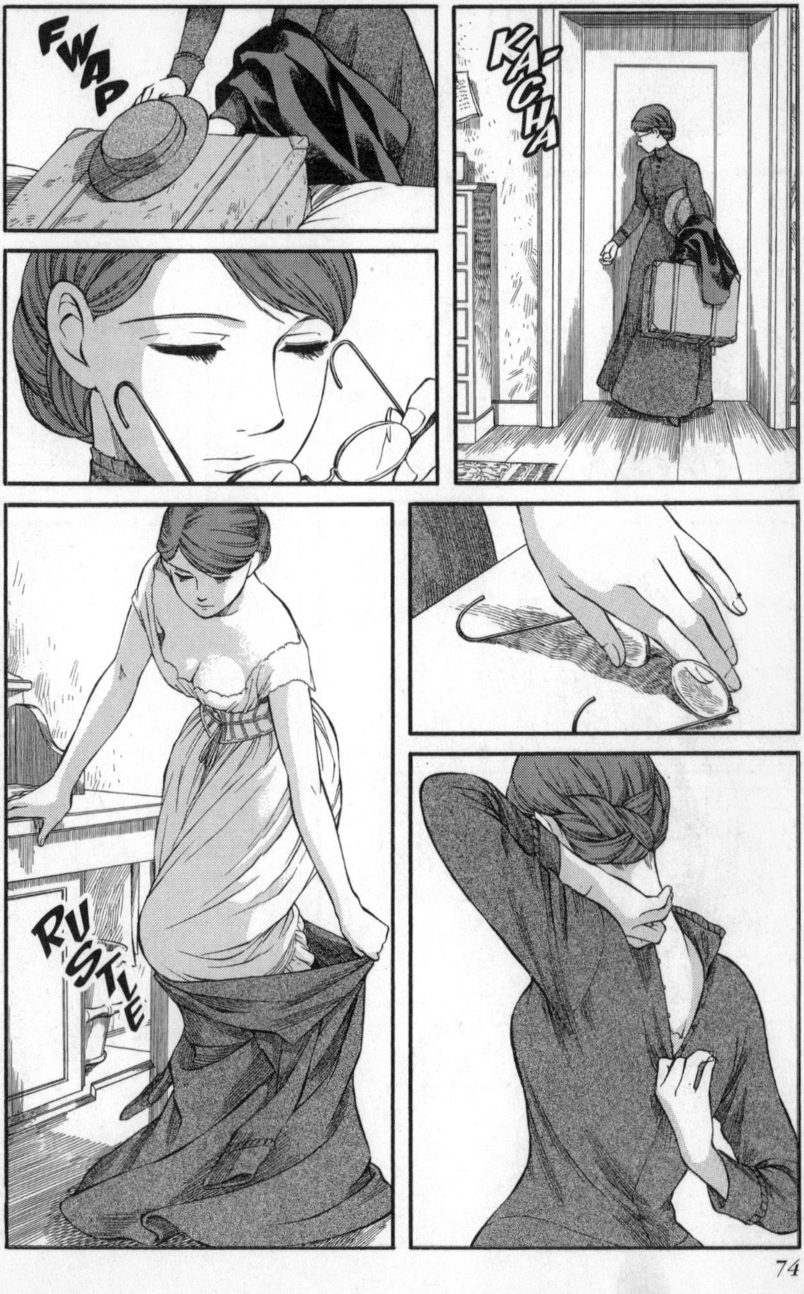
KA-CHA
FWAP
RUSTLE

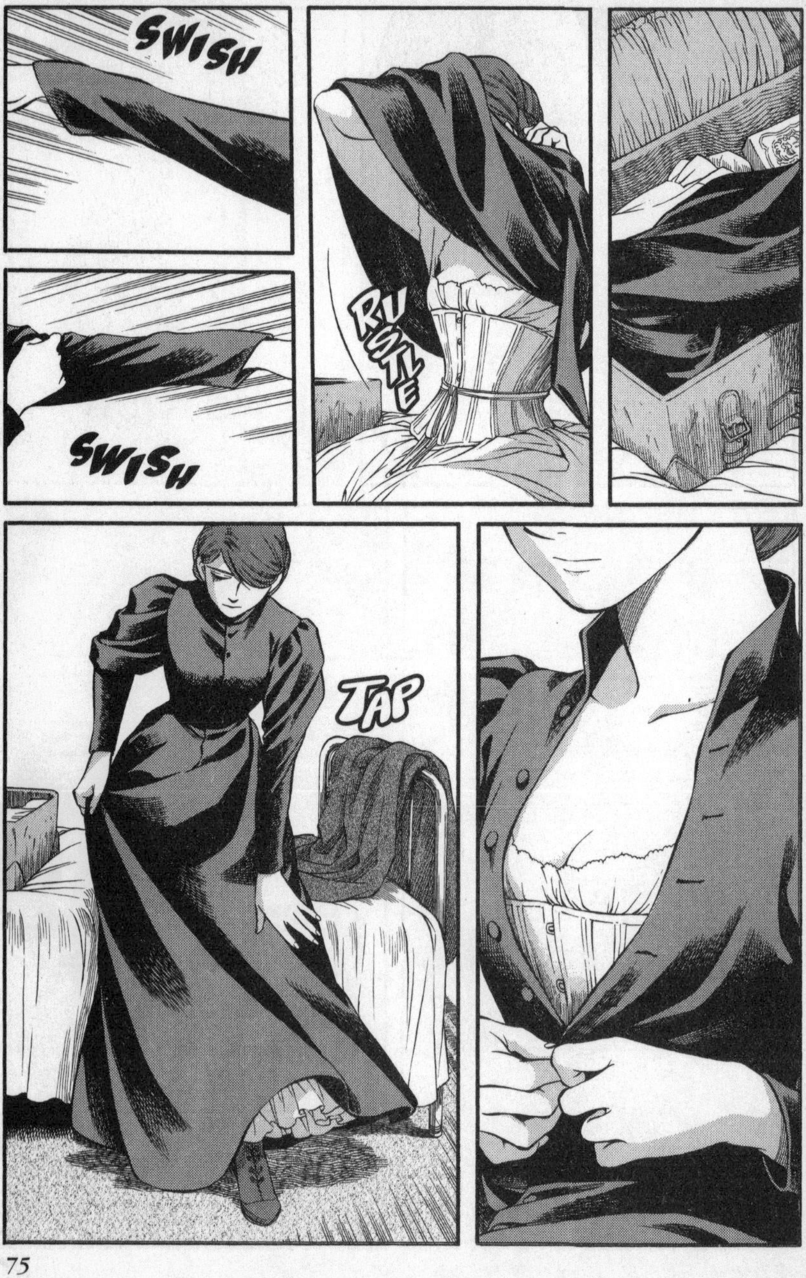
RUSTLE
SWISH
SWISH
TAP

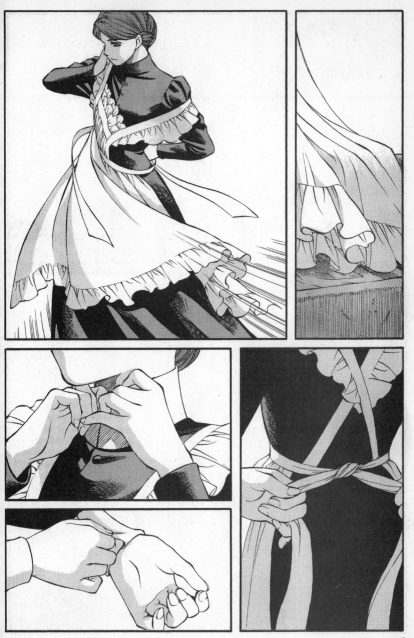

76

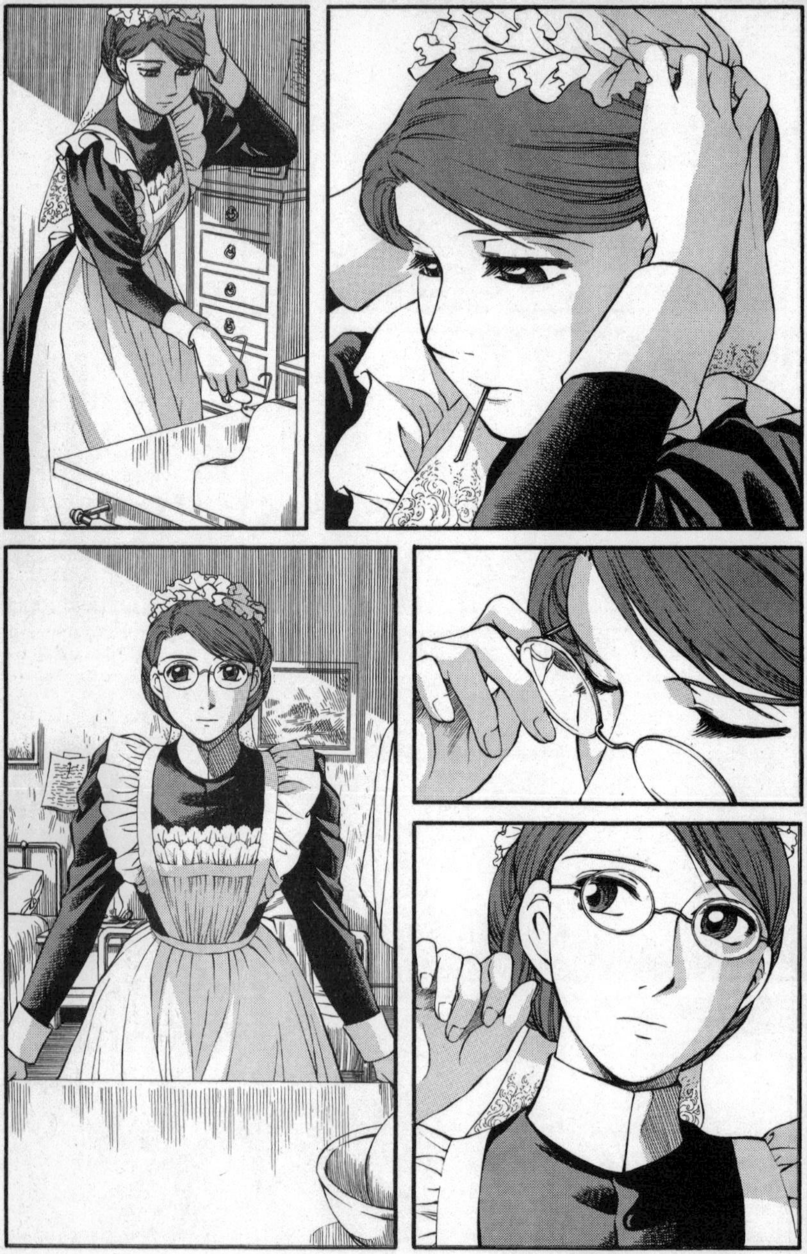

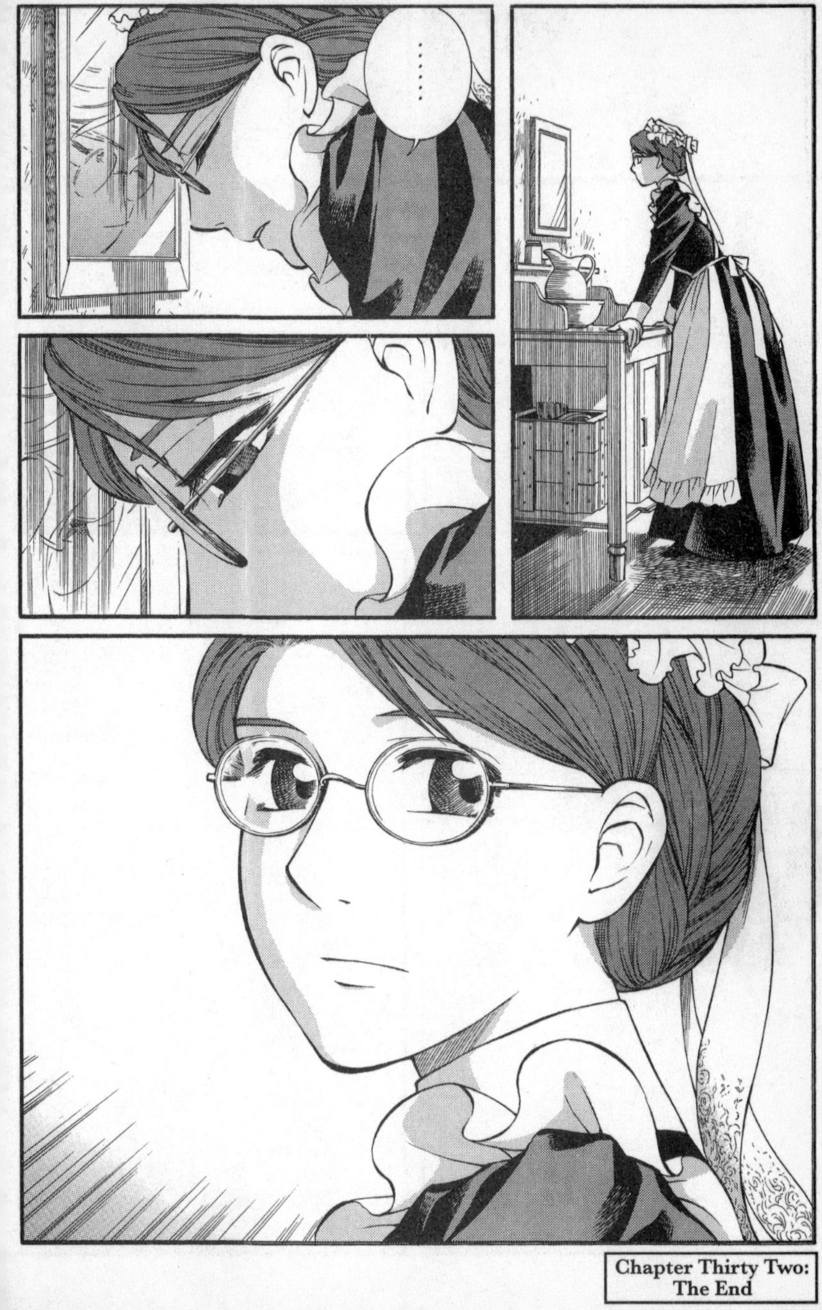
......

Chapter Thirty Two: The End

EPILOGUE

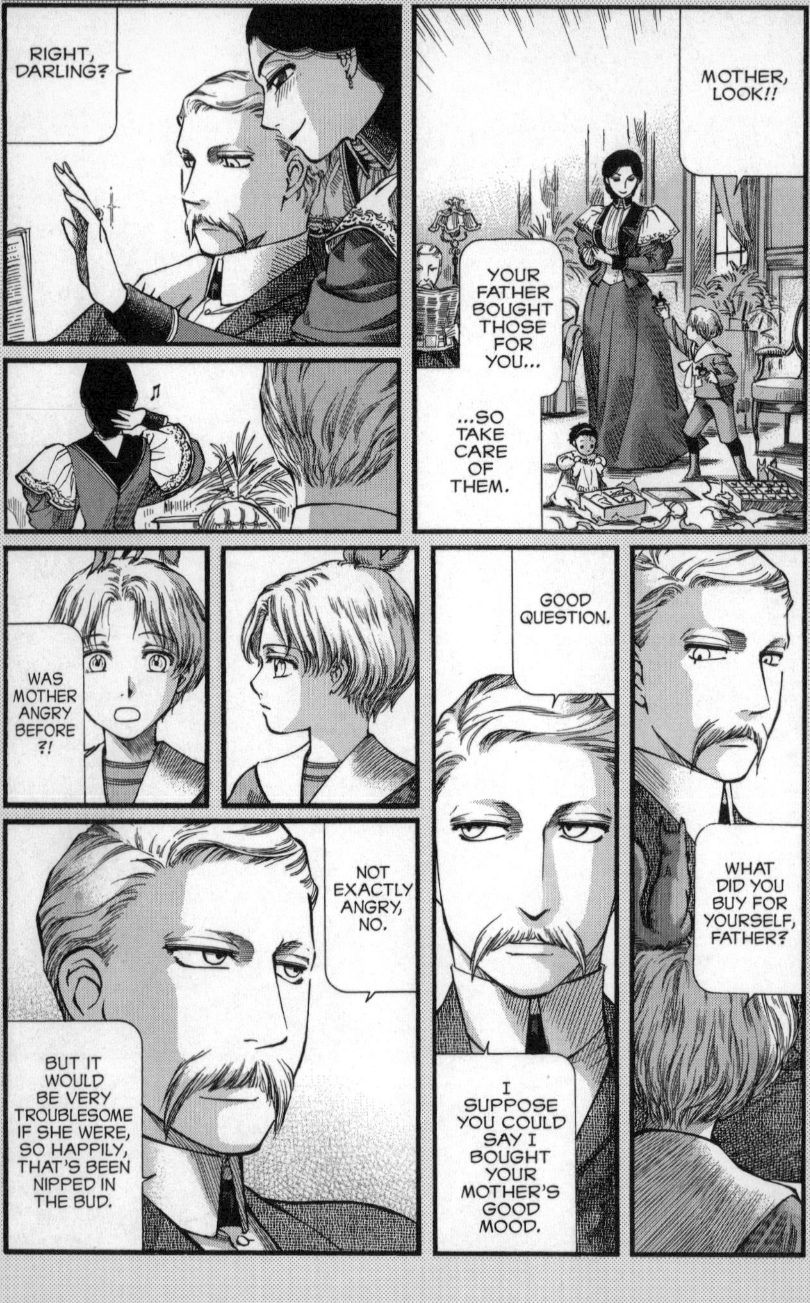
MOTHER, LOOK!!
YOUR FATHER BOUGHT THOSE FOR YOU...
...SO TAKE CARE OF THEM.
RIGHT, DARLING?
WHAT DID YOU BUY FOR YOURSELF, FATHER?
GOOD QUESTION.
I SUPPOSE YOU COULD SAY I BOUGHT YOUR MOTHER'S GOOD MOOD.
WAS MOTHER ANGRY BEFORE?!
NOT EXACTLY ANGRY, NO.
BUT IT WOULD BE VERY TROUBLESOME IF SHE WERE, SO HAPPILY, THAT'S BEEN NIPPED IN THE BUD.

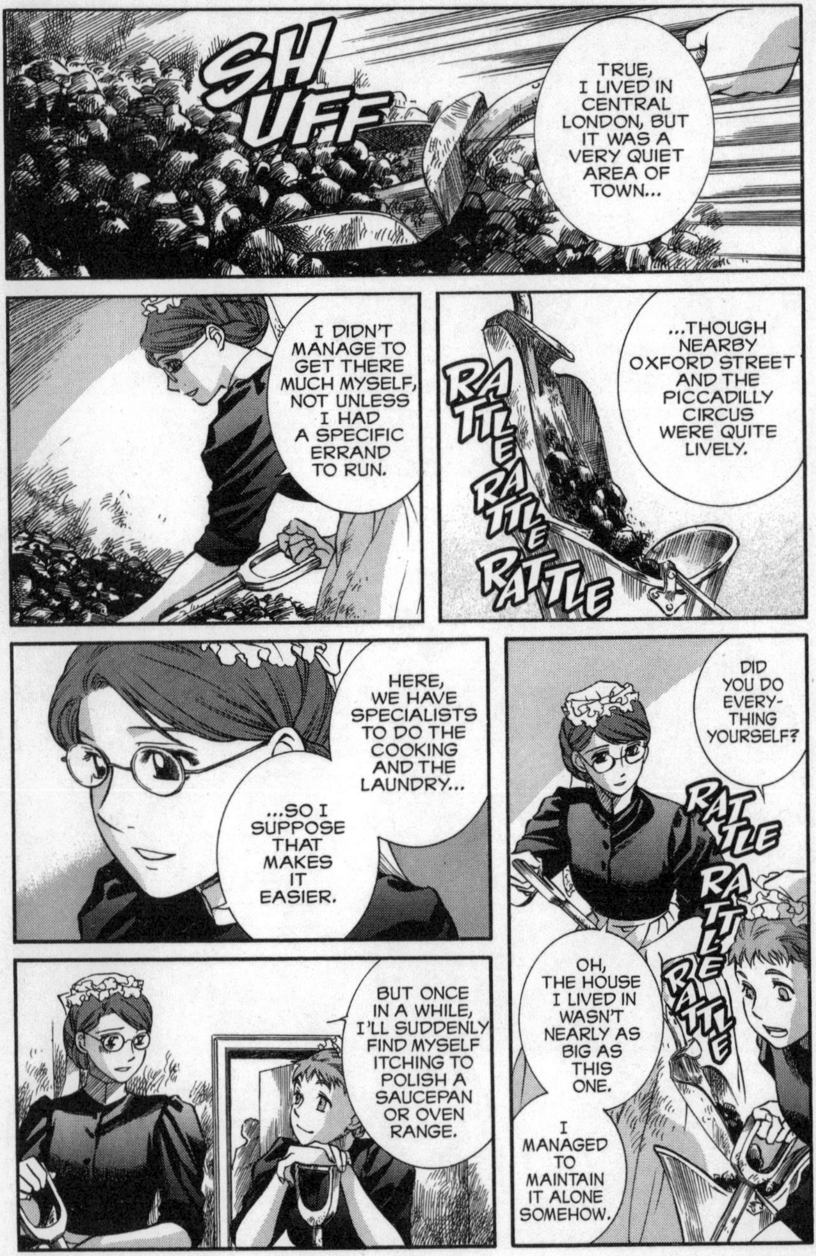
SHUFF
TRUE, I LIVED IN CENTRAL LONDON, BUT IT WAS A VERY QUIET AREA OF TOWN...
...THOUGH NEARBY OXFORD STREET AND THE PICCADILLY CIRCUS WERE QUITE LIVELY.
RATTLE RATTLE RATTLE
I DIDN'T MANAGE TO GET THERE MUCH MYSELF, NOT UNLESS I HAD A SPECIFIC ERRAND TO RUN.
DID YOU DO EVERYTHING YOURSELF?
RATTLE RATTLE RATTLE
OH, THE HOUSE I LIVED IN WASN'T NEARLY AS BIG AS THIS ONE.
I MANAGED TO MAINTAIN IT ALONE SOMEHOW.
HERE, WE HAVE SPECIALISTS TO DO THE COOKING AND THE LAUNDRY...
...SO I SUPPOSE THAT MAKES IT EASIER.
BUT ONCE IN A WHILE, I'LL SUDDENLY FIND MYSELF ITCHING TO POLISH A SAUCEPAN OR OVEN RANGE.

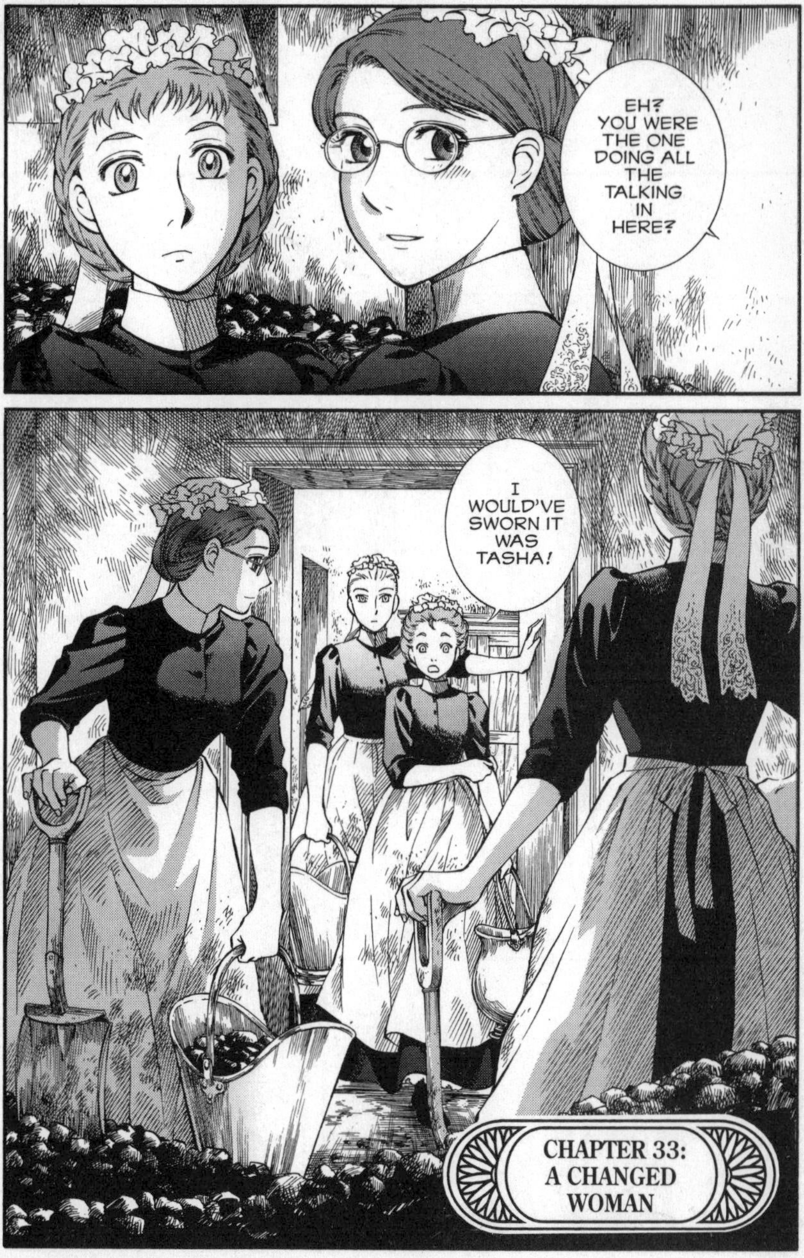
EH? YOU WERE THE ONE DOING ALL THE TALKING IN HERE?
I WOULD'VE SWORN IT WAS TASHA!
CHAPTER 33: A CHANGED WOMAN

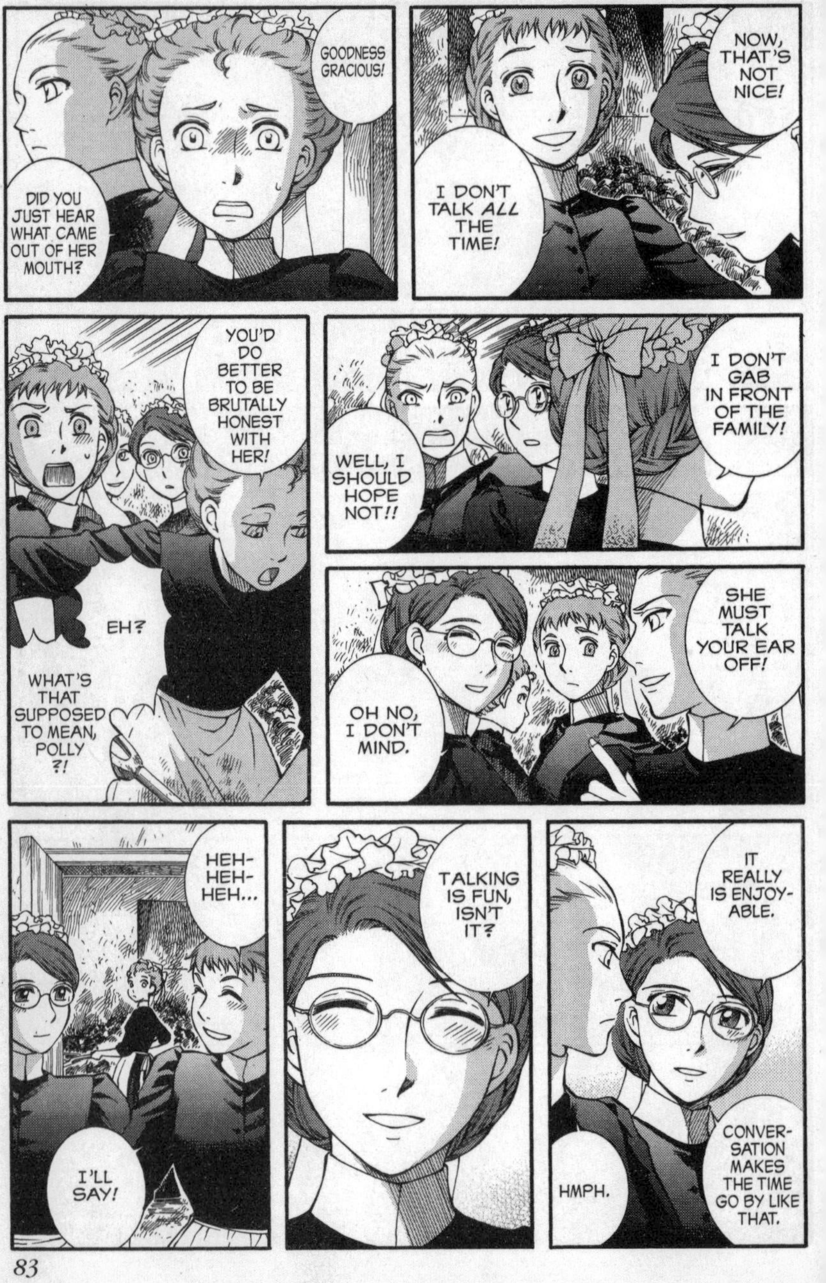
NOW, THAT'S NOT NICE!
I DON'T TALK *ALL* THE TIME!
GOODNESS GRACIOUS!
DID YOU JUST HEAR WHAT CAME OUT OF HER MOUTH?
I DON'T GAB IN FRONT OF THE FAMILY!
WELL, I SHOULD HOPE NOT!!
SHE MUST TALK YOUR EAR OFF!
OH NO, I DON'T MIND.
YOU'D DO BETTER TO BE BRUTALLY HONEST WITH HER!
EH?
WHAT'S THAT SUPPOSED TO MEAN, POLLY?!
IT REALLY IS ENJOY-ABLE.
CONVER-SATION MAKES THE TIME GO BY LIKE THAT.
HMPH.
TALKING IS FUN, ISN'T IT?
HEH-HEH-HEH...
I'LL SAY!

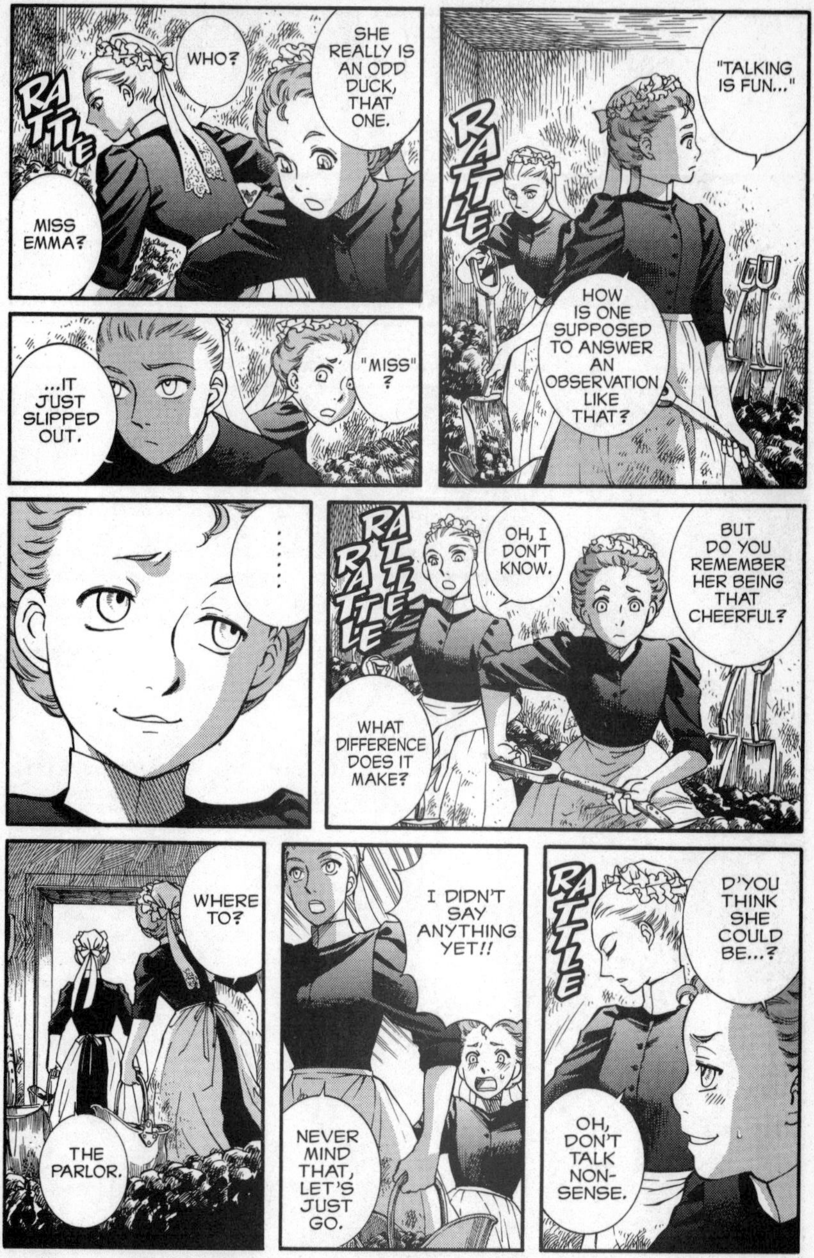
"TALKING IS FUN..."
RATTLE
HOW IS ONE SUPPOSED TO ANSWER AN OBSERVATION LIKE THAT?
SHE REALLY IS AN ODD DUCK, THAT ONE.
WHO?
RATTLE
MISS EMMA?
"MISS"?
...IT JUST SLIPPED OUT.
BUT DO YOU REMEMBER HER BEING THAT CHEERFUL?
OH, I DON'T KNOW.
RATTLE RATTLE
WHAT DIFFERENCE DOES IT MAKE?
......
D'YOU THINK SHE COULD BE...?
RATTLE
OH, DON'T TALK NONSENSE.
I DIDN'T SAY ANYTHING YET!!
NEVER MIND THAT, LET'S JUST GO.
WHERE TO?
THE PARLOR.

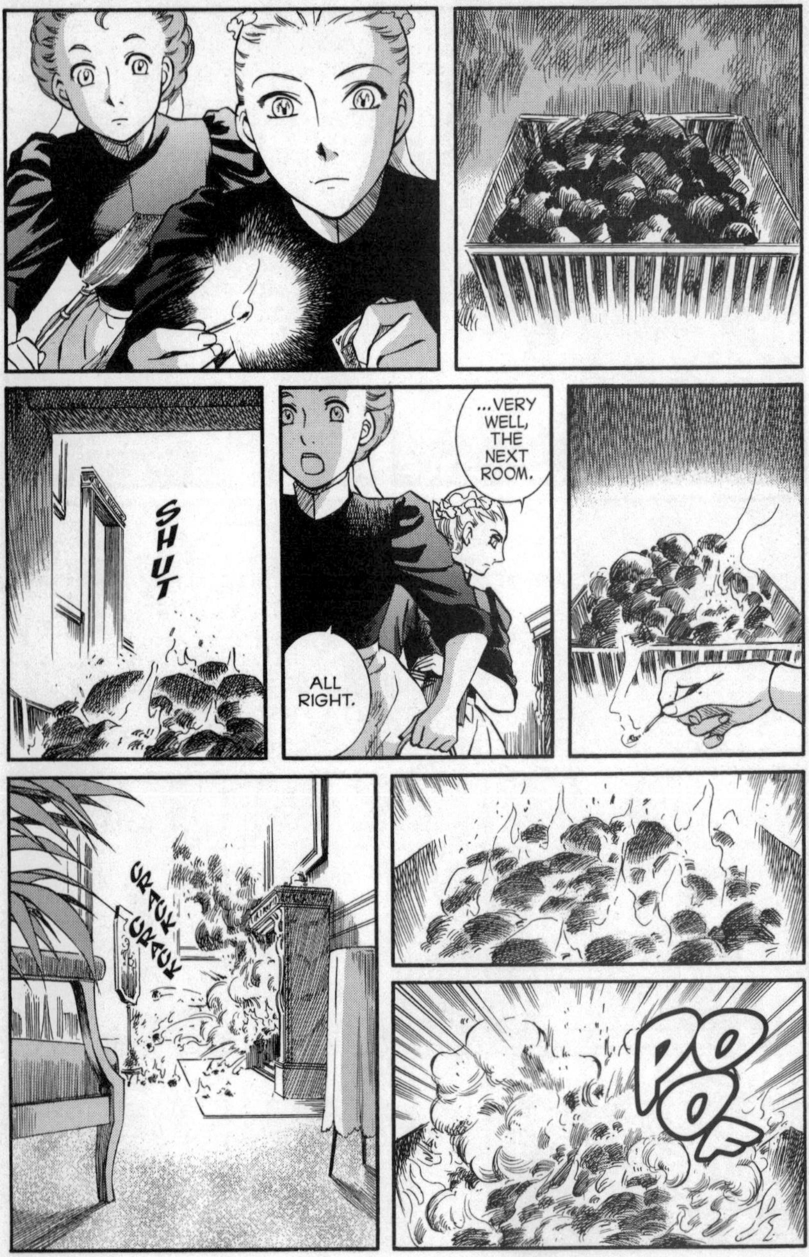
...VERY WELL, THE NEXT ROOM.
ALL RIGHT.
SHUT
POOF
CRACK CRACK

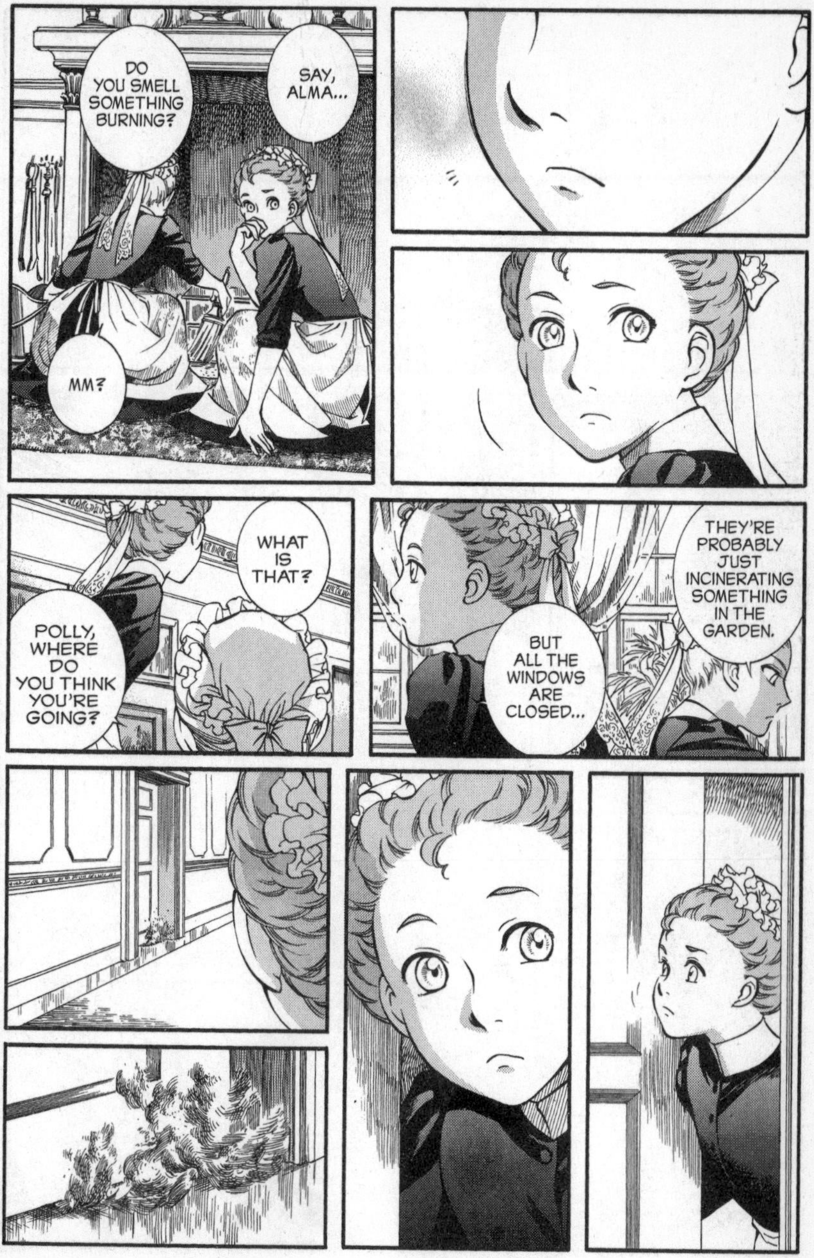
SAY, ALMA...
DO YOU SMELL SOMETHING BURNING?
MM?
THEY'RE PROBABLY JUST INCINERATING SOMETHING IN THE GARDEN.
BUT ALL THE WINDOWS ARE CLOSED...
WHAT IS THAT?
POLLY, WHERE DO YOU THINK YOU'RE GOING?

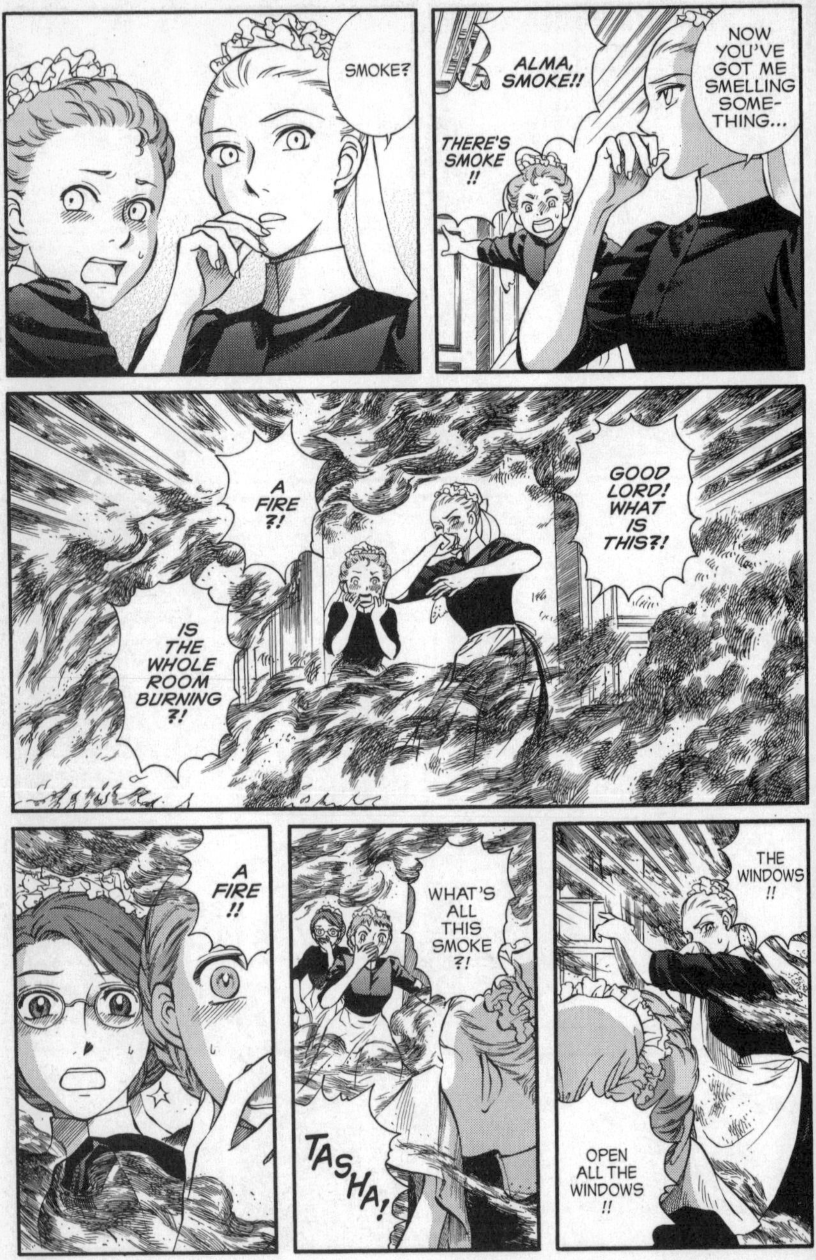
NOW YOU'VE GOT ME SMELLING SOME-THING...
ALMA, SMOKE!!
THERE'S SMOKE!!
SMOKE?
GOOD LORD! WHAT IS THIS?!
A FIRE?!
IS THE WHOLE ROOM BURNING?!
THE WINDOWS!!
OPEN ALL THE WINDOWS!!
WHAT'S ALL THIS SMOKE?!
TASHA!
A FIRE!!

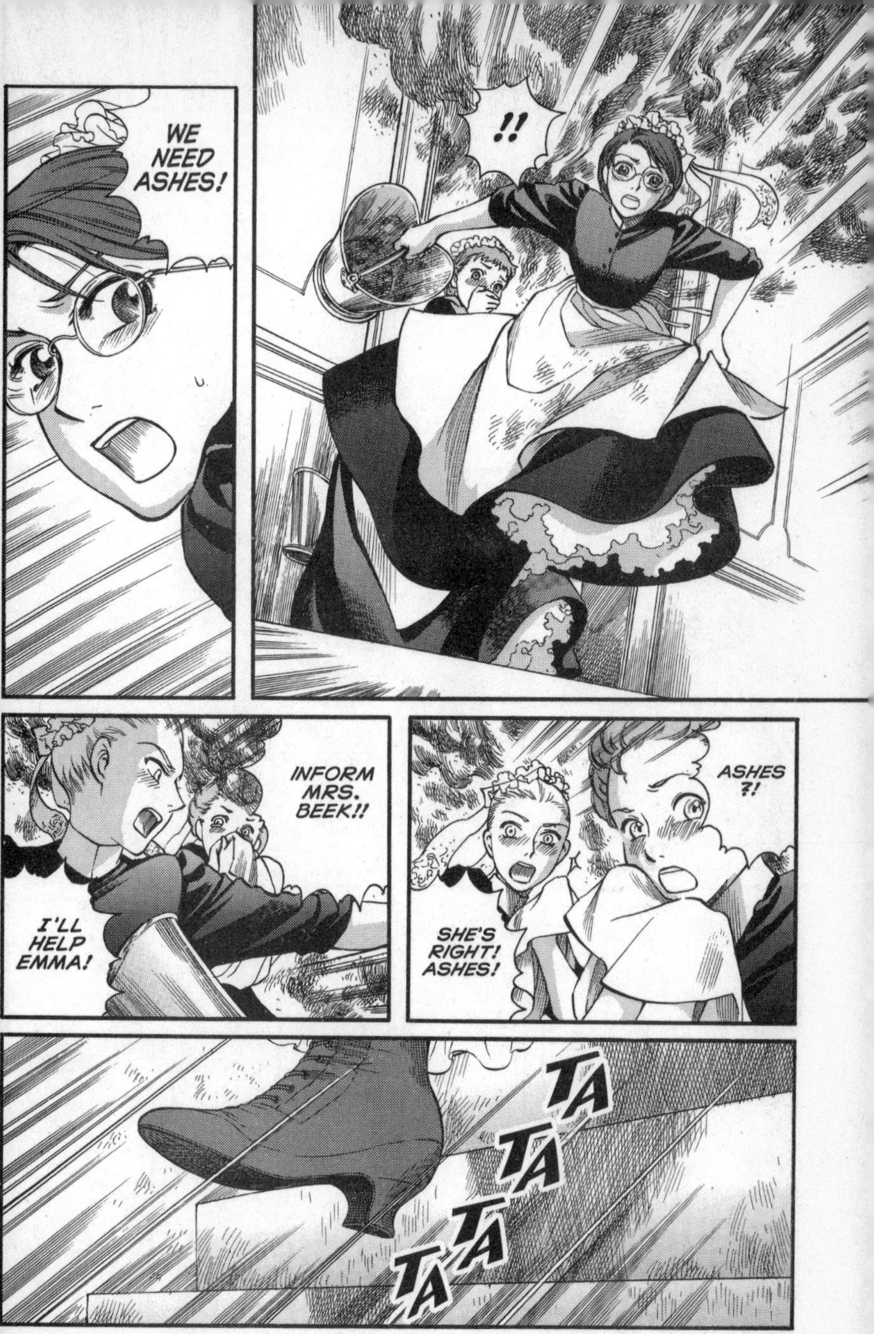
!!
WE NEED ASHES!
ASHES ?!
SHE'S RIGHT! ASHES!
INFORM MRS. BEEK!!
I'LL HELP EMMA!
TA TA TA TA TA

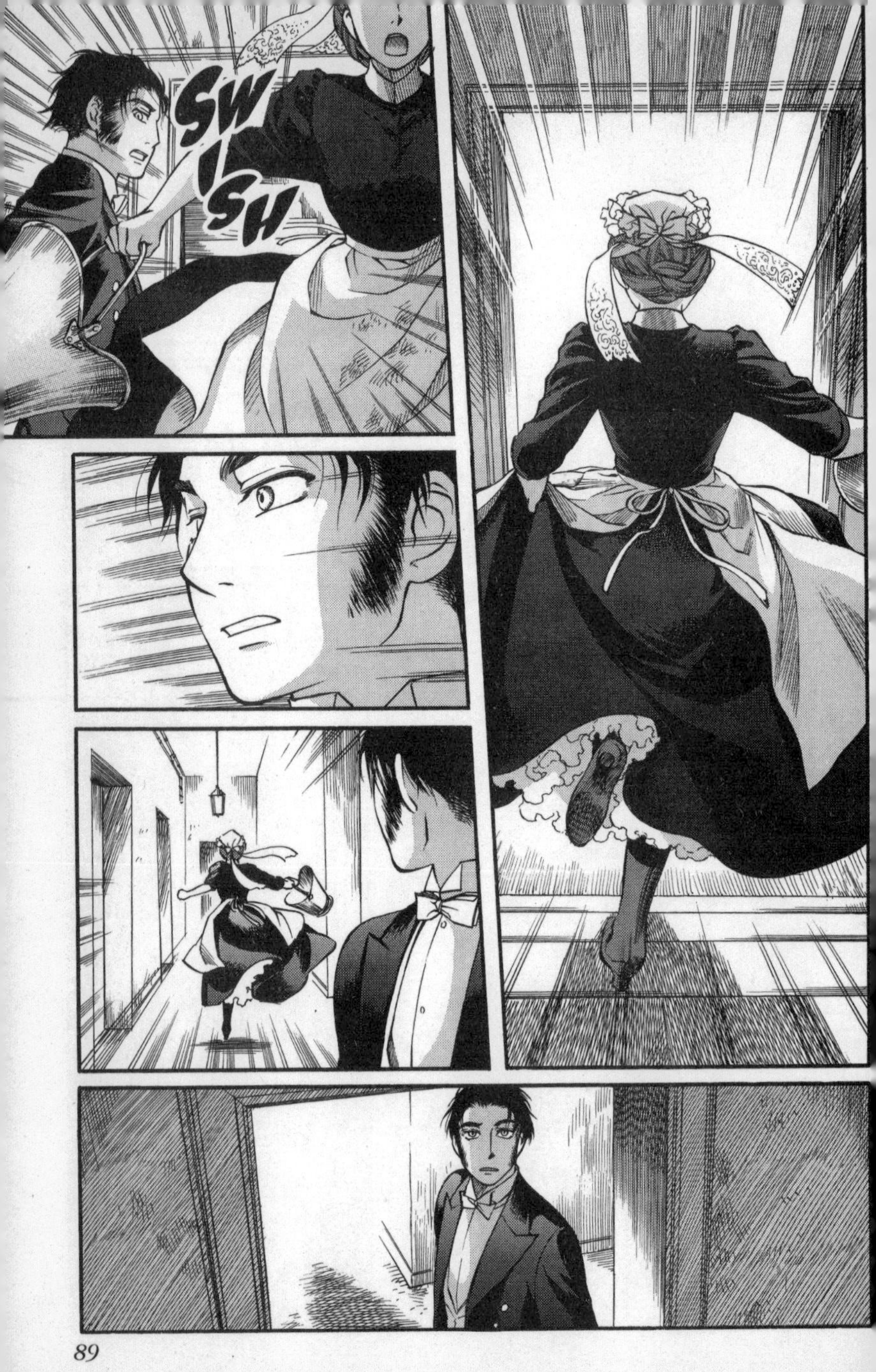
SWISH

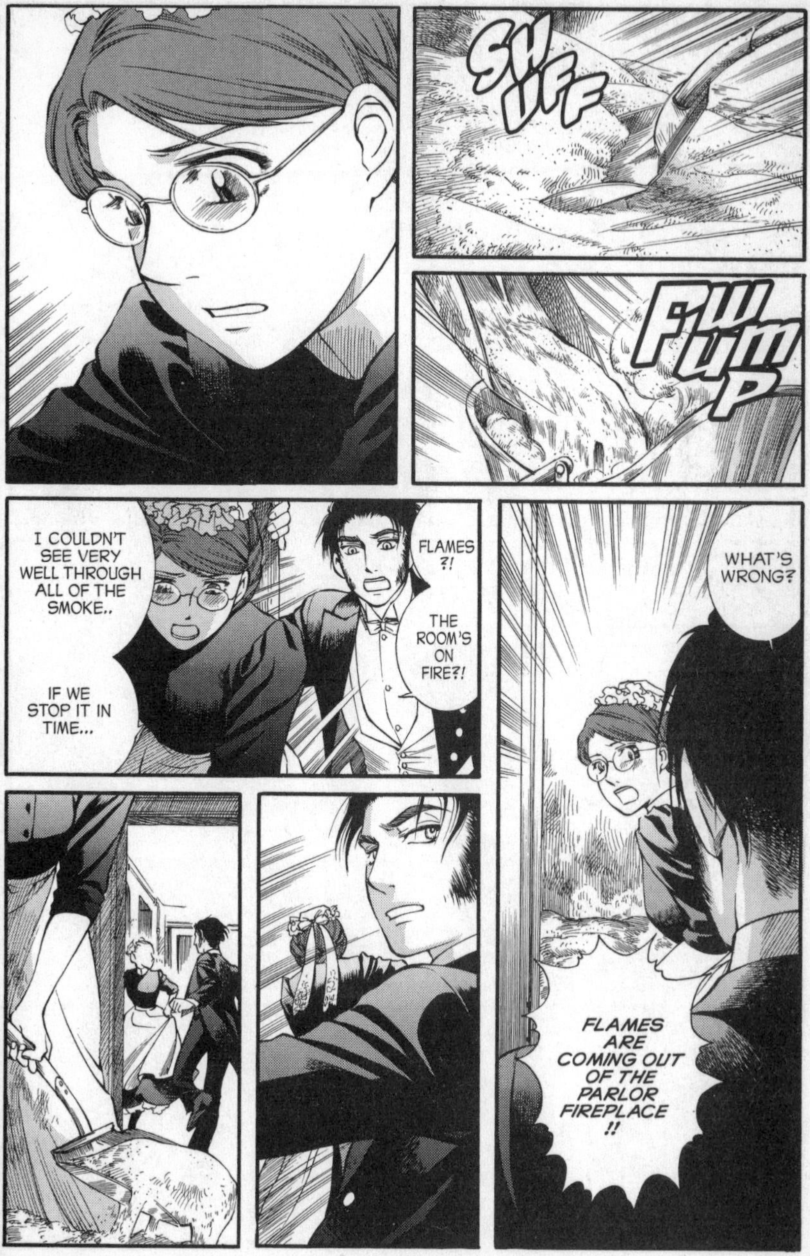
SHUFF
FWUMP
WHAT'S WRONG?
FLAMES ARE COMING OUT OF THE PARLOR FIREPLACE !!
FLAMES ?!
THE ROOM'S ON FIRE?!
I COULDN'T SEE VERY WELL THROUGH ALL OF THE SMOKE..
IF WE STOP IT IN TIME...

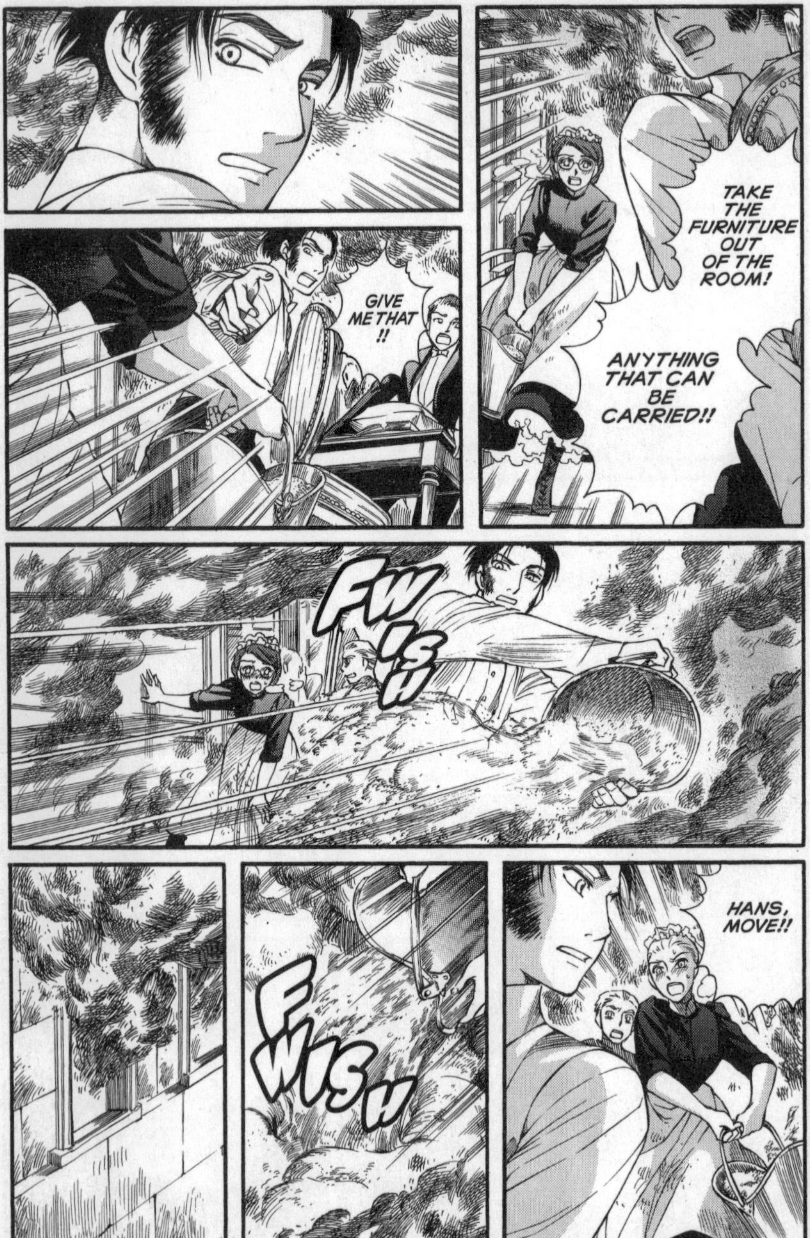
TAKE THE FURNITURE OUT OF THE ROOM!
ANYTHING THAT CAN BE CARRIED!!
GIVE ME THAT !!
FWISH
HANS, MOVE!!
FWISH

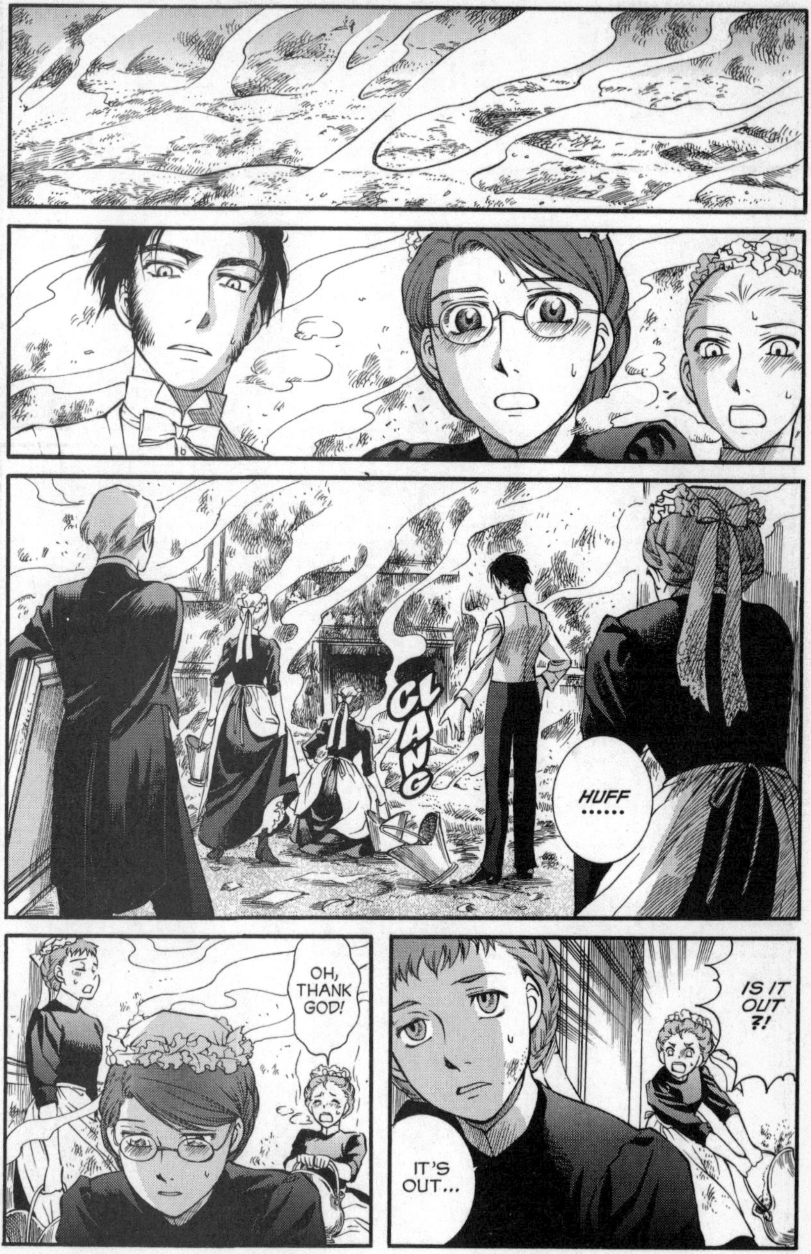
HUFF ......
CLANG
IS IT OUT ?!
IT'S OUT...
OH, THANK GOD!

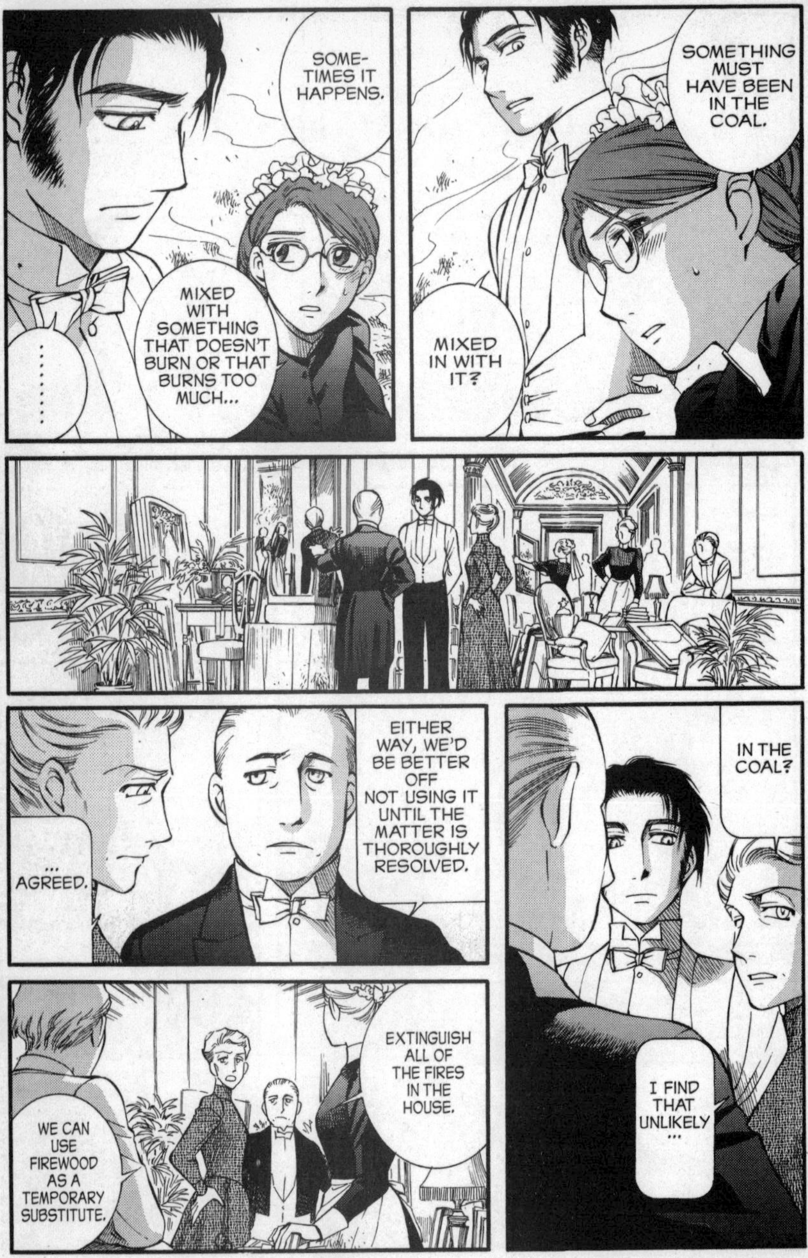
SOMETHING MUST HAVE BEEN IN THE COAL.
MIXED IN WITH IT?
SOME-TIMES IT HAPPENS.
MIXED WITH SOMETHING THAT DOESN'T BURN OR THAT BURNS TOO MUCH...
....
IN THE COAL?
I FIND THAT UNLIKELY ...
EITHER WAY, WE'D BE BETTER OFF NOT USING IT UNTIL THE MATTER IS THOROUGHLY RESOLVED.
... AGREED.
EXTINGUISH ALL OF THE FIRES IN THE HOUSE.
WE CAN USE FIREWOOD AS A TEMPORARY SUBSTITUTE.

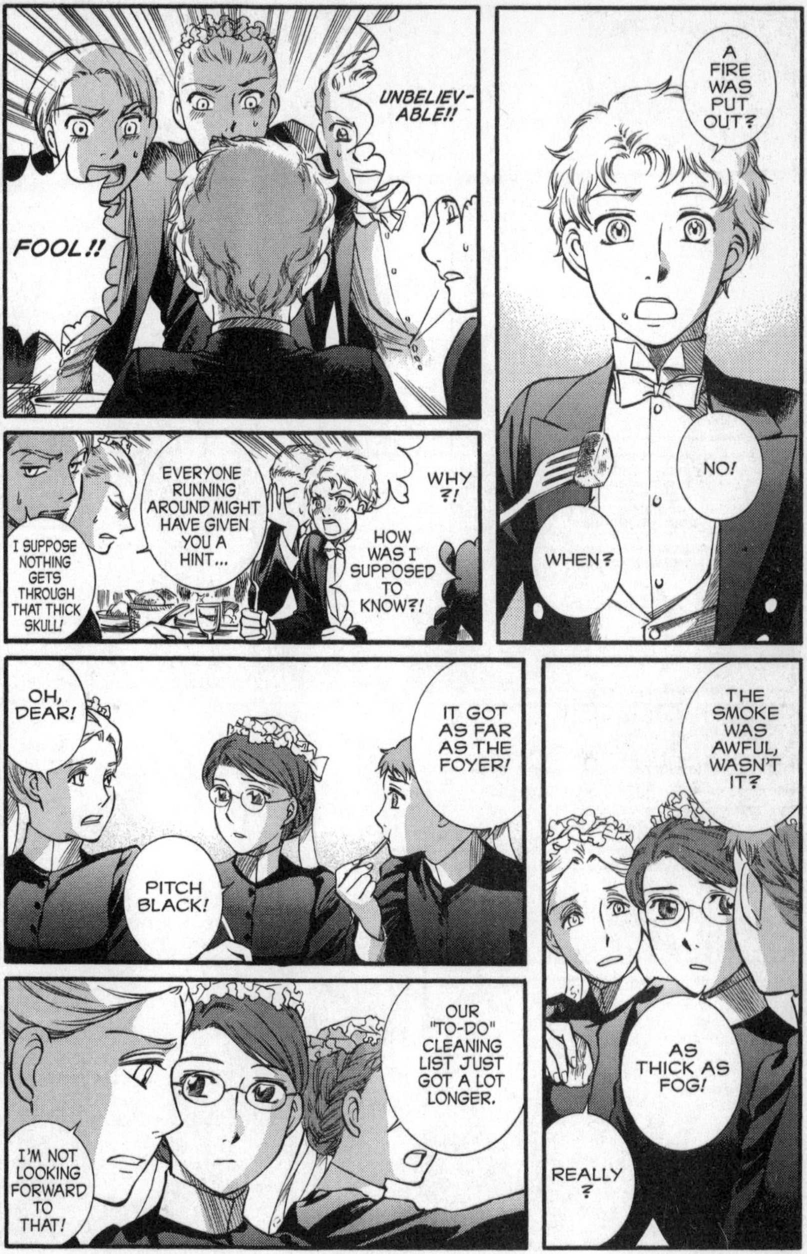
A FIRE WAS PUT OUT?
NO!
WHEN?
UNBELIEVABLE!!
FOOL!!
WHY?!
HOW WAS I SUPPOSED TO KNOW?!
EVERYONE RUNNING AROUND MIGHT HAVE GIVEN YOU A HINT...
I SUPPOSE NOTHING GETS THROUGH THAT THICK SKULL!
THE SMOKE WAS AWFUL, WASN'T IT?
AS THICK AS FOG!
REALLY?
IT GOT AS FAR AS THE FOYER!
PITCH BLACK!
OH, DEAR!
OUR "TO-DO" CLEANING LIST JUST GOT A LOT LONGER.
I'M NOT LOOKING FORWARD TO THAT!

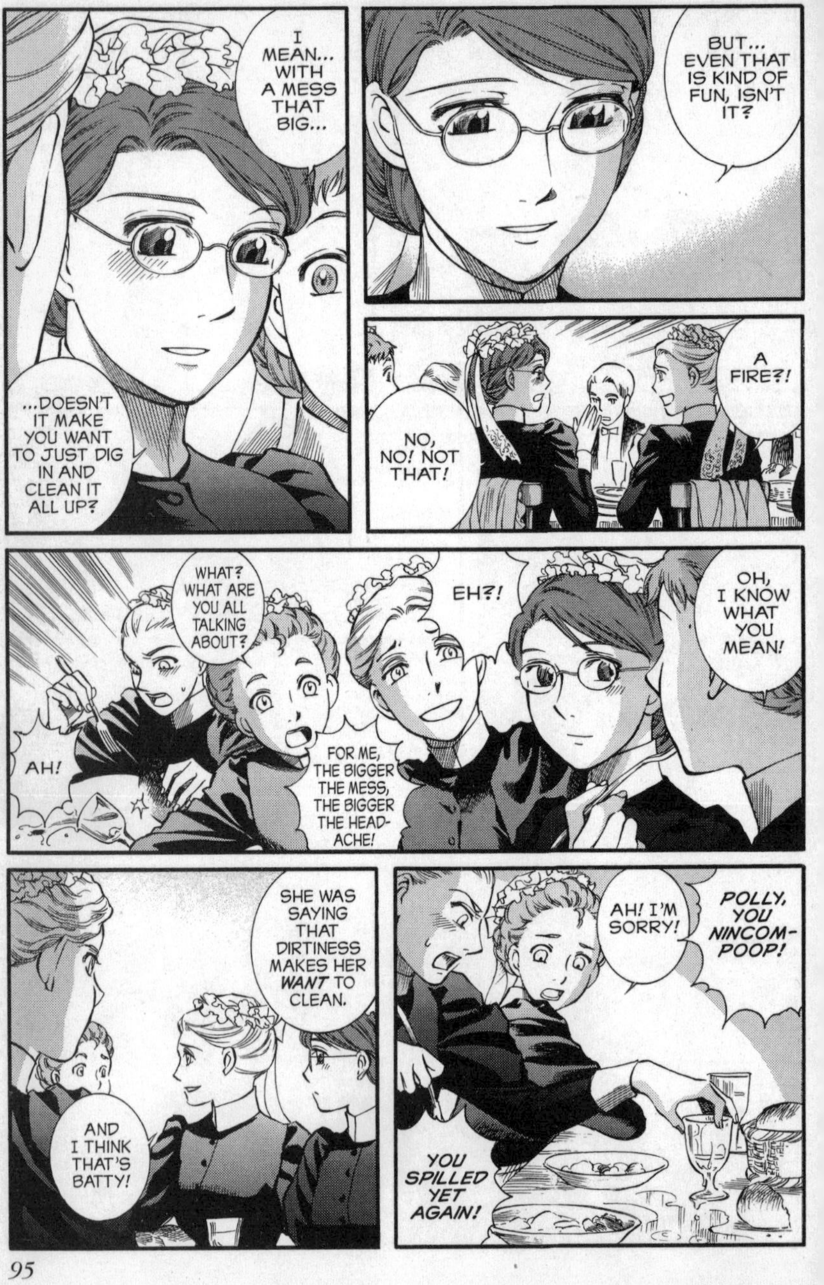
BUT... EVEN THAT IS KIND OF FUN, ISN'T IT?
A FIRE?!
NO, NO! NOT THAT!
I MEAN... WITH A MESS THAT BIG...
...DOESN'T IT MAKE YOU WANT TO JUST DIG IN AND CLEAN IT ALL UP?
OH, I KNOW WHAT YOU MEAN!
EH?!
WHAT? WHAT ARE YOU ALL TALKING ABOUT?
FOR ME, THE BIGGER THE MESS, THE BIGGER THE HEAD-ACHE!
AH!
POLLY, YOU NINCOMPOOP!
AH! I'M SORRY!
YOU SPILLED YET AGAIN!
SHE WAS SAYING THAT DIRTINESS MAKES HER *WANT* TO CLEAN.
AND I THINK THAT'S BATTY!

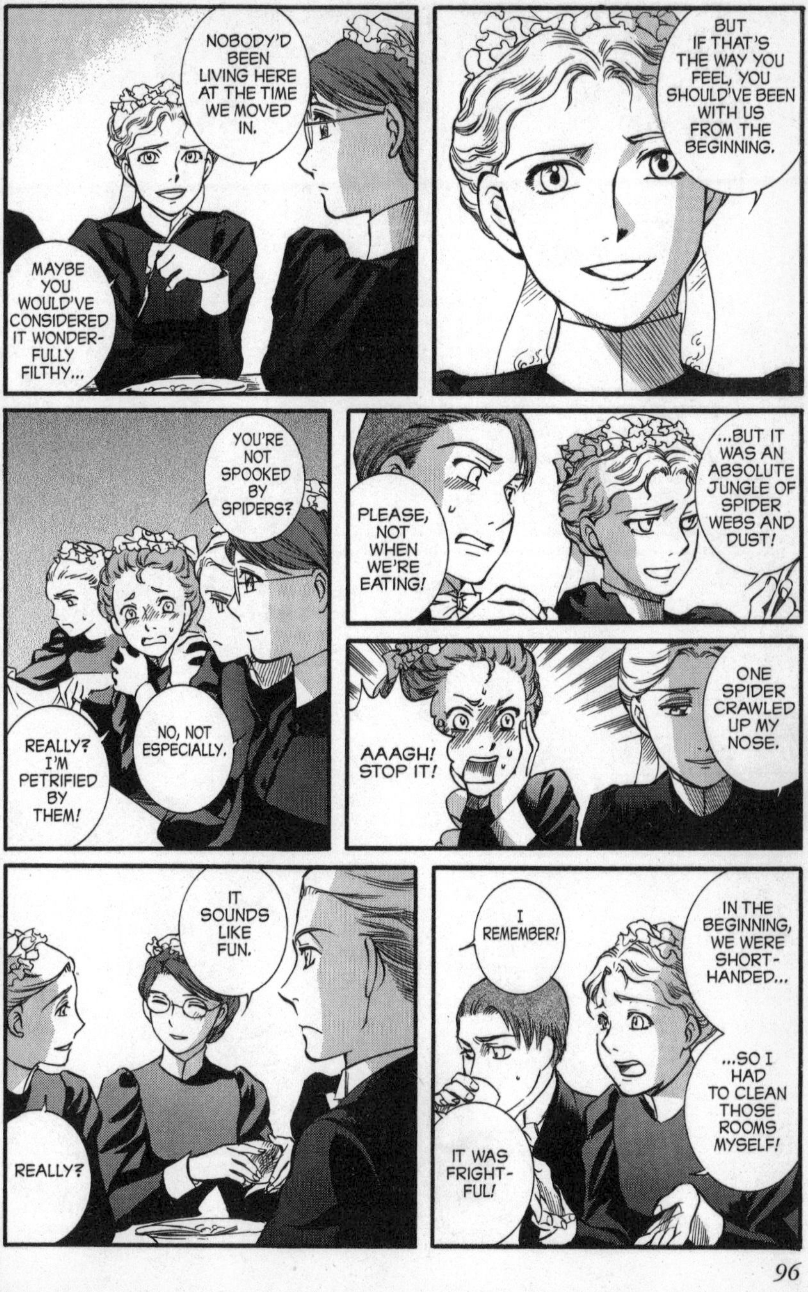
BUT IF THAT'S THE WAY YOU FEEL, YOU SHOULD'VE BEEN WITH US FROM THE BEGINNING.
NOBODY'D BEEN LIVING HERE AT THE TIME WE MOVED IN.
MAYBE YOU WOULD'VE CONSIDERED IT WONDER-FULLY FILTHY...
...BUT IT WAS AN ABSOLUTE JUNGLE OF SPIDER WEBS AND DUST!
PLEASE, NOT WHEN WE'RE EATING!
ONE SPIDER CRAWLED UP MY NOSE.
AAAGH! STOP IT!
YOU'RE NOT SPOOKED BY SPIDERS?
NO, NOT ESPECIALLY.
REALLY? I'M PETRIFIED BY THEM!
IN THE BEGINNING, WE WERE SHORT-HANDED...
I REMEMBER!
...SO I HAD TO CLEAN THOSE ROOMS MYSELF!
IT WAS FRIGHT-FUL!
IT SOUNDS LIKE FUN.
REALLY?

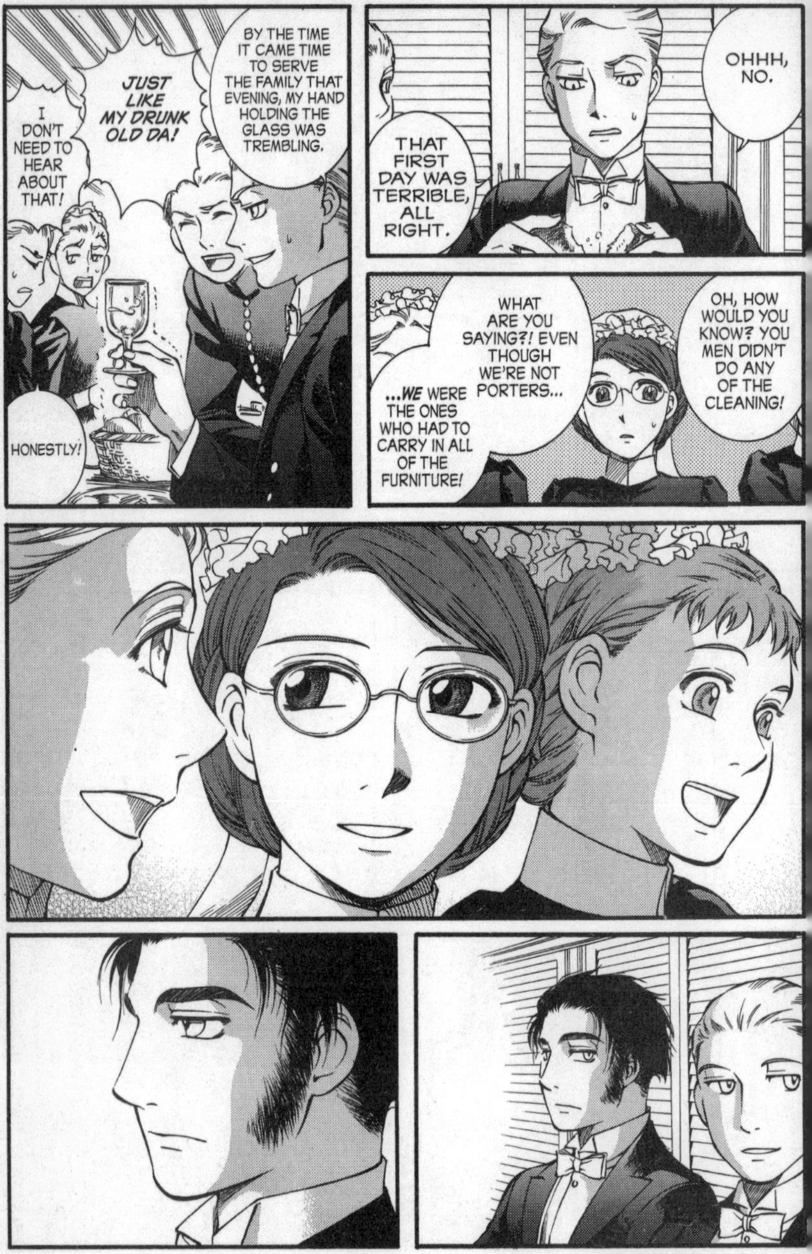
OHHH, NO.
THAT FIRST DAY WAS TERRIBLE, ALL RIGHT.
OH, HOW WOULD YOU KNOW? YOU MEN DIDN'T DO ANY OF THE CLEANING!
WHAT ARE YOU SAYING?! EVEN THOUGH WE'RE NOT PORTERS...
...WE WERE THE ONES WHO HAD TO CARRY IN ALL OF THE FURNITURE!
BY THE TIME IT CAME TIME TO SERVE THE FAMILY THAT EVENING, MY HAND HOLDING THE GLASS WAS TREMBLING.
JUST LIKE MY DRUNK OLD DA!
I DON'T NEED TO HEAR ABOUT THAT!
HONESTLY!

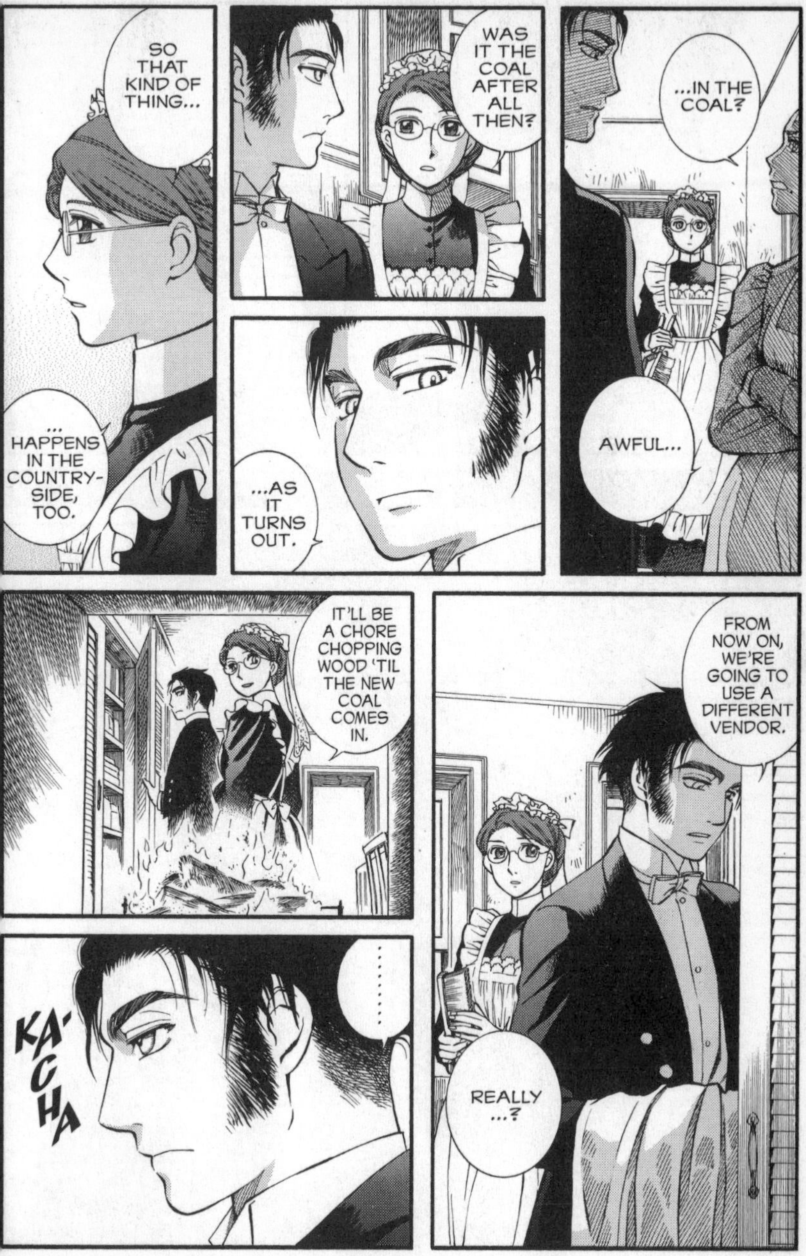
...IN THE COAL?
AWFUL...
WAS IT THE COAL AFTER ALL THEN?
...AS IT TURNS OUT.
SO THAT KIND OF THING...
...HAPPENS IN THE COUNTRY-SIDE, TOO.
FROM NOW ON, WE'RE GOING TO USE A DIFFERENT VENDOR.
REALLY ...?
IT'LL BE A CHORE CHOPPING WOOD 'TIL THE NEW COAL COMES IN.
......
KA-CHA

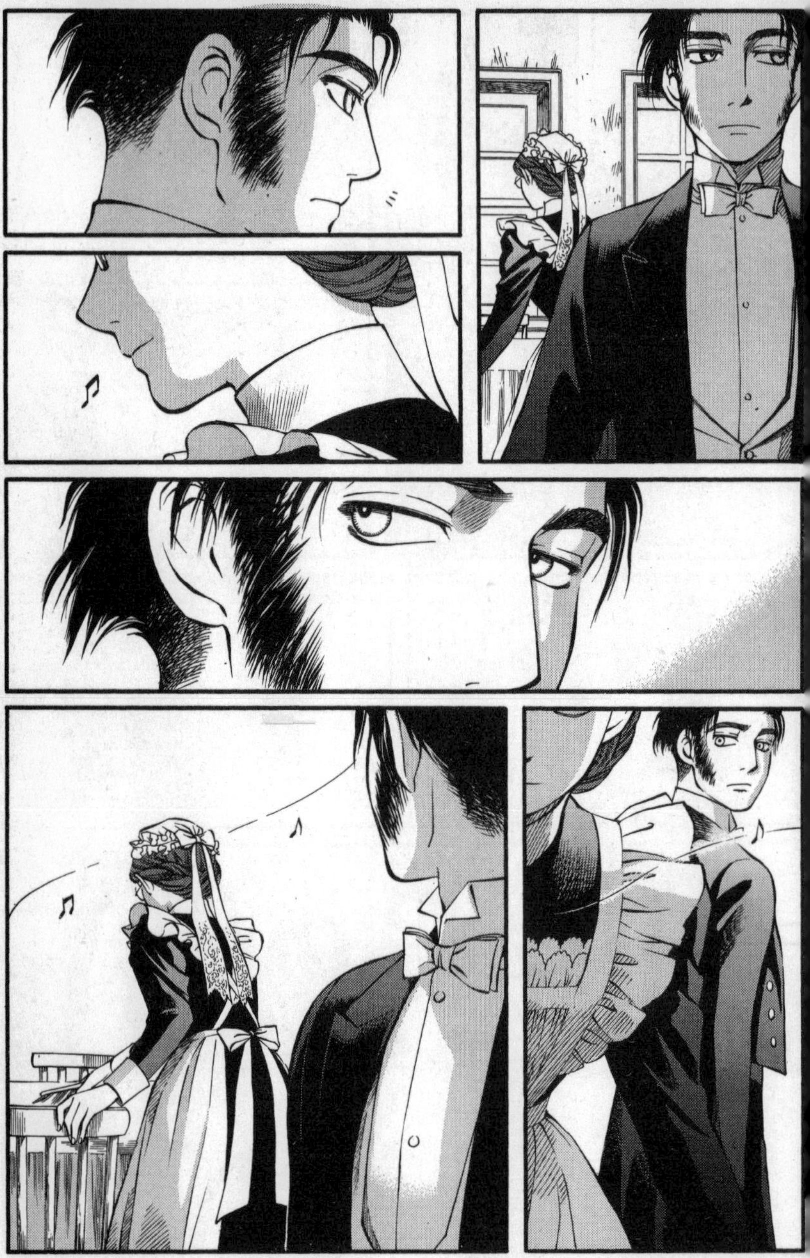

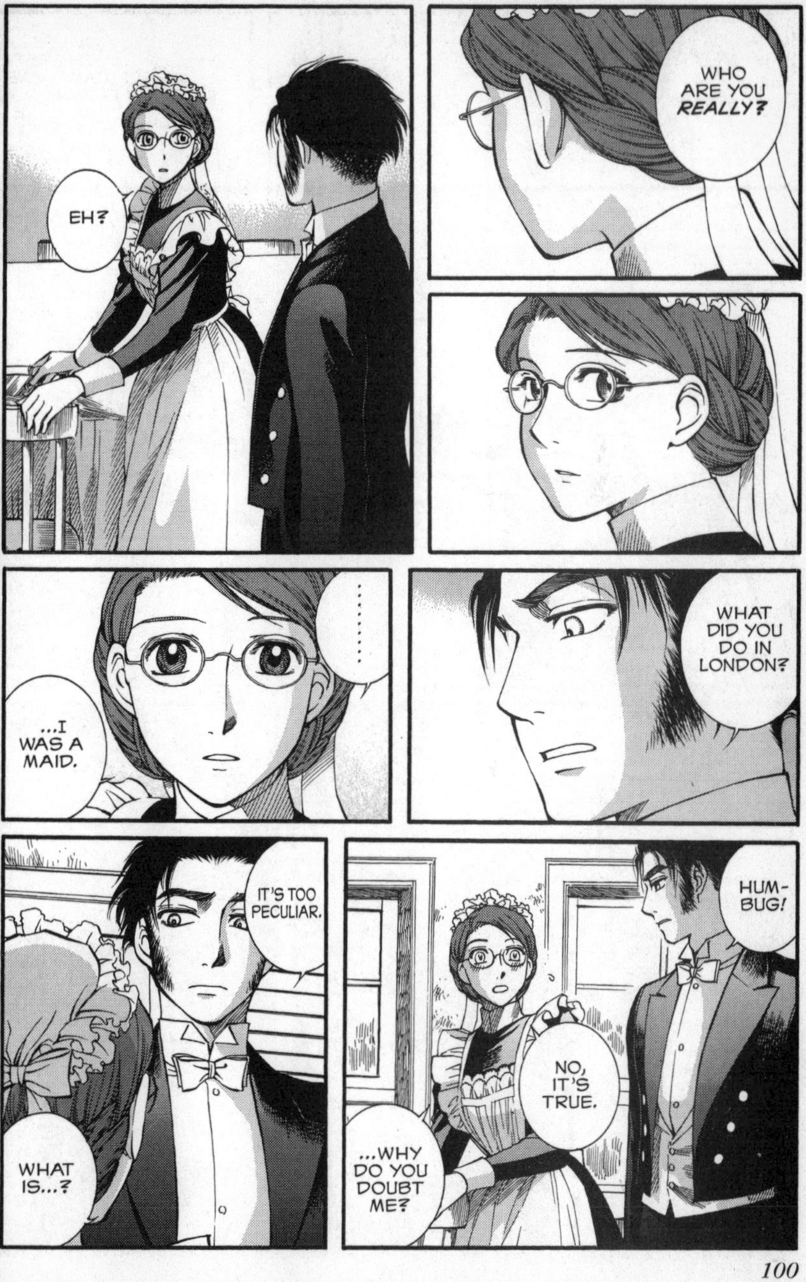
WHO ARE YOU *REALLY*?
EH?
WHAT DID YOU DO IN LONDON?
......
...I WAS A MAID.
HUM-BUG!
NO, IT'S TRUE.
...WHY DO YOU DOUBT ME?
IT'S TOO PECULIAR.
WHAT IS...?

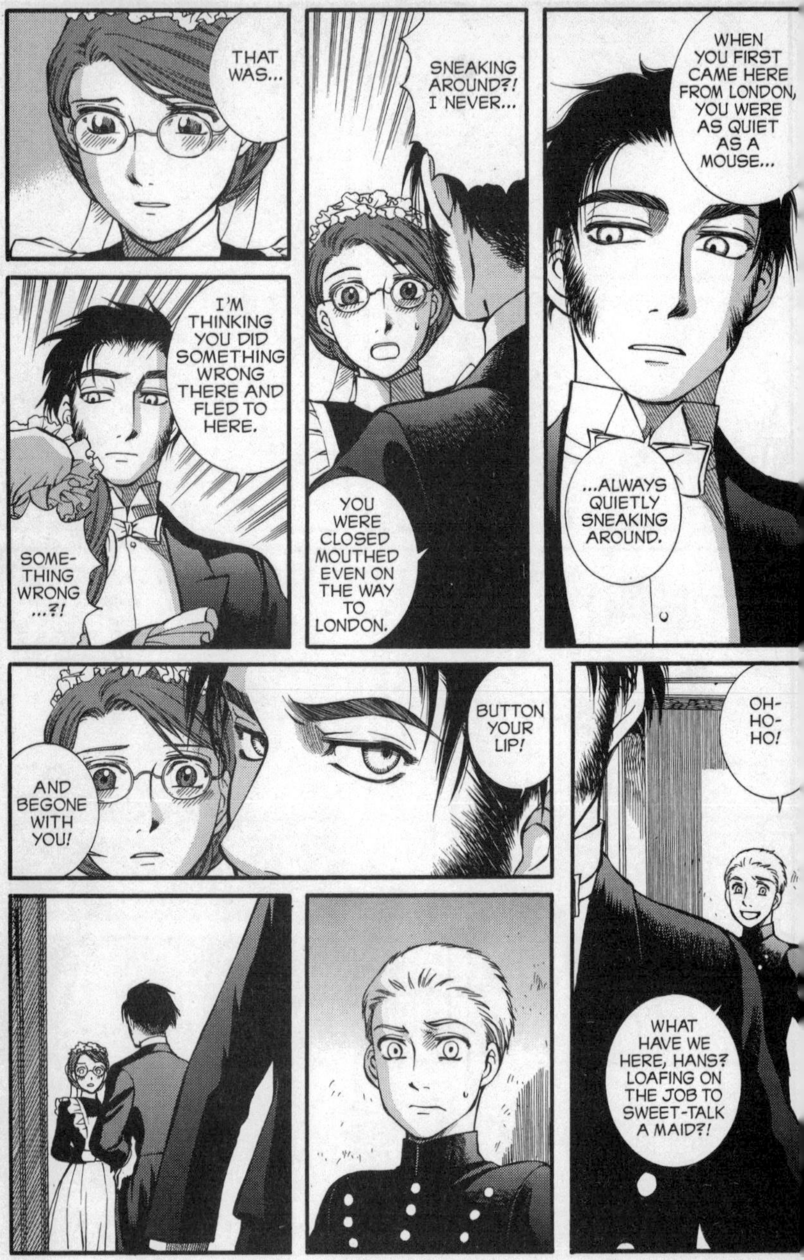
WHEN YOU FIRST CAME HERE FROM LONDON, YOU WERE AS QUIET AS A MOUSE...
...ALWAYS QUIETLY SNEAKING AROUND.
SNEAKING AROUND?! I NEVER...
YOU WERE CLOSED MOUTHED EVEN ON THE WAY TO LONDON.
THAT WAS...
I'M THINKING YOU DID SOMETHING WRONG THERE AND FLED TO HERE.
SOME-THING WRONG ...?!
OH-HO-HO!
WHAT HAVE WE HERE, HANS? LOAFING ON THE JOB TO SWEET-TALK A MAID?!
BUTTON YOUR LIP!
AND BEGONE WITH YOU!

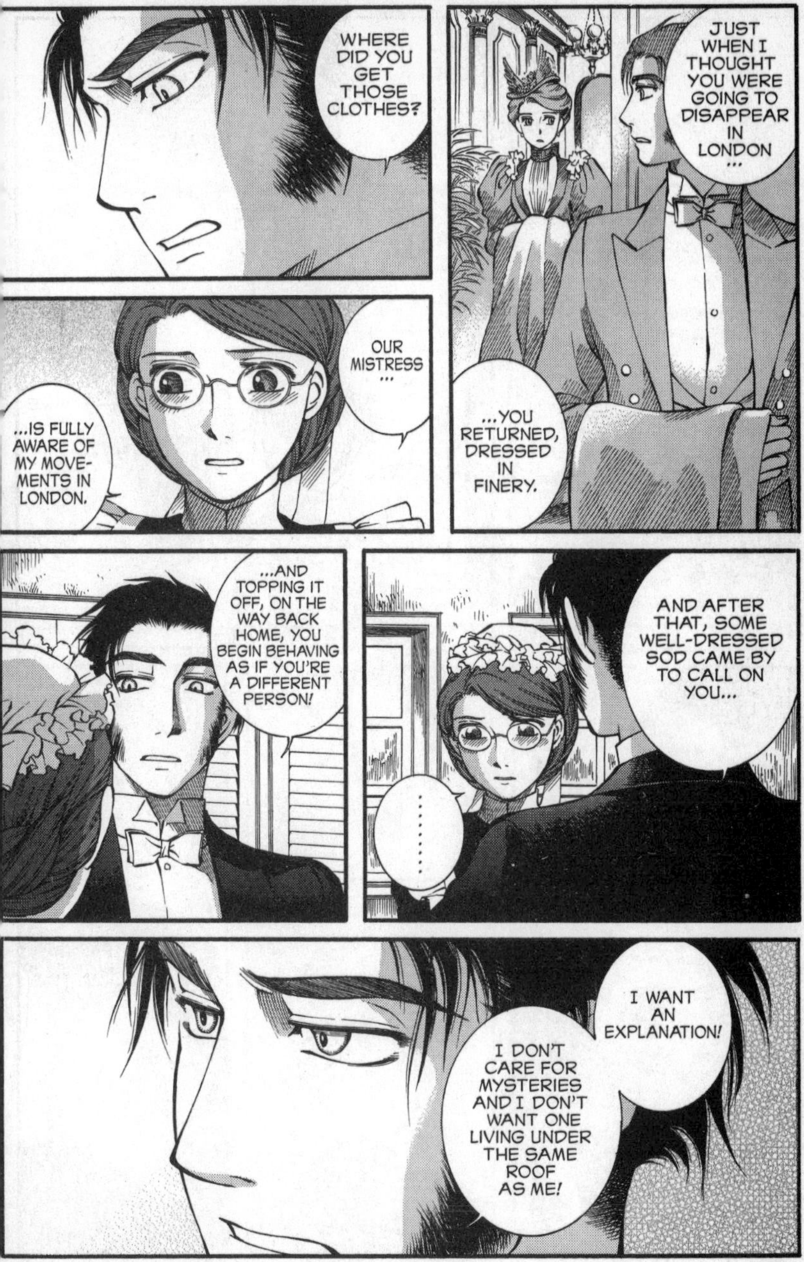
JUST WHEN I THOUGHT YOU WERE GOING TO DISAPPEAR IN LONDON ...
...YOU RETURNED, DRESSED IN FINERY.
WHERE DID YOU GET THOSE CLOTHES?
OUR MISTRESS ...
...IS FULLY AWARE OF MY MOVEMENTS IN LONDON.
AND AFTER THAT, SOME WELL-DRESSED SOD CAME BY TO CALL ON YOU...
....
...AND TOPPING IT OFF, ON THE WAY BACK HOME, YOU BEGIN BEHAVING AS IF YOU'RE A DIFFERENT PERSON!
I WANT AN EXPLANATION!
I DON'T CARE FOR MYSTERIES AND I DON'T WANT ONE LIVING UNDER THE SAME ROOF AS ME!

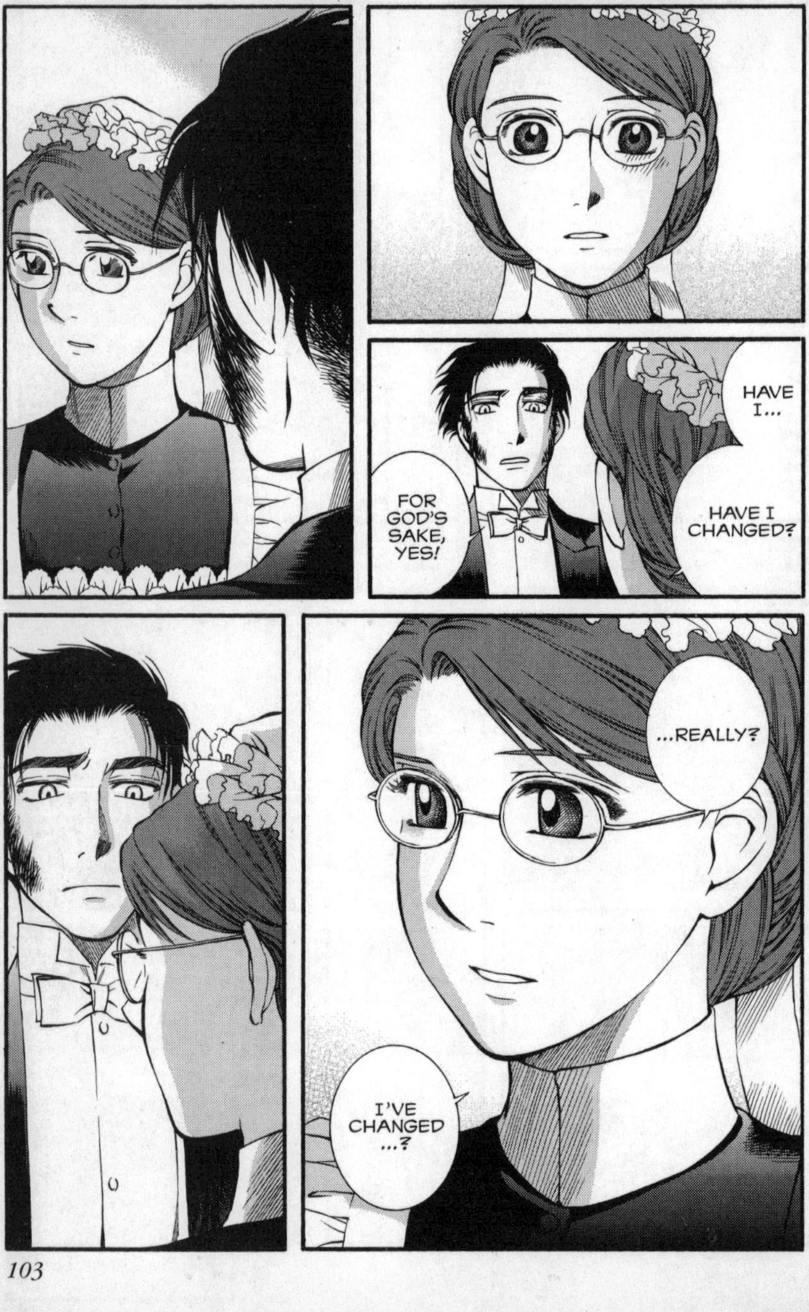
HAVE I...
HAVE I CHANGED?
FOR GOD'S SAKE, YES!
...REALLY?
I'VE CHANGED ...?

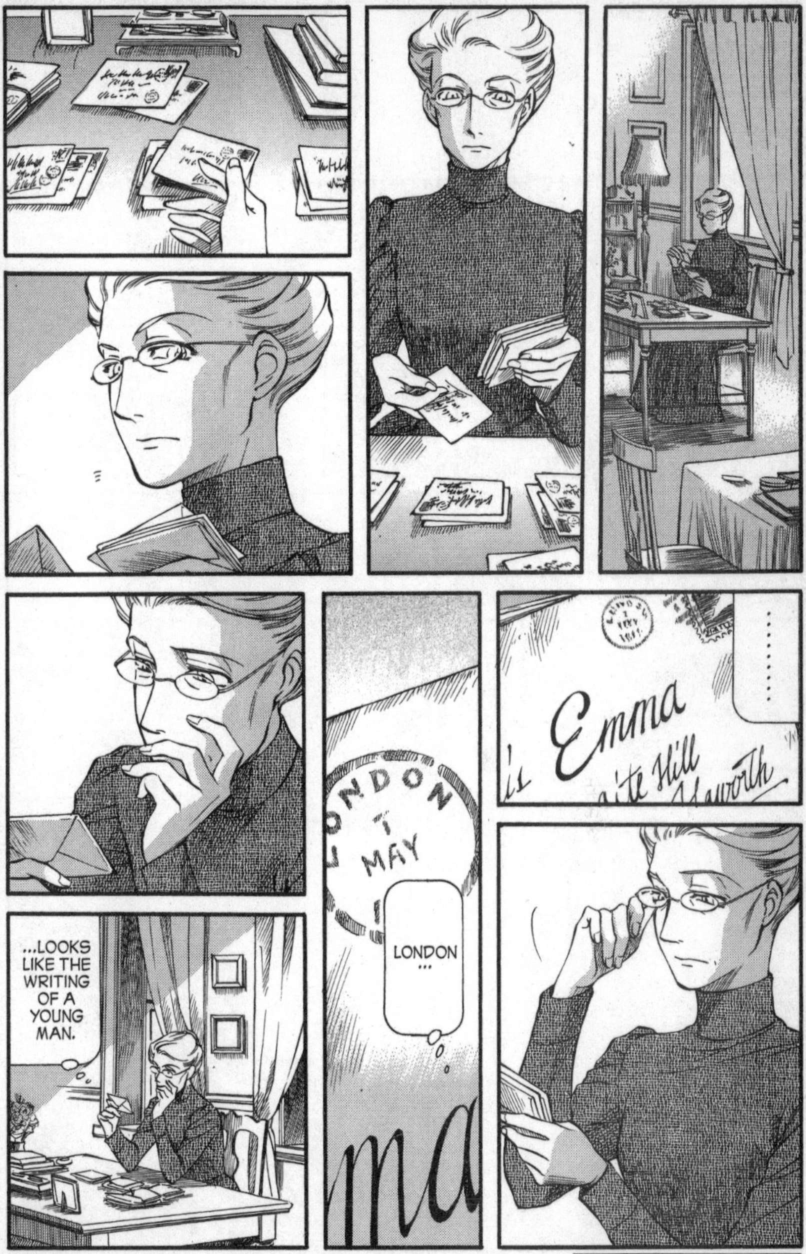
Emma
LONDON 1 MAY
LONDON ...
...LOOKS LIKE THE WRITING OF A YOUNG MAN.

Chapter Thirty Three: The End

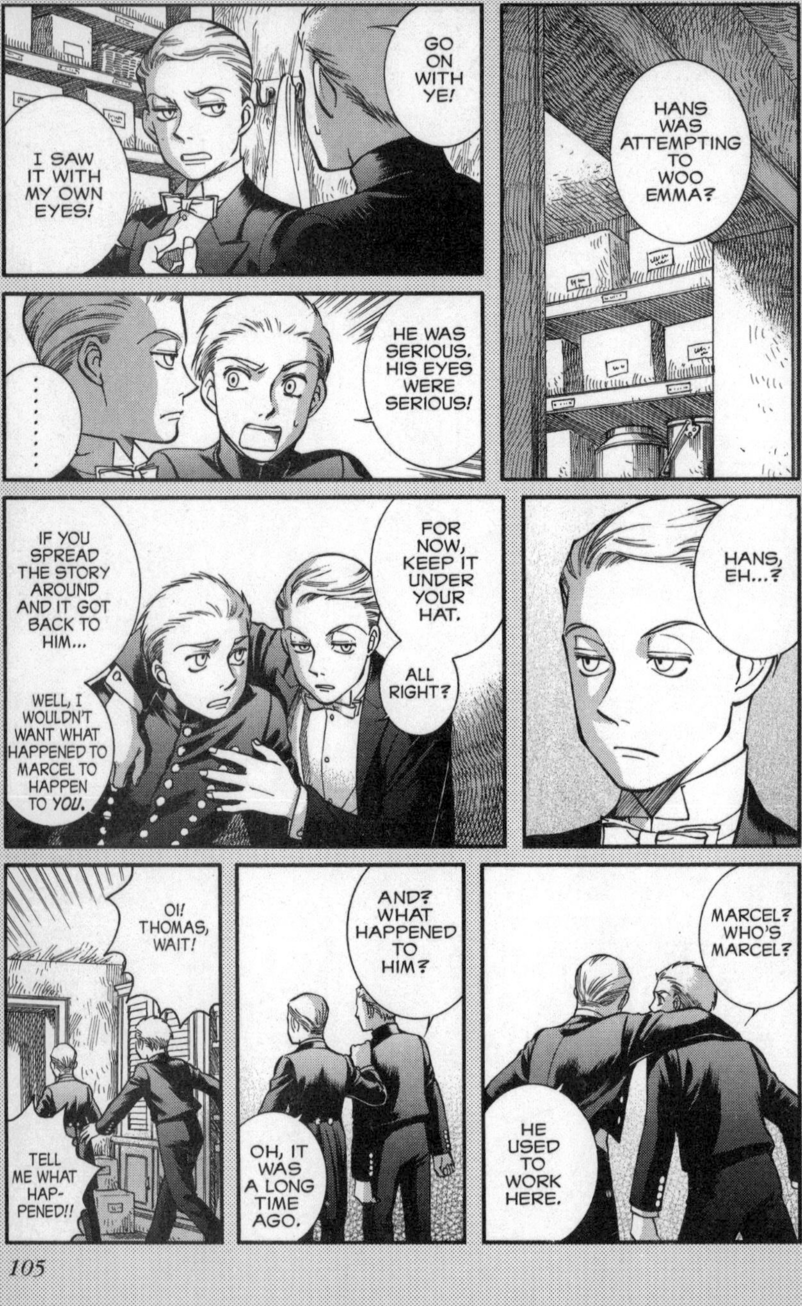
HANS WAS ATTEMPTING TO WOO EMMA?
GO ON WITH YE!
I SAW IT WITH MY OWN EYES!
HE WAS SERIOUS. HIS EYES WERE SERIOUS!
......
HANS, EH...?
FOR NOW, KEEP IT UNDER YOUR HAT.
ALL RIGHT?
IF YOU SPREAD THE STORY AROUND AND IT GOT BACK TO HIM...
WELL, I WOULDN'T WANT WHAT HAPPENED TO MARCEL TO HAPPEN TO *YOU*.
MARCEL? WHO'S MARCEL?
HE USED TO WORK HERE.
AND? WHAT HAPPENED TO HIM?
OH, IT WAS A LONG TIME AGO.
OI! THOMAS, WAIT!
TELL ME WHAT HAP-PENED!!

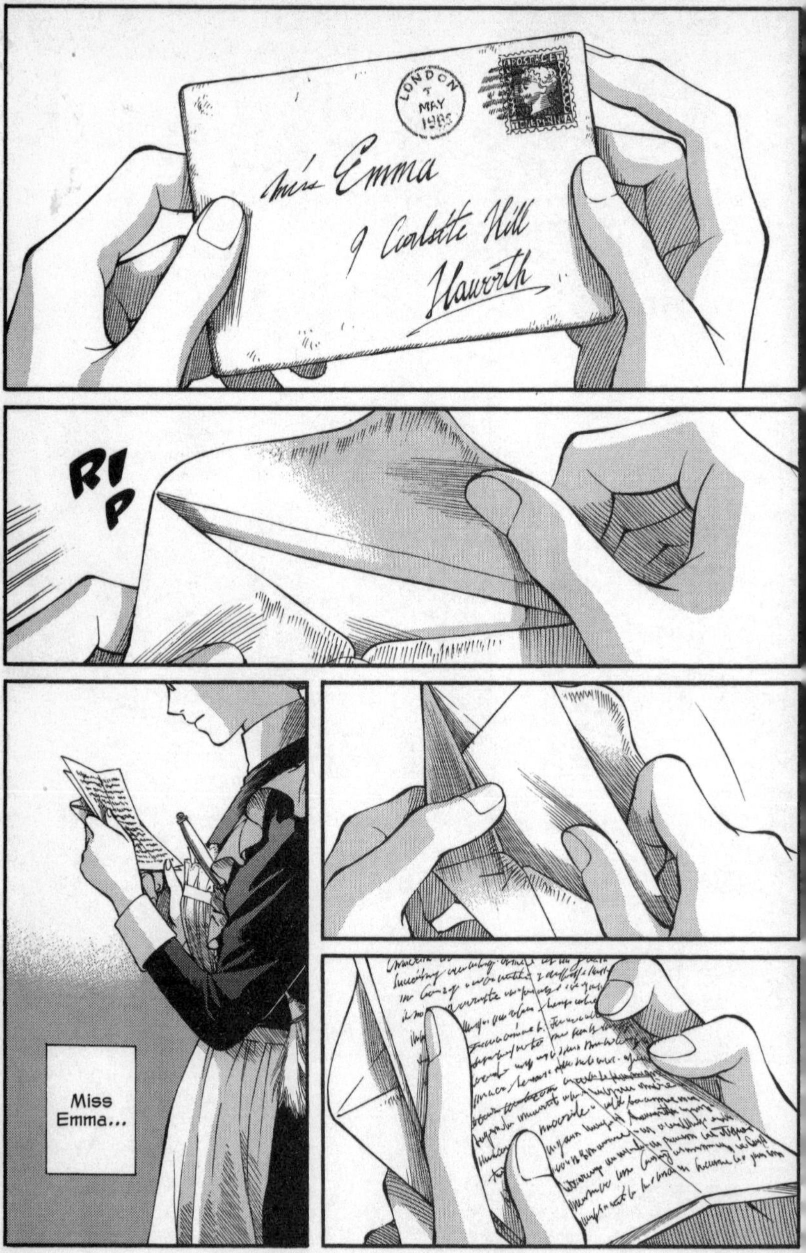
RIP
Miss Emma...

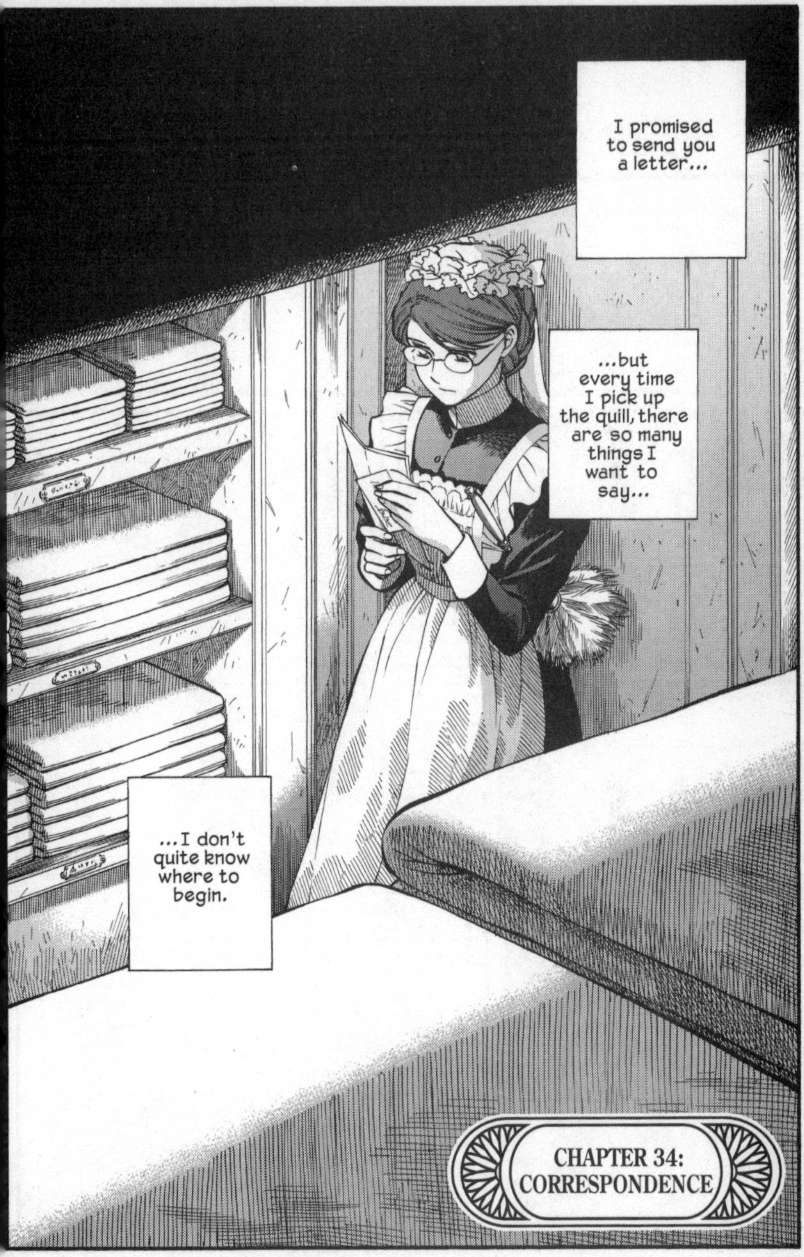
I promised to send you a letter...
...but every time I pick up the quill, there are so many things I want to say...
...I don't quite know where to begin.
CHAPTER 34: CORRESPONDENCE

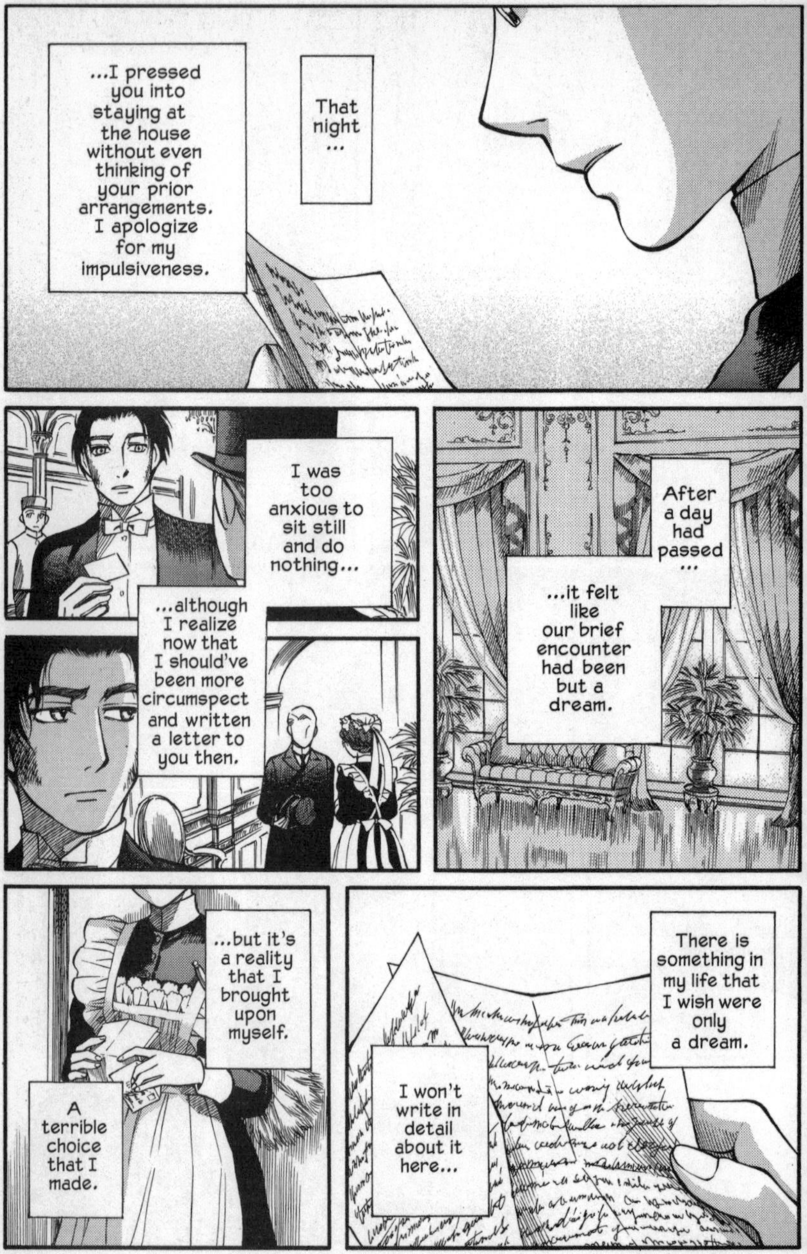

That night...
...I pressed you into staying at the house without even thinking of your prior arrangements. I apologize for my impulsiveness.
After a day had passed...
...it felt like our brief encounter had been but a dream.
I was too anxious to sit still and do nothing...
...although I realize now that I should've been more circumspect and written a letter to you then.
There is something in my life that I wish were only a dream.
I won't write in detail about it here...
...but it's a reality that I brought upon myself.
A terrible choice that I made.

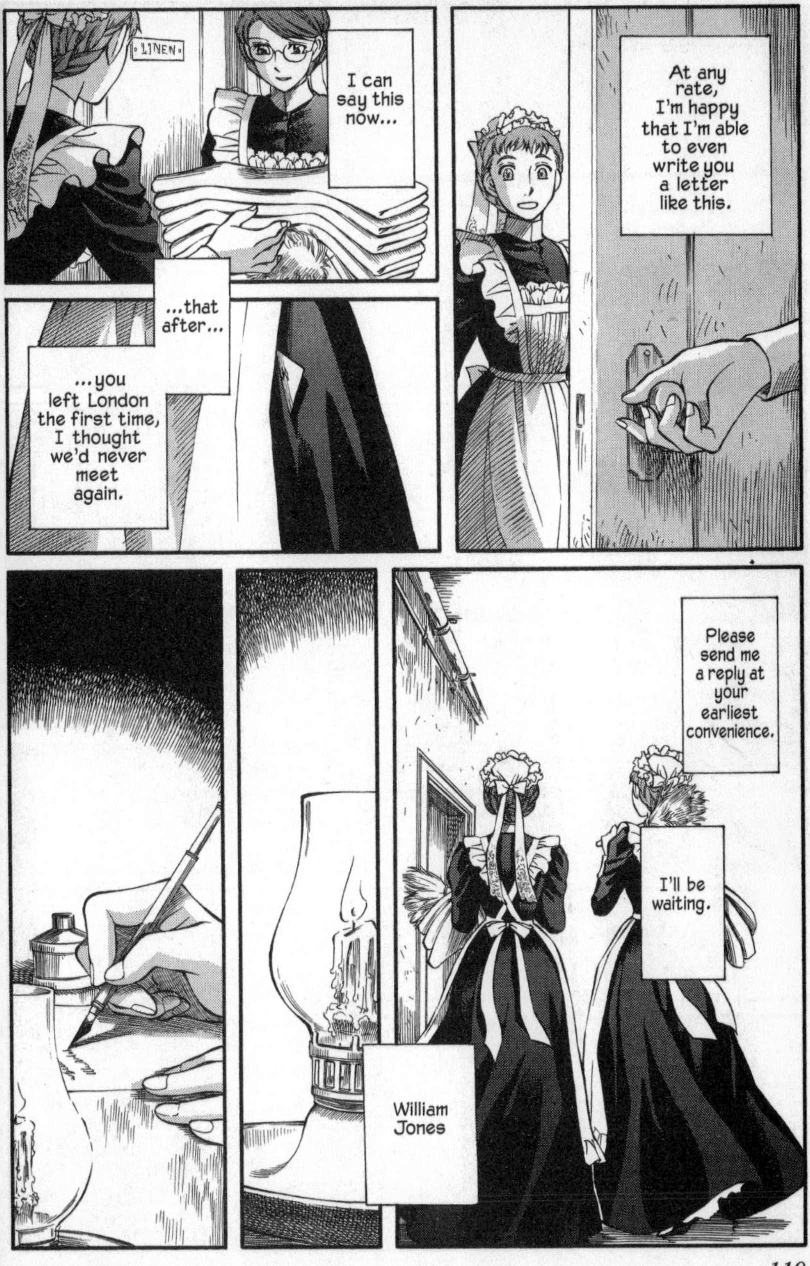

At any rate, I'm happy that I'm able to even write you a letter like this.
LINEN
I can say this now...
...that after...
...you left London the first time, I thought we'd never meet again.
Please send me a reply at your earliest convenience.
I'll be waiting.
William Jones

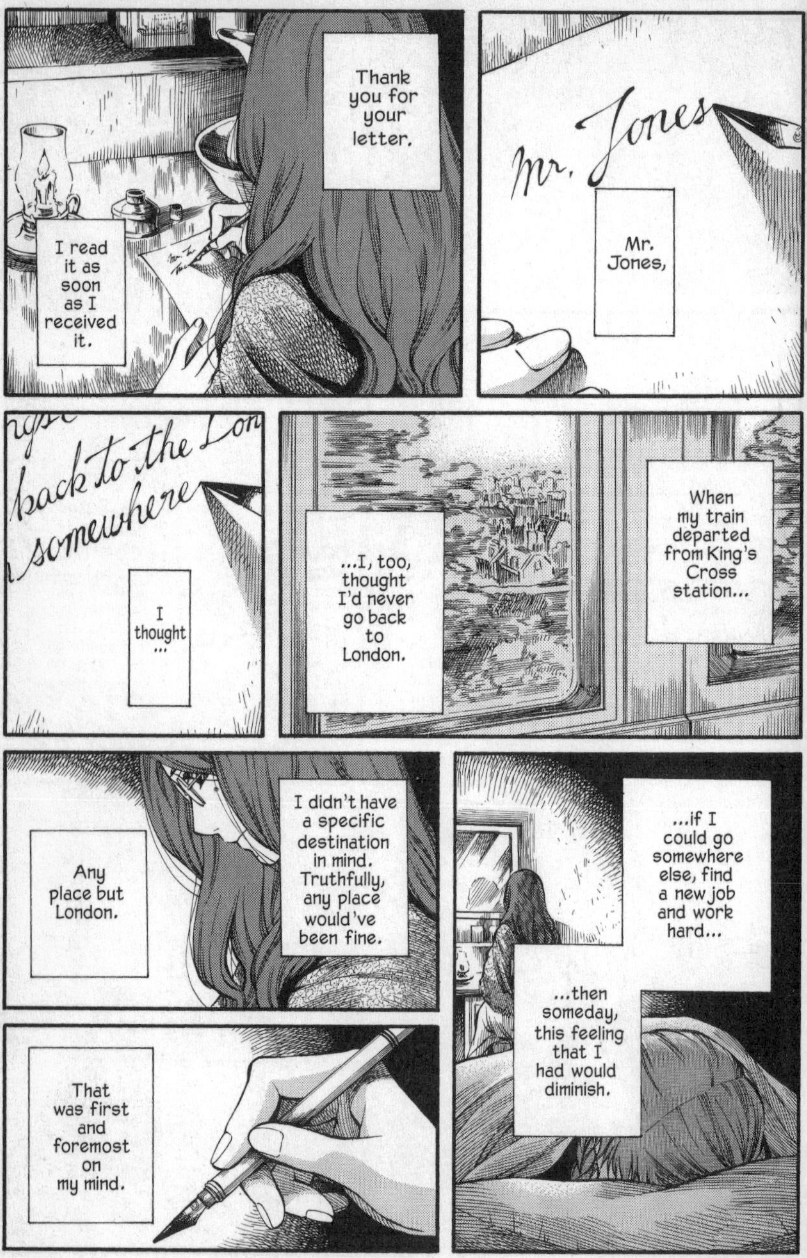
Mr. Jones
Mr. Jones,
Thank you for your letter.
I read it as soon as I received it.
When my train departed from King's Cross station...
...I, too, thought I'd never go back to London.
back to the
somewhere
I thought...
...if I could go somewhere else, find a new job and work hard...
...then someday, this feeling that I had would diminish.
I didn't have a specific destination in mind. Truthfully, any place would've been fine.
Any place but London.
That was first and foremost on my mind.

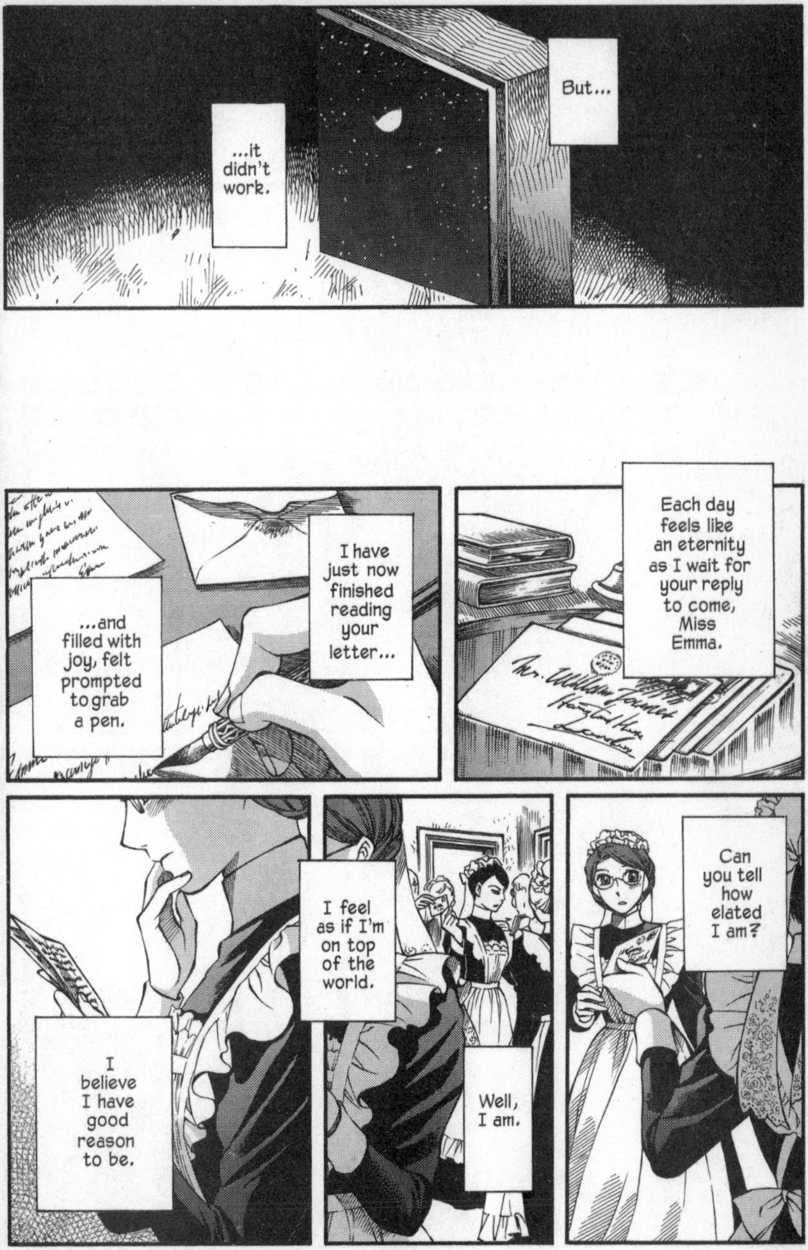
But...
...it didn't work.
Each day feels like an eternity as I wait for your reply to come, Miss Emma.
I have just now finished reading your letter...
...and filled with joy, felt prompted to grab a pen.
Can you tell how elated I am?
I feel as if I'm on top of the world.
Well, I am.
I believe I have good reason to be.

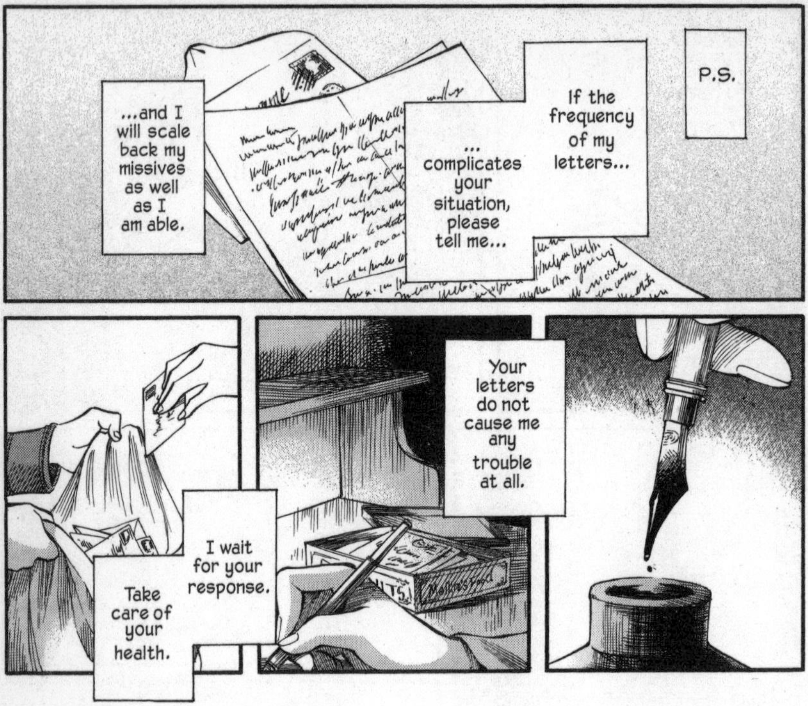
P.S.
If the frequency of my letters...
... complicates your situation, please tell me...
...and I will scale back my missives as well as I am able.
Your letters do not cause me any trouble at all.
I wait for your response.
Take care of your health.

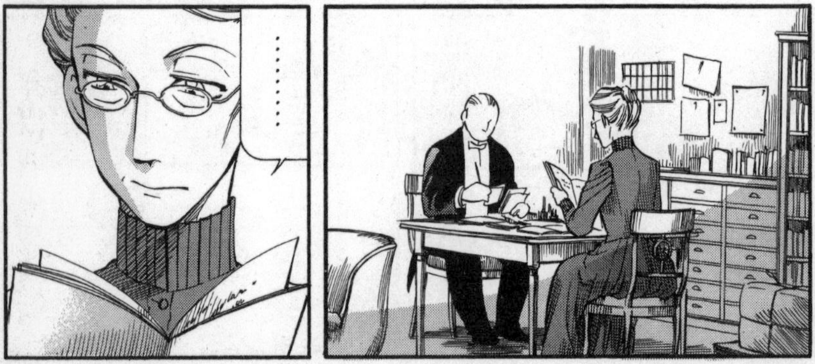
......

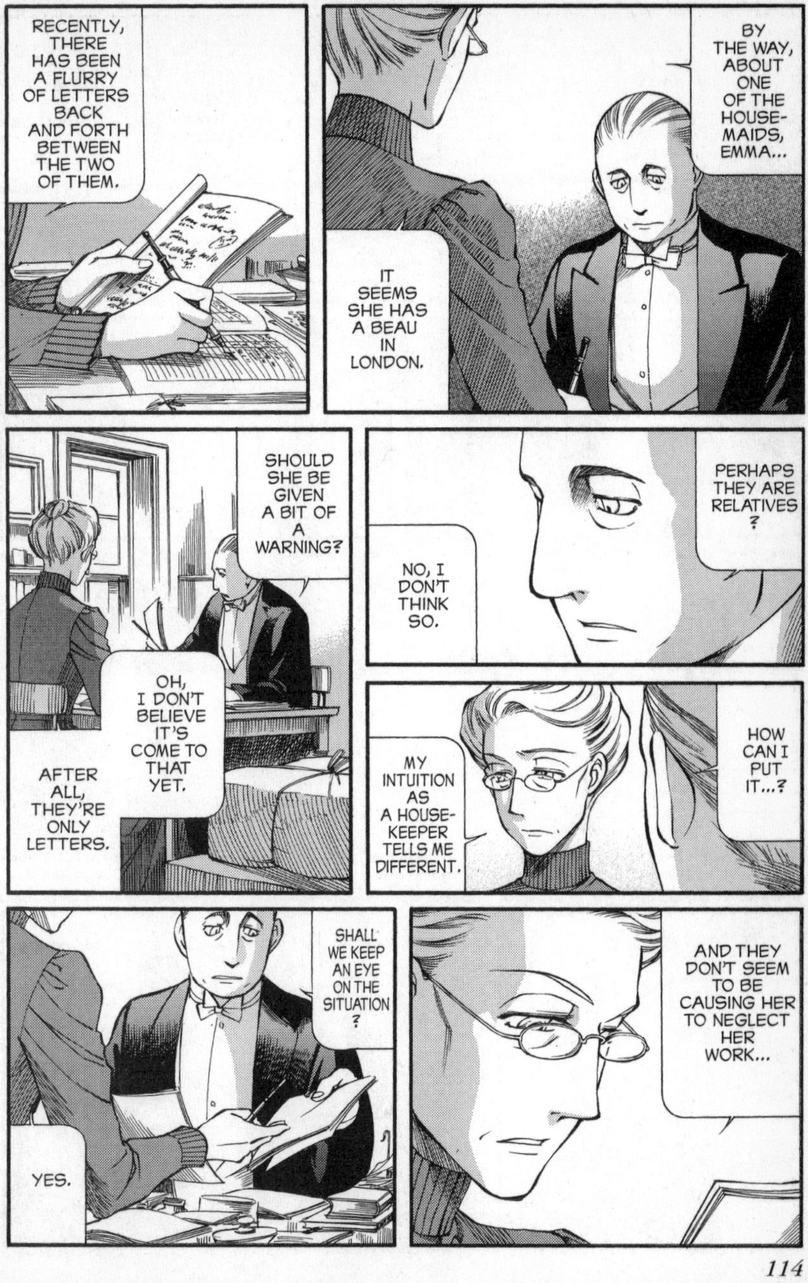
BY THE WAY, ABOUT ONE OF THE HOUSE-MAIDS, EMMA...
IT SEEMS SHE HAS A BEAU IN LONDON.
RECENTLY, THERE HAS BEEN A FLURRY OF LETTERS BACK AND FORTH BETWEEN THE TWO OF THEM.
PERHAPS THEY ARE RELATIVES?
NO, I DON'T THINK SO.
HOW CAN I PUT IT...?
MY INTUITION AS A HOUSE-KEEPER TELLS ME DIFFERENT.
SHOULD SHE BE GIVEN A BIT OF A WARNING?
OH, I DON'T BELIEVE IT'S COME TO THAT YET.
AFTER ALL, THEY'RE ONLY LETTERS.
AND THEY DON'T SEEM TO BE CAUSING HER TO NEGLECT HER WORK...
SHALL WE KEEP AN EYE ON THE SITUATION?
YES.

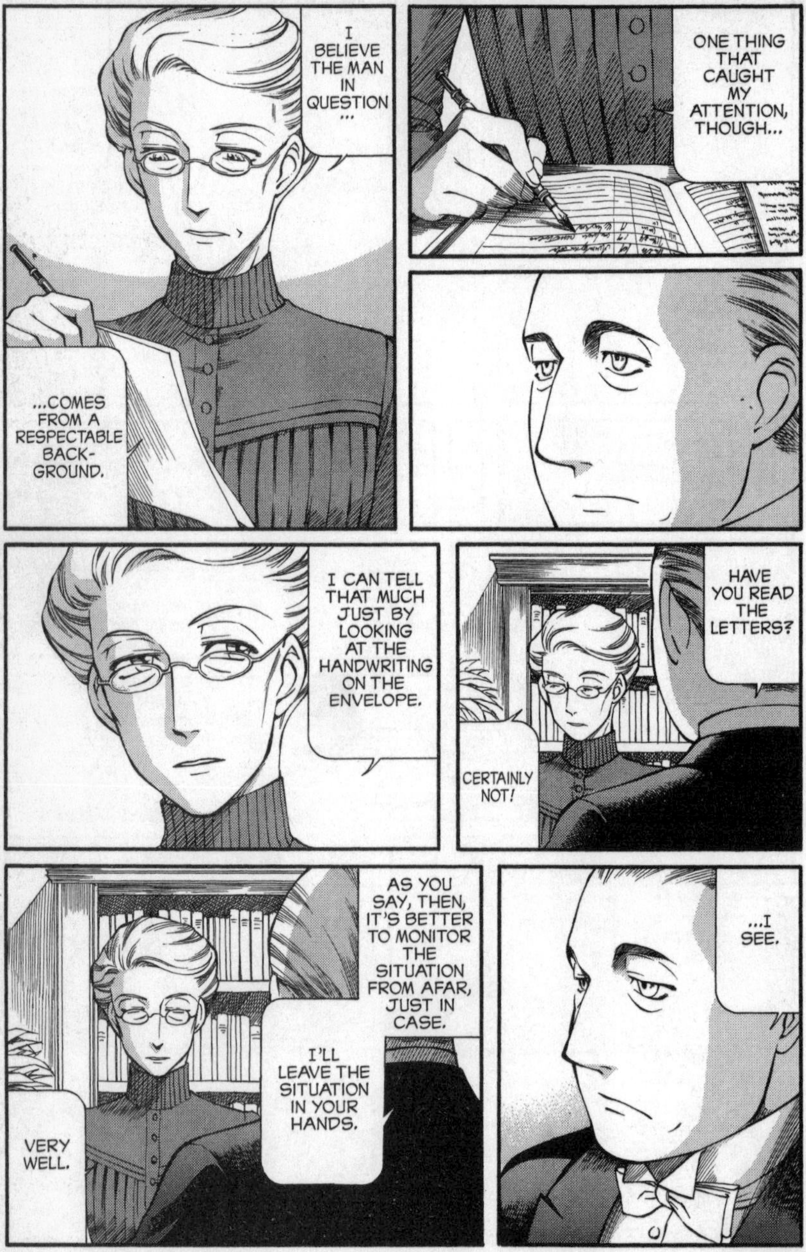
ONE THING THAT CAUGHT MY ATTENTION, THOUGH...
I BELIEVE THE MAN IN QUESTION ...
...COMES FROM A RESPECTABLE BACK-GROUND.
HAVE YOU READ THE LETTERS?
CERTAINLY NOT!
I CAN TELL THAT MUCH JUST BY LOOKING AT THE HANDWRITING ON THE ENVELOPE.
...I SEE.
AS YOU SAY, THEN, IT'S BETTER TO MONITOR THE SITUATION FROM AFAR, JUST IN CASE.
I'LL LEAVE THE SITUATION IN YOUR HANDS.
VERY WELL.

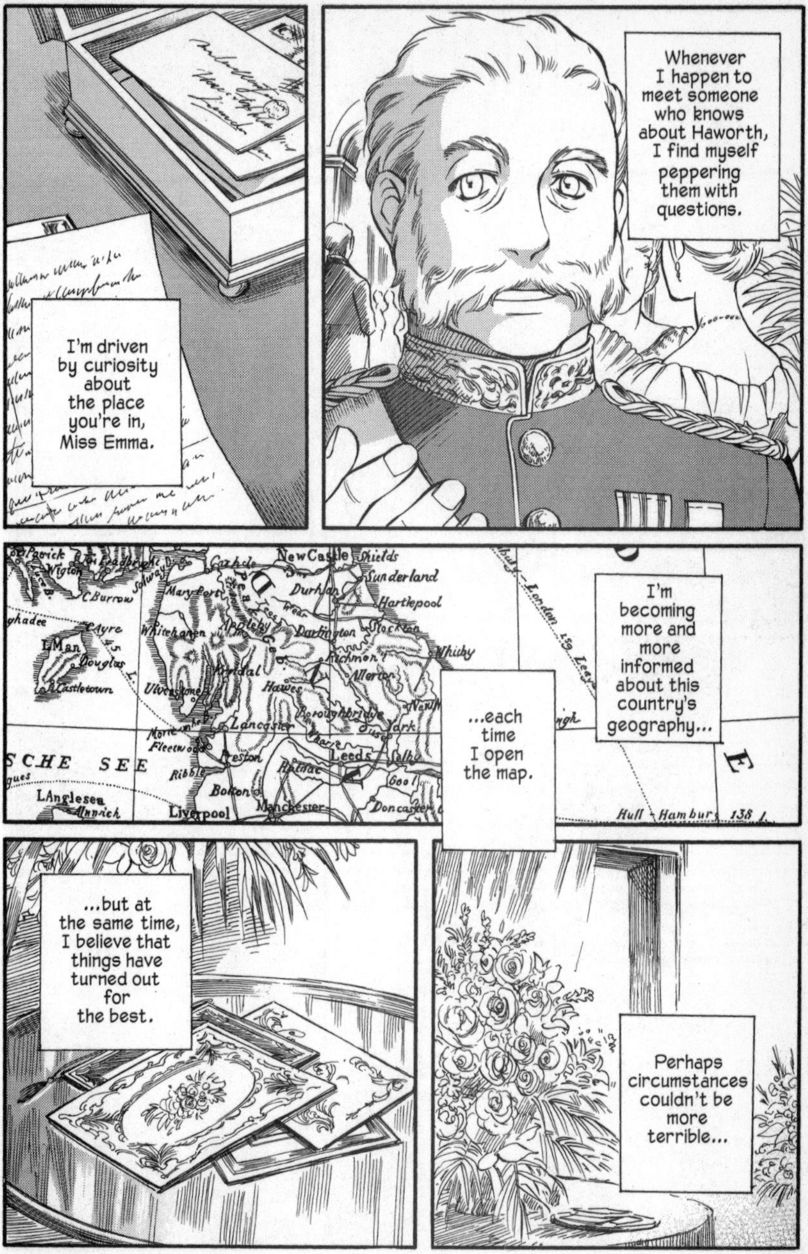
Whenever I happen to meet someone who knows about Haworth, I find myself peppering them with questions.
I'm driven by curiosity about the place you're in, Miss Emma.
I'm becoming more and more informed about this country's geography...
...each time I open the map.
Perhaps circumstances couldn't be more terrible...
...but at the same time, I believe that things have turned out for the best.

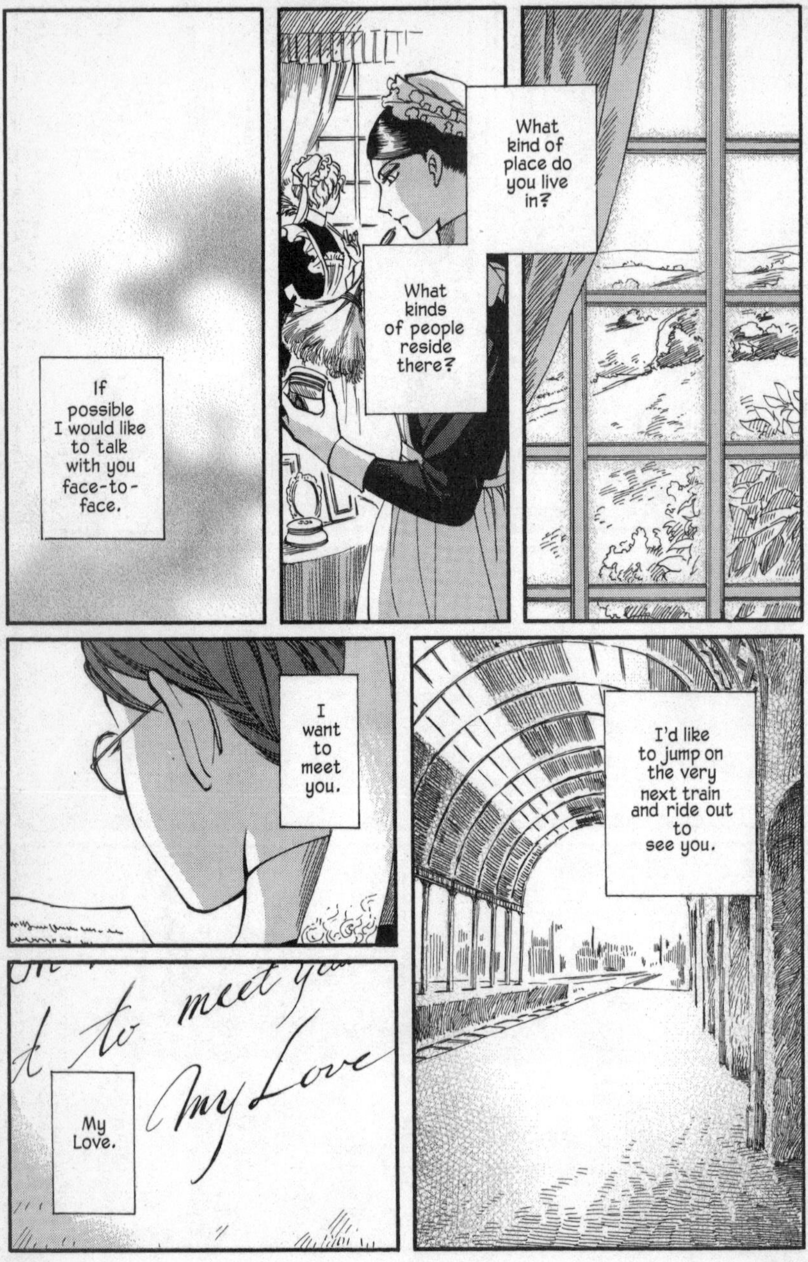

What kind of place do you live in?
What kinds of people reside there?
If possible I would like to talk with you face-to-face.
I'd like to jump on the very next train and ride out to see you.
I want to meet you.
My Love.

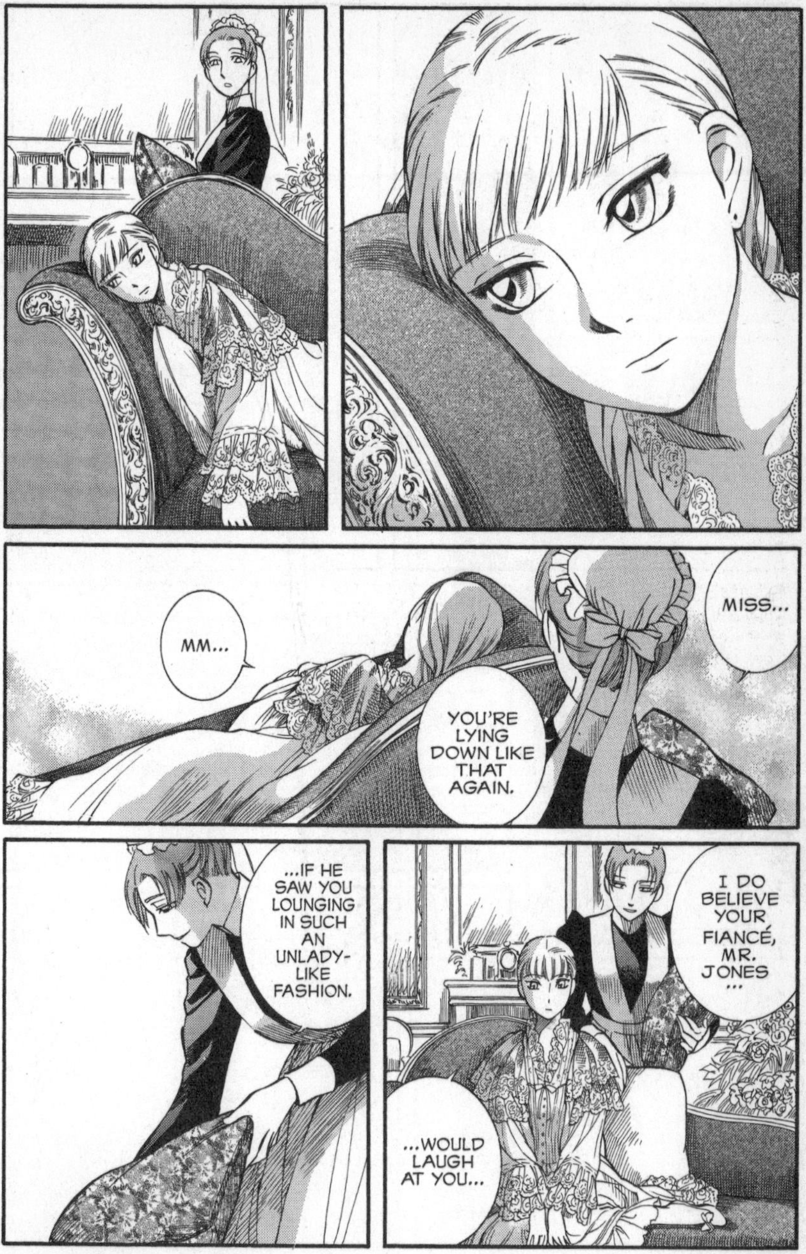
MISS...
MM...
YOU'RE LYING DOWN LIKE THAT AGAIN.
I DO BELIEVE YOUR FIANCÉ, MR. JONES ...
...WOULD LAUGH AT YOU...
...IF HE SAW YOU LOUNGING IN SUCH AN UNLADY-LIKE FASHION.

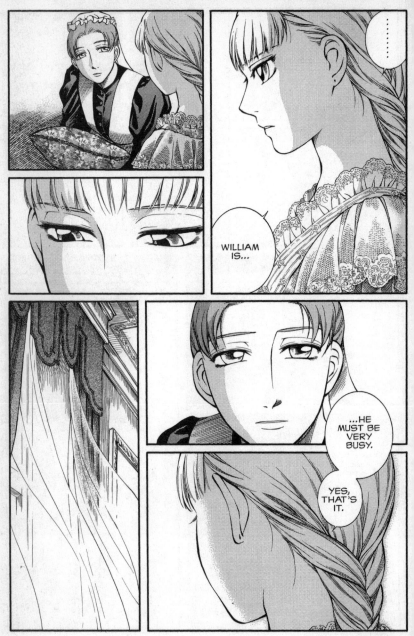

WILLIAM IS...

...HE MUST BE VERY BUSY.

YES, THAT'S IT.

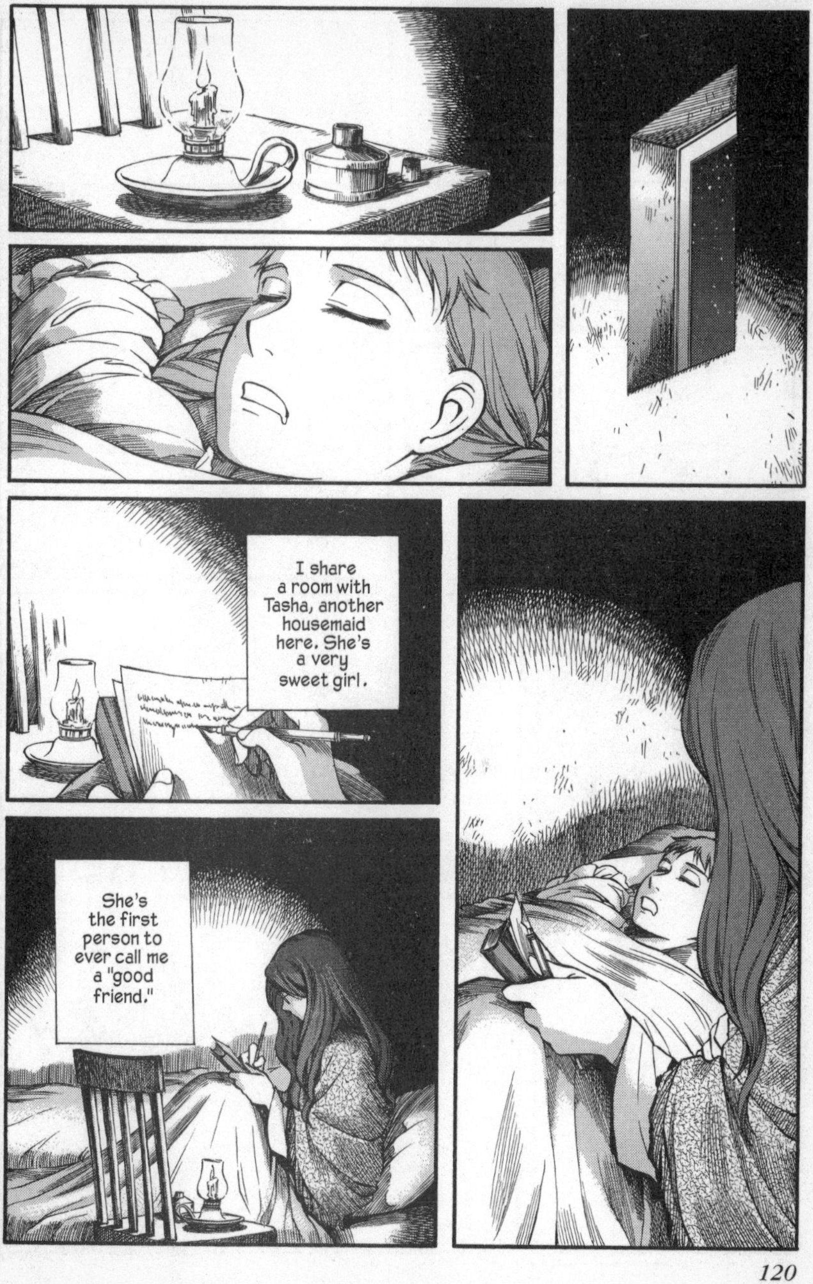
I share a room with Tasha, another housemaid here. She's a very sweet girl.
She's the first person to ever call me a "good friend."

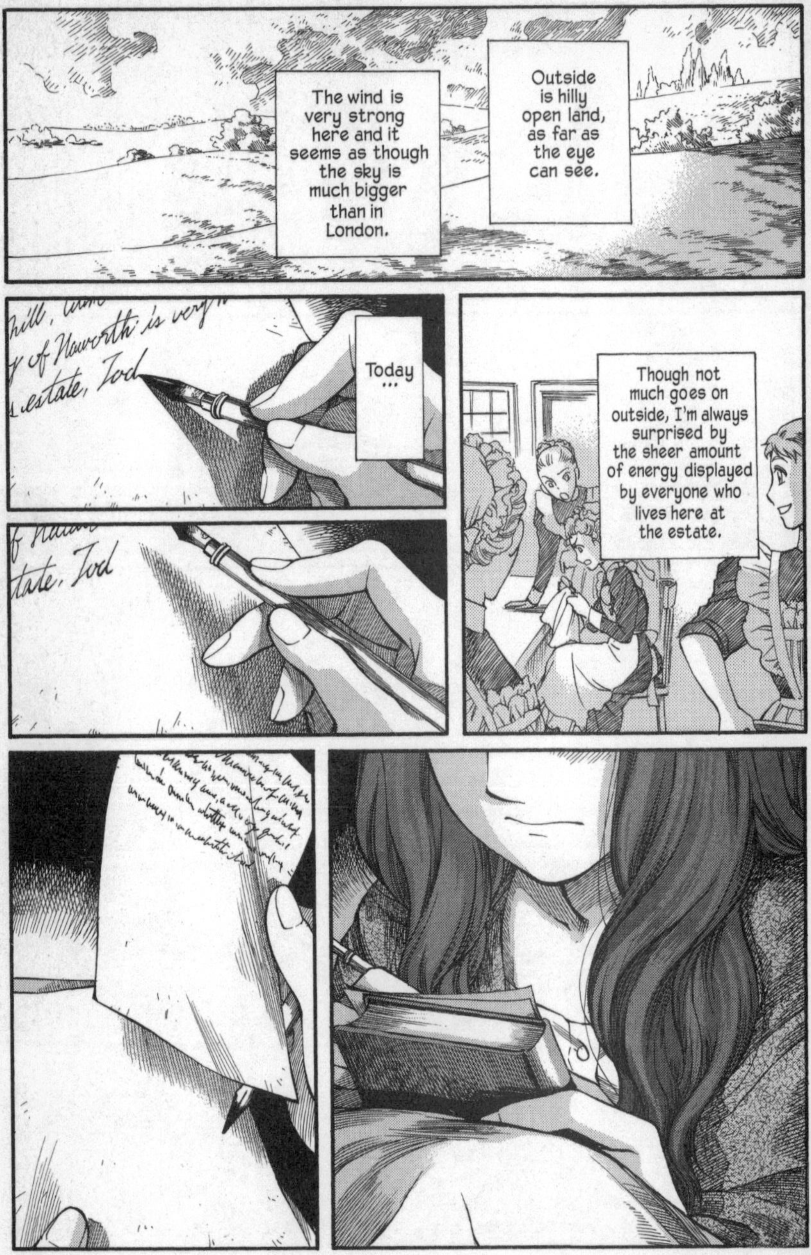
Outside is hilly open land, as far as the eye can see.
The wind is very strong here and it seems as though the sky is much bigger than in London.
Though not much goes on outside, I'm always surprised by the sheer amount of energy displayed by everyone who lives here at the estate.
Today...

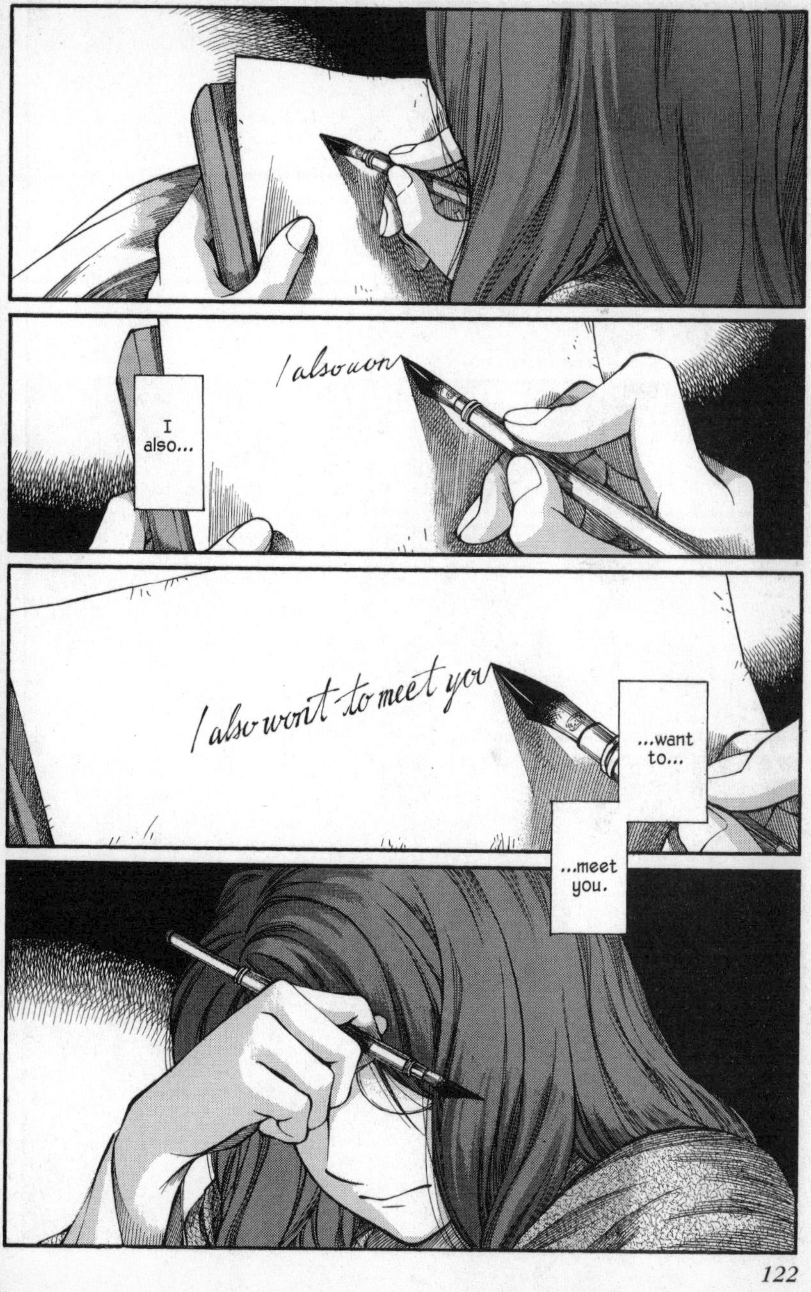
I also won
I also...
I also want to meet you
...want to...
...meet you.

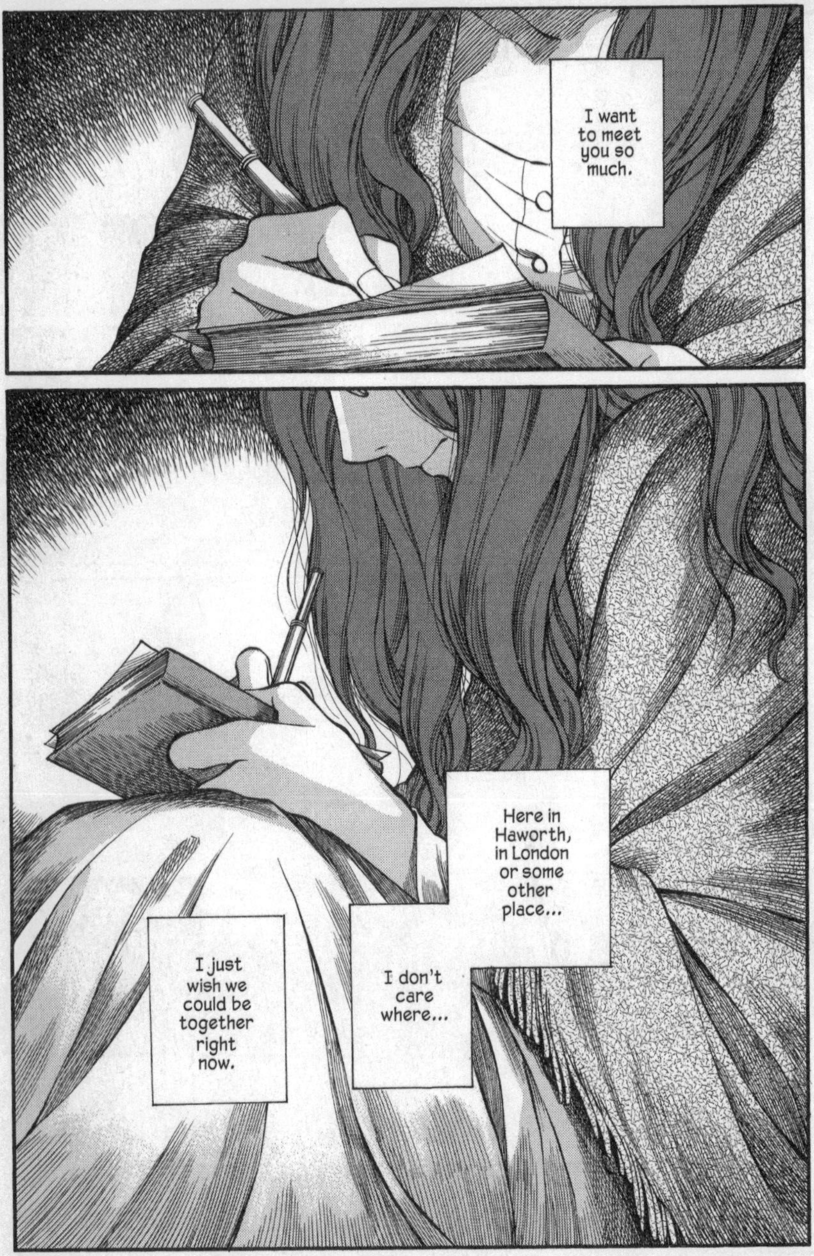
I want to meet you so much.
Here in Haworth, in London or some other place...
I don't care where...
I just wish we could be together right now.

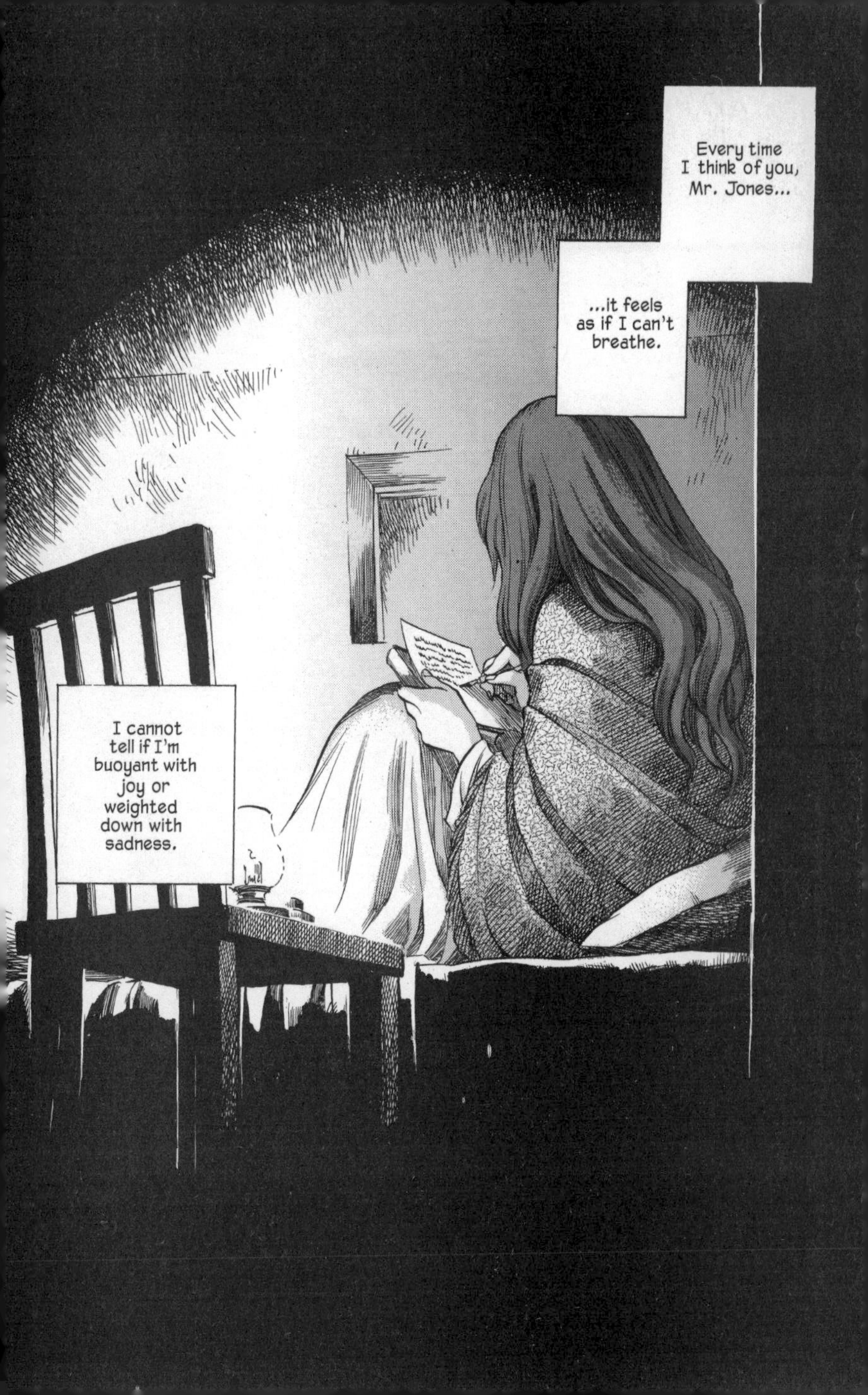
Every time I think of you, Mr. Jones...
...it feels as if I can't breathe.
I cannot tell if I'm buoyant with joy or weighted down with sadness.

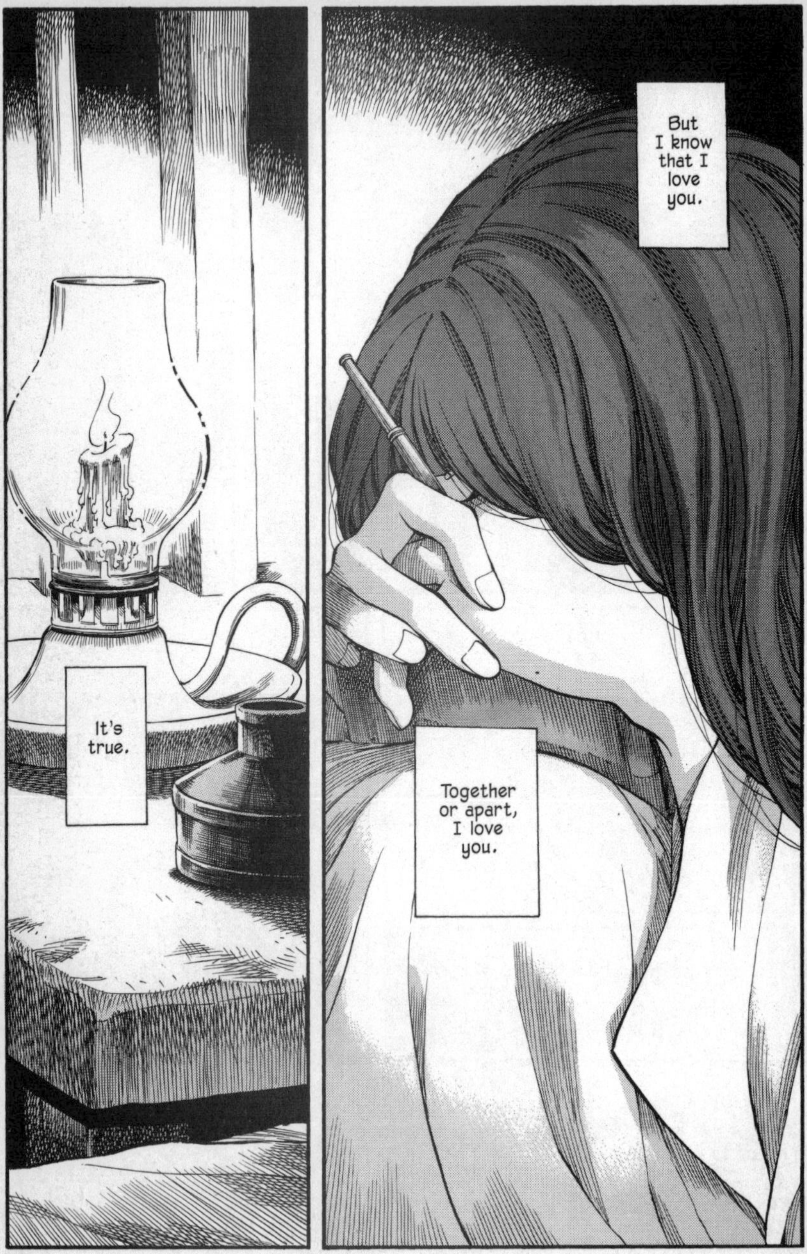
But I know that I love you.
Together or apart, I love you.
It's true.

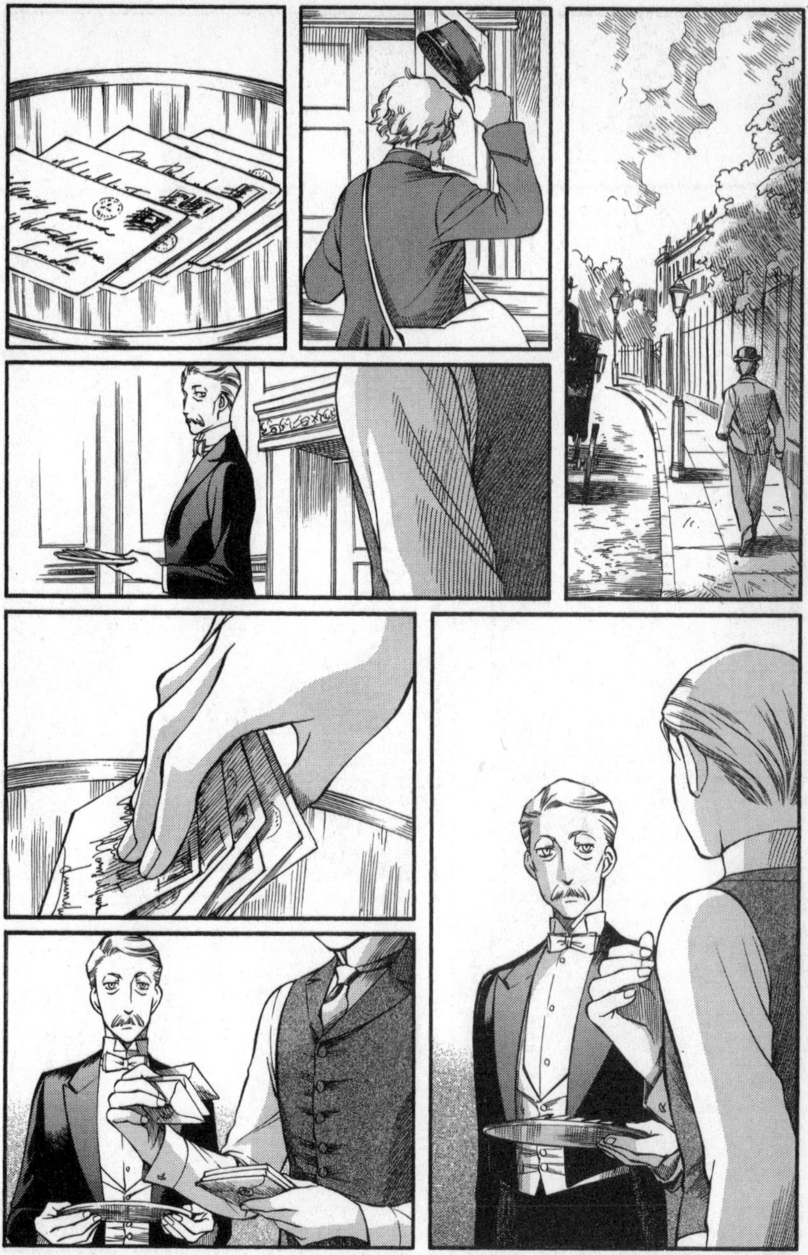

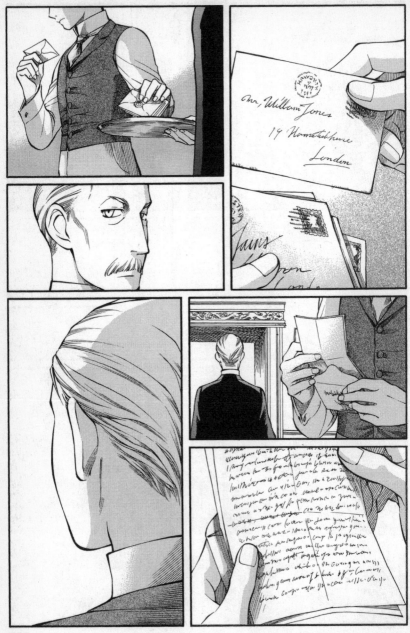

Mr. William Jones

19 Hamstishine

London

127

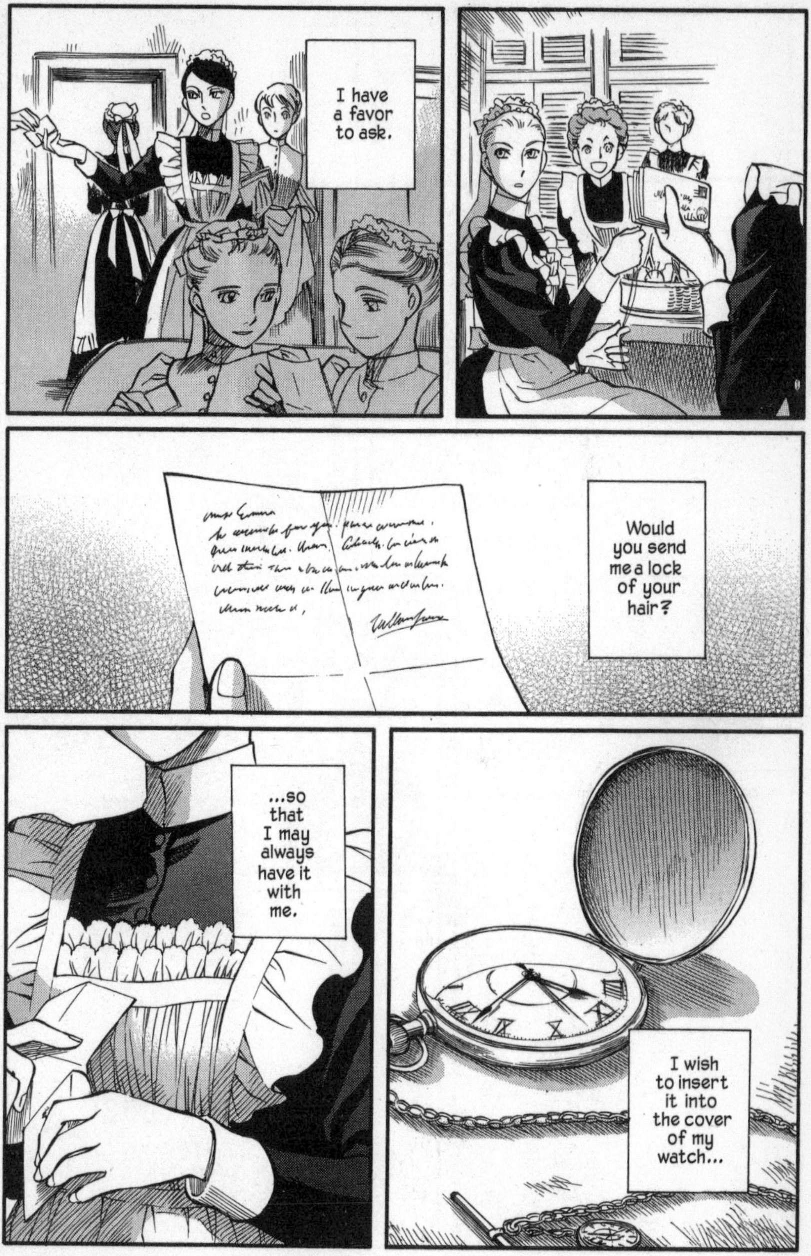
I have a favor to ask.
Would you send me a lock of your hair?
I wish to insert it into the cover of my watch...
...so that I may always have it with me.

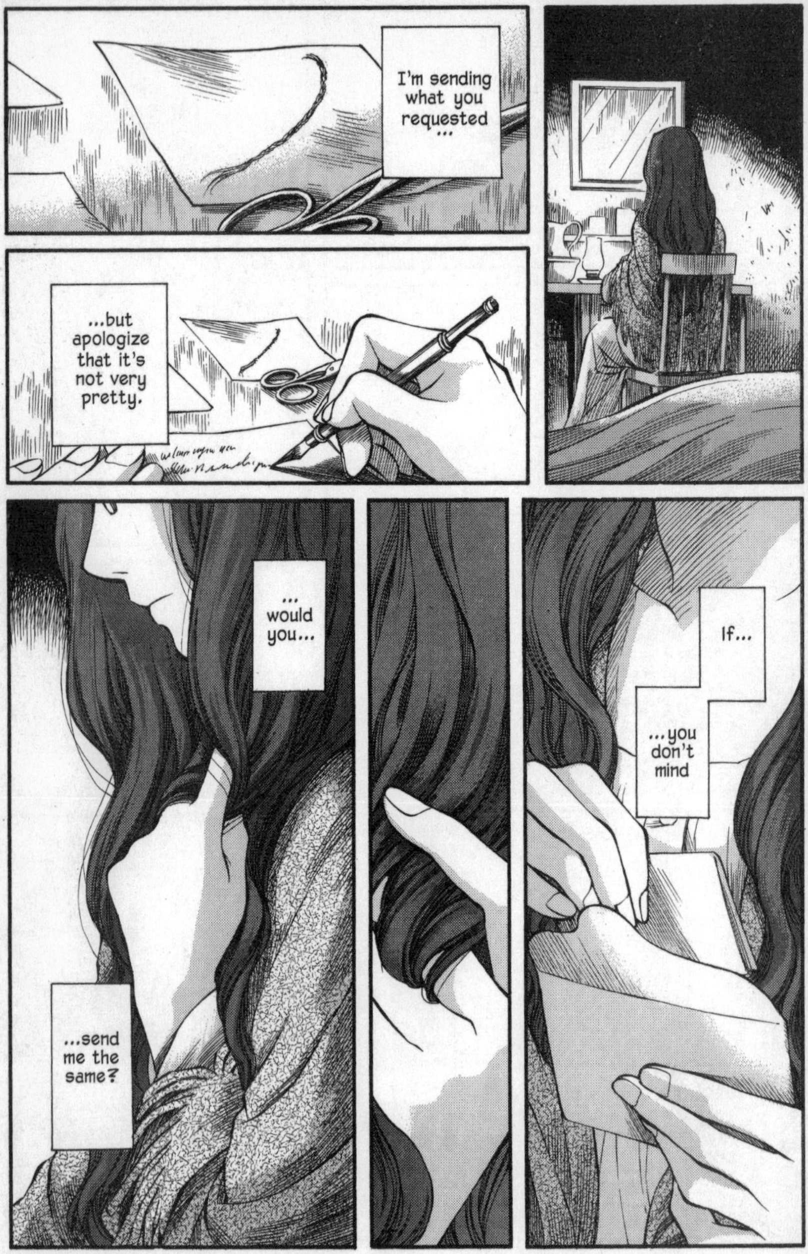
I'm sending what you requested ...
...but apologize that it's not very pretty.
If...
...you don't mind
... would you...
...send me the same?

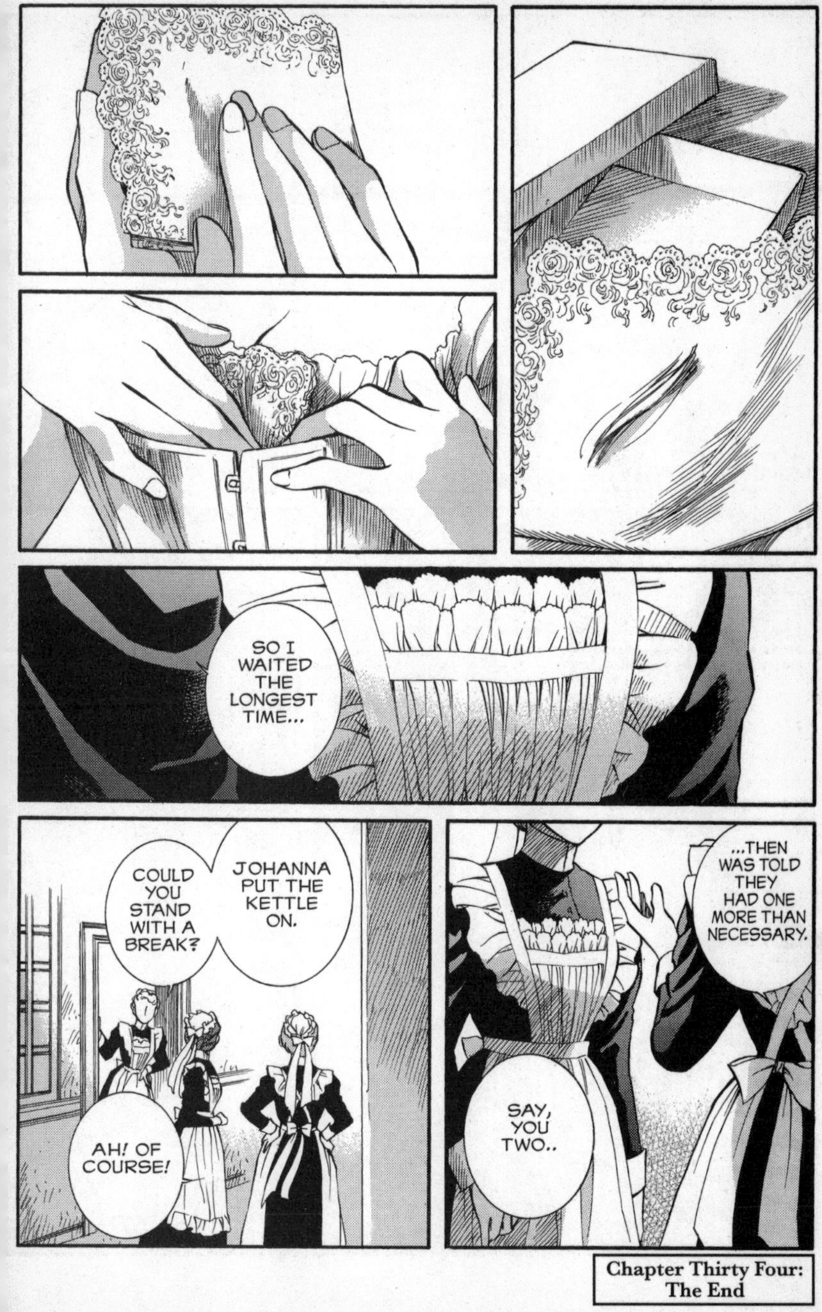
SO I WAITED THE LONGEST TIME...
...THEN WAS TOLD THEY HAD ONE MORE THAN NECESSARY.
SAY, YOU TWO..
JOHANNA PUT THE KETTLE ON.
COULD YOU STAND WITH A BREAK?
AH! OF COURSE!

Chapter Thirty Four: The End

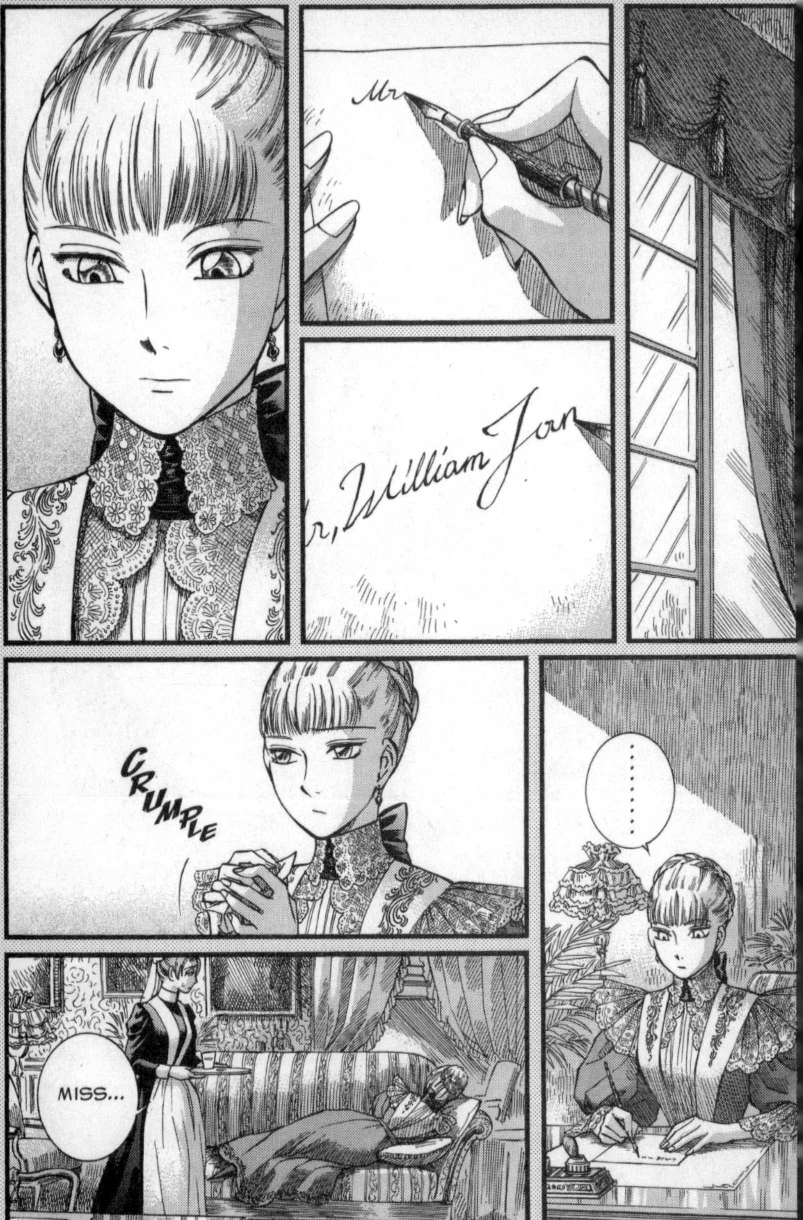
Mr
r, William Jon
CRUMPLE
......
MISS...

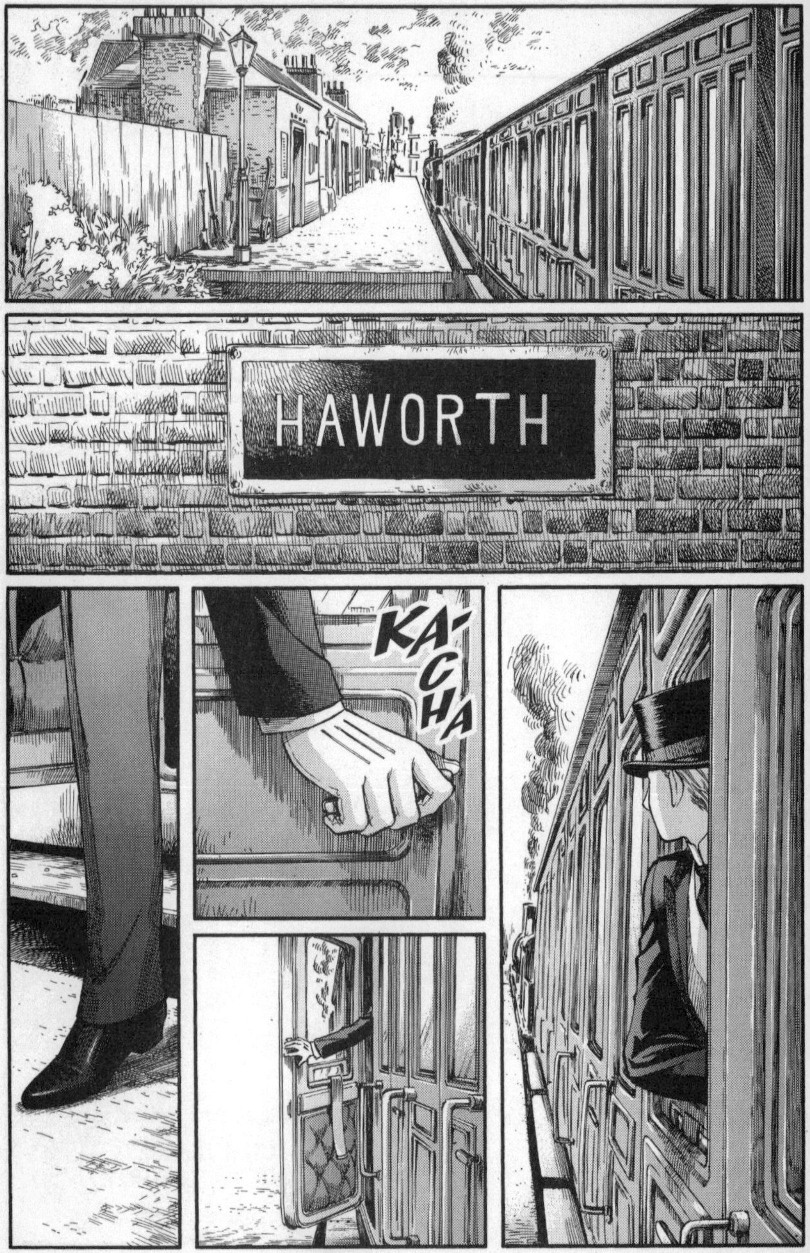
HAWORTH
KA-CHA

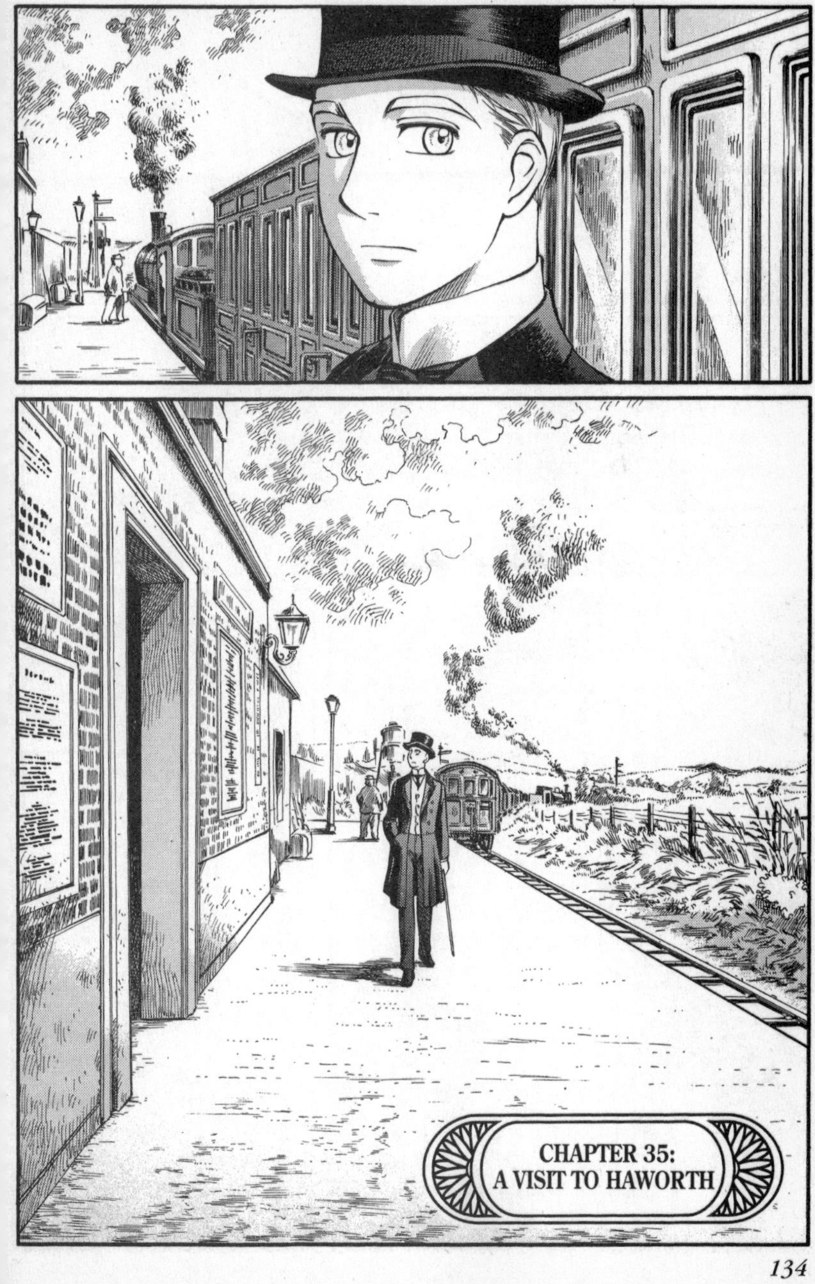
CHAPTER 35:
A VISIT TO HAWORTH

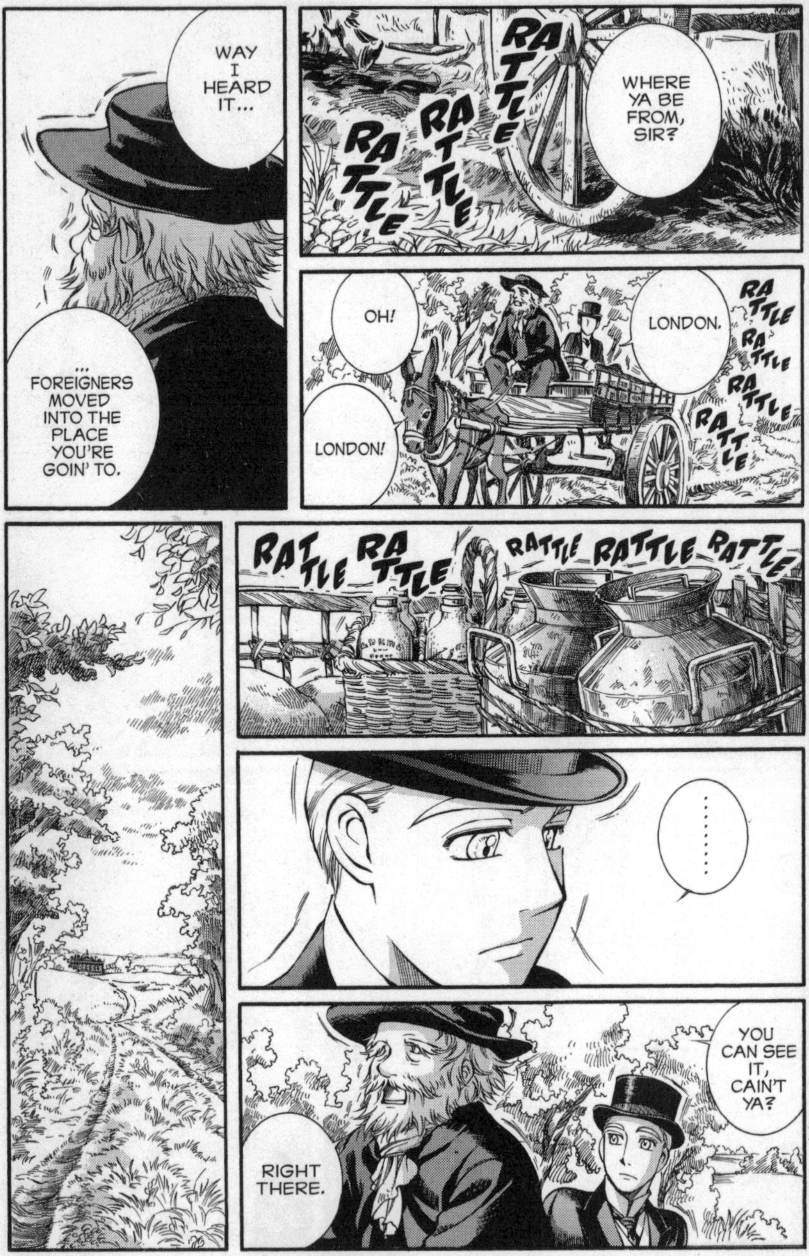
WHERE YA BE FROM, SIR?
RATTLE
RATTLE
RATTLE
RATTLE
RATTLE
RATTLE
RATTLE
LONDON.
OH!
LONDON!
WAY I HEARD IT...
...FOREIGNERS MOVED INTO THE PLACE YOU'RE GOIN' TO.
RATTLE
RATTLE
RATTLE
RATTLE
RATTLE
......
YOU CAN SEE IT, CAIN'T YA?
RIGHT THERE.

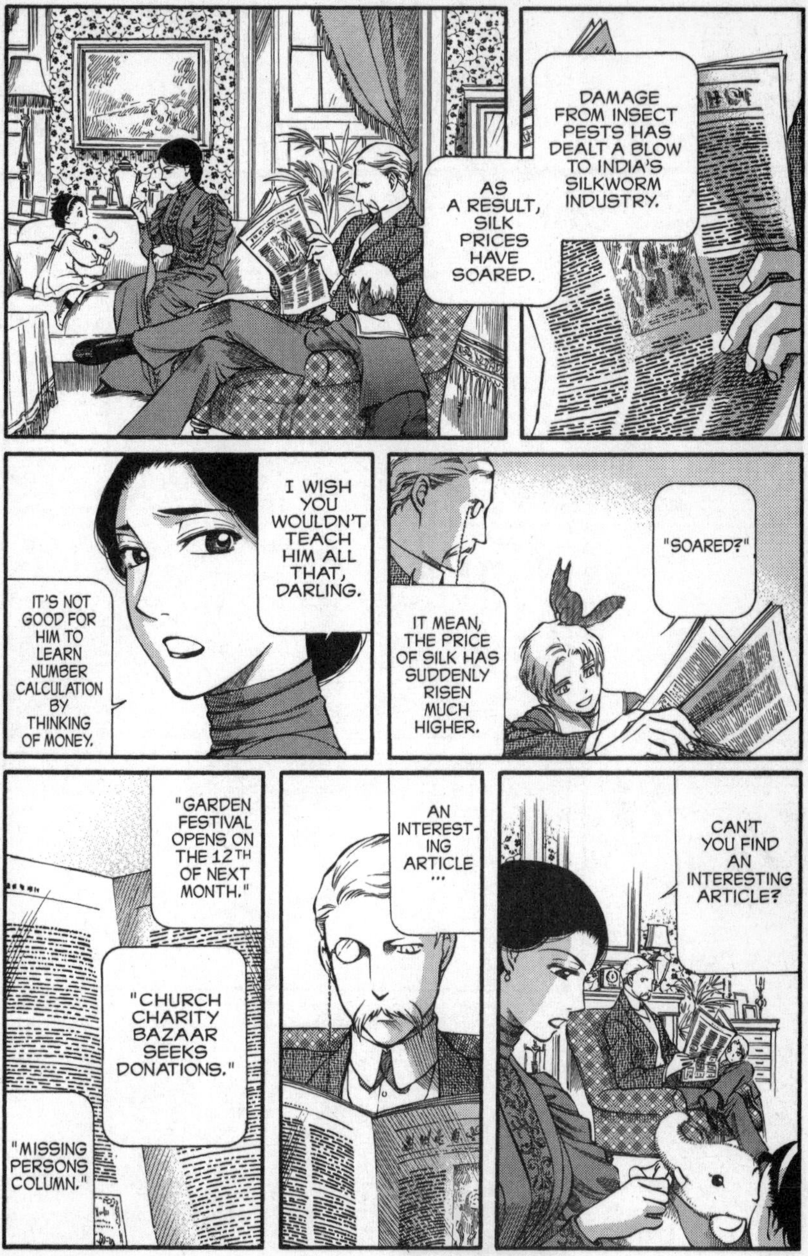
DAMAGE FROM INSECT PESTS HAS DEALT A BLOW TO INDIA'S SILKWORM INDUSTRY.
AS A RESULT, SILK PRICES HAVE SOARED.
"SOARED?"
IT MEAN, THE PRICE OF SILK HAS SUDDENLY RISEN MUCH HIGHER.
I WISH YOU WOULDN'T TEACH HIM ALL THAT, DARLING.
IT'S NOT GOOD FOR HIM TO LEARN NUMBER CALCULATION BY THINKING OF MONEY.
CAN'T YOU FIND AN INTERESTING ARTICLE?
AN INTEREST-ING ARTICLE ...
"GARDEN FESTIVAL OPENS ON THE 12TH OF NEXT MONTH."
"CHURCH CHARITY BAZAAR SEEKS DONATIONS."
"MISSING PERSONS COLUMN."

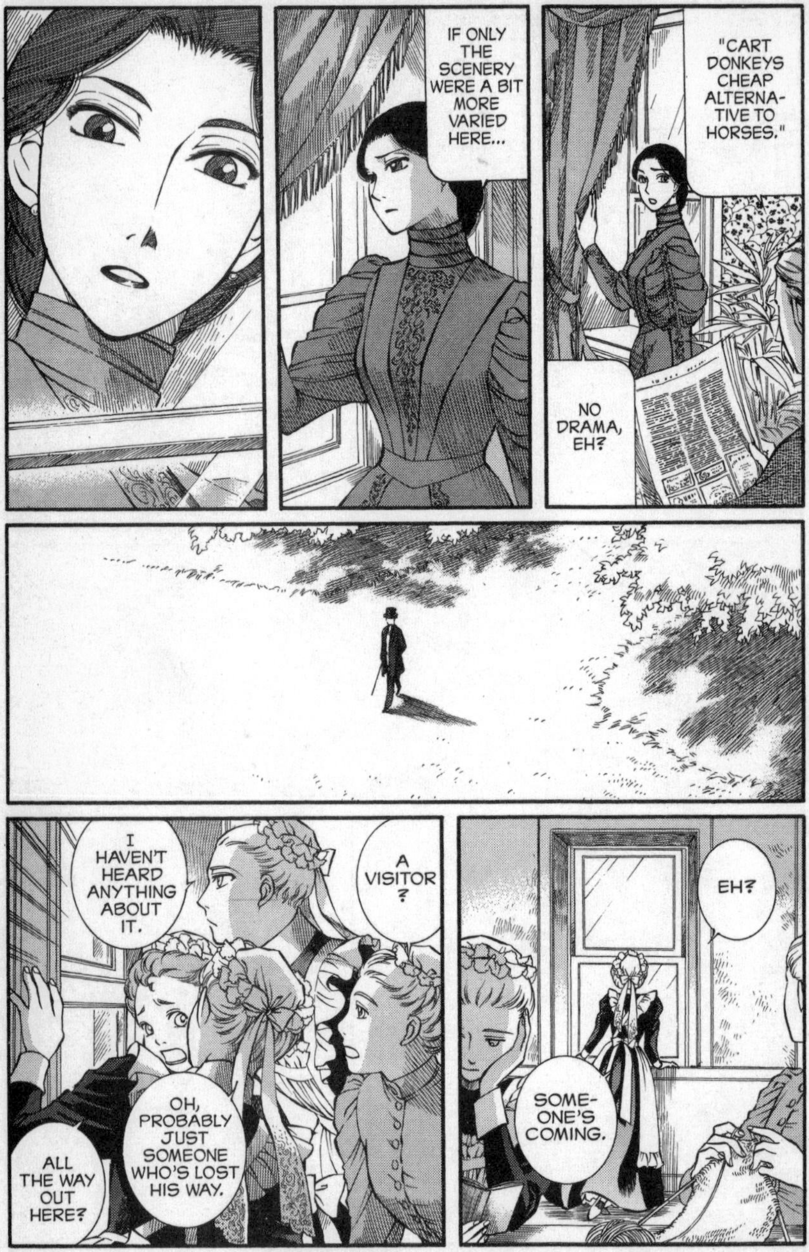

"CART DONKEYS CHEAP ALTERNATIVE TO HORSES."
NO DRAMA, EH?
IF ONLY THE SCENERY WERE A BIT MORE VARIED HERE...
EH?
SOMEONE'S COMING.
A VISITOR?
I HAVEN'T HEARD ANYTHING ABOUT IT.
OH, PROBABLY JUST SOMEONE WHO'S LOST HIS WAY.
ALL THE WAY OUT HERE?

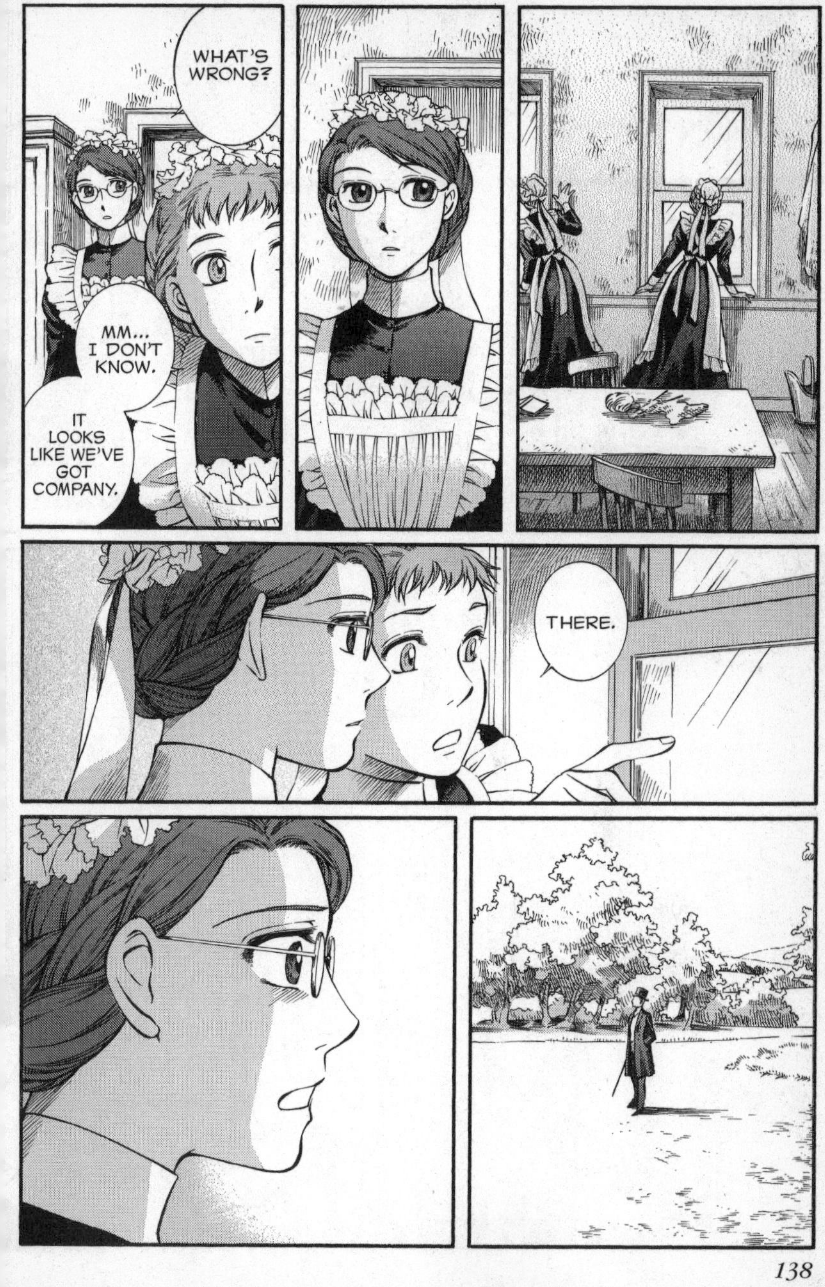
WHAT'S WRONG?
MM... I DON'T KNOW.
IT LOOKS LIKE WE'VE GOT COMPANY.
THERE.

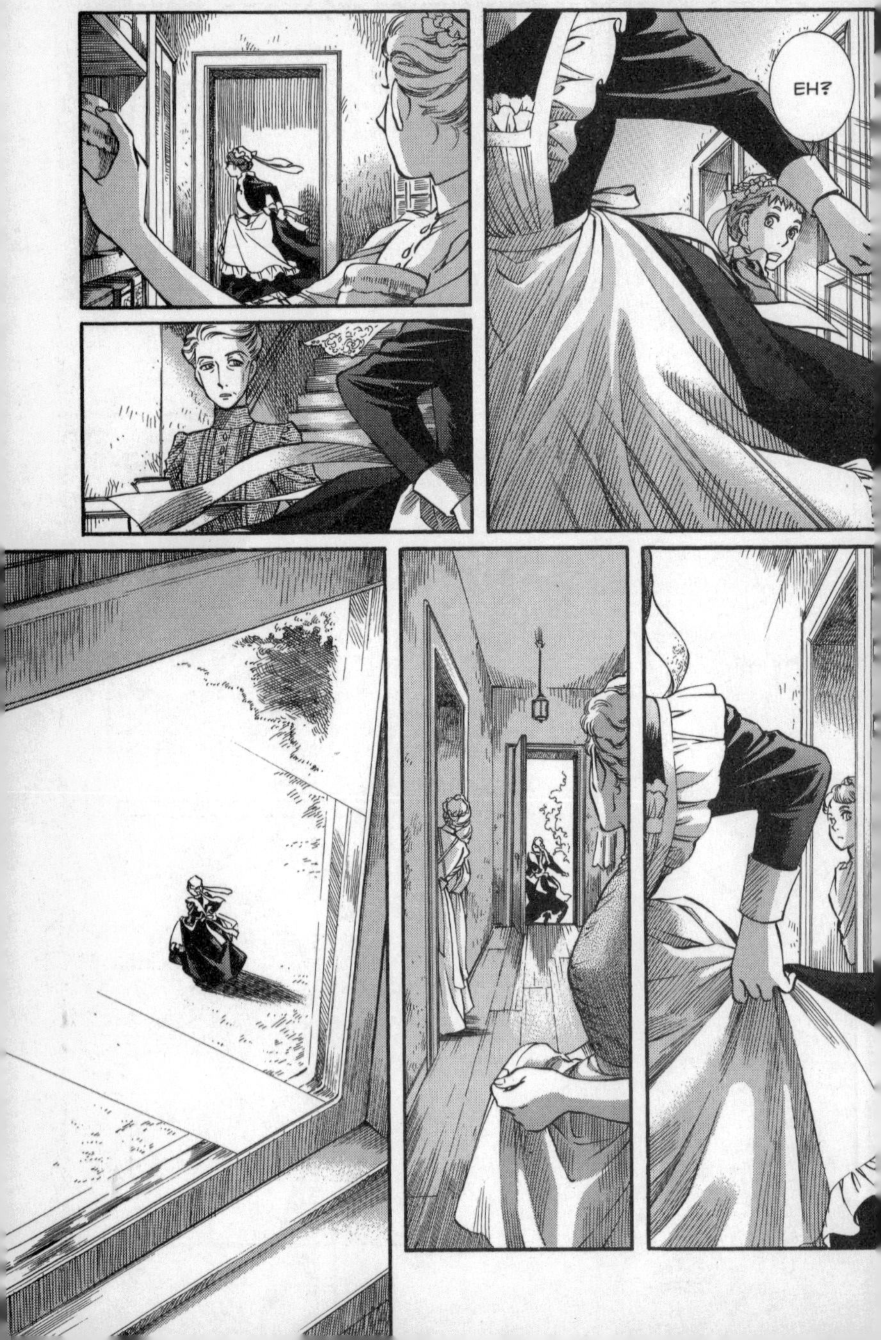
EH?

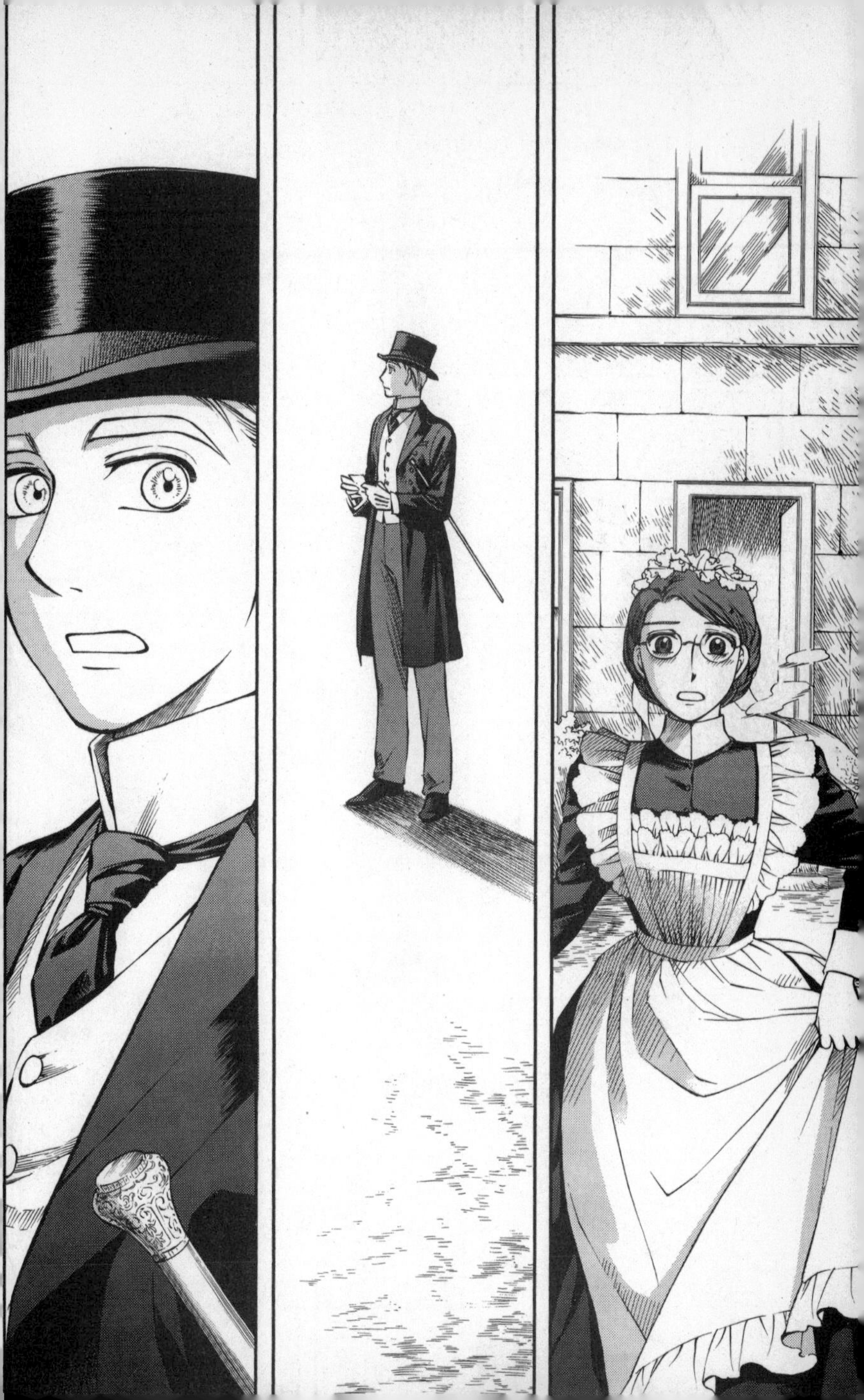

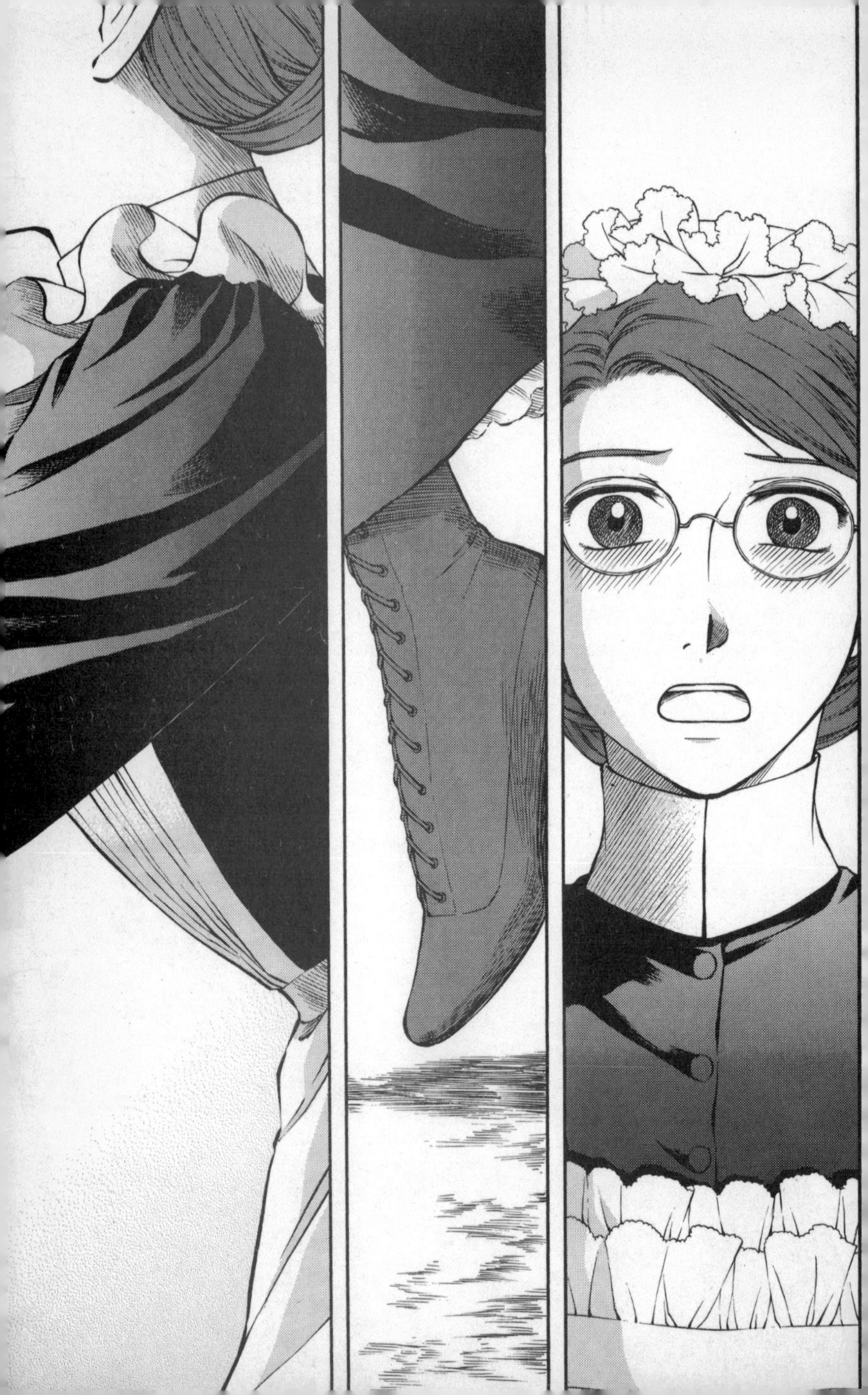

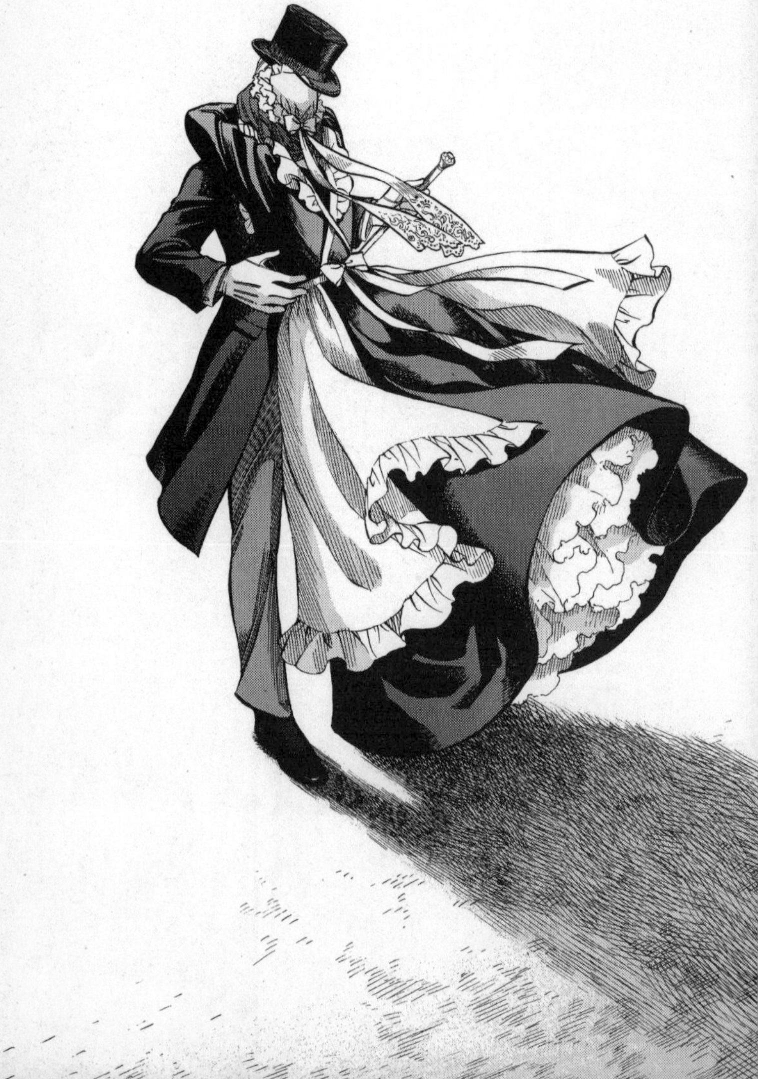

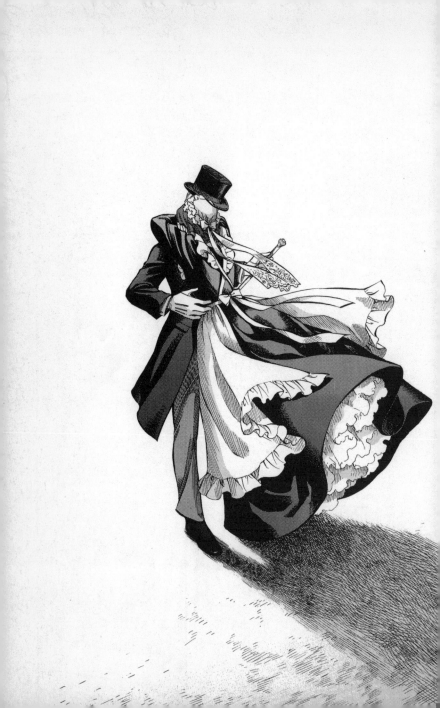

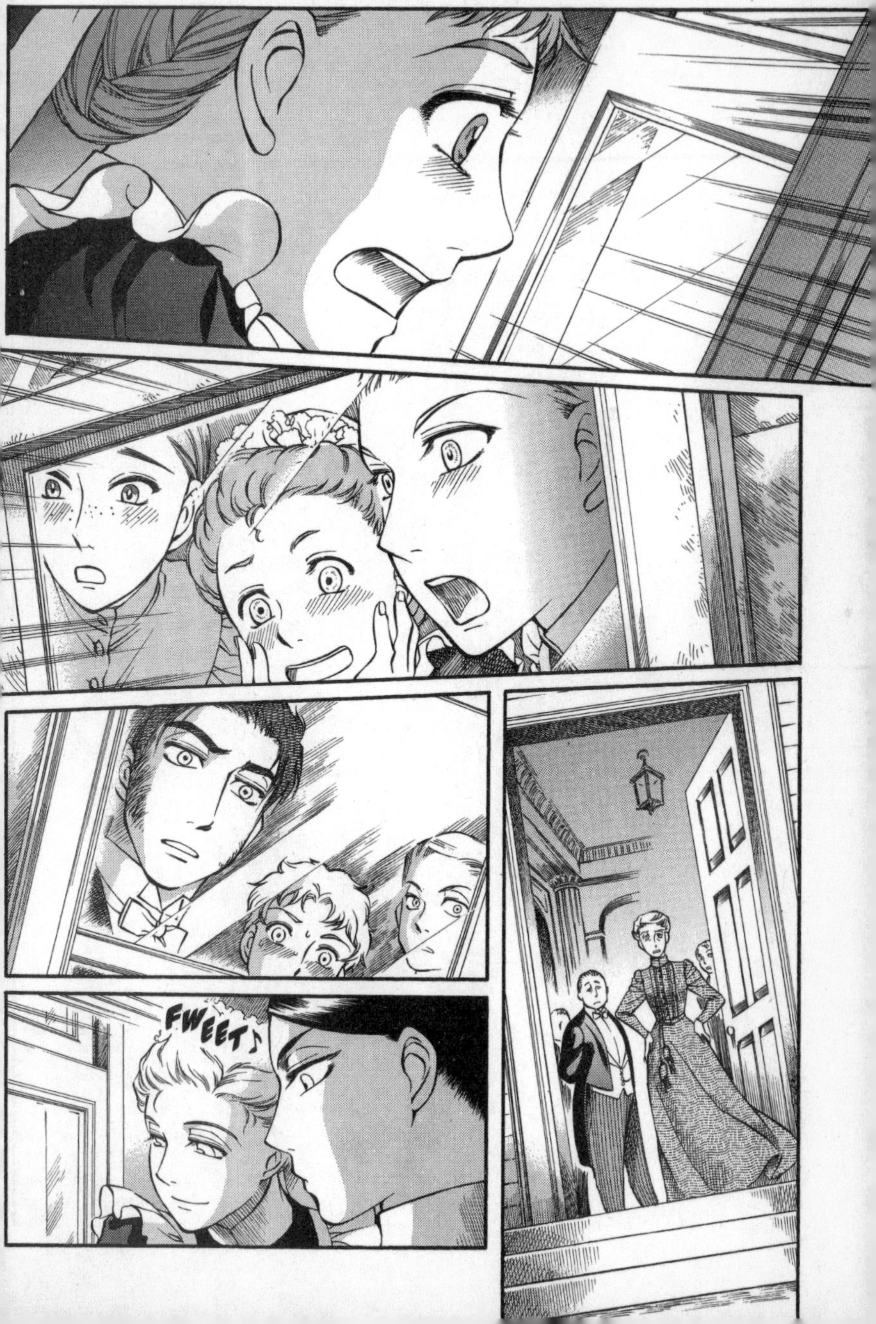
FWEET♪

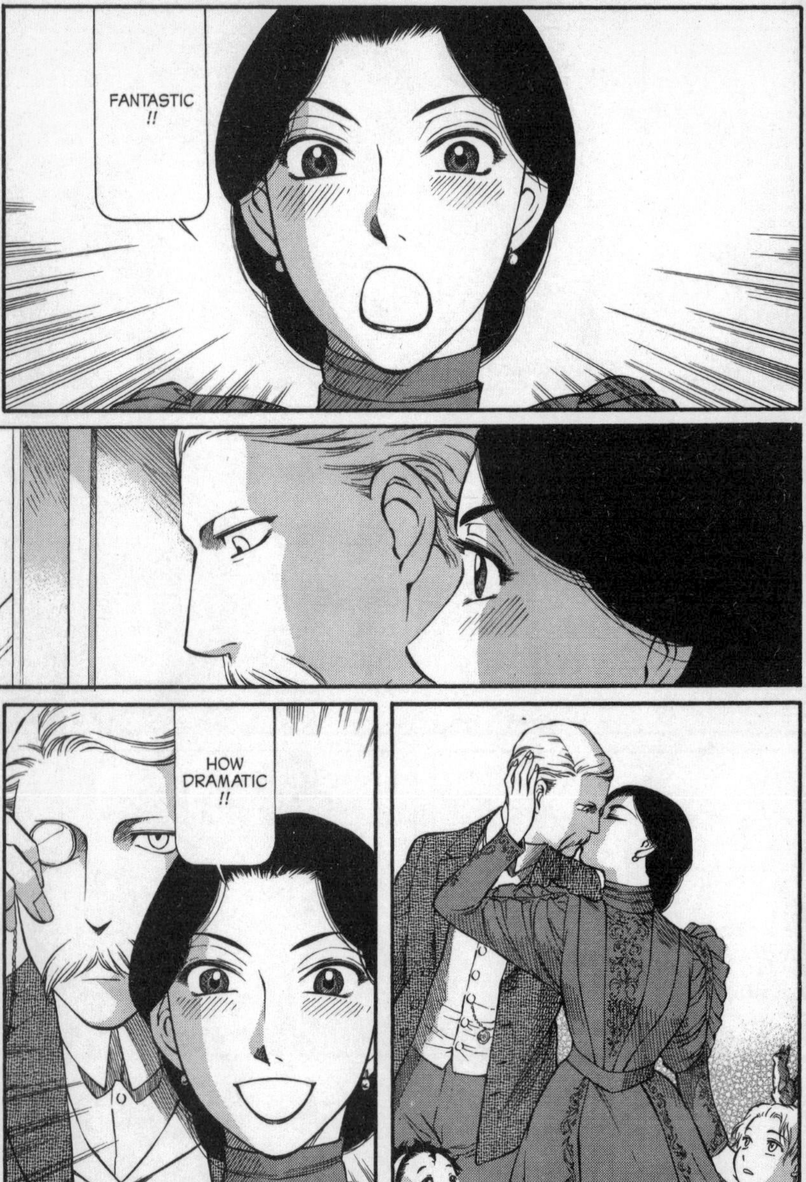
FANTASTIC !!
HOW DRAMATIC !!

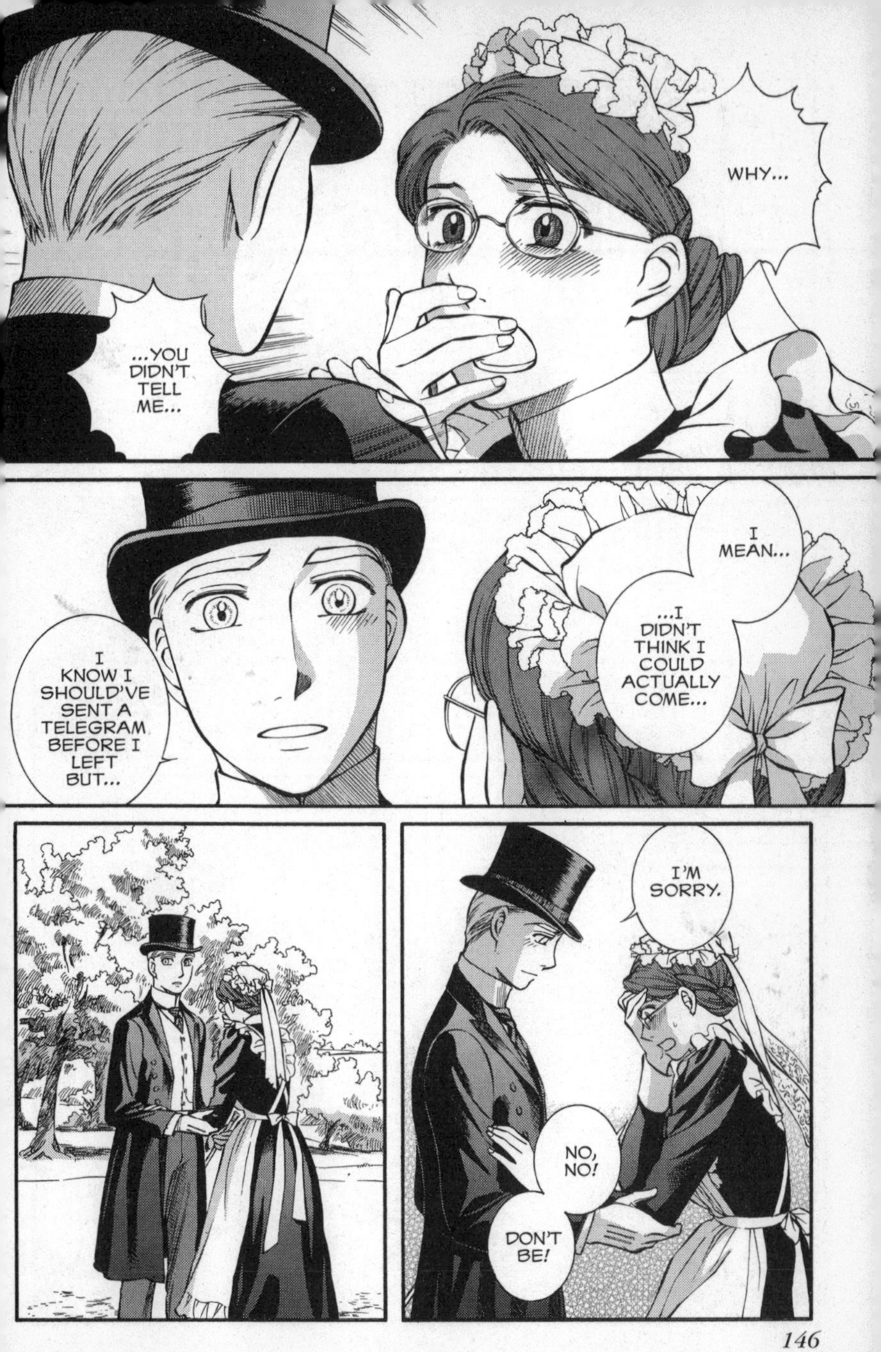
WHY...
...YOU DIDN'T TELL ME...
I MEAN...
...I DIDN'T THINK I COULD ACTUALLY COME...
I KNOW I SHOULD'VE SENT A TELEGRAM BEFORE I LEFT BUT...
I'M SORRY.
NO, NO!
DON'T BE!

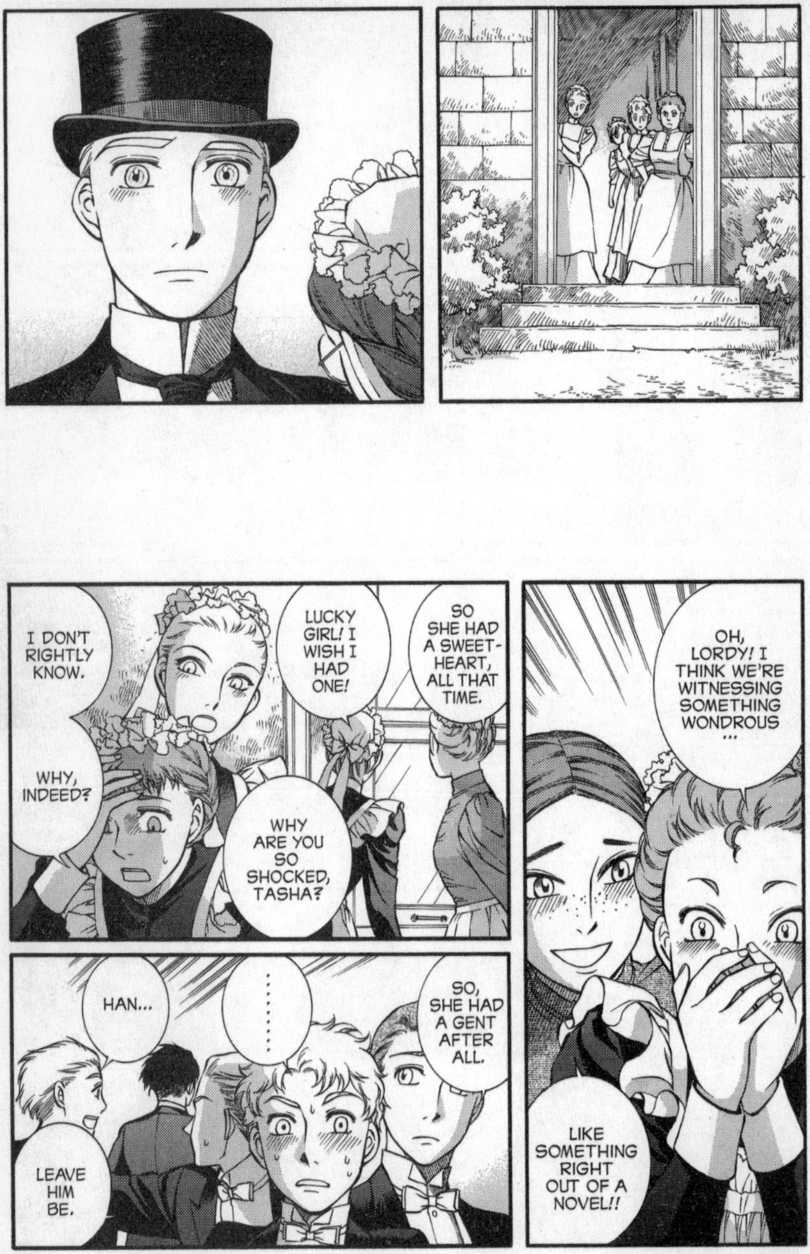
OH, LORDY! I THINK WE'RE WITNESSING SOMETHING WONDROUS ...
LIKE SOMETHING RIGHT OUT OF A NOVEL!!
SO SHE HAD A SWEET-HEART, ALL THAT TIME.
LUCKY GIRL! I WISH I HAD ONE!
WHY ARE YOU SO SHOCKED, TASHA?
I DON'T RIGHTLY KNOW.
WHY, INDEED?
SO, SHE HAD A GENT AFTER ALL.
......
HAN...
LEAVE HIM BE.

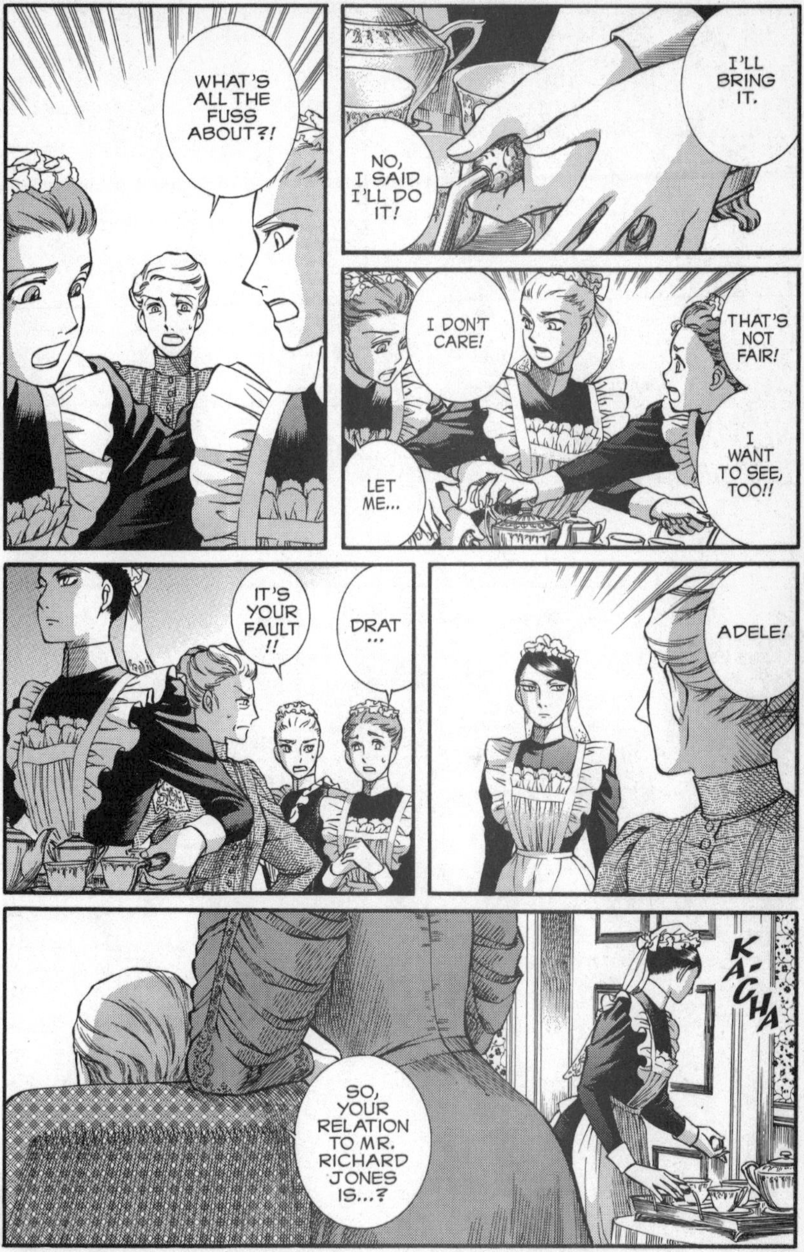
I'LL BRING IT.
NO, I SAID I'LL DO IT!
THAT'S NOT FAIR!
I WANT TO SEE, TOO!!
I DON'T CARE!
LET ME...
WHAT'S ALL THE FUSS ABOUT?!
ADELE!
DRAT...
IT'S YOUR FAULT!!
KA-CHA
SO, YOUR RELATION TO MR. RICHARD JONES IS...?

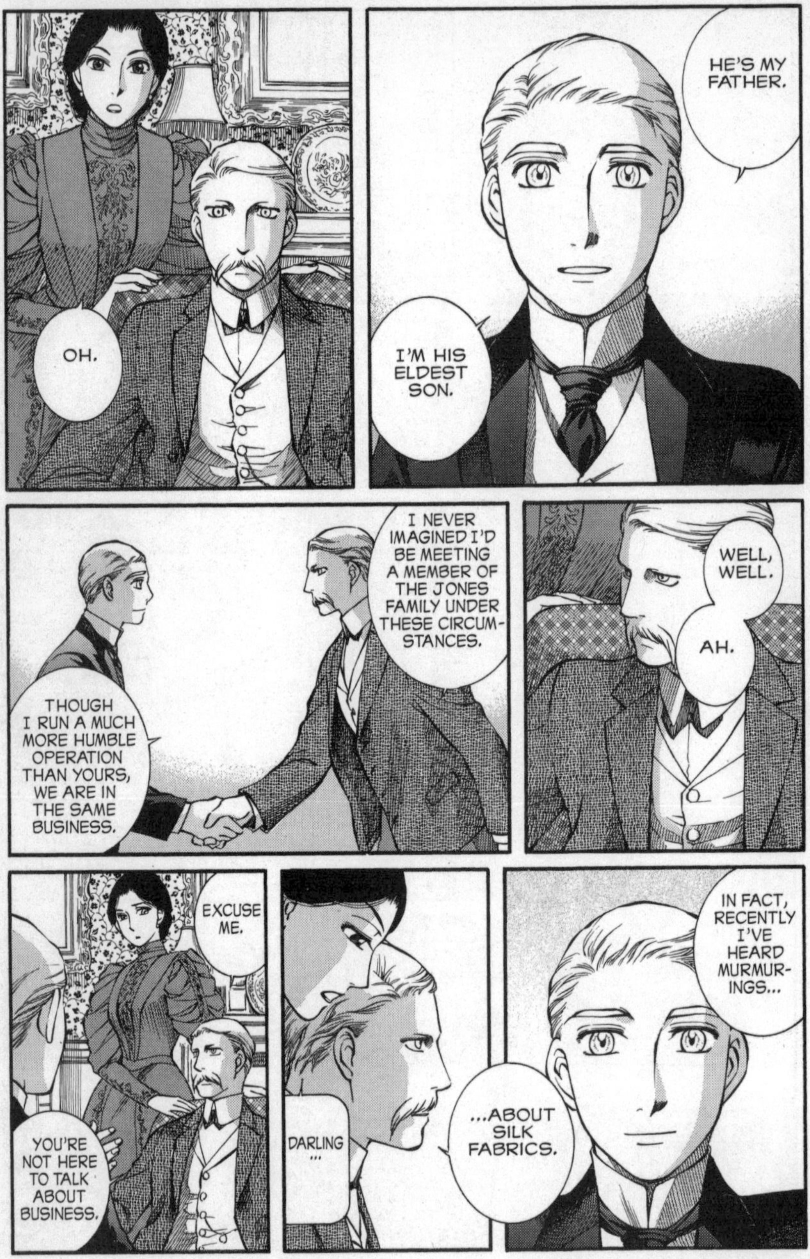
HE'S MY FATHER.
I'M HIS ELDEST SON.
OH.
WELL, WELL.
AH.
I NEVER IMAGINED I'D BE MEETING A MEMBER OF THE JONES FAMILY UNDER THESE CIRCUM-STANCES.
THOUGH I RUN A MUCH MORE HUMBLE OPERATION THAN YOURS, WE ARE IN THE SAME BUSINESS.
IN FACT, RECENTLY I'VE HEARD MURMUR-INGS...
...ABOUT SILK FABRICS.
DARLING ...
EXCUSE ME.
YOU'RE NOT HERE TO TALK ABOUT BUSINESS.

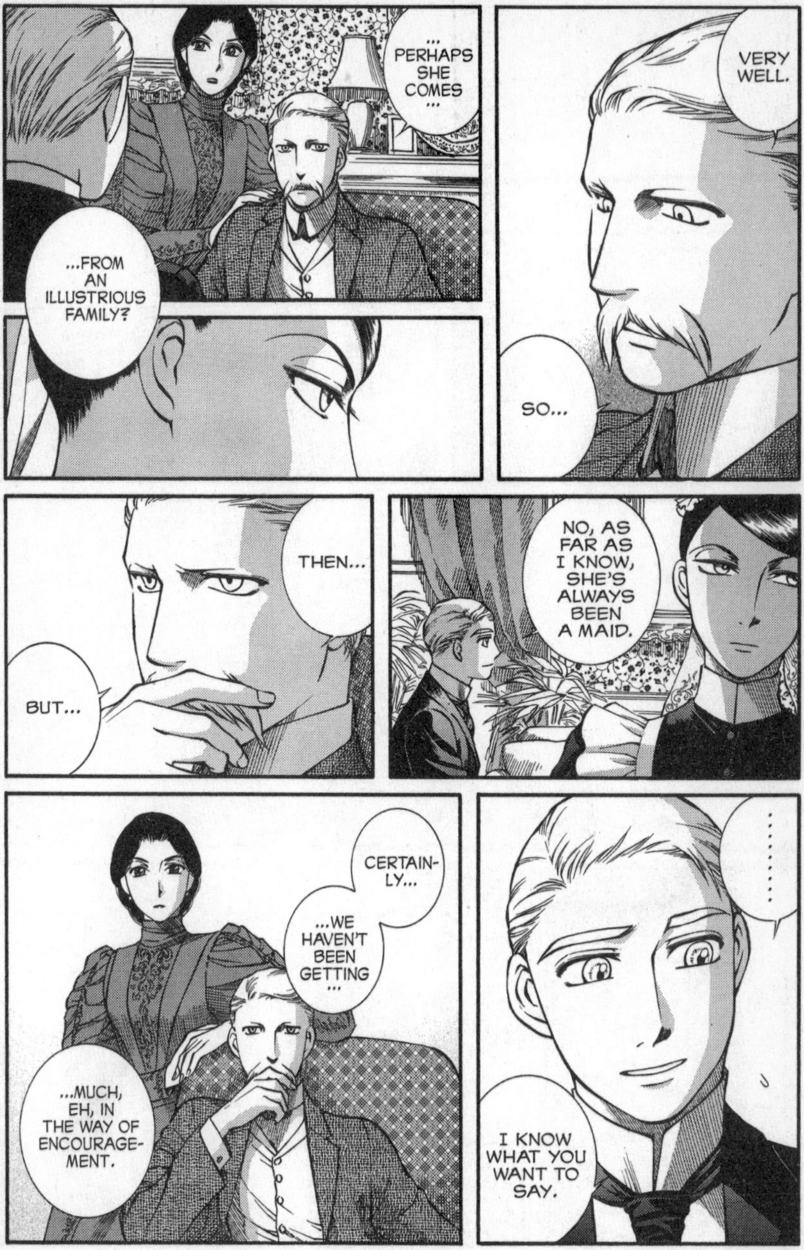
VERY WELL.
SO...
...PERHAPS SHE COMES...
...FROM AN ILLUSTRIOUS FAMILY?
NO, AS FAR AS I KNOW, SHE'S ALWAYS BEEN A MAID.
THEN...
BUT...
....
I KNOW WHAT YOU WANT TO SAY.
CERTAIN-LY...
...WE HAVEN'T BEEN GETTING...
...MUCH, EH, IN THE WAY OF ENCOURAGE-MENT.

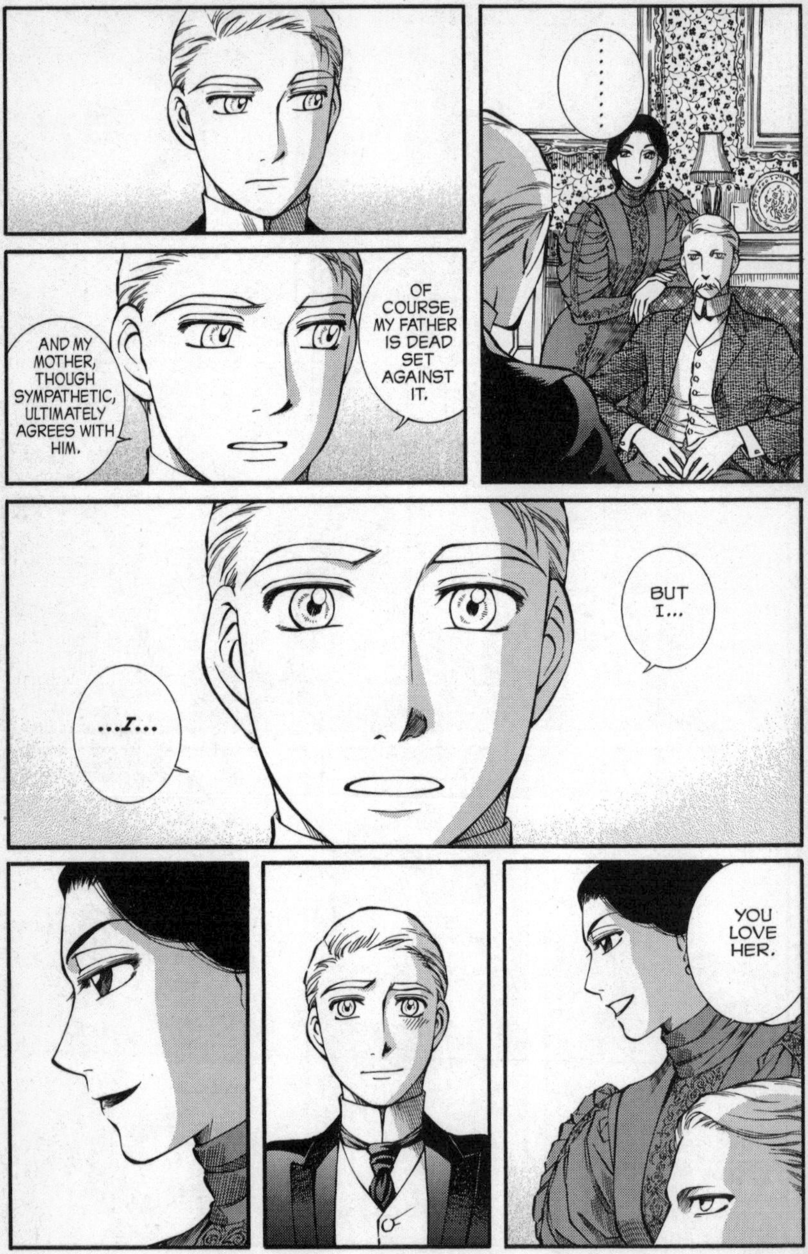
......
OF COURSE, MY FATHER IS DEAD SET AGAINST IT.
AND MY MOTHER, THOUGH SYMPATHETIC, ULTIMATELY AGREES WITH HIM.
BUT I...
...I...
YOU LOVE HER.

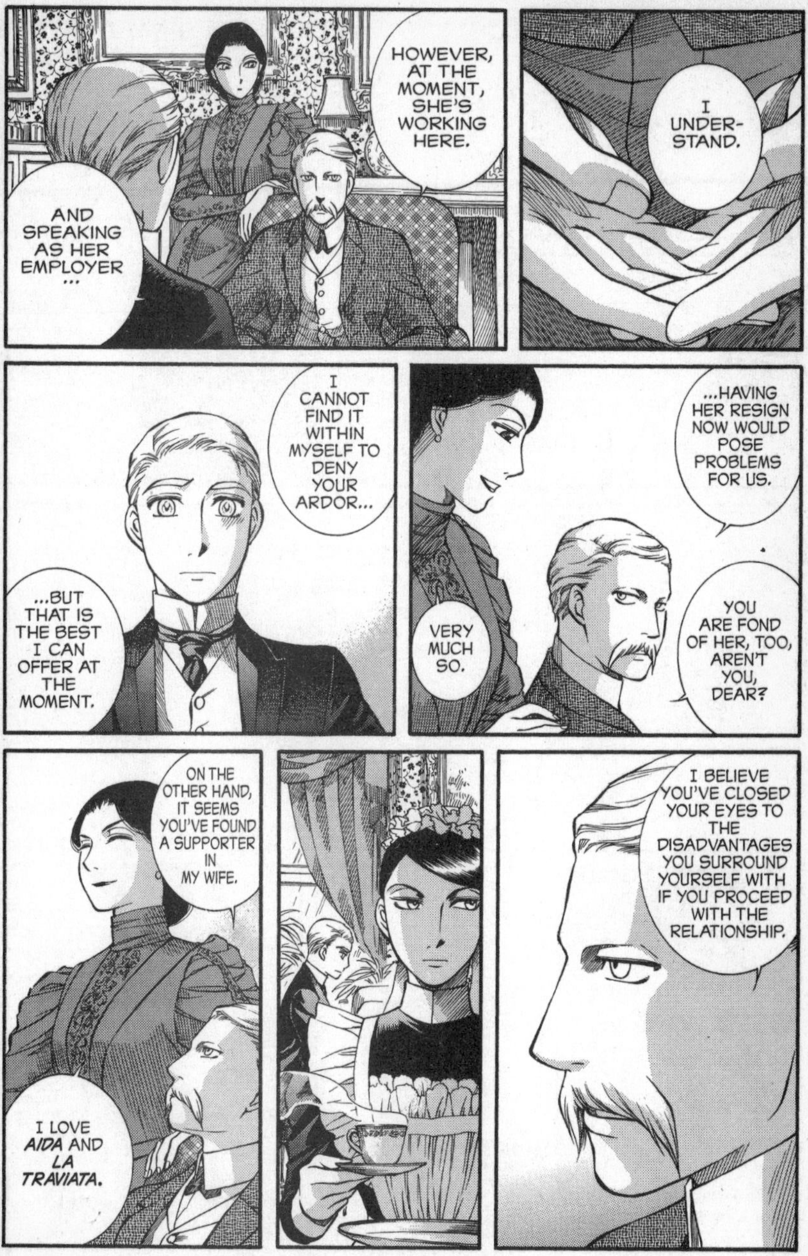
I UNDERSTAND.
HOWEVER, AT THE MOMENT, SHE'S WORKING HERE.
AND SPEAKING AS HER EMPLOYER ...
...HAVING HER RESIGN NOW WOULD POSE PROBLEMS FOR US.
YOU ARE FOND OF HER, TOO, AREN'T YOU, DEAR?
VERY MUCH SO.
I CANNOT FIND IT WITHIN MYSELF TO DENY YOUR ARDOR...
...BUT THAT IS THE BEST I CAN OFFER AT THE MOMENT.
I BELIEVE YOU'VE CLOSED YOUR EYES TO THE DISADVANTAGES YOU SURROUND YOURSELF WITH IF YOU PROCEED WITH THE RELATIONSHIP.
ON THE OTHER HAND, IT SEEMS YOU'VE FOUND A SUPPORTER IN MY WIFE.
I LOVE *AIDA* AND *LA TRAVIATA*.

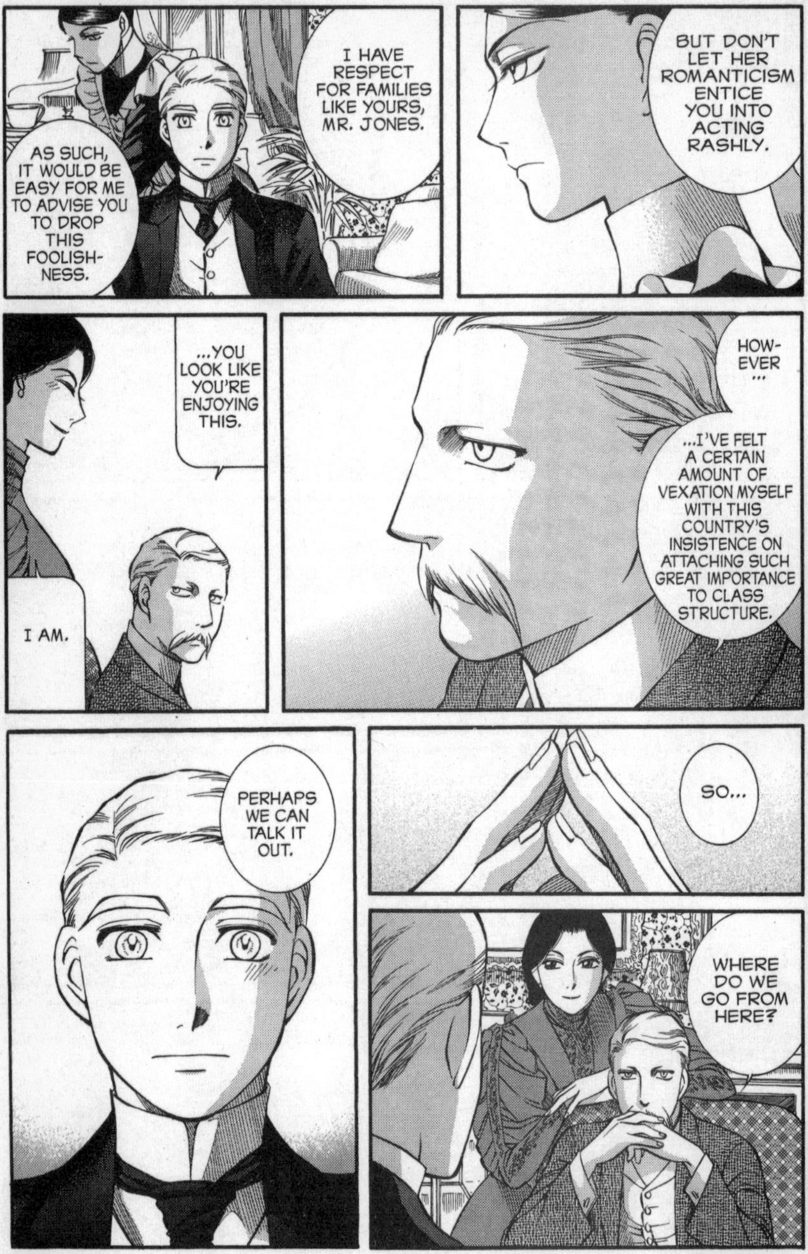
BUT DON'T LET HER ROMANTICISM ENTICE YOU INTO ACTING RASHLY.
I HAVE RESPECT FOR FAMILIES LIKE YOURS, MR. JONES.
AS SUCH, IT WOULD BE EASY FOR ME TO ADVISE YOU TO DROP THIS FOOLISHNESS.
HOWEVER...
...I'VE FELT A CERTAIN AMOUNT OF VEXATION MYSELF WITH THIS COUNTRY'S INSISTENCE ON ATTACHING SUCH GREAT IMPORTANCE TO CLASS STRUCTURE.
...YOU LOOK LIKE YOU'RE ENJOYING THIS.
I AM.
SO...
WHERE DO WE GO FROM HERE?
PERHAPS WE CAN TALK IT OUT.

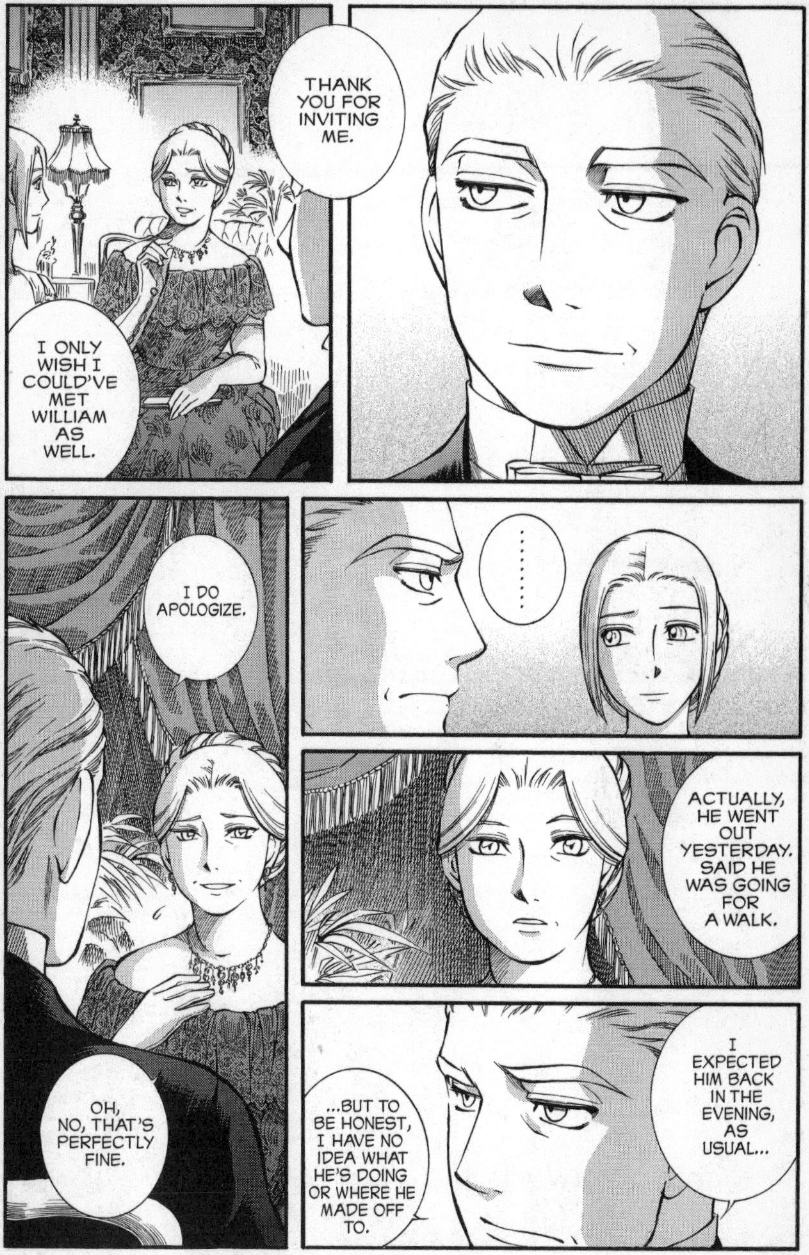
THANK YOU FOR INVITING ME.
I ONLY WISH I COULD'VE MET WILLIAM AS WELL.
......
ACTUALLY, HE WENT OUT YESTERDAY. SAID HE WAS GOING FOR A WALK.
I EXPECTED HIM BACK IN THE EVENING, AS USUAL...
...BUT TO BE HONEST, I HAVE NO IDEA WHAT HE'S DOING OR WHERE HE MADE OFF TO.
I DO APOLOGIZE.
OH, NO, THAT'S PERFECTLY FINE.

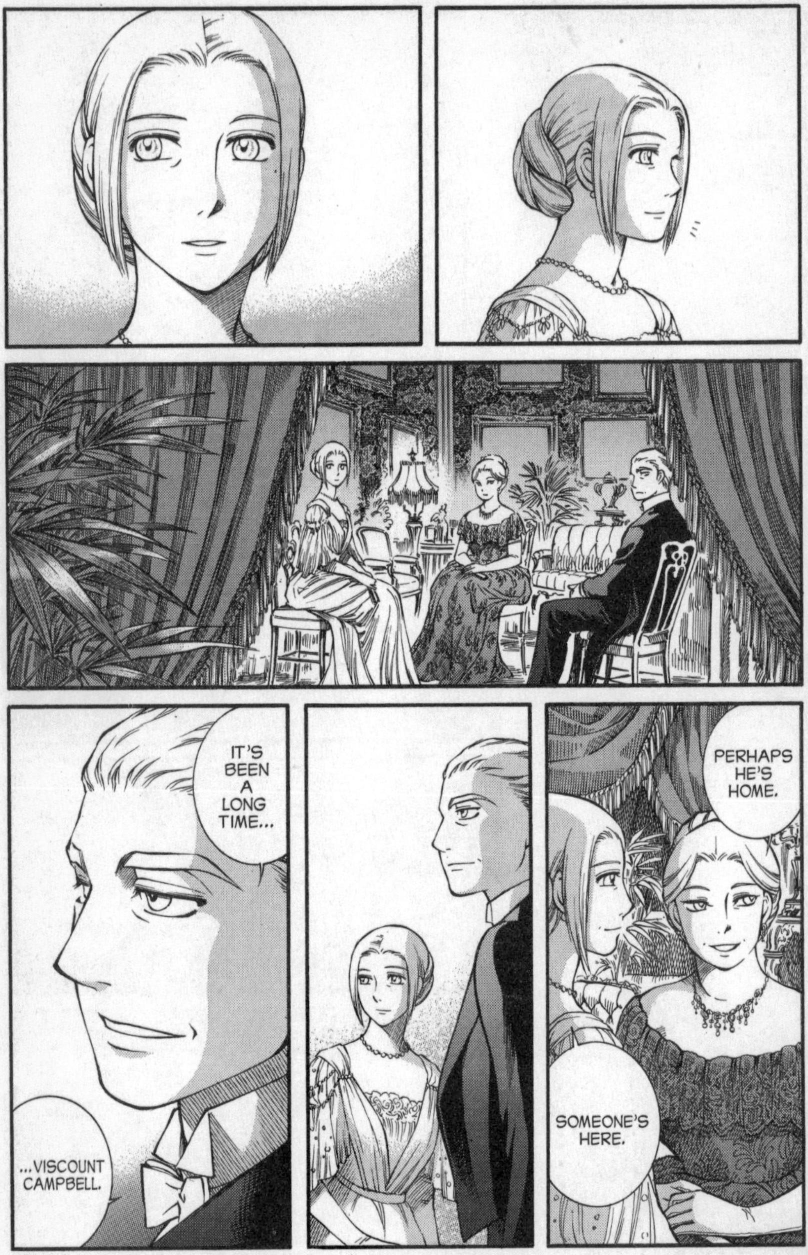
PERHAPS HE'S HOME.
SOMEONE'S HERE.
IT'S BEEN A LONG TIME...
...VISCOUNT CAMPBELL.

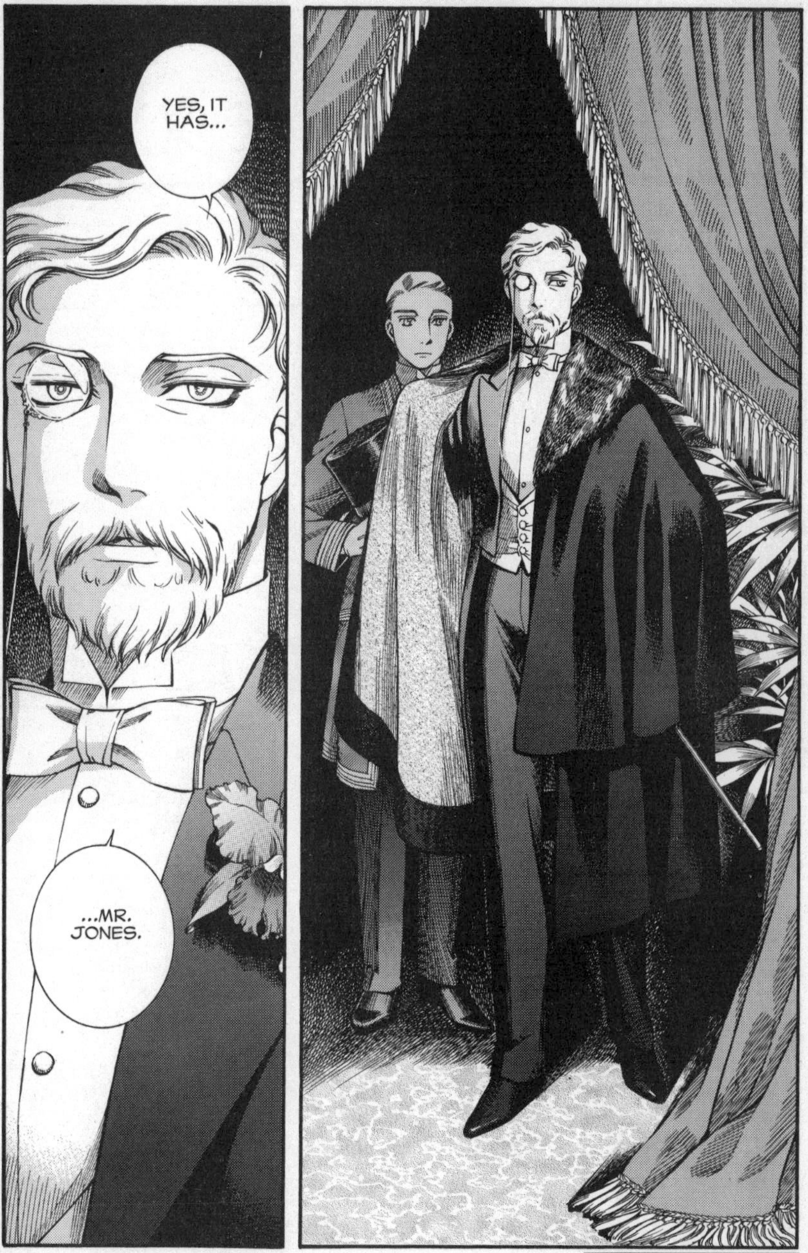
YES, IT HAS...
...MR. JONES.

Chapter Thirty-Five:
The End

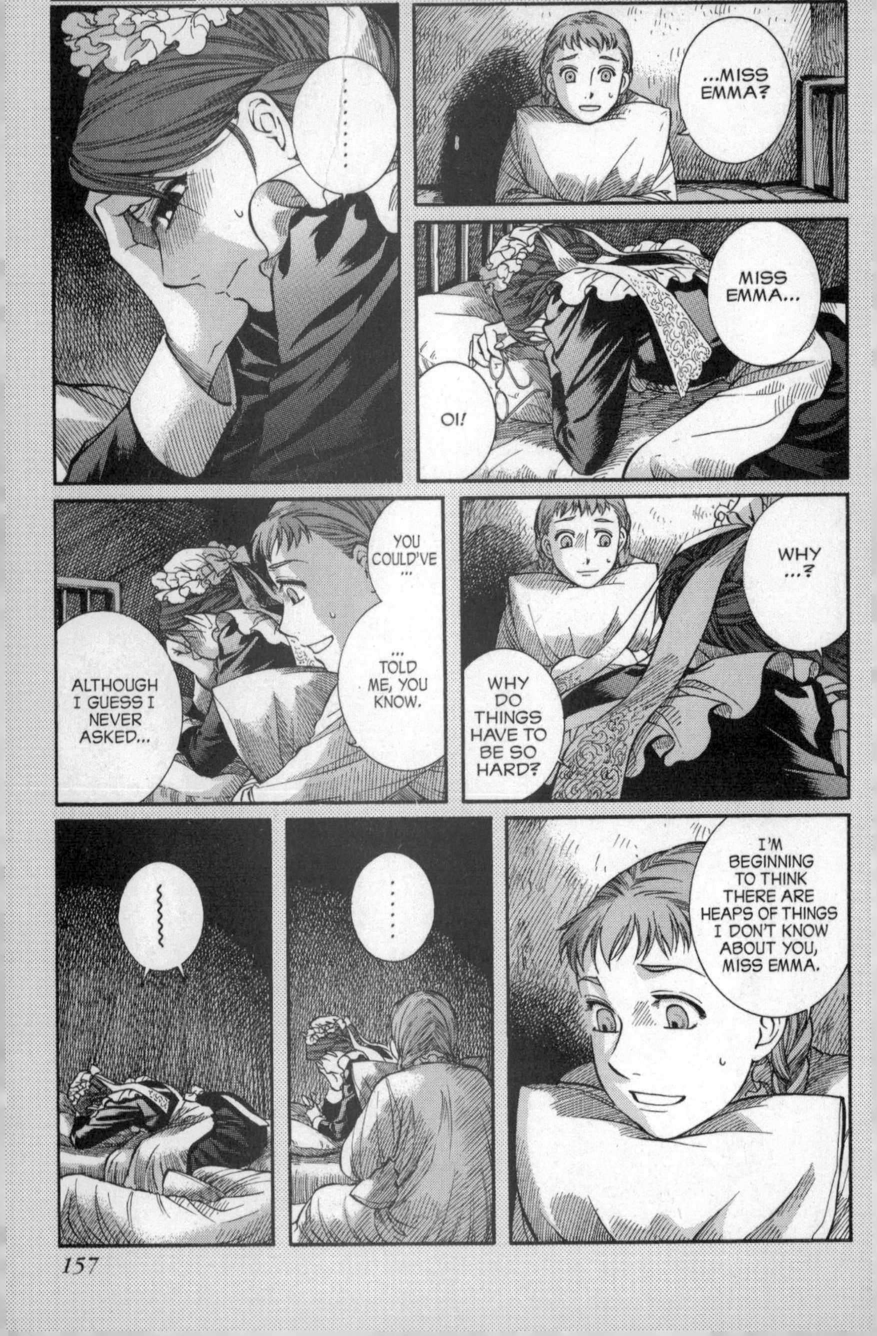
...MISS EMMA?
MISS EMMA...
OI!
......
WHY ...?
WHY DO THINGS HAVE TO BE SO HARD?
YOU COULD'VE ...
... TOLD ME, YOU KNOW.
ALTHOUGH I GUESS I NEVER ASKED...
I'M BEGINNING TO THINK THERE ARE HEAPS OF THINGS I DON'T KNOW ABOUT YOU, MISS EMMA.
......

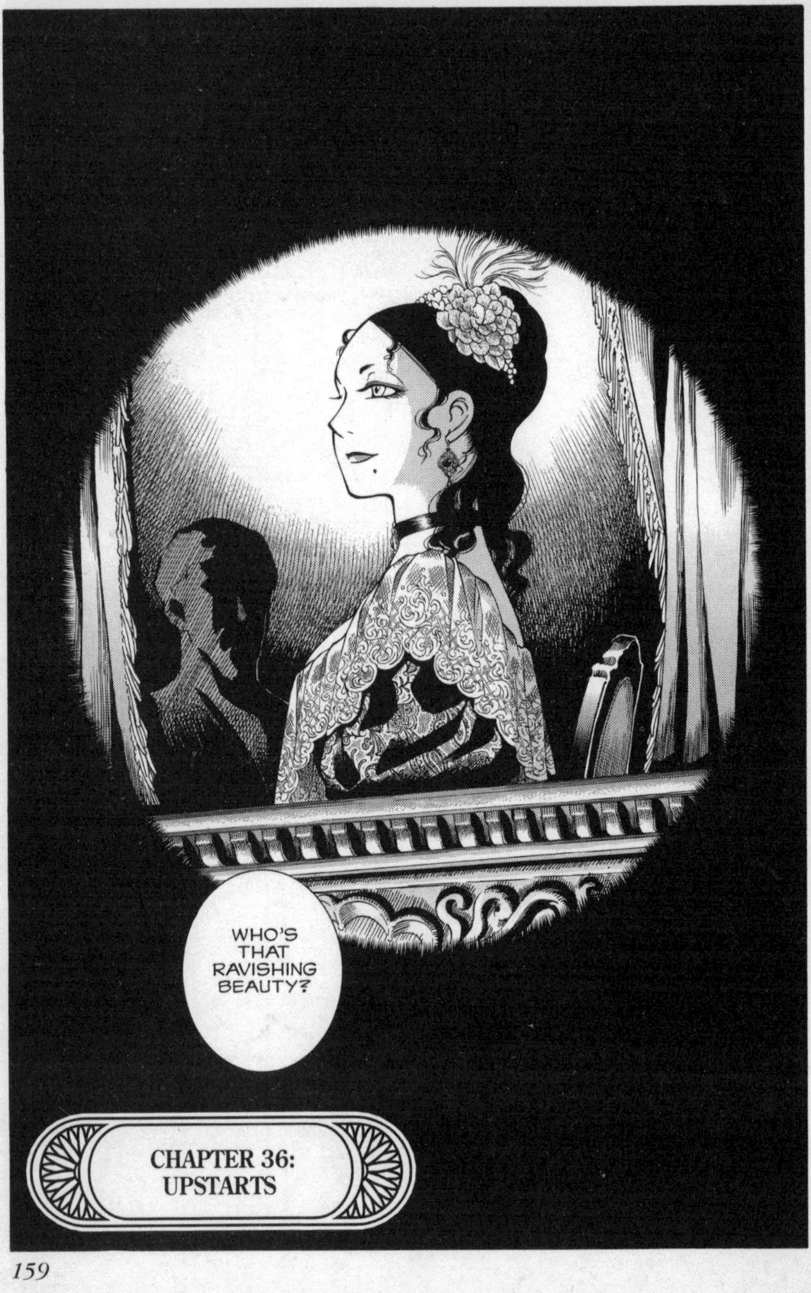
WHO'S THAT RAVISHING BEAUTY?
CHAPTER 36: UPSTARTS

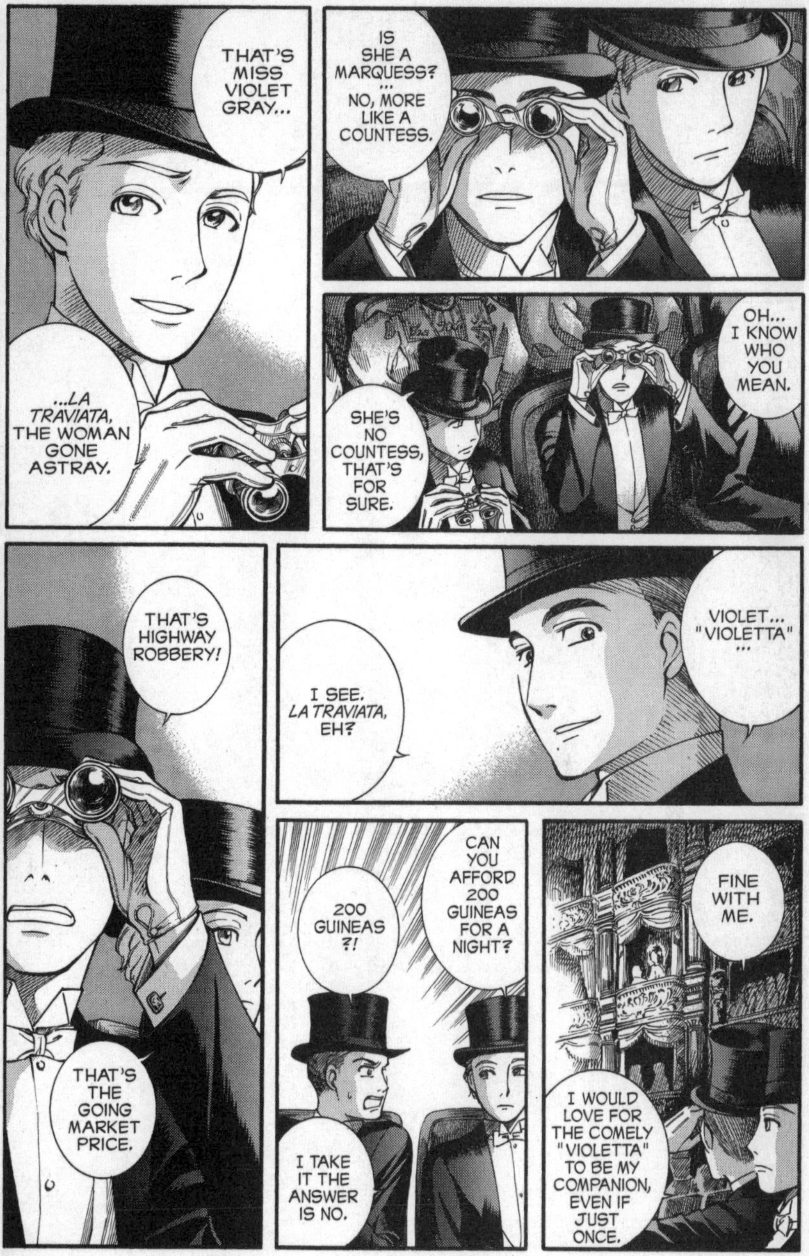
IS SHE A MARQUESS? ... NO, MORE LIKE A COUNTESS.
OH... I KNOW WHO YOU MEAN.
SHE'S NO COUNTESS, THAT'S FOR SURE.
THAT'S MISS VIOLET GRAY...
...*LA TRAVIATA*, THE WOMAN GONE ASTRAY.
VIOLET... "VIOLETTA" ...
I SEE. *LA TRAVIATA*, EH?
FINE WITH ME.
I WOULD LOVE FOR THE COMELY "VIOLETTA" TO BE MY COMPANION, EVEN IF JUST ONCE.
CAN YOU AFFORD 200 GUINEAS FOR A NIGHT?
200 GUINEAS?!
I TAKE IT THE ANSWER IS NO.
THAT'S HIGHWAY ROBBERY!
THAT'S THE GOING MARKET PRICE.

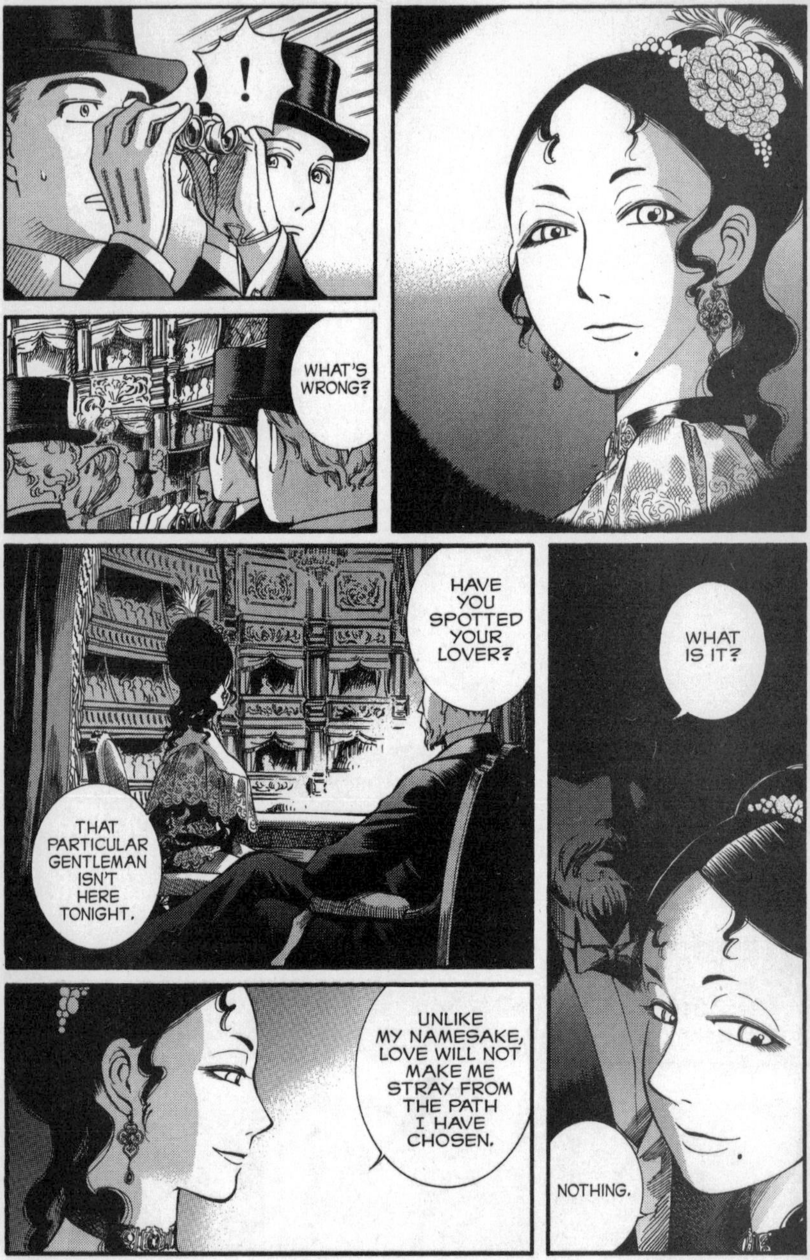
!
WHAT'S WRONG?
WHAT IS IT?
NOTHING.
HAVE YOU SPOTTED YOUR LOVER?
THAT PARTICULAR GENTLEMAN ISN'T HERE TONIGHT.
UNLIKE MY NAMESAKE, LOVE WILL NOT MAKE ME STRAY FROM THE PATH I HAVE CHOSEN.

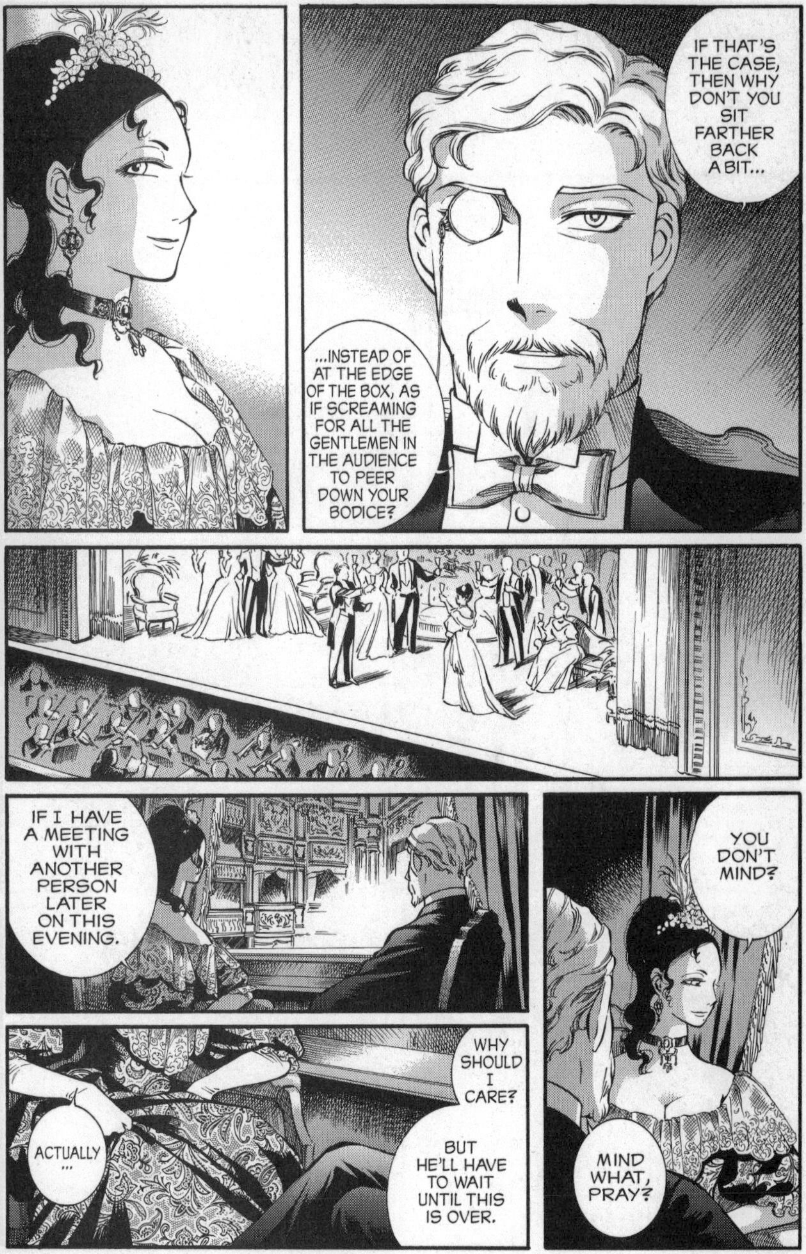
IF THAT'S THE CASE, THEN WHY DON'T YOU SIT FARTHER BACK A BIT...
...INSTEAD OF AT THE EDGE OF THE BOX, AS IF SCREAMING FOR ALL THE GENTLEMEN IN THE AUDIENCE TO PEER DOWN YOUR BODICE?
YOU DON'T MIND?
MIND WHAT, PRAY?
IF I HAVE A MEETING WITH ANOTHER PERSON LATER ON THIS EVENING.
WHY SHOULD I CARE?
BUT HE'LL HAVE TO WAIT UNTIL THIS IS OVER.
ACTUALLY...

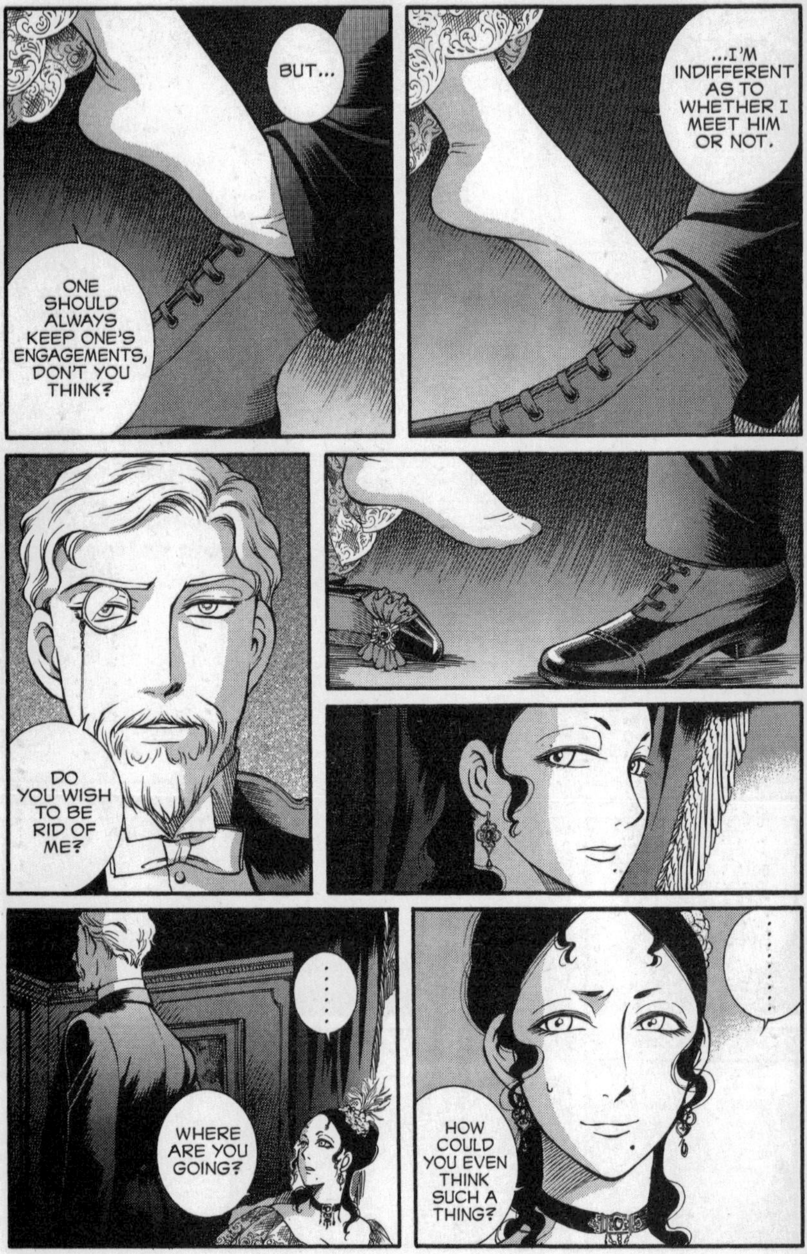
...I'M INDIFFERENT AS TO WHETHER I MEET HIM OR NOT.
BUT...
ONE SHOULD ALWAYS KEEP ONE'S ENGAGEMENTS, DON'T YOU THINK?
DO YOU WISH TO BE RID OF ME?
......
HOW COULD YOU EVEN THINK SUCH A THING?
......
WHERE ARE YOU GOING?

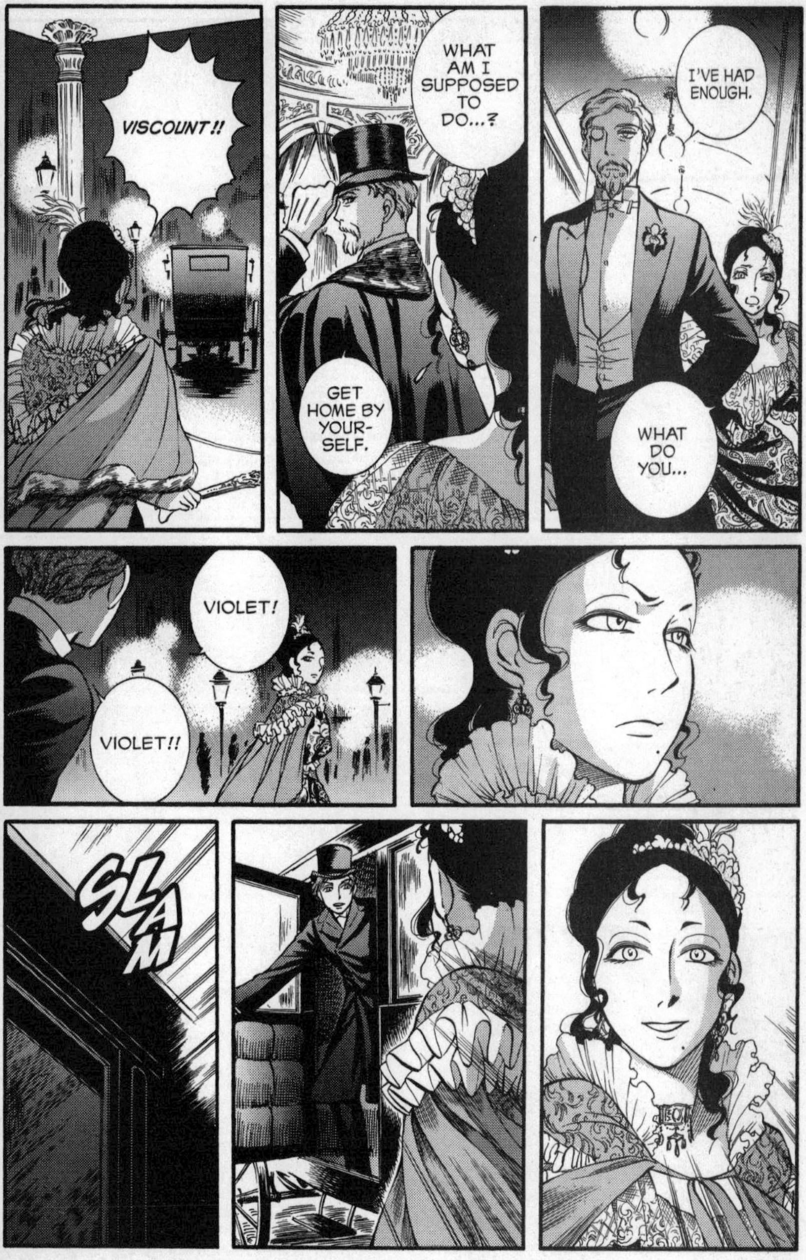
I'VE HAD ENOUGH.
WHAT DO YOU...
WHAT AM I SUPPOSED TO DO...?
GET HOME BY YOURSELF.
VISCOUNT!!
VIOLET!
VIOLET!!
SLAM

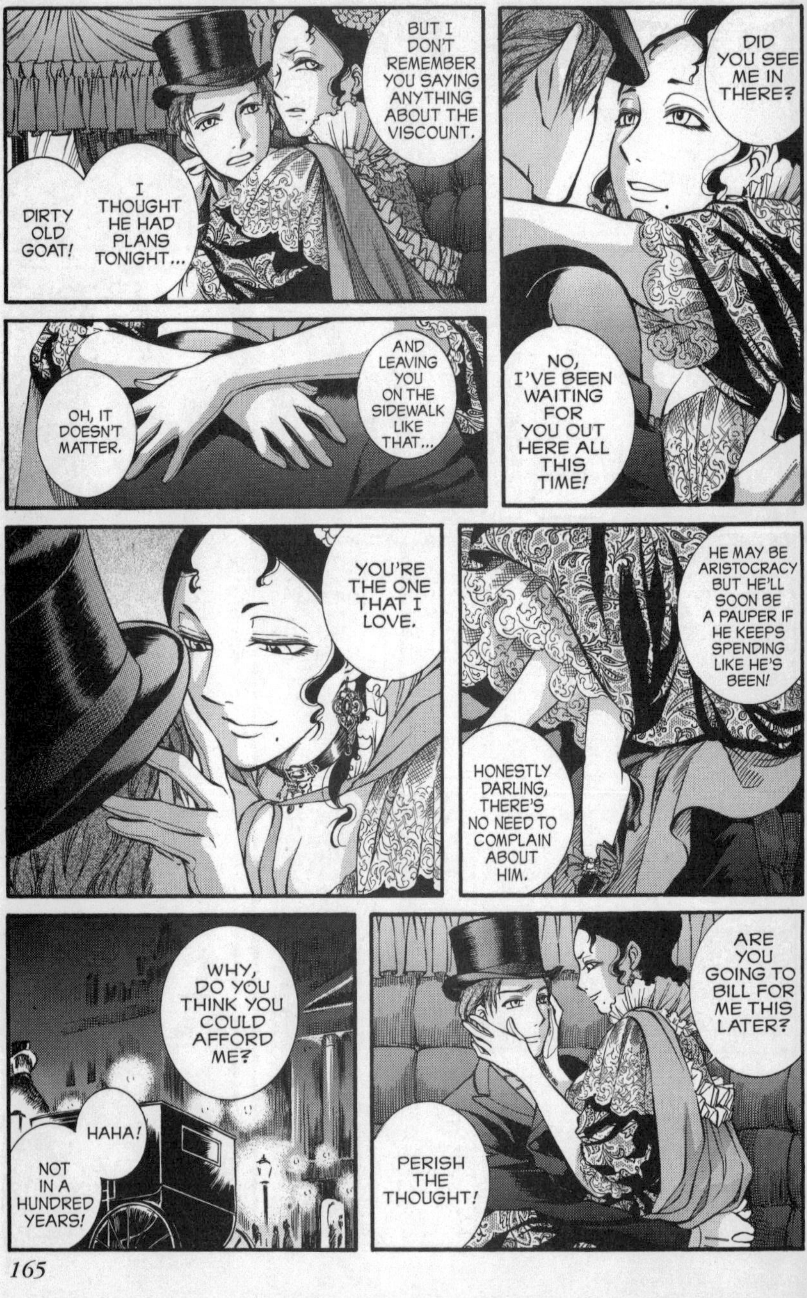
DID YOU SEE ME IN THERE?
NO, I'VE BEEN WAITING FOR YOU OUT HERE ALL THIS TIME!
BUT I DON'T REMEMBER YOU SAYING ANYTHING ABOUT THE VISCOUNT.
I THOUGHT HE HAD PLANS TONIGHT...
DIRTY OLD GOAT!
AND LEAVING YOU ON THE SIDEWALK LIKE THAT...
OH, IT DOESN'T MATTER.
HE MAY BE ARISTOCRACY BUT HE'LL SOON BE A PAUPER IF HE KEEPS SPENDING LIKE HE'S BEEN!
HONESTLY DARLING, THERE'S NO NEED TO COMPLAIN ABOUT HIM.
YOU'RE THE ONE THAT I LOVE.
ARE YOU GOING TO BILL FOR ME THIS LATER?
PERISH THE THOUGHT!
WHY, DO YOU THINK YOU COULD AFFORD ME?
HAHA!
NOT IN A HUNDRED YEARS!

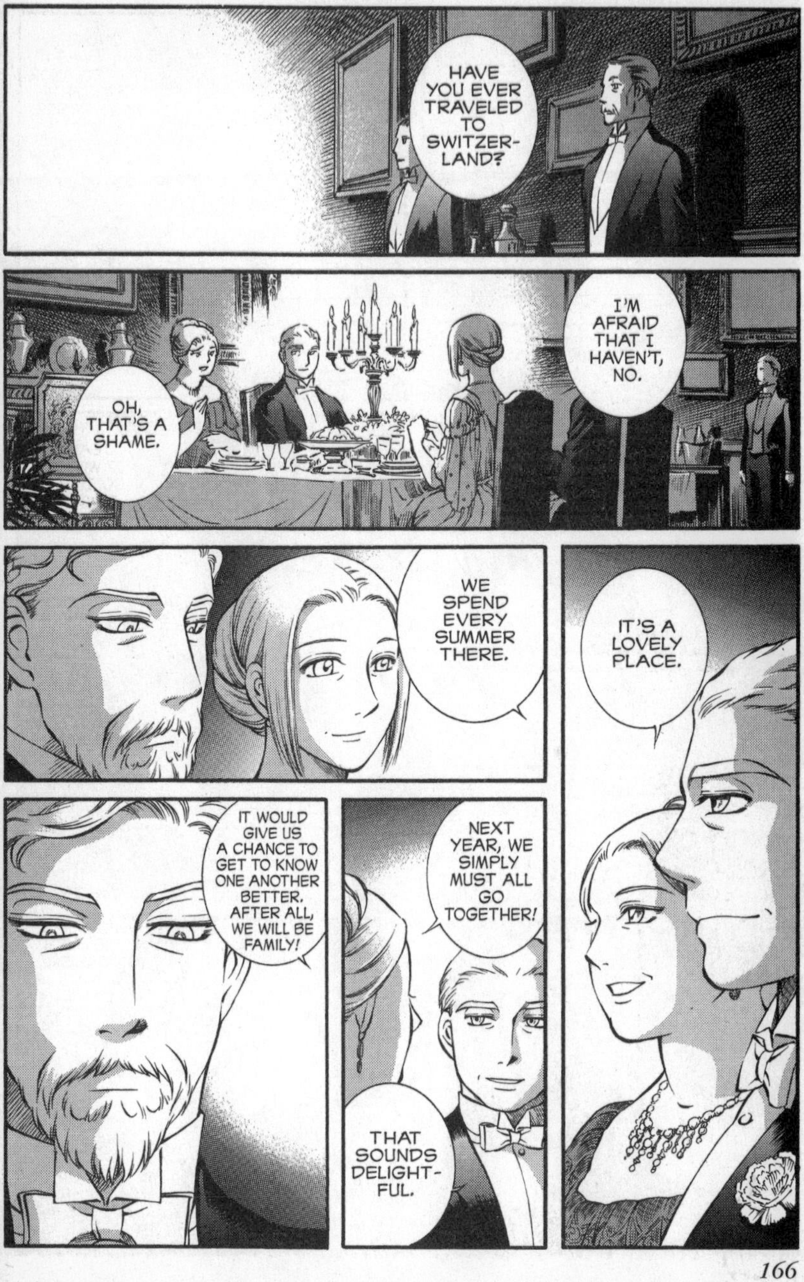

HAVE YOU EVER TRAVELED TO SWITZER-LAND?
I'M AFRAID THAT I HAVEN'T, NO.
OH, THAT'S A SHAME.
IT'S A LOVELY PLACE.
WE SPEND EVERY SUMMER THERE.
NEXT YEAR, WE SIMPLY MUST ALL GO TOGETHER!
THAT SOUNDS DELIGHT-FUL.
IT WOULD GIVE US A CHANCE TO GET TO KNOW ONE ANOTHER BETTER. AFTER ALL, WE WILL BE FAMILY!

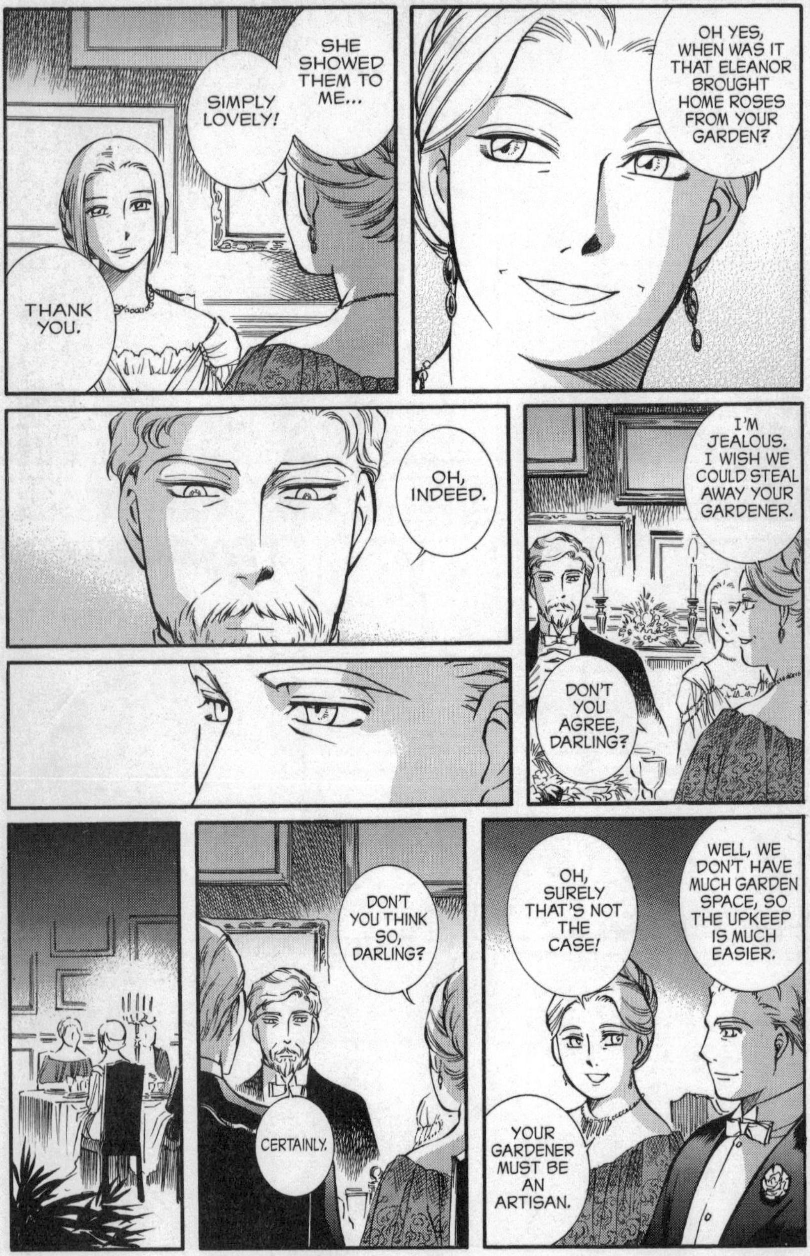
OH YES, WHEN WAS IT THAT ELEANOR BROUGHT HOME ROSES FROM YOUR GARDEN?
SHE SHOWED THEM TO ME...
SIMPLY LOVELY!
THANK YOU.
I'M JEALOUS. I WISH WE COULD STEAL AWAY YOUR GARDENER.
DON'T YOU AGREE, DARLING?
OH, INDEED.
WELL, WE DON'T HAVE MUCH GARDEN SPACE, SO THE UPKEEP IS MUCH EASIER.
OH, SURELY THAT'S NOT THE CASE!
YOUR GARDENER MUST BE AN ARTISAN.
DON'T YOU THINK SO, DARLING?
CERTAINLY.

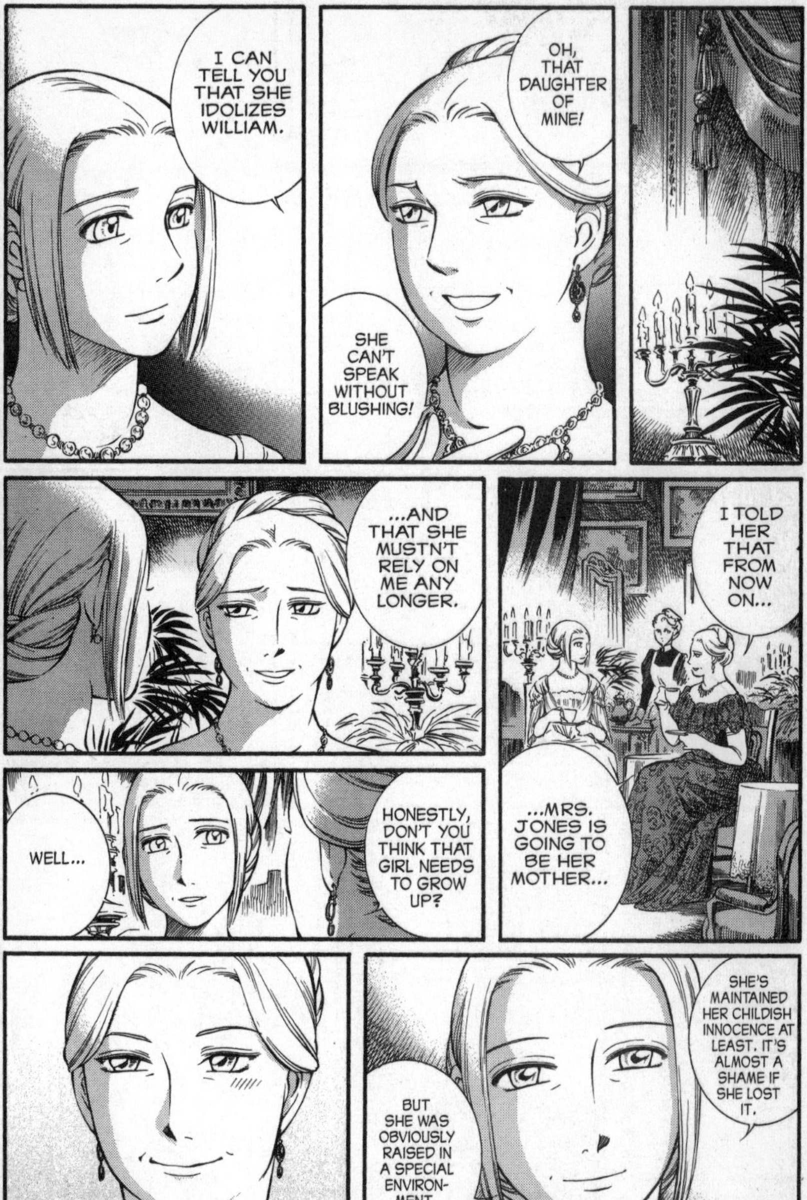
OH, THAT DAUGHTER OF MINE!
SHE CAN'T SPEAK WITHOUT BLUSHING!
I CAN TELL YOU THAT SHE IDOLIZES WILLIAM.
I TOLD HER THAT FROM NOW ON...
...MRS. JONES IS GOING TO BE HER MOTHER...
...AND THAT SHE MUSTN'T RELY ON ME ANY LONGER.
HONESTLY, DON'T YOU THINK THAT GIRL NEEDS TO GROW UP?
WELL...
SHE'S MAINTAINED HER CHILDISH INNOCENCE AT LEAST. IT'S ALMOST A SHAME IF SHE LOST IT.
BUT SHE WAS OBVIOUSLY RAISED IN A SPECIAL ENVIRONMENT.

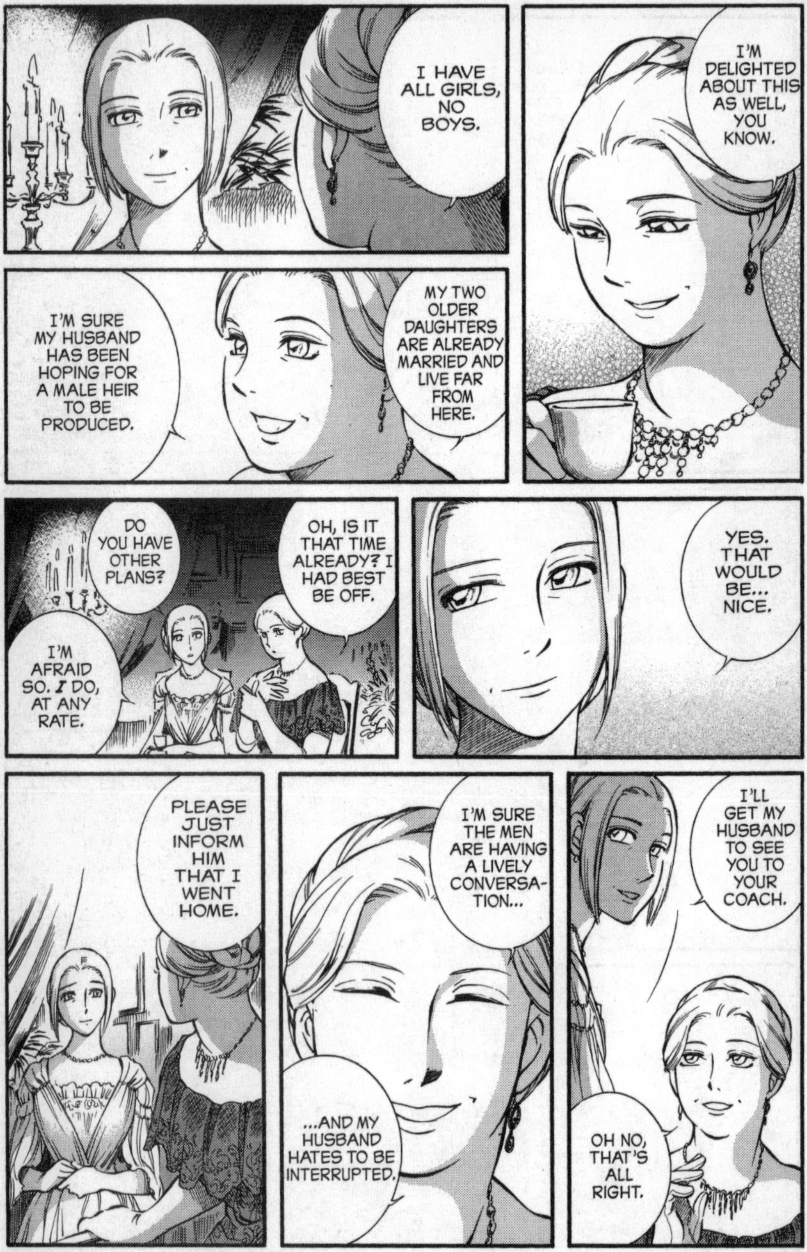
I'M DELIGHTED ABOUT THIS AS WELL, YOU KNOW.
I HAVE ALL GIRLS, NO BOYS.
MY TWO OLDER DAUGHTERS ARE ALREADY MARRIED AND LIVE FAR FROM HERE.
I'M SURE MY HUSBAND HAS BEEN HOPING FOR A MALE HEIR TO BE PRODUCED.
YES. THAT WOULD BE... NICE.
OH, IS IT THAT TIME ALREADY? I HAD BEST BE OFF.
DO YOU HAVE OTHER PLANS?
I'M AFRAID SO. *I* DO, AT ANY RATE.
I'LL GET MY HUSBAND TO SEE YOU TO YOUR COACH.
OH NO, THAT'S ALL RIGHT.
I'M SURE THE MEN ARE HAVING A LIVELY CONVERSATION...
...AND MY HUSBAND HATES TO BE INTERRUPTED.
PLEASE JUST INFORM HIM THAT I WENT HOME.

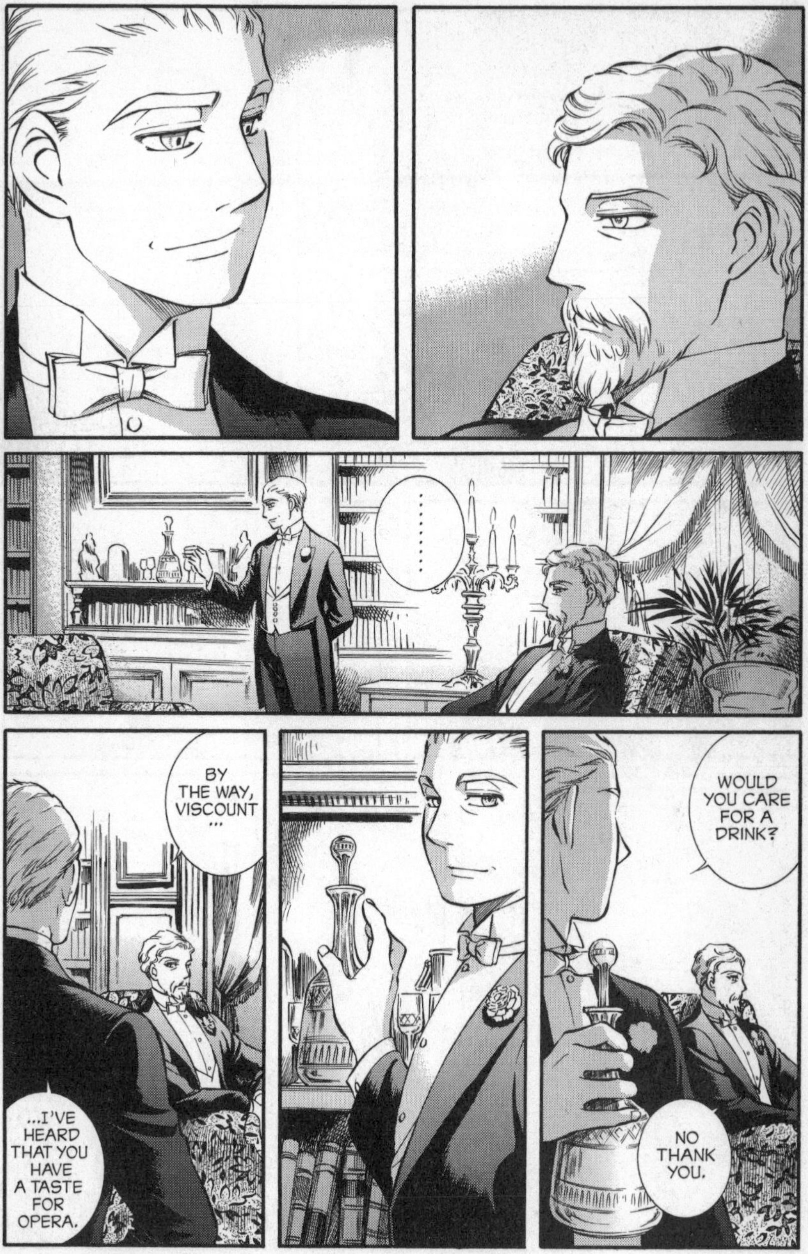
......
WOULD YOU CARE FOR A DRINK?
NO THANK YOU.
BY THE WAY, VISCOUNT ...
...I'VE HEARD THAT YOU HAVE A TASTE FOR OPERA.

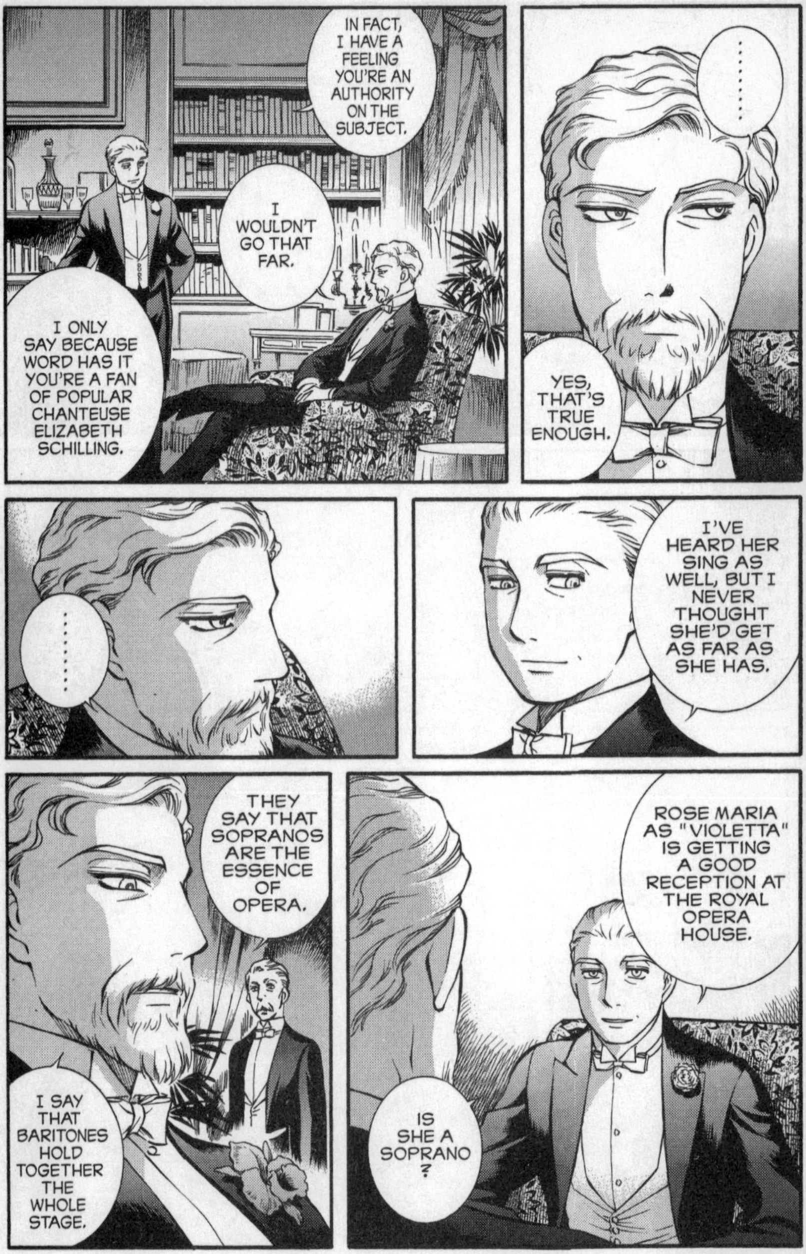
......
YES, THAT'S TRUE ENOUGH.
IN FACT, I HAVE A FEELING YOU'RE AN AUTHORITY ON THE SUBJECT.
I WOULDN'T GO THAT FAR.
I ONLY SAY BECAUSE WORD HAS IT YOU'RE A FAN OF POPULAR CHANTEUSE ELIZABETH SCHILLING.
I'VE HEARD HER SING AS WELL, BUT I NEVER THOUGHT SHE'D GET AS FAR AS SHE HAS.
......
ROSE MARIA AS "VIOLETTA" IS GETTING A GOOD RECEPTION AT THE ROYAL OPERA HOUSE.
IS SHE A SOPRANO?
THEY SAY THAT SOPRANOS ARE THE ESSENCE OF OPERA.
I SAY THAT BARITONES HOLD TOGETHER THE WHOLE STAGE.

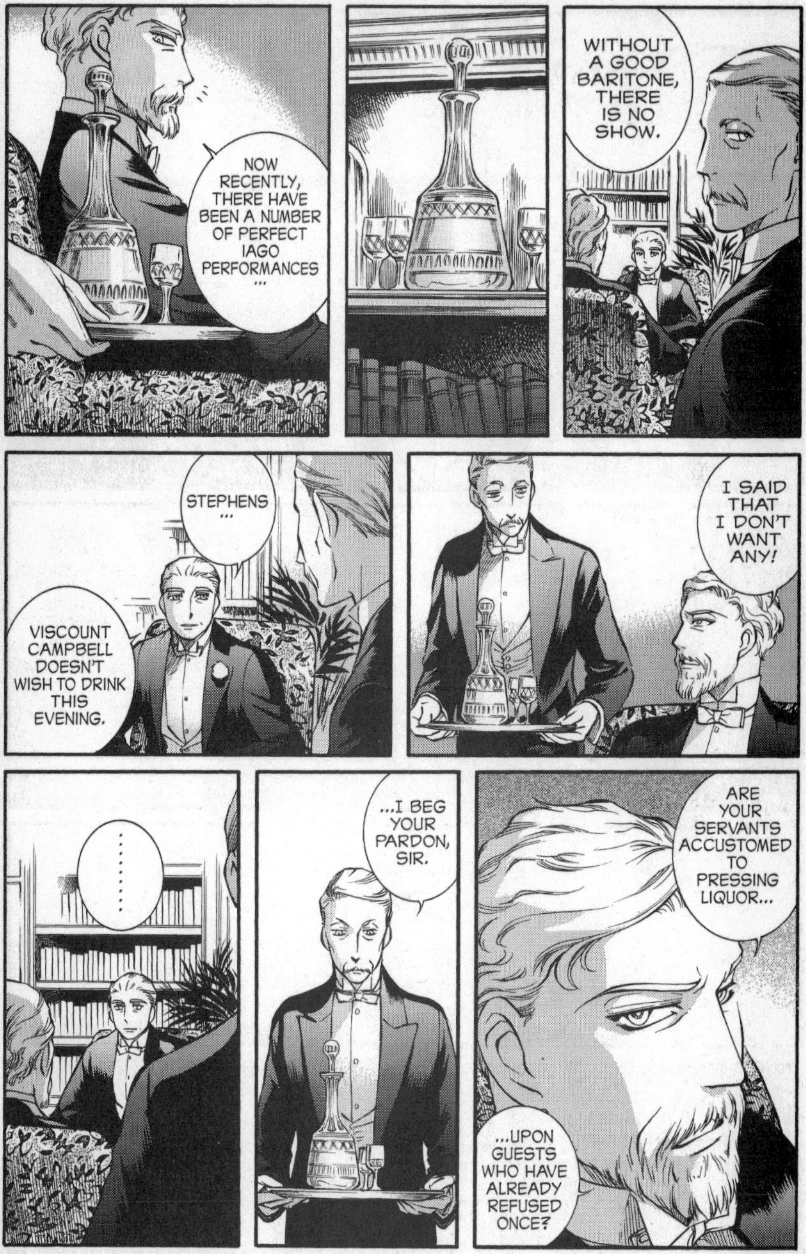
WITHOUT A GOOD BARITONE, THERE IS NO SHOW.
NOW RECENTLY, THERE HAVE BEEN A NUMBER OF PERFECT IAGO PERFORMANCES ...
I SAID THAT I DON'T WANT ANY!
STEPHENS ...
VISCOUNT CAMPBELL DOESN'T WISH TO DRINK THIS EVENING.
ARE YOUR SERVANTS ACCUSTOMED TO PRESSING LIQUOR...
...UPON GUESTS WHO HAVE ALREADY REFUSED ONCE?
...I BEG YOUR PARDON, SIR.
......

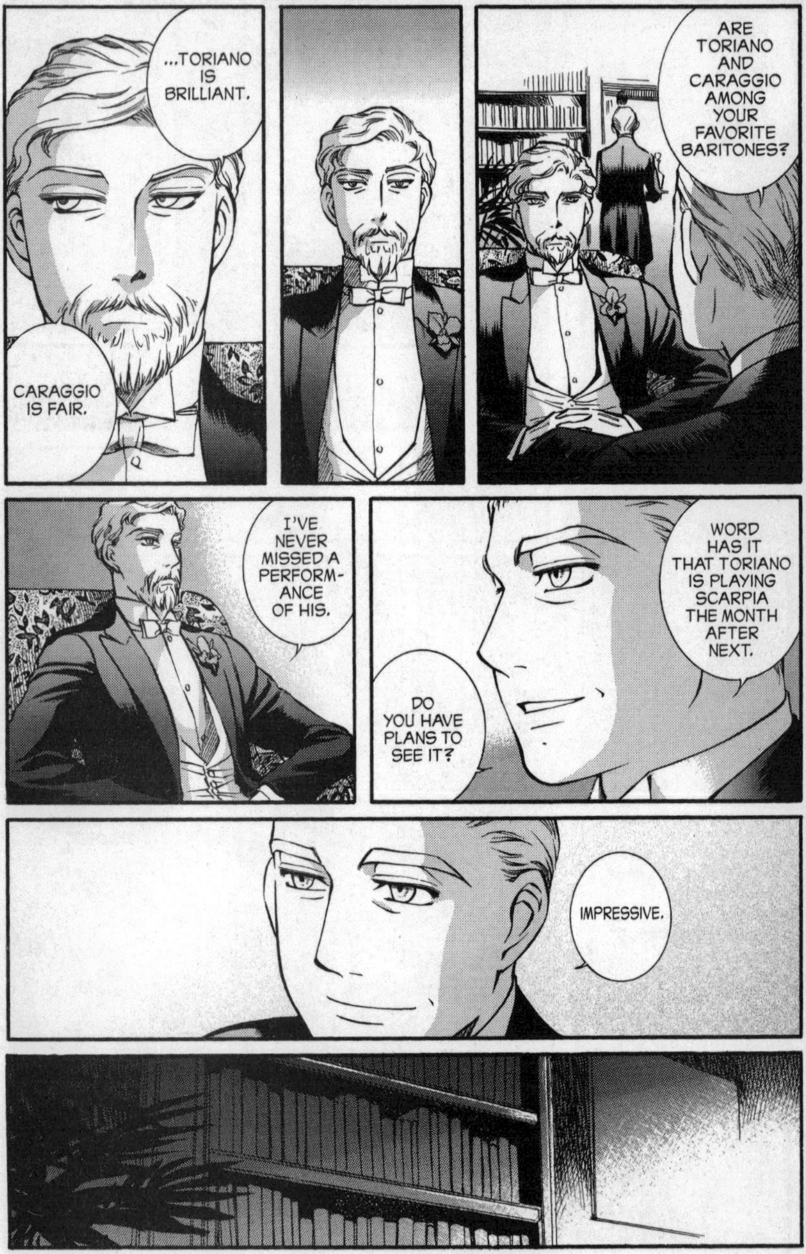
ARE TORIANO AND CARAGGIO AMONG YOUR FAVORITE BARITONES?
...TORIANO IS BRILLIANT.
CARAGGIO IS FAIR.
WORD HAS IT THAT TORIANO IS PLAYING SCARPIA THE MONTH AFTER NEXT.
DO YOU HAVE PLANS TO SEE IT?
I'VE NEVER MISSED A PERFORM-ANCE OF HIS.
IMPRESSIVE.

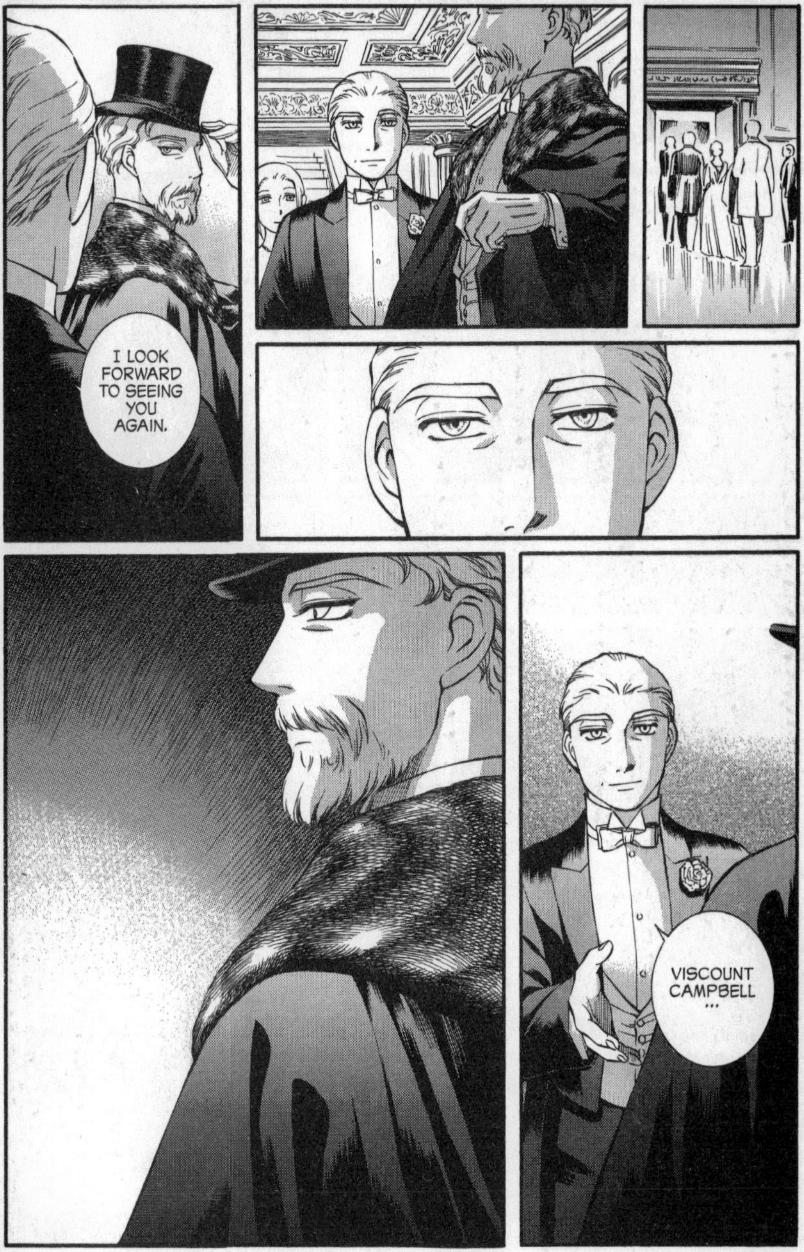
I LOOK FORWARD TO SEEING YOU AGAIN.
VISCOUNT CAMPBELL ...

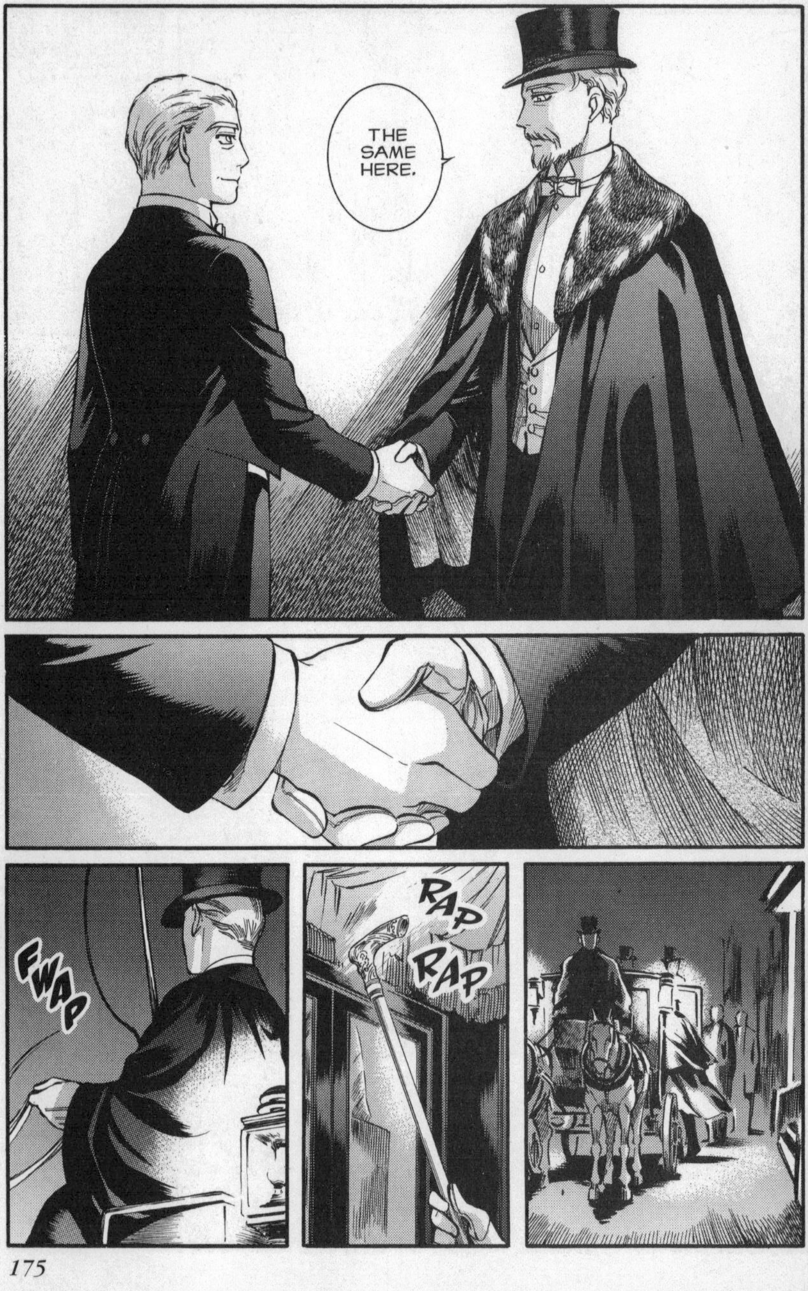
THE SAME HERE.
RAP RAP
FWAP

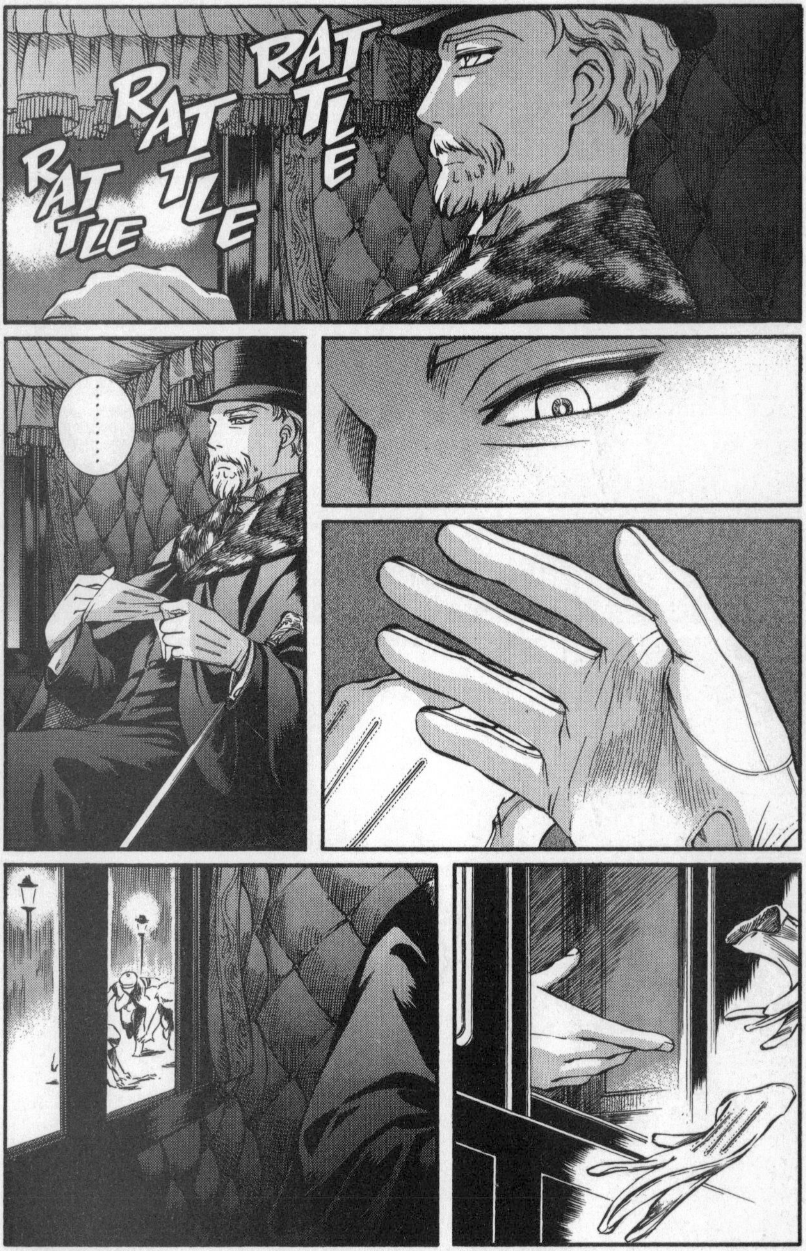
RATTLE
RATTLE
RATTLE
......

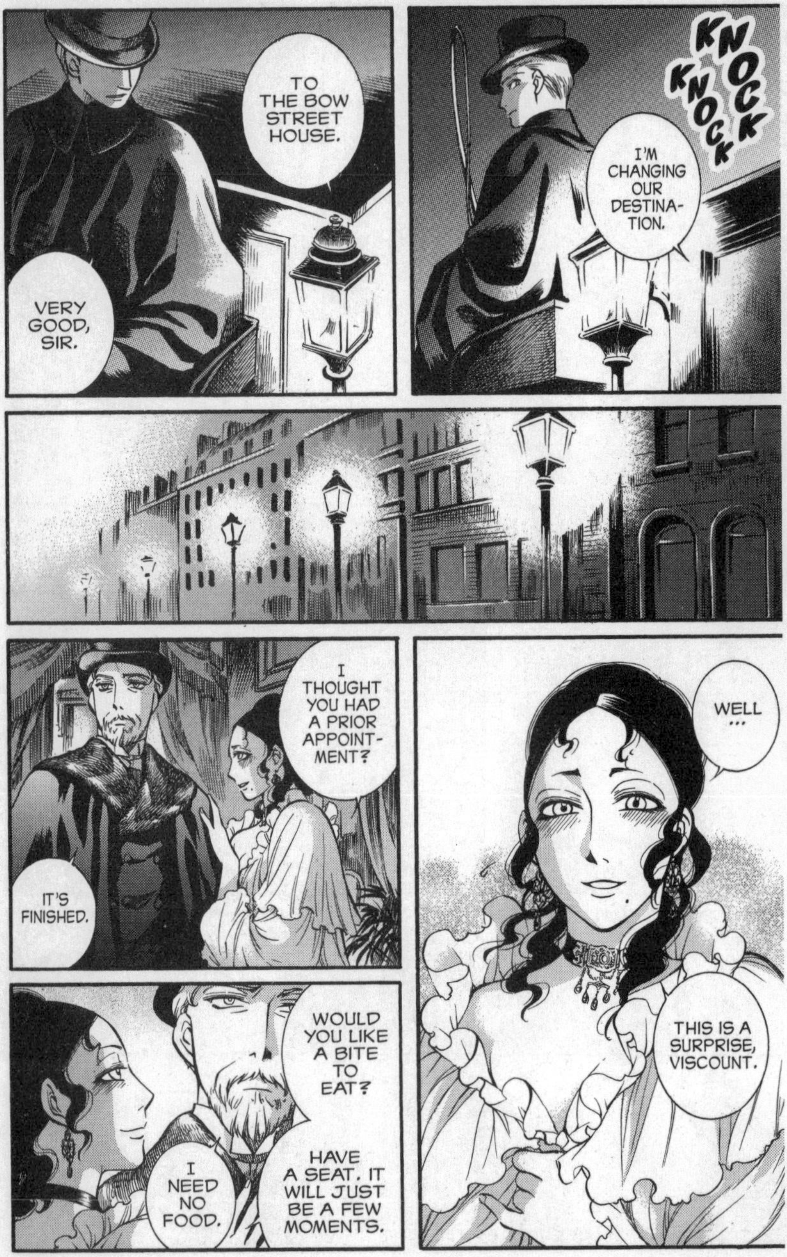
KNOCK
KNOCK
I'M CHANGING OUR DESTINATION.
TO THE BOW STREET HOUSE.
VERY GOOD, SIR.
WELL...
THIS IS A SURPRISE, VISCOUNT.
I THOUGHT YOU HAD A PRIOR APPOINTMENT?
IT'S FINISHED.
WOULD YOU LIKE A BITE TO EAT?
HAVE A SEAT. IT WILL JUST BE A FEW MOMENTS.
I NEED NO FOOD.

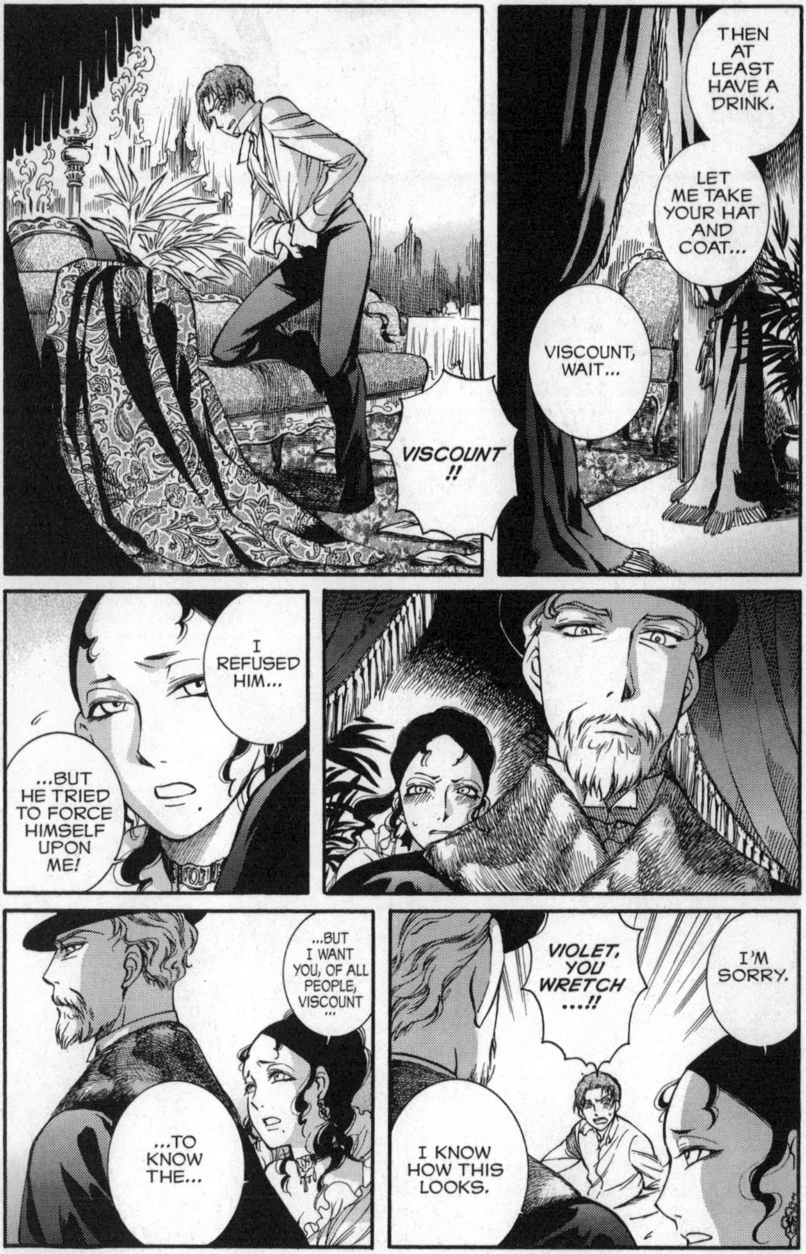
THEN AT LEAST HAVE A DRINK.
LET ME TAKE YOUR HAT AND COAT...
VISCOUNT, WAIT...
VISCOUNT!!
I REFUSED HIM...
...BUT HE TRIED TO FORCE HIMSELF UPON ME!
I'M SORRY.
VIOLET, YOU WRETCH...!!
I KNOW HOW THIS LOOKS.
...BUT I WANT YOU, OF ALL PEOPLE, VISCOUNT...
...TO KNOW THE...

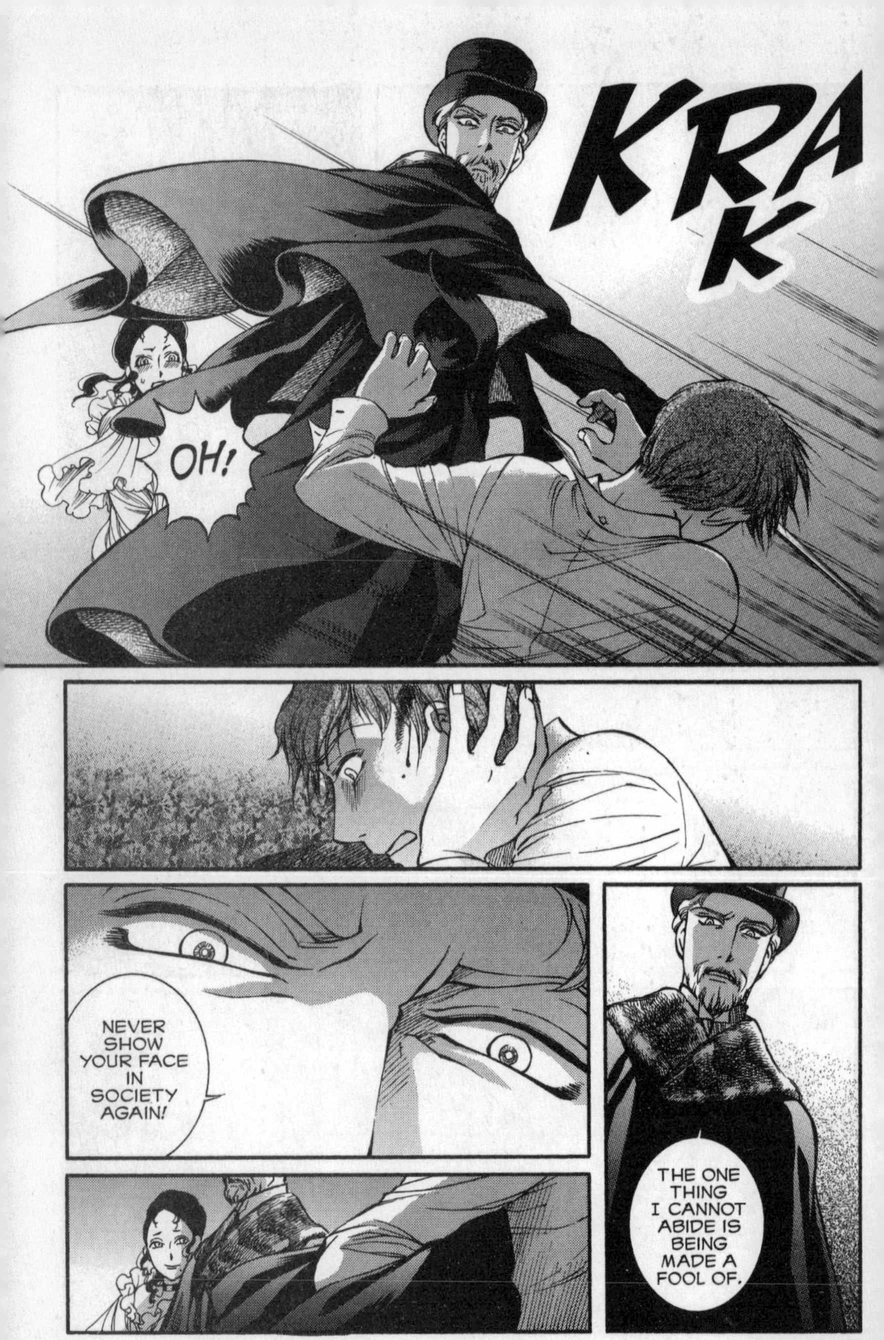
KRAK
OH!
THE ONE THING I CANNOT ABIDE IS BEING MADE A FOOL OF.
NEVER SHOW YOUR FACE IN SOCIETY AGAIN!

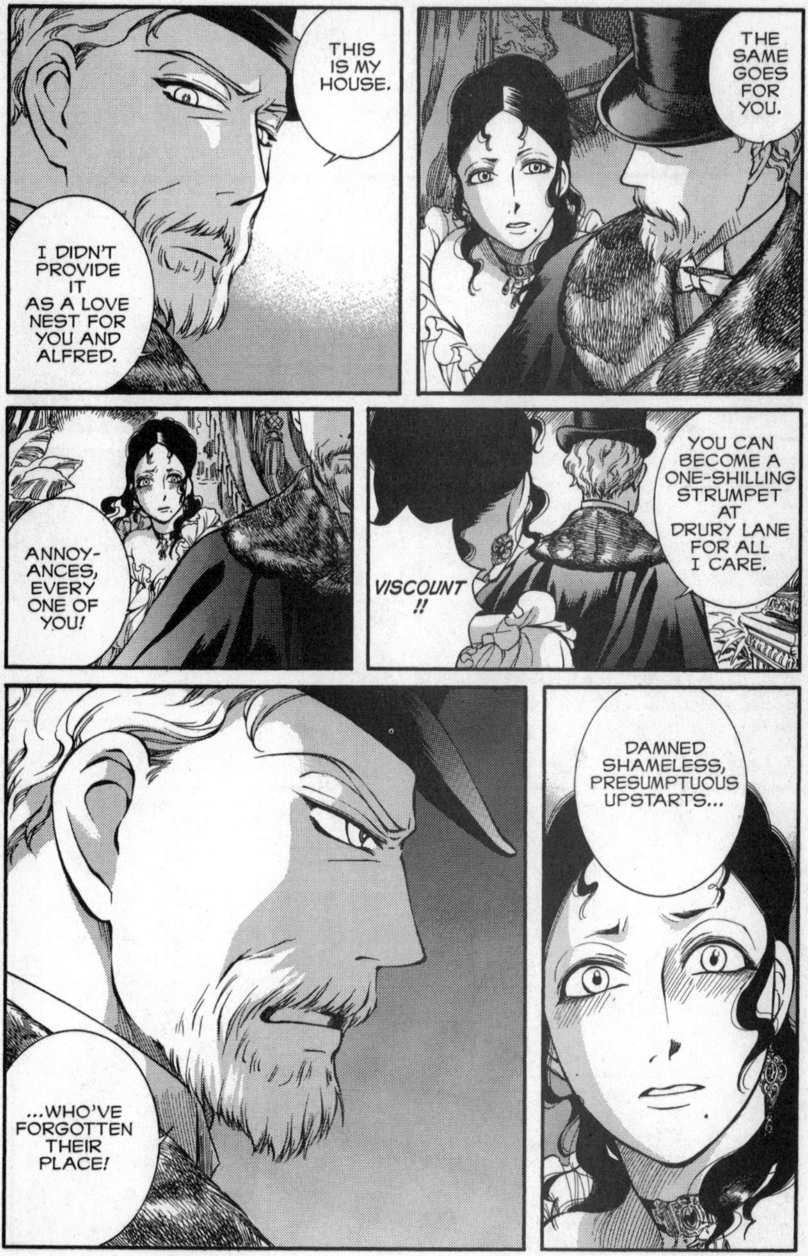
THE SAME GOES FOR YOU.
THIS IS MY HOUSE.
I DIDN'T PROVIDE IT AS A LOVE NEST FOR YOU AND ALFRED.
YOU CAN BECOME A ONE-SHILLING STRUMPET AT DRURY LANE FOR ALL I CARE.
VISCOUNT!!
ANNOY-ANCES, EVERY ONE OF YOU!
DAMNED SHAMELESS, PRESUMPTUOUS UPSTARTS...
...WHO'VE FORGOTTEN THEIR PLACE!

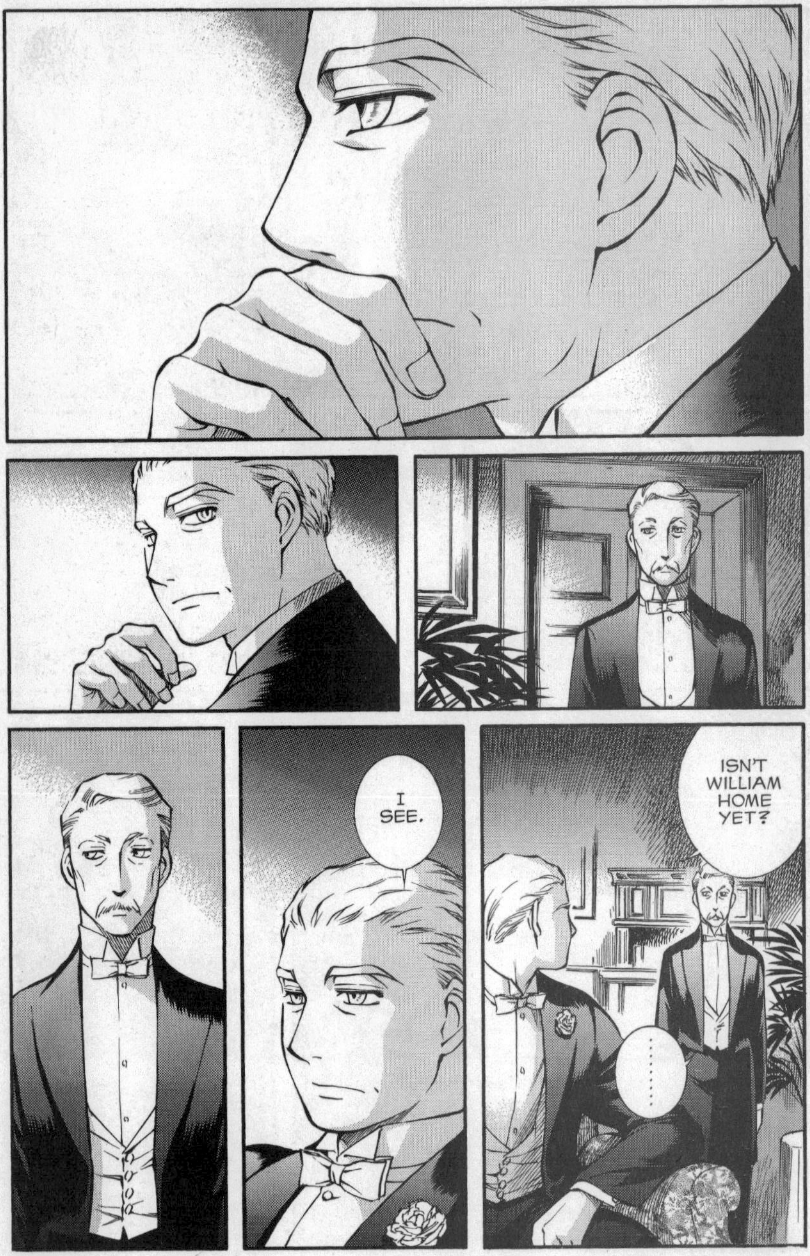
ISN'T WILLIAM HOME YET?
......
I SEE.

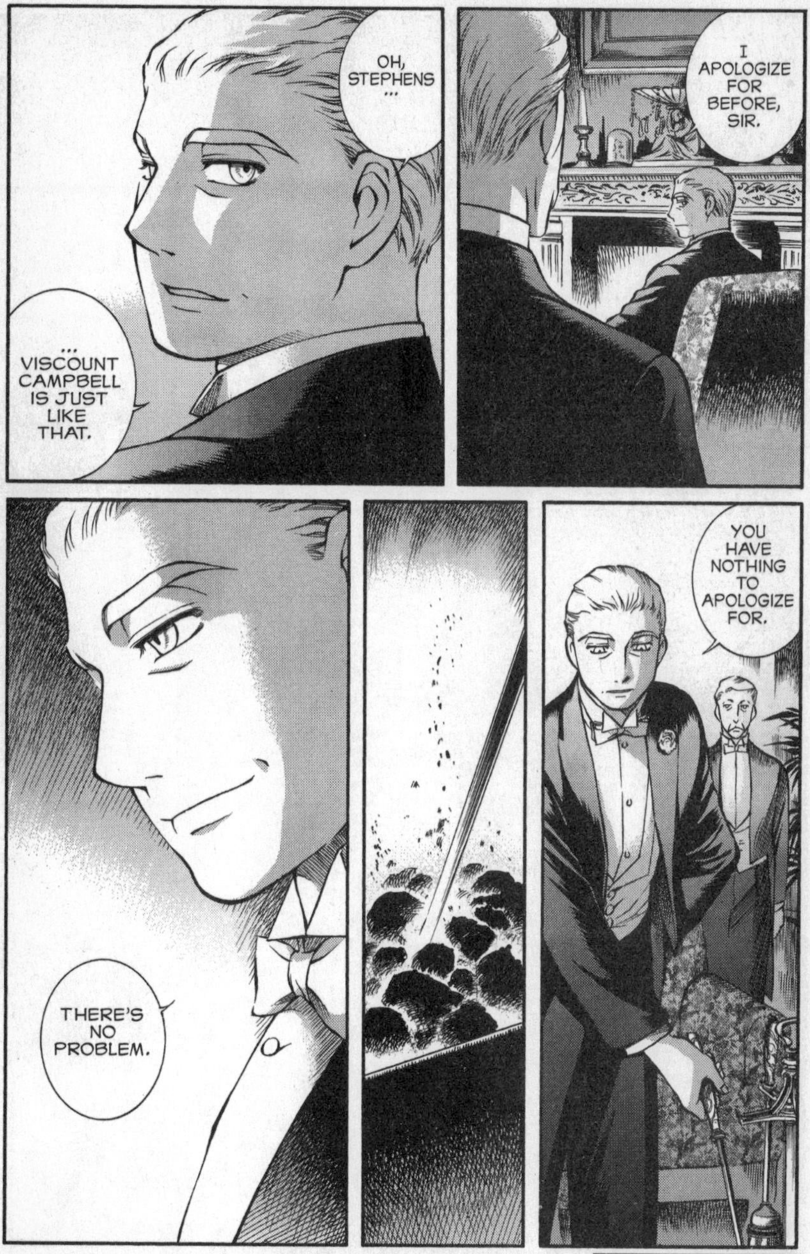
I APOLOGIZE FOR BEFORE, SIR.
OH, STEPHENS...
...VISCOUNT CAMPBELL IS JUST LIKE THAT.
YOU HAVE NOTHING TO APOLOGIZE FOR.
THERE'S NO PROBLEM.

Chapter Thirty Six: The End

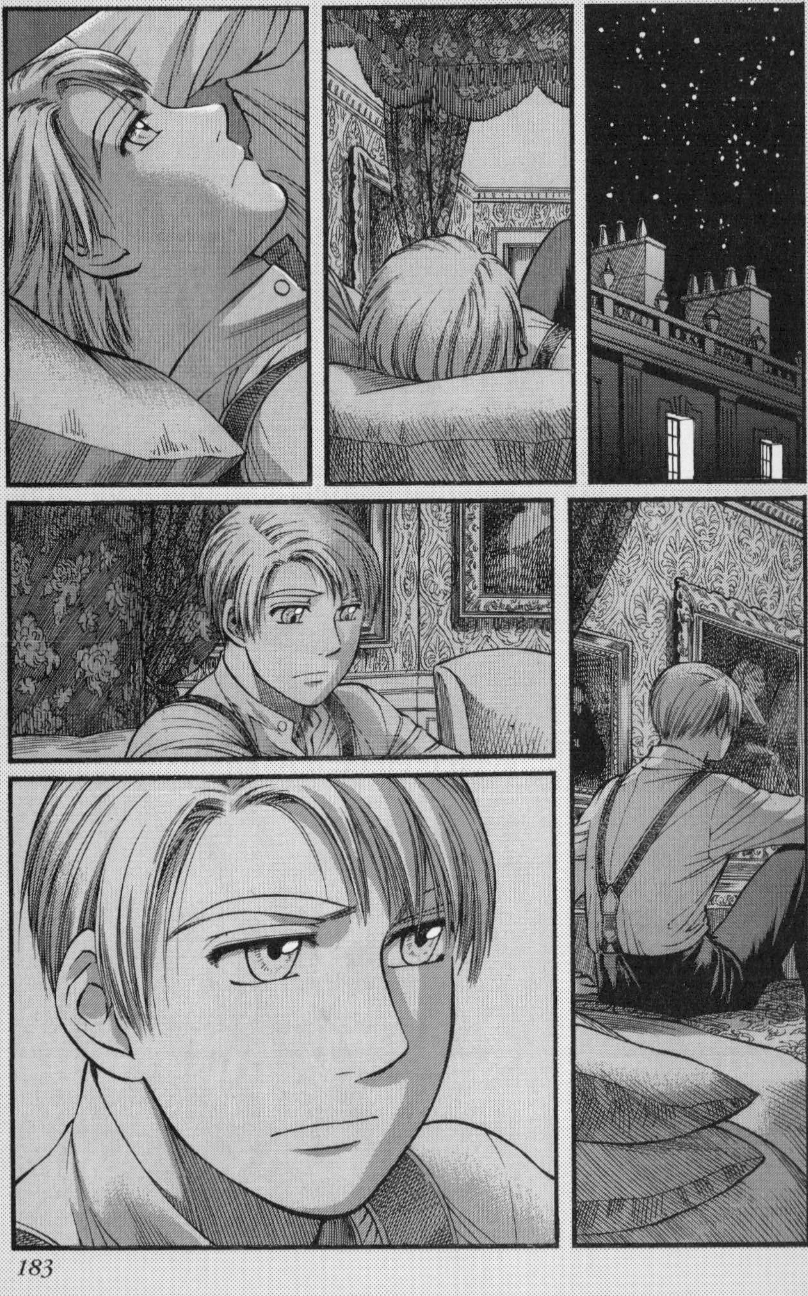

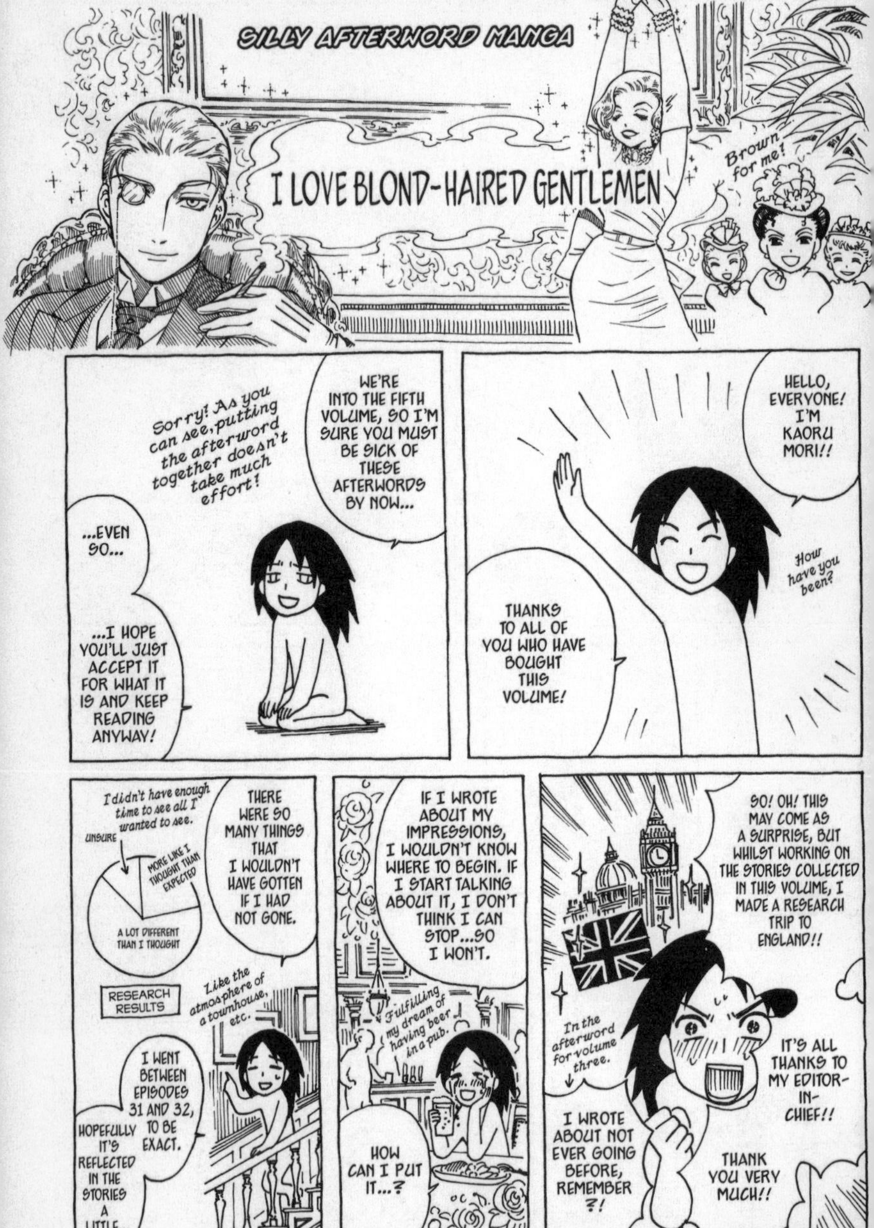
SILLY AFTERWORD MANGA
I LOVE BLOND-HAIRED GENTLEMEN
Brown for me!
HELLO, EVERYONE! I'M KAORU MORI!!
How have you been?
THANKS TO ALL OF YOU WHO HAVE BOUGHT THIS VOLUME!
WE'RE INTO THE FIFTH VOLUME, SO I'M SURE YOU MUST BE SICK OF THESE AFTERWORDS BY NOW...
Sorry! As you can see, putting the afterword together doesn't take much effort!
...EVEN SO...
...I HOPE YOU'LL JUST ACCEPT IT FOR WHAT IT IS AND KEEP READING ANYWAY!
SO! OH! THIS MAY COME AS A SURPRISE, BUT WHILST WORKING ON THE STORIES COLLECTED IN THIS VOLUME, I MADE A RESEARCH TRIP TO ENGLAND!!
In the afterword for volume three.
I WROTE ABOUT NOT EVER GOING BEFORE, REMEMBER ?!
IT'S ALL THANKS TO MY EDITOR-IN-CHIEF!!
THANK YOU VERY MUCH!!
IF I WROTE ABOUT MY IMPRESSIONS, I WOULDN'T KNOW WHERE TO BEGIN. IF I START TALKING ABOUT IT, I DON'T THINK I CAN STOP...SO I WON'T.
Fulfilling my dream of having beer in a pub.
HOW CAN I PUT IT...?
THERE WERE SO MANY THINGS THAT I WOULDN'T HAVE GOTTEN IF I HAD NOT GONE.
I didn't have enough time to see all I wanted to see.
UNSURE
MORE LIKE I THOUGHT THAN EXPECTED
A LOT DIFFERENT THAN I THOUGHT
RESEARCH RESULTS
Like the atmosphere of a townhouse, etc.
I WENT BETWEEN EPISODES 31 AND 32, TO BE EXACT.
HOPEFULLY IT'S REFLECTED IN THE STORIES A LITTLE...

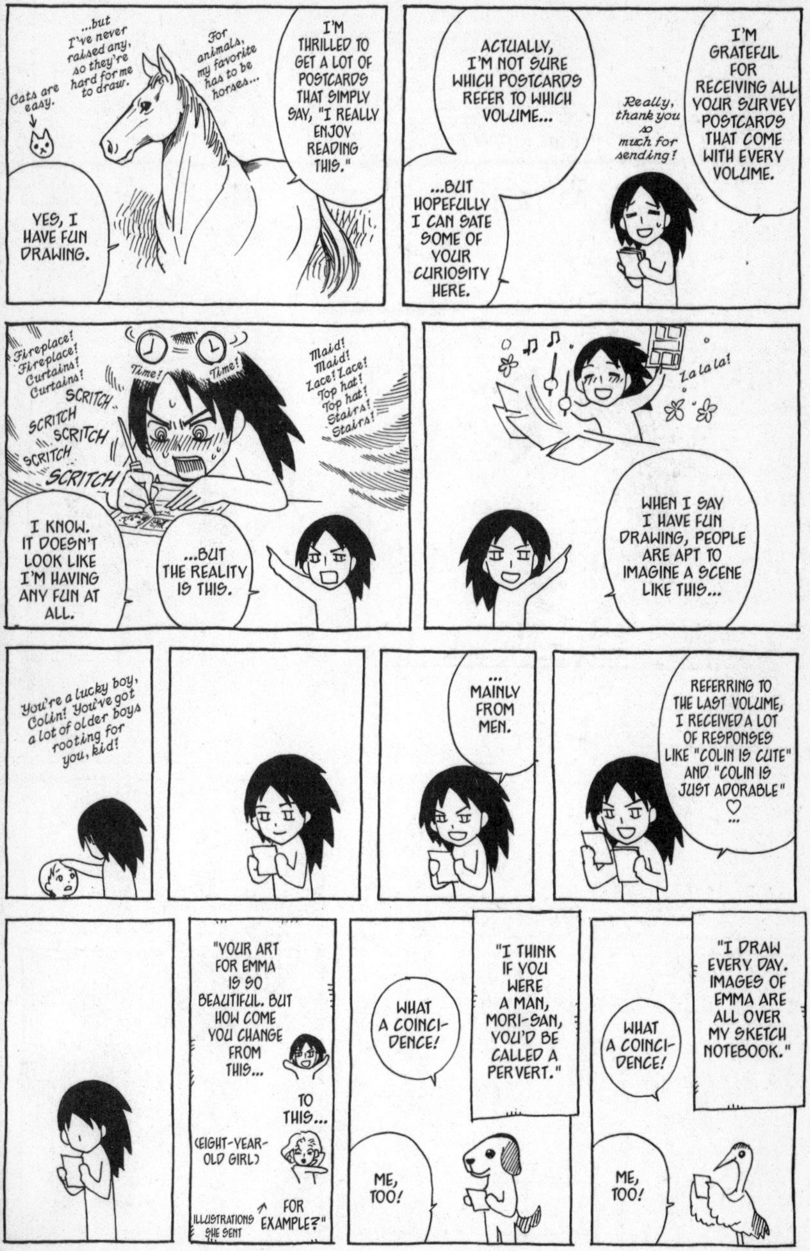

I'M GRATEFUL FOR RECEIVING ALL YOUR SURVEY POSTCARDS THAT COME WITH EVERY VOLUME.
Really, thank you so much for sending!
ACTUALLY, I'M NOT SURE WHICH POSTCARDS REFER TO WHICH VOLUME...
...BUT HOPEFULLY I CAN SATE SOME OF YOUR CURIOSITY HERE.
I'M THRILLED TO GET A LOT OF POSTCARDS THAT SIMPLY SAY, "I REALLY ENJOY READING THIS."
For animals, my favorite has to be horses...
...but I've never raised any, so they're hard for me to draw.
Cats are easy.
YES, I HAVE FUN DRAWING.
WHEN I SAY I HAVE FUN DRAWING, PEOPLE ARE APT TO IMAGINE A SCENE LIKE THIS...
La la la!
Maid! Maid! Lace! Lace! Top hat! Top hat! Stairs! Stairs!
Time! Time!
Fireplace! Fireplace! Curtains! Curtains!
SCRITCH SCRITCH SCRITCH SCRITCH SCRITCH
...BUT THE REALITY IS THIS.
I KNOW. IT DOESN'T LOOK LIKE I'M HAVING ANY FUN AT ALL.
REFERRING TO THE LAST VOLUME, I RECEIVED A LOT OF RESPONSES LIKE "COLIN IS CUTE" AND "COLIN IS JUST ADORABLE" ♡...
...MAINLY FROM MEN.
You're a lucky boy, Colin! You've got a lot of older boys rooting for you, kid!
"I DRAW EVERY DAY. IMAGES OF EMMA ARE ALL OVER MY SKETCH NOTEBOOK."
WHAT A COINCIDENCE!
ME, TOO!
"I THINK IF YOU WERE A MAN, MORI-SAN, YOU'D BE CALLED A PERVERT."
WHAT A COINCI-DENCE!
ME, TOO!
"YOUR ART FOR EMMA IS SO BEAUTIFUL. BUT HOW COME YOU CHANGE FROM THIS...
TO THIS...
(EIGHT-YEAR-OLD GIRL)
FOR EXAMPLE?"
ILLUSTRATIONS SHE SENT

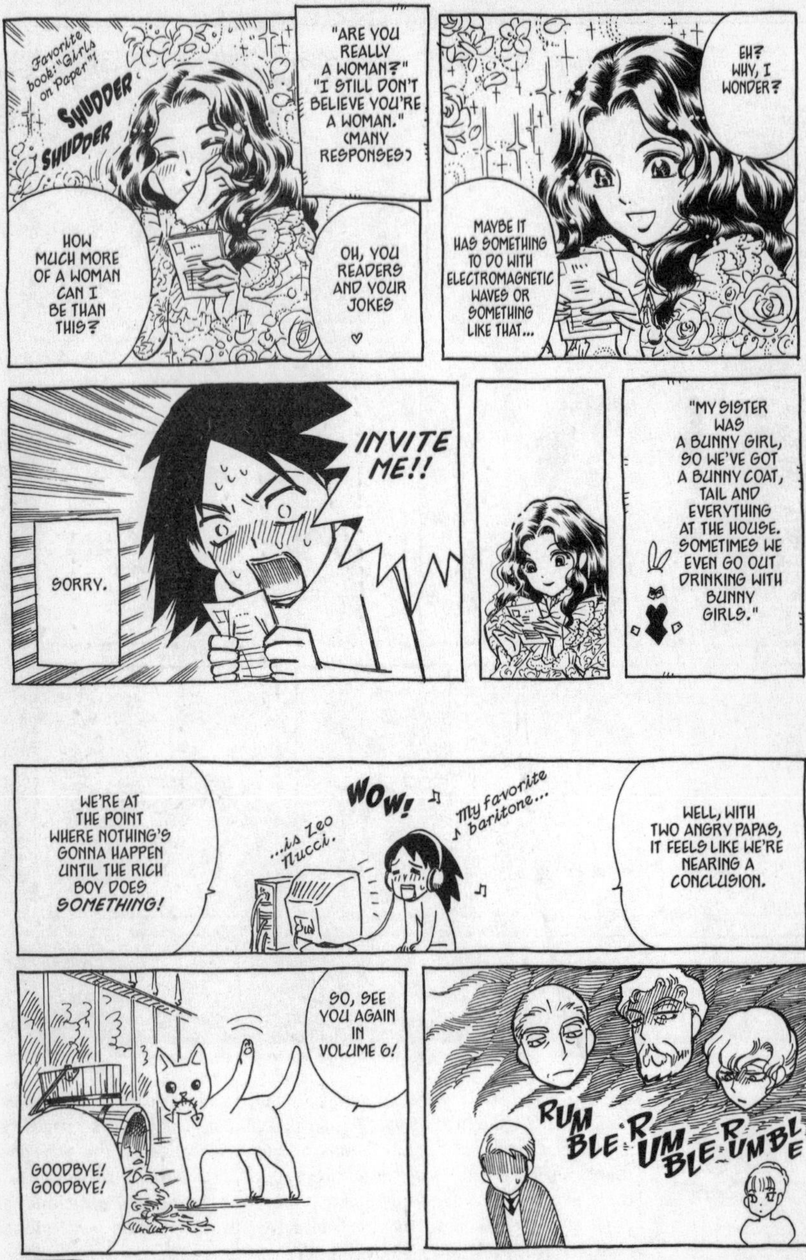
EH? WHY, I WONDER?
MAYBE IT HAS SOMETHING TO DO WITH ELECTROMAGNETIC WAVES OR SOMETHING LIKE THAT...
"ARE YOU REALLY A WOMAN?" "I STILL DON'T BELIEVE YOU'RE A WOMAN." (MANY RESPONSES)
OH, YOU READERS AND YOUR JOKES ♡
Favorite book: "Girls on Paper"!
SHUDDER SHUDDER
HOW MUCH MORE OF A WOMAN CAN I BE THAN THIS?
"MY SISTER WAS A BUNNY GIRL, SO WE'VE GOT A BUNNY COAT, TAIL AND EVERYTHING AT THE HOUSE. SOMETIMES WE EVEN GO OUT DRINKING WITH BUNNY GIRLS."
INVITE ME!!
SORRY.
WELL, WITH TWO ANGRY PAPAS, IT FEELS LIKE WE'RE NEARING A CONCLUSION.
My favorite baritone...
WOW!
...is Zeo Nucci.
WE'RE AT THE POINT WHERE NOTHING'S GONNA HAPPEN UNTIL THE RICH BOY DOES SOMETHING!
RUMBLE RUMBLE RUMBLE
SO, SEE YOU AGAIN IN VOLUME 6!
GOODBYE! GOODBYE!
THE END

IS EMMA IN GRAVE DANGER?!
FIND OUT IN DECEMBER.

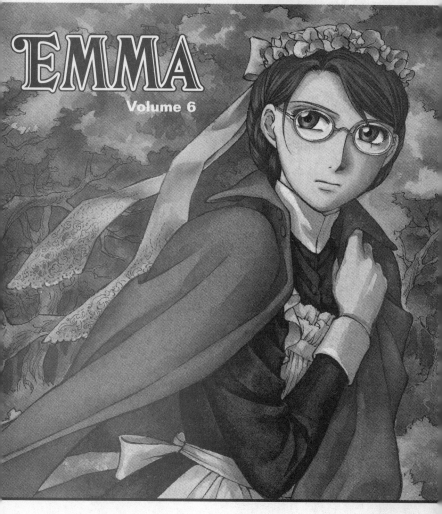

EMMA

Volume 6

By Kaoru Mori. While publicly declaring his intentions to marry Eleanor, the daughter of the Viscount, William is still not so secretly carrying a torch for Emma. Finally deciding to break off the engagement, he is surprised by the calm reaction of Eleanor's parents. But their exterior demeanor disguises their true response; anticipating such a turn of events, they have already put into motion a nefarious plan involving William's beloved maid.

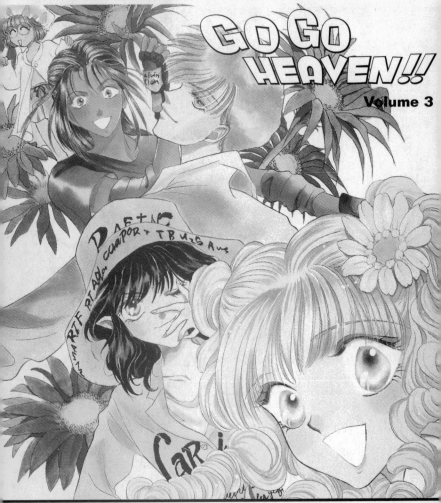

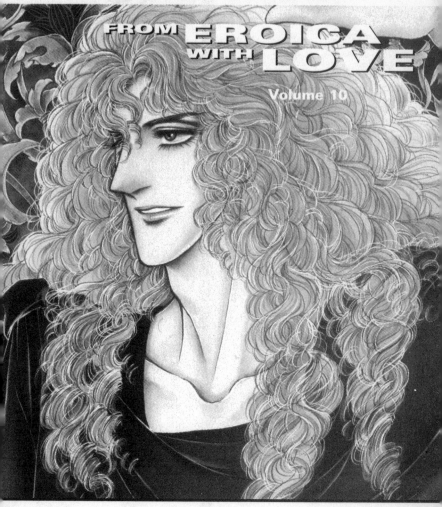

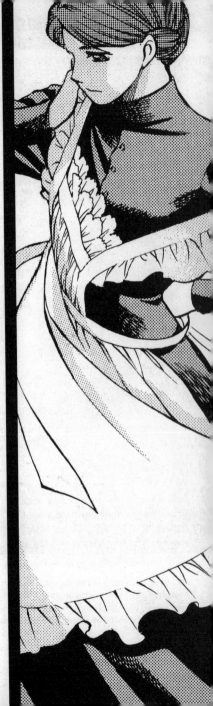

EMMA Vol. 5 © 2005 Kaoru Mori. All Rights Reserved. First
published in Japan in 2005 by ENTERBRAIN, INC.

EMMA Volume 5, published by WildStorm Productions, an
imprint of DC Comics, 888 Prospect St. #240, La Jolla, CA
92037. English Translation © 2007. All Rights Reserved.
English translation rights in U.S.A. and Canada arranged by
ENTERBRAIN, INC. through Tuttle-Mori Agency, Inc., Tokyo.
CMX is a trademark of DC Comics. The stories, characters,
and incidents mentioned in this magazine are entirely
fictional. Printed on recyclable paper. WildStorm does not
read or accept unsolicited submissions of ideas, stories or
artwork. Printed in Canada.

DC Comics, a Warner Bros. Entertainment Company.

Sheldon Drzka – Translation and Adaptation
Janice Chiang – Lettering
Larry Berry – Design
Jim Chadwick – Editor

ISBN:1-4012-1136-4
ISBN-13: 978-1-4012-1136-3

All the pages in this book were created—and are printed here—in Japanese RIGHT-to-LEFT format. No artwork has been reversed or altered, so you can read the stories the way the creators meant for them to be read.

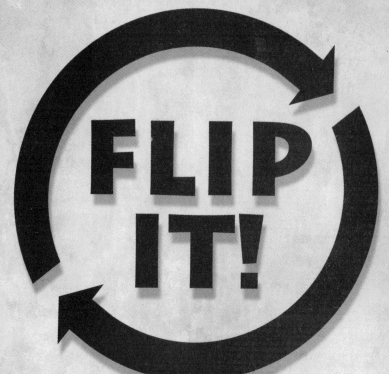

RIGHT TO LEFT?!

Traditional Japanese manga starts at the upper right-hand corner, and moves right-to-left as it goes down the page. Follow this guide for an easy understanding.

For more information and sneak previews, visit cmxmanga.com. Call 1-888-COMIC BOOK for the nearest comics shop or head to your local book store.

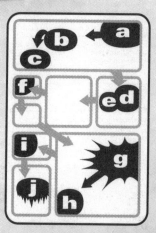